THE LIBRARY
ST. MARY'S COLLEGE OF MARYLAND
ST. MARY'S CITY, MARYLAND 20686

D1570167

# Modern European History

## A Garland Series of Outstanding Dissertations

General Editor
**William H. McNeill**
University of Chicago

Associate Editors

*Eastern Europe*
**Charles Jelavich**
Indiana University

*Great Britain*
**Peter Stansky**
Stanford University

*France*
**David H. Pinkney**
University of Washington

*Russia*
**Barbara Jelavich**
Indiana University

*Germany*
**Enno E. Kraehe**
University of Virginia

MODERN EUROPEAN HISTORY

# Samuel Smiles and the Victorian Work Ethic

Tim Travers

Garland Publishing, Inc.
New York and London 1987

Copyright © 1987 Tim Travers
All rights reserved

Library of Congress Cataloging-in-Publication Data

Travers, Timothy.
Samuel Smiles and the Victorian work ethic.

(Modern European history)
Bibliography: p.
Includes index.
1. Work ethic—Great Britain—History—19th century. 2. Labor and laboring classes—Great Britain—History—19th century. 3. Conduct of life.
4. Smiles, Samuel, 1812–1904. 5. Radicals—Great Britain—Biography. I. Title. II. Series.
HD4905.T73 19897 306′.36′0924
[B] 87-25803
ISBN 0-8240-7835-7 (alk. paper)

All volumes in this series are printed on acid-free, 250-year-life paper.

Printed in the United States of America

# SAMUEL SMILES AND THE VICTORIAN WORK ETHIC

Tim Travers

University of Calgary

PORTRAIT OF SAMUEL SMILES by GEORGE REID, c. 1880 (NPG 1377)

NATIONAL PORTRAIT GALLERY, LONDON

TABLE OF CONTENTS

## SUMMARY

Those Victorians who emphasised the meaning and value of work frequently did so as a reaction to industrial and social change. Four attitudes toward work were frequently expressed - a Traditional attitude which sought to retain the hierarchical *status quo* of work roles; a Promethean attitude which attempted to spiritualise and give a transcendent meaning to the task of work; a Rational attitude which set the seal of approval upon industrial needs and upon the commercial work and reward symbiosis; and a Protean attitude, very often expressed by the clergy, who tried to reintegrate work and religion through the internalisation of work, and through the linkage of work and character formation. Over and above these four attitudes, there was a general attempt to regulate the pace of social change by elevating the value of work, but moderating the reward of such work.

Samuel Smiles (1812-1904) is best known for his book *Self-Help* (1859), which many have assumed to be an encouragement to social and financial success. However, Smiles actually argued against the single-minded pursuit of success, and in favour of the Protean formation of character as the ultimate goal in life. *Self-Help*, as the epitome of Smiles' ideal of self-help, was in reality an attempt to reform and improve society through the moral reform of the individual. Nor was Smiles' ideal of self-help an isolated phenomenon; there were a number of other books written in the same self-help tradition of moral reform, character formation and the value of work in opposition to an idle aristocracy. Smiles' ideal of self-help evolved from the individualism of a Dissenting radical. The formation of the ideal can be traced through Smiles' early (1830-1859) ideas on Religion, Ethics, Psychology, Economics, Politics, and a final disillusionment with political reform, coupled with a strengthening of his individualism. After the publication of *Self-Help*, Smiles wrote biographies of engineers, inventors, scientists and philanthropists, whom he considered to be the members of a "natural aristocracy" of work and merit, better suited to lead the country than the idle and useless aristocracy of birth.

Smiles' ideal of work and self-help was challenged in the 1880s by the contrasting Socialist idea of work. Three Socialists, Carpenter, Blatchford and Sidney Webb, present views both attacking and at variance with Smiles'. It was also in the 1880s that Smiles' books began to lose popularity, and the sales of *Self-Help* fell off. In the last analysis both the ideal of self-help and the Victorian work ethic were reactions to change, as was Smiles' journey from radical to conservative principles. In the middle of this journey *Self-Help* appeared, and reflected Smiles' combination of authoritarian and progressive ideas. Smiles' life was a microcosm of an early radical and reforming generation that in general retained its certainty but lost its relevance after mid century.

## FOOTNOTE ABBREVIATIONS

The following abbreviations are used in the footnotes:

*Eliza Cook's Journal* has been abbreviated to *ECJ*.

The Smiles Collection (Archives, Leeds Public Library) has been abbreviated to *Smiles Correspondence*. Because much of Smiles' correspondence is to and from his children, and there are often no surnames, the following is a list of Smiles' children, with their nicknames:

| | |
|---|---|
| Janet Hartree (nee Smiles) | Gingers |
| William Smiles | Willie, Billio |
| Samuel Smiles | Duff |
| Jack Hartree (son-in-law) | Jack |

The Eva Hartree Collection (Fitzwilliam Museum, Cambridge), had been abbreviated to *Hartree Collection*.

The Works of Thomas Carlyle used are the collection of his *Works* put together by Dana Estes and Co., Boston, as the Centennial Memorial Edition in 26 volumes. In this study, the articles and books used from these *Works* have been given volume numbers relating to the entire series (e.g. Carlyle, "Jean Paul Frederick Richter" (1827), *Works*, vol. XV, p. 20; this article is in vol. I of Critical and Miscellaneous Essays, which are vols. XV, XVI, XVII, XVIII of the whole series).

The Cobden Papers (West Sussex Record Office, Chichester) are all from vol. 17.

# PREFACE

Work has compelled the time and energy of man for a major portion of his existence. Yet there have been few investigations of the history of work, apart from such studies as Weber and Tawney (and their critics) on the Protestant ethic, and in France an exceptional group of social studies, for example, P. Jaccard, Histoire Sociale du Travail (1960) and P. Wolff, Histoire générale du travail: l'âge de l'artisanat (1960). In English, such enquiries are few and far between, but include a sketchy historical outline, translated from the Italian, A. Tilgher, Homo Faber, Work through the Ages (1930), the philosophical approach by H. Arendt, The Human Condition (1958), and two overviews, Stanley Udy, Work in Traditional and Modern Society (1970), and Edward Shorter (ed.), Work & Community in the West (1973). The lack of enthusiasm for historical investigations of the problem of work is the more interesting in view of the stimulus given by the publication and translation of Karl Marx's brilliant reflections on work and alienation in his philosophical and economic manuscripts, written during 1844. The reason seems to be that in general, modern industrial society has so conditioned its members to conceive of work as the normal expectation of life, that few have stopped to reflect on the nature of work and its historical evolution.

This was not so true of 19th Century Britain where the pace of industrialisation and social change released a considerable amount of discussion and publication on the subject of work. Perhaps it would be more accurate to say that the Victorians tried to emphasise and elevate the value of work, rather than reflect on its meaning - nevertheless, as one student of the period has noted, after 'God,' the most popular word in the

Victorian vocabulary must have been 'work' (Walter Houghton, The Victorian Frame of Mind, 1830-1870 (1957), p. 242). However, no studies devoted specifically to the analysis of Victorian attitudes toward work have been published, and so this study ventures to fill the gap through the investigation of the life and ideas of one of the most notable Victorian popularisers of the value of work - Samuel Smiles. The study has therefore a double purpose around the theme of 'work': firstly and principally, to examine the forces in the first half of the 19th Century that formed and were reflected in Smiles' attitudes toward work as expressed through his concept of self-help, and the evolution of that concept through the 19th Century; and secondly, to explore the meaning of the Victorian work ethic and suggest some relationships between Smiles' ideas and Victorian attitudes toward work as a whole. In this respect the study also pursues the contrast between Smiles' concepts of work and self-help and the ideals of the late Victorian Socialist movement.

Samuel Smiles occupies a curious position in the historiography of 19th Century Britain. Modern studies of the social history of the Victorian era usually feel obliged to mention Smiles' best known book, Self-Help (1859), because of its great popularity (some quarter of a million copies printed by the turn of the century), and because his ideal of self-help seemed to be unusually representative of mid-Victorian culture. Yet there have been no full length critical studies of Smiles and his message - at present there are three or four articles and a subjective monograph by his granddaughter - and so Smiles' reputation has had to rest on a limited apprehension of a small percentage of the material available. In consequence, Smiles has been cast in the role of an author dedicated to the advocacy of success in life. Indeed this reputation has been repeated so often that it has grown into something of a myth, and it has been customary to see Smiles as a sort of British Horatio Alger, and thus as a paradigm author of 'how to get on' literature (see Introduction, Chapter II and Critical Bibliography). But an assessment of his background before the publication of Self-Help (1859), a careful reading of all his numerous articles and books, and an acquaintance with his private correspondence, leaves a contrary impression, and enables this study to reach a very different evaluation of Smiles' ideals.

The significance of Samuel Smiles is that he was one of the foremost apostles of the work ethic in Victorian Britain, and that he can be seen as broadly representative of much that went into the making of what Asa Briggs has called the 'Age of Improvement.' In fact, Smiles was particularly involved with one of the most dynamic elements in 19th Century society, those self-educators who formed Mutual Improvement Societies, entered (originally at least) Mechanics Institutes and bought the 'improving' literature of Eliza Cook, William Chambers, the S.D.U.K. (Society for the Diffusion of Useful Knowledge) and others. Smiles was also a leading figure in various reform movements in Leeds in the 1840s (especially the Anti Corn Law League, and the drive for suffrage extension) while his training and professional status as a medical doctor, his experience as a newspaper editor in the Industrial North, and his involvement with the expansion of the railways gave him a unique relationship to some of the most powerful forces of change in society.

Smiles was born early enough in the 19th Century (1812) to inherit certain principles of the Enlightenment, and a radical Dissenters' attitude toward politics and society. But in contrast, his Scottish parents and an early training in Calvinism gave him a somewhat conservative morality and ethics. The years between 1830 and 1859 were marked by Smiles' efforts to resolve the often conflicting traditions and currents of thought that he had inherited and acquired. The final synthesis of these early efforts was achieved in Self-Help. Because of the importance in Smiles' thought of these years, a large section of the study (Chapter II) is devoted to this formative period, which is examined through Smiles' thinking in regard to religion, ethics, psychology, economics and politics. The years 1830 to 1859 present Smiles' life as a microcosm of what was happening to other Dissenting radicals in Victorian Britain - the radicalism being chipped away and leaving only a bare bones individualism. After 1859 Smiles turned to an optimistic survey of Britain's industrial and moral power through his biographies of engineers, inventors and amateur scientists - and here again Smiles mirrors the confidence of the mid-Victorian generation - a confidence that was, however, soon to be undermined by a variety of challenges, including the Socialist movement.

Smiles and his ideals of work and self-help must be seen against the background of the Victorian work ethic. Because the Victorian concern with work has not been the object of particular study, historians of the period have not separated out the problem of work, and thus most of their sources and comments are limited to selective references to leading authors, and in particular, references to that earnest advocate of industry, Thomas Carlyle. Intentionally, therefore, a wide variety of Victorian literature was used as source material in order to provide a reasonable basis for conclusions in regard to Victorian attitudes to work, and also to offset the predominance of Carlyle's influence. Using Sampson Low's Indexes to the British and English Catalogue of Books (1837-1889), it was possible to find, under subject headings such as 'work,' 'success,' 'self-improvement,' etc., relevant periodicals, pamphlets, novels, works by Dissenting and Anglican ministers, popular 'success' and 'self-improvement' books, etiquette pamphlets, and general literature connected with the condition of the working classes. Much of this material had no lasting literary merit, some of the authors were anonymous, and many others were not well known even in the 19th Century, so that on occasion the study will not be able to identify all the individuals whose views are presented. But it was just for these reasons that these sources were used, for they represented an undercurrent of what may be called Victorian 'sub-literature,' providing a much broader range of public opinion and attitudes toward work than has previously been heard from. This 'sub-literature' also supplies an essential framework and context for Smiles' popular books, and can be used as a counterweight, not only to Carlyle, but to the practice of using leading authors as representative of Victorian attitudes toward work.

The source material used in this work is divided roughly into three areas (Smiles, Victorian 'work' literature, Socialism), and is adequately covered in the Critical Bibliography. But a brief note on the originality of the sources may help to explain the structure and direction of the study. Victorian 'work' literature has already received comment above. The sources for the investigation of Smiles are many and varied, but because most of Smiles' better known work was published from 1859 onward, secondary material on Smiles tends to concentrate on this period to the detriment of the pre-1859 sources. These earlier and hitherto unused sources include Smiles' correspondence in the National Library of Scotland; Fitzwilliam Museum, Cambridge (the Hartree Collection); and several smaller groups of letters in such places as the Cobden Papers (Sussex) and the British Museum. Other material that has not been used before includes

Smiles' articles from Eliza Cook's Journal (1849-1854) and the Owenite periodical, The Union (1842-1843); and a number of earlier pamphlets and books, especially Physical Education (1838). Published work on Smiles has also generally failed to use material from Smiles' editorship of the Leeds Times (1839-1842) and from the large Smiles Collection (1,000 letters) in the Leeds Public Library (mostly post 1859). It might also be noted that the wide chronological span of Smiles' material carries the story through from the 1830s to approximately 1890.

Toward the end of the 19th Century, Smiles' ideal of self-help was challenged by opposing theories put forward by the late Victorian Socialists. The intellectual history of late 19th Century British Socialism has been overshadowed by the study of the political aspects of Socialism, and by the many-sided talents of G.B. Shaw and William Morris, so that even Sidney Webb, the guiding light of Fabian Socialism, has yet to receive a modern biography to himself, intellectual or otherwise. For reasons explained in Appendix G, three Socialists (Carpenter, Blatchford and Sidney Webb) were selected as representative of the Socialist movement, and their views on work contrasted with Smiles'. Because of the lack of reliable secondary works when this dissertation was written, sources for these Socialists were largely drawn from manuscript collections, together with newspapers and printed pamphlets.

Samuel Smiles and many other Victorians tried to enhance the value and prestige of work in the 19th Century. But perhaps more than anything else the study reflects the loss of any inherent meaning or value to work by the close of the 19th Century - a problem that has revealed itself even more acutely in contemporary British arguments over productivity. The meaning that many Victorians gave to life and work has been lost by a less confident and uncertain 20th Century Britain, and thus the study of Samuel Smiles and the Victorian work ethic may also carry some implications for the future.

* * *

I am indebted to Frank Turner for taking the time to read this work in its early stages, and to Joseph Ellis and Charles Bright for their original encouragement and discussion. John Murray Ltd., publishers, kindly opened their financial records, which my father, Lt. Col. T.H. Travers, was good enough to evaluate. I was especially thankful to my adviser, Dr. Franklin Baumer, for his patience when faced with the prospect of changes, for his encouragement when it was most needed, and for his comments on the dissertation which helped to give it structure and life. It was also with unfailing courtesy that he gave up so much of his hardpressed time to discussion and reading of various drafts. To those who know her, it will come as no surprise to learn how much my wife, Heather, has supported my endeavours, and how much of her own time and opportunities she has given up. For this I am most grateful.

## Introduction: Samuel Smiles and self-help, a re-evaluation

Over 15 years have passed since this study was presented in 1970, and the task of bringing certain areas up-to-date has proved an interesting, if occasionally humbling, endeavour. The thesis was originally composed of four major areas of investigation: (i) the life of Samuel Smiles and the origins of his ideal of self-help, (ii) Self-Help and the self-help tradition at mid-century, and (iii) the decline of the self-help ideal, partly via the emergence of a genuine 'success' literature, but more specifically through the creation of an opposite ideal in the Socialist movement. The thesis also tried (iv) to set the ideal of self-help within the whole context of the Victorian work ethic.

To take the last point first, it is curious that the discussion of Victorian attitudes to work which opens the thesis, remains one of the very few attempts to analyse the topic. From the point of view of the worker, John Burnett has edited an unusual collection of working class autobiographies.[1] According to Burnett: "Work was a means to an end, not an end in itself . . . ," and for most working people, what mattered was not the work itself or the search for it, but personal relationships . . ." More doubtfully, Burnett argues that workers wrote little about their work, and that "work was not a central life-interest of the working classes." Finally, Burnett stresses that the working class rejected the new Victorian cult of work as an unpalatable and alien notion.[2] Another approach to Victorian work attitudes is through Henry Mayhew, and his frank interviews with working people, together with his Morning Chronicle articles.[3] Apart from these sources, and the occasional analysis in overviews such as J.F.C. Harrison, The Early Victorians 1832-51 (1971) and Geoffrey Best,

Mid-Victorian Britain 1851-75 (1971), the historian can only turn to more general accounts like Edward Shorter, ed., Work and Community in the West (New York, 1973). Essentially, the sheer acceptance of work as an unremarkable and inevitable part of Victorian life by historians has diverted attention away from this cultural topic.

In contrast, the central thrust of the thesis, the life of Samuel Smiles and the origins of his concept of self-help, has continued to attract the interest of historians. In 1970 Alexander Tyrrell published an article which emphasised Smiles' radical origins and placed him more firmly within the class structure of Leeds. However, his explanation of Smiles' turn to self-help indicates more of a break with the radical past than this author would presently agree with.[4] More recently R.J. Morris published an extensive review of Smiles' career and the origins of self-help.[5] Morris argues that Smiles viewed politics through his status as a petit bourgeois, a member of the lower middle "uneasy class." But Smiles' views and ambitions met political and social reality in the 1840s and 1850s, claimed Morris, which forced a narrowing of Smiles' radical and social aspirations, and thus produced the self-help ideal. Morris threfore stresses the failures of the 1840s in achieving suffrage reform and in relieving the plight of the unemployed as motivating factors in the creation of Self-Help. Similarly the union of middle and working classes did not succeed in the 1840s, and thus self-help emerged, not as an apologia for middle class values, but as a lower middle class sublimation of frustrated political ambitions. This process continued with the failure of cooperative efforts in the late 1840s, such as the Woodhouse Temperance Hall and Mechanics Institute, the Zion School, and the Leeds Redemption Society. Consequently by the 1850s, the only way by which Smiles could continue to press for working class self respect, independence of patronage, class consensus, and improvement was through a narrowing of goals into a lower middle class utopia of self-respect and self-culture. In other words, self-help was not mid-Victorian confidence, nor an attempt at instilling middle class ideals, but a means of restoring working class self-respect after the defeats of the 1840s.

Morris' analysis is on the right track, and may only be revised in two respects: (i) by pushing back the emergence of the concept of self-help to Lovett's 1841 address and even earlier, and (ii) in stressing the unity of Smiles' thought, rather than seeing self-help as either a swing to the right or as simply a reaction to political and social defeats. In two articles subsequent to the thesis, the present author argues that 18th Century influences on Smiles were fundamental to the creation of the concept of self-help. In addition, it is argued that self-help really comprised 2 interdependent and permanently linked strands, namely 'active' self-help (self-education, self-culture, self-improvement, independence), and 'passive' self-help (the removal of evils by legislation and intervention, Bentham's 'artificial' harmony of interests). Smiles could emphasise one or the other, or both together, but the shift from 'passive' self-help to 'active' self-help in the 1850s did not mean a change in the concept of self-help, or a retreat. Finally, Smiles' links to 'knowledge' or 'self-help' Chartism should be stressed, as well as the impact of William Lovett's 1841 Address on Smiles. In summary, Smiles' ideal of self-help can be seen as double-edged, active <u>and</u> passive, combining both deterministic and individualistic elements, and bearing a strong relationship to Benthamism's two aspects of 'natural' versus 'artificial' harmony of interests, i.e., 'active' and 'passive' elements. The real thrust of self-help was toward the education and fulfillment of the divinely granted faculties present in every individual, and the various means by which this could be achieved, both active and passive. Thus the thesis' basic interpretation of the self-help ideal is toward continuity rather than change, although acknowledging the importance of Smiles' perception of the more favourable class relations of the 1850s.[6]

The middle section of the thesis stresses the fact that Smiles' book, Self-Help, was received as favourably abroad as it was in Britain. A recent article in the American Historical Review shows just how popular the self-help 'character' message was in Japan. The Japanese translation of Self-Help appealed to middle and low ranking samurai, who were politically disgruntled by their status, and who saw the Self-Help translation Saikoku risshi hen as a way out of their predicament. The book could appeal to Japanese readers because they viewed it as establishing a relationship between individual and national character, but within the Confucian tradition.[7]

Within Britain, the readership and influence of Self-Help, and the following books in the series, was hard to assess in the thesis. The actual sales figures of Self-Help were available, but to whom did the book appeal? Fortunately Jeffrey Richards and others have led the way in showing how G.A. Henty, Charles Dickens and George Eliot were all able to make use of or react against the self-help ideal.[8] Although Richards mistakenly sees self-help as a success ideal rather than character formation, nevertheless G.A. Henty found the values of work, perseverence and thrift useful in such novels as Facing Death (1882), Through the Fray (1886), and Sturdy and Strong (1888). The last volume in particular was interesting because, according to Richards, Sturdy and Strong emphasised the virtues of self-help, paternalism, the peaceful pursuit of mutual aims by middle and working class protagonists, and also came out strongly against trades unions and strikes.[9]

The message of Sturdy and Strong raises an area (ii) that was not particularly well-handled in the thesis, namely the place of Self-Help and the self-help tradition in the decline of working class radicalism of the 1850s. Much of the very recent scholarship on mid-Victorian Britain is presently struggling with the reasons for the shift to moderation in the 1850s from the radical politics of the 1840s. R.J. Morris, for example, sees two central arguments. Firstly, was there a successful attempt by the middle class to influence and capture working class values - a middle class attempt at hegemony and cultural aggression? In other words was this a middle class cultural conspiracy, in which Self-Help would have played its part? Or, secondly, in the words of R.J. Morris, did the turn to moderation in the 1850s evolve out of "a thriving independent culture which coincided with middle-class values at many points but which selected from the values and organisations offered by the middle and ruling classes only those that suited artisan interests"?[10] Once again, Self-Help could fill this role too, but in a way that was more congruent with working class interests.

A more complicated scenario was proposed in 1985 by Neville Kirk. He sees three possible explanations for the turn to mid-Victorian respectability and the transformation of radicals into Liberals. These explanations range from working class collaboration with the middle class (a consensus model) to working class attempts at independence (a conflict model). The first argument is that middle class values were adopted by the skilled workers - the labour aristocracy. This was essentially middle class cultural capture of working class values. The second argument sees the emergence of a system of values that cut across middle and working class lines. This really meant the submergence of radicalism within a pervasive middle class culture. The third argument emphasises the complex nature of mid-Victorian respectability - "on the one hand, class pride, independence and opposition to middle class control, and, on the other conscious dissociation from the non-respectable and acceptance of the broad customs of a socio-cultural world dominated by the middle class." This represents a kind of independent reformism within the system.[11]

Smiles' own position would certainly be closest to the third analysis - indeed in the 1850s Smiles was still lobbying for government reform in the areas of health and education - but only so that an independent-minded working class could help themselves. It also seems very likely that the readers of Self-Help to a large extent came from the education-minded, 'respectable,' working class members of the various cooperative, mutual aid and self-education societies of the late 1850s and 1860s. For example, Kirk points to an 1863 article entitled "Self-help: or Work, Wait and Win" in the Oddfellows Magazine, in which the aim was not so much 'escape' from the working class, as attempts to rise within the class.[12] Clearly, the third analysis would best fit Smiles' own aims at working class independence, but within the economic system. However, it must be emphasised again that like Robert Lowery and many others such as Vincent, Cooper and Lovett, Smiles had not abandoned his earlier radicalism in seeing moral reform as complementary to social and political reform - the goals of both sides of self-help were mutually supportive, not mutually exclusive.[13]

Finally, the area in the thesis dealing with the decline of the self-help ideal, (iii), offered an original look at previously unused primary sources in regard to the socialist challenge (ms. material on Edward Carpenter, Robert Blatchford and Sidney Webb). The thesis also presented a not very convincing account of the demise of self-help. In fact the end of the self-help genre might well have been placed in the post-World War I period,[14] rather than earlier in the 1880s, while the reasons given for the decline in the popularity of Smiles' ideal might well have included the parallel rise and decline of the Friendly Society movement.[15] In addition, the challenge to the self-help ideal toward the end of the century was of course wider than the opposite image evolved by the socialists, and in this respect Martin Wiener offers some useful insights. Wiener argues, for example, that the triumph of the middle class was a phyrric victory, since the middle class soon produced a new concept of the gentleman who gave up work, money making and business. In fact the middle class soon reshaped itself into the image of the class it was replacing. Other anti-industrial forces came into play also, such as nostalgia for the countryside, and a public school ethos which eschewed attention to production and profit. Moreover, towards the end of the century other voices were raised against single minded competition and the pursuit of material production as an end in itself, such as Arnold Toynbee and Alfred Marshall. While Martin Wiener's account probably over-emphasises the decline of the industrial spirit, it is one of the few attempts to take a wider look at cultural change.[16]

Turning to the analysis of the three major socialists contained in the thesis, it would seem that recent publications have not substantially altered the analysis presented in 1970. Edward Carpenter has now become something of a cult figure due to his interest in homosexual and feminist issues, but in 1970 he was a largely unknown figure. Since then two biographies have appeared, but neither really alters the thesis' interpretation of Carpenter's views on work and human nature, which was based upon Carpenter's Ms. lectures in Sheffield Public Library.[17] Robert Blatchford has yet to attract an up-to-date biography, and again the thesis' account of Blatchford's attitudes toward work and human nature remains viable. In particular, the discussion of Blatchford's two lively but often unread utopias [Merrie England (1893/94) and The Sorcerer's Shop (1906/07)], and Blatchford's 'Nunquam' columns in the Manchester Sunday Chronicle, continues to have some value.[18]

The treatment of the third socialist, Sidney Webb, was original in its early use of the Passfield Papers and the Ms. diaries of Beatrice Potter/Webb[19], but needs to be brought up-to-date. One area of Sidney Webb's thought that the thesis did not emphasise enough was his debt to Comtean Positivism, and here the research of Willard Wolfe has been important, especially in revealing Positivism as the source of Fabian 'permeation,' and in the value of Positivism as a substitute religion.[20] Very recently there has also been a scholarly trend that 'rescues' the Webbs from the early unflattering image of them provided by H.G. Wells, and now imparts to them an emotional content and a greater sense of humanity than had hitherto been suspected.[21] The thesis went some way towards this interpretation, although still seeing the Webbs on the right wing of the Socialist movement, with Sidney Webb especially revealing authoritarian tendencies in his unpublished lectures.

* * * * * *

In conclusion, this opportunity to review an extensive piece of work after fifteen years gives a unique sense of the historiographical movement of the Victorian field of study. Cultural concerns such as the Victorian work-ethic tend to receive little attention, while the political aspects of self-help and the radical career of Samuel Smiles have aroused more interest. However, the focus has been on the political 'shift to the right' of the 1850s rather than on the cultural origins of self-help. This is because the nature of working class consciousness and politics at mid-century has become a major area of study. Even so, the real meaning of Self-Help has continued to be a puzzle. Later in the century, the socialist movement predictably has seen much greater research, although 'trendier' topics and available material has focussed attention on individuals such as Edward Carpenter and Beatrice Webb, while Robert Blatchford and Sidney Webb remain without major biographies. Moreover, the socialist material has tended to overshadow other late 19th Century reactions against the Victorian age.[22] A final comment would be that self-help as a concept has a curious staying power - the popular books of the 1970s and 1980s that deal with diet, health, exercise, self-analysis, sex and work roles, and individual ways to a better, happier life, are really our own successors to an earlier tradition of self-culture first set out by Smiles' Self-Help.

## Introduction - Footnotes

[1]John Burnett, ed., Useful Toil: Autobiographies of working people from the 1820s to the 1920s (London, 1974).

[2]Ibid., "Preface," pp. 14-19.

[3]E.P. Thompson and Eileen Yeo, eds., The Unknown Mayhew (London, 1971).

[4]Alexander Tyrrell, "Class Consciousness in Early Victorian Britain: Samuel Smiles, Leeds Politics and the Self-Help Creed," Journal of British Studies, vol. 9 (May 1970), pp. 102-115.

[5]R.J. Morris, "Samuel Smiles and the Genesis of Self-Help; the Retreat to a Petit Bourgeois Utopia," Historical Journal, vol. 24, no. 1 (1981), pp. 89-109.

[6]T.H.E. Travers, "Samuel Smiles and the Origins of 'Self-Help': Reform and the New Enlightenment," Albion, vol. 9, no. 2 (1977), pp. 161-187; and Travers, T.H.E., "Samuel Smiles (1812-1904)," Biographical Dictionary of Modern British Radicals, Sussex: Harvester Press, 1984, pp. 455-460. Of great value in looking at the 2 sides of self-help was E.C. Midwi Victorian Social Reform (London, 1968), especially chapter 3, "New thinking," on the split of Bentham's followers into the two schools of 'natural' versus 'artificial' harmony of interests (roughly the 'active' and 'passive' elements of self-help), and the concept of the tutelary state. Very useful, too, are the studies by Patricia Hollis, ed., Class and Class-conflict in Nineteenth Century England, 1815-1850 (London, 1973), especially "Self-Help Chartism," pp. 248-267; and Brian Harrison and Patricia Hollis, eds., Robert Lowery, Radical and Chartist (London, 1979), "Introduction," pp. 1-35; and Patricia Hollis, ed., Pressure from Without

in early Victorian England (London, 1974), especially chapter 5, "William Lovett." The 18th Century origins of self-help have also been easier to see with the publication of research on phrenology, e.g., David de Giustino, Conquest of Mind: Phrenology and Victorian Social Thought (London, 1975).

[7]Earl H. Kinmouth, "Nakamura Keiu and Samuel Smiles: A Victorian Confucian and a Confucian Victorian," American Historical Review, vol. 85, no. 3 (1980), pp. 535-556.

[8]Jeffrey Richards, "Spreading the Gospel of Self-Help: G.A. Henty and Samuel Smiles," Journal of Popular Culture, vol. 16, no. 2 (1982), pp. 52-65; Robin Gilmour, "Dickens and the self-help idea," in J. Butt and I.F. Clarke, eds., The Victorians and Social Protest (Newton Abbott, 1973), pp. 71-101 (Dickens had a negative view!); David Molstad, "George Eliot's Adam Bede and Smiles' Life of George Stephenson," English Language Notes, vol. 14 (1977), pp. 189-192. The contribution of Smiles and self-help to the late Victorian adventure story is evaluated in Martin Green, Dreams of Adventure: Deeds of Empire (London, 1980), pp. 204-212.

[9]Richards, op cit, p. 64.

[10]R.J. Morris, Class and Class Consciousness in the Industrial Revolution 1780-1850 (London, 1979), pp. 60-61.

[11]Neville Kirk, The Growth of Working Class Reformism in Mid-Victorian England (London & Sydney, 1985), pp. 176-177, and 229. Kirk sees J. Foster proposing the first argument, T.W. Laqueur and Brian Harrison the second, and T.R. Tholfsen, J.F.C. Harrison, G. Crossick and R.Q. Gray the third. For references, see footnotes in Kirk, ibid., pp. 231 ff

[12]Kirk, op cit, pp. 224-225.

[13]Harrison & Hollis, "Introduction," Robert Lowery, pp. 5, 19.

[14]Ibid., p. 20.

[15]P.H.J.H. Gosden, Self-Help: Voluntary Associations in Nineteenth Century Britain (London, 1973), especially chapter 9: "The Crisis at the End of the Century"; Dot Jones, "Self-Help in Nineteenth Century Wales: the Rise and Fall of the Female Friendly Society," Llafur, vol. 4, no. 1 (1984), pp. 14-26.

[16]Martin Wiener, English Culture and the Decline of the Industrial Spirit, 1850-1950 (Cambridge University Press, 1981), pp. 13-14, 20 ff, 47, 82, 90.

[17]Sheila Rowbotham and Jeffrey Weeks, Socialism and the New Life: The Personal and Sexual Politics of Edward Carpenter and Havelock Ellis (London, 1977); Chushichi Tsuzuki, Edward Carpenter, 1844-1929: Prophet of Human Fellowship (Cambridge University Press, 1980). See also the brief but useful section on Carpenter in Stanley Pierson, Marxism and the Origins of British Socialism: The Struggle for a New Consciousness (Ithaca and London, 1973), pp. 97-105.

[18]For Blatchford, see Pierson, ibid., pp. 149-161; Stanley Pierson, British Socialists: The Journey from Fantasy to Politics (Cambridge, Mass., 1979), pp. 71-79 and passim (Pierson here concentrates on Blatchford's anti-Christian crusade, but does make a passing reference to Blatchford's more fundamental attitudes).

[19]The Passfield Papers and the Potter/Webb diaries are in the British Library of Political and Economic Science.

[20]Willard Wolfe, From Radicalism to Socialism: Men and Ideas in the Formation of Fabian Socialist Doctrines, 1881-1889 (New Haven & London, 1975), chapter 6.

[21]Pierson, Marxism and the Origins of British Socialism, pp. 112-118; but more particularly Lisanne Radice, Beatrice and Sidney Webb (London,

1984), and Deborah Nord, The Apprenticeship of Beatrice Webb (Amherst, 1985). See also Norman Mackenzie, ed., The Letters of Sidney and Beatrice Webb, 3 vols. (Cambridge, 1978), and Jeanne Mackenzie, A Victorian Courtship: The Story of Beatrice Potter and Sidney Webb (London, 1979). There still is no single biography of Sidney Webb.

[22]For example, the theosophy movement, Harley Trudeau, Theosophy and the late Victorian Revolt (MA Thesis, University of Calgary, 1977).

CHAPTER I

# SAMUEL SMILES AND THE VICTORIAN WORK ETHIC

## Work and Labour[1]: a brief history

In 1968 the leader of the British Conservative Party, Edward Heath, wrote:

> we must change our whole attitude to work and its rewards . . . If we want to make the people of our country richer, if we want to provide the material basis for the better life for which everyone longs, then economic policy must be directed at encouraging and rewarding industrial skill, hard work and initiative.[2]

Such an attitude is wholly modern, and illustrates the fact that in Britain, as in any other industrial society, the need to define work roles and work sanctions is of paramount importance. It also illustrates a conscious acceptance of the pursuit of wealth and material production as the ultimate criteria of the "better life" for which "everyone longs." The distance between this position and the early years of the 19th Century points up the way in which attitudes toward work have been transformed from work as moral imperative to work as secular reward. In fact, the 19th Century can be seen as the battleground in which a traditional belief in work as a value in itself, and as a means of both forming and judging internal character or "identity," was defeated both by the concept of work as a measurable commodity (leading to the early 20th Century work and time study programmes), and by the utility of work as an amoral and secular route to social mobility and financial success. Samuel Smiles was caught up in these changing patterns, and (for his own reasons) sought to provide explanations for the distribution of work, and a rationalisation for the necessity and positive value of labour, at a time when labour was often spiritually degrading and physically exhausting.

However, work and labour had not always been so complicated. A very brief history of work and labour will serve to place the 19th Century in perspective. The Greeks found a negative value in work and labour, because to labour meant to be enslaved by necessity, and slaves were therefore required in order to defeat necessity. Slave owners sought to escape labour, not only because it dehumanised man to something approaching the level of animal life, but also because it prevented the use of leisure [schole] for more worthy occupations - as Aristotle would have it, music and contemplation. Christianity moderated the Greek escape from work, particularly through the concept of sin - man must work by the sweat of his brow in order to atone for his guilt in the Garden of Eden. But for Thomas Aquinas, although work was a necessary part of human life, yet the highest pursuit was still religious activity. Nevertheless, there were attempts in the Middle Ages to investigate and understand the secrets of Nature through alchemy, medicine and natural science. Men like the 13th Century Franciscan, Roger Bacon, were prepared to experiment, and to consider transforming the material elements of Nature. Grosseteste's mathematical physics, Roger Bacon's interest in applied knowledge, and the rationalism of Occam's _via moderna_, all helped to place an emphasis on experience and discovery - to turn some attention away from contemplation of the eternal heavenly order toward an active involvement with the changeable material world.

The creativity and appreciation of human life expressed by the Renaissance, together with the roughly contemporaneous development of rationalised commercial activity, led to an increased awareness of the endeavours and occupations of the individual. But it was only after the Reformation that an atmosphere truly conducive to hard work emerged. It is true that previous to the Reformation, various orders of monks, particularly the order of St. Benedict, had used work and labour as a form of discipline and as an approved activity. But it is also true that monasteries used lay labourers as widely as possible to provide the necessaries of life. However, Max Weber has claimed that it was the Reformation which produced an 'innerwordly asceticism' and specific sanctions for the value of persistent work; useful, as it transpired, for the future of capitalism. This is not to argue that the Reformation produced capitalism, or to deny that economic activity existed before Luther's time, or that Catholic countries did not also engage in successful commercial enterprise, but only that certain forms of Protestantism, particularly Calvinism, were conducive and congruent to hard work among Protestant sects and the commercial classes - two groups that were often synonymous. Salvation was not promised to Calvinists on account of earthly fruits, but the presence of material success might well indicate a favourable chance of salvation.[3]

It was, however, the labour theory of value developed by John Locke in the 17th Century that gave a rationalised explanation to the value of work and labour in the acquisition of property, as opposed to the more abstract religious connection devised by the theologians and interpreters of the Reformation. Locke declared that "every man has a 'property' in his own 'person' . . . The 'labour' of his body and the 'work' of his hands . . . are properly his . . ."[4] This position was reinforced by Adam Smith in the 18th Century, who asserted that labour was the source of all wealth, and by Marx in the 19th Century, who considered labour to be the measure of all productive value, although recognising that man was also exploited by the quantification and measurement of labour.

Marx lived and wrote for the most part in Britain, and his considerable interest in the problems of work and labour was an indication of the rapid industrialisation of that country. Industralisation requires a disciplined work force, and so for this reason (as well as various others to be discussed) the Victorians raised the value and status of work and labour to a new and higher level. In 1857, a children's story related how a young girl had learnt at Sunday School that British missionaries abroad were teaching "the heathens how to read, and work, and fear God." Indeed, besides being articles of export, these three commodities, education, work and religion, were also the subject of intense debate within 19th Century Britain and it is significant that for Samuel Smiles (as for many other Victorians) these three were interrelated and each possessed overwhelming positive value. But of the three, work held a special place in Victorian literature, for it was often deemed capable of encompassing both education and religion: "Work, then, ye young," advised Maria Edgeworth (author of many didactic tales),

> for work is your best friend; work it is that saves you. It is for you a source of grace, virtue, and happiness. That is the great secret of living well; work instructs and amends; it renders us habitually industrious and clever, always estimable and honourable. In fine, work, with the blessing of God and a pure intention, procures peace upon earth and leads to happiness in heaven.[5]

Maria Edgeworth's homily revealed some of the work traditions that had come down to the 19th Century - work was honourable, valuable in itself, a means of salvation, and an education as well as a discipline (roughly the Protestant tradition) - but work was valuable also as a productive and earthly pursuit (Locke and Adam Smith). However, these traditions were complicated in four essential ways during the 19th Century: the labour of the mass of the people shifted from agricultural and home labour to factory labour; there was a new questioning and discussion of the nature of work and its distribution; almost all sections of the nation became involved in work of some kind - so that as one philosopher has noted, not only "must the man of the bourgeois epoch work, he desires to work, for a life without work would seem to him not worth living, lived 'in vain'."[6] And by the same token, if, by the end of the 19th Century work had become as secularised as its traditions would allow, yet, paradoxically, work as production and manufacture - the Gross National Product - was elevated into a new 20th Century religion.

But the proponents of this new religion should beware, for systems of production rest upon ideals, and as the late Victorians discovered, such ideals must be accepted by the majority of the people involved in this production, or the ideals and the system of production itself will be challenged.

## The Victorian Work Ethic

The problems of a society in rapid industrial and social change, then as now, require definitions of social roles and work roles, as well as a re-evaluation of political, moral and religious guides to social behaviour and conduct. This was particularly the case in regard to the emergence of the working class in 19th Century Britain, for as one historian has noted: "Pre-industrial experience, tradition, wisdom and morality, provided no adequate guide for the kind of behaviour which a capitalist economy required."[7] The result was an outpouring of books designed for the guidance of the new reading public, and at the same time, an underlying attempt to discover and redefine moral values as a basis for a stable society. In a disguised fashion this was to be the role of Samuel Smiles, author of _Self-Help; with illustrations of character and conduct_ (1859) and numerous other books of a biographic and inspiring tendency. But more specifically, these redefinitions, and the books of Samuel Smiles, posed a fundamental question - fundamental to any society at any time - the relationship of work and work roles to the social structure. The social, political, and industrial changes in 19th Century Britain thus raised a series of issues around this fundamental question. Who works and who does not? Why work? What kind of work and for how long? It is in this context that the Victorian emphasis on work (also termed work ethic) must be seen, and it is in this context that Smiles' attitude to work and his concept of self-help must be understood.

There have been few specific attempts to study the Victorian work ethic, and those few have usually referred either to a revitalisation of the Puritan ethic, or have approached the subject through the medium of major Victorian figures such as Thomas Carlyle.[8] This study of the work ethic uses as wide a range of literature as possible, including works by clergymen - both Anglicans and Dissenters - which raises again the question of the Puritan ethic, and hence the relevance of the studies of Max Weber and R.H. Tawney.

Tawney has remarked that the "astonishing outburst of industrial activity after 1760" did _not_ produce a new type of economic character, nor a new system of economic organisation, but that in reality "the ideal which was to carry all before it, in the person of the inventor and engineer and captain of industry, was well established among Englishment before the end of the 17th Century." And Weber has declared that "one of the fundamental elements of the spirit of modern capitalism, . . . rational conduct on the basis of the idea of the calling, was born . . . from the spirit of Christian asceticism." Essentially Weber argued that ascetic Protestantism created a spirit or ethos sympathetic to the development of rational economic conduct, while Tawney broadened the discussion and included other political, social and economic conditions, but still reached a similar conclusion, at least in regard to the later Puritans - the "capitalist spirit" found in certain aspects of later Puritanism a tonic and an encouragement for its already existant vigour.[9]

Both Tawney and Weber have been subjected to strong (and usually justified) criticism, but the cultural congruence of such diverse elements as religion and economics has not been disputed, merely the existence and nature of the connecting links. What of the relevance of Weber and Tawney to the 19th Century work ethic and to Samuel Smiles? To anticipate, it is true that Weber's characterisation of Calvinist conduct in the phrase "God helps those who help themselves" was a favourite maxim of Smiles', and that Tawney believed the "ethics of the Puritan bore some resemblances to those associated later with the name of Smiles."[10] It is also true that the virtues expressed by many 19th Century moralists, and especially the Dissenting clergy, were the same as the virtues extolled by some of the post-Restoration Puritans - work, the formation of character through self-control and self-discipline, a certain individualism, thrift and rational calculation, and a consciousness of the value of life and time. Less obviously, however, did the 19th Century dedicate itself to the service of God and the hope of salvation (although of course still a matter of major concern) and less obvious too are the parallels between the economic and industrial requirements of the 17th Century and the 19th Century.

Nevertheless, one student of the 17th Century Puritans does offer an analysis that is suggestive in the 19th Century context. Michael Walzer maintains that the Puritan demand for methodical and continuous activity was "a reaction to the breakdown of country stability, and . . . to the sudden appearance of the mobile urban man." The Puritan work ethic was "at least as much a response to the overriding problem of social order as it is to the individual's anxiety with regard to his fate in the life to come."[11] In the same way, the 19th Century work ethic can also be seen as a response to the disruption of social order, from Peterloo (1819) onwards, and a response to the emergence of the volatile and (to other classes) often fearsome working class. Hence it can be argued that the 19th Century work ethic was less a result of Evangelical influence, transmitted Puritan ideals, or the religious revival, than a response to the question of social order. It would not be surprising, therefore, to find that many Victorians reacted to social discontent by emphasising the value of work according to traditional and *status quo* work roles, and such was indeed the case. Others (most often the clergy) also reacted to changing social and moral values by stressing the nees for a link between individual self-discipline and morality, character formation and steady work. There *was* a relationship, therefore, between work and religion in Victorian Britain, but the relationship was peculiar to the 19th Century, and often seemed to be a negative reaction to social change rather than a positive enthusiasm for the alliance of work, commerce and religion. Indeed there is strong evidence that many clergy feared the secularism thought to be inherent in an over-commitment to commerce - and the frequent criticism of the single-minded drive for money and success in Victorian literature bears out their warnings.

This would still be a very one-sided explanation, however, without taking into account the industrial needs of an expanding economy: namely, a large well-disciplined labour force, and the accumulation of capital for reinvestment through the medium of low wages and high profits. Moreover, these needs clashed with the aristocratic ideal of the leisured gentlemen - in an age of production, a functionless class was anachronistic. The result of all these requirements and reactions was an emphasis on work either negative or positive), and ultimately an often reluctant search for a _via media_ between the old society and the new. This solution sought to find a compromise that would grant a measure of social and financial mobility without endangering social stability - a middle way that would accommodate social change but not social revolution. In this process of adjusting and legitimising work roles within the parameters of social stability, four attitudes toward work became especially evident and will be discussed, namely Traditional, Promethean, Rational and Protean attitudes. In the end, however, three elements stand out: the contempt for labour among the upper classes, the fear of secularisation, and the very carefully moderated encouragements to work in the shape of cautious promises of social mobility and financial reward.

Firstly, and despite the precedents of the Puritan era (a favourite period of study for Victorians), many did believe that the 19th Century was uniquely an age of work. In 1853 an anonymous author for the Sunday School Union pronounced his understanding of the times, recognising both good and evil:

> This is an age of work. All hands and heads are busy. Some for good and some for evil. Some for God and

> some for Satan. High and low, rich and poor, young and old, wise and simple all are at it. Knowledge is being rapidly increased. Inventions, curious and many, are rapidly brought out. Men are <u>running</u> to and fro in the earth. It is a busy age in which we live.

The age was so busy, in fact, that many simply accepted that which was evil as inevitable, as did William Unsworth (Methodist) in 1861:

> One is heartily sorry that any man should be under the necessity of working twelve or more hours a day . . . But this is an age when all is going at railway speed. Every energy is called forth in business, trade and profession.

Another clergyman, writing in 1862, believed that the Victorian age was remarkable for its faith in power - the power to produce astounding achievements through work. But the result, an almost irrational pursuit of work for its own sake, without any idea of future goals, did not immediately dismay him:

> . . . the entire age is stamped with an unmistakable energy and force. It is an age of gigantic and universal toil, possessed with the idea that there is work to be done; restless and insatiable, resolute and quiet, in pursuing this idea . . . Work is lauded and glorified, even for its own sake, and without regard to its end. It is held to be something sacred, a thoroughly manly and almost devout pursuit. Nay, it has been exalted into a kind of deity in our day, to be worshipped with a pure and rigorous devotion. Life is to be doing, because it is felt more than ever that there is power in life.[12]

Indeed the Victorians were working so hard and so long that there were frequent efforts (including the 10 Hours Bill) to channel and to slacken the effort. The Rev. J. Kennedy, writing for the Religious Tract Society in 1860, recognised the strong desire of the age to work, which he hoped was for the sake of internal conscience, and not for any other reasons:

> We need not that the orator or poet should tell us of the dignity of labour; or the economist, of its necessity; or the casuist, of its lawfulness.[13]

In fact the problem came to be not so much to encourage work activity, as to control the excess of work and its accompaniment, anxiety. The Journal of Health published an article in 1853 entitled "Effects of Over-Confinement to Business" (incidentally anticipating the stress theory of disease): "The great source of disease among the middle class is ANXIETY. The mind of the tradesmen, constantly fluctuating between hope and fear, is ever in an unsettled condition." By the 1860s some even placed an equal emphasis on rest and relaxation as an antidote to work: "Overwork has plainly had its day. Medical people have plainly set their faces against it . . ."[14]

Given that the Victorian age was one of hard work, there is still a distinction to be made between the hard work that was self-enforced, and the labour induced by the industrial system. Self-enforced work could be either self-disciplined work seen as a value in itself, or the self-enforced drive for success in the shape of wealth or status. Self-disciplined work for its own sake will be considered below, but the difference between the self-enforced pursuit of wealth and the necessary work of the working class was only too clear to one observer in 1866:

> Wealth is the only aim of life - gold the only true worship. Gold is the measure of men's importance, the badge of distinction, while the working man is treated with contempt, abandonment and sneers. True, many people talk of the dignity of labour, but not a soul believes in it.[15]

One the one hand, the enforced labour of the factory system is too well known to require more documentation than Engels' The Condition of the Working Classes in England in 1844, although it is well to remember that cases of long hours of work occurred as frequently outside the factory as within, namely, among the store clerks and domestic servants. However, the hard work engendered by the self-enforced pursuit of success, while equally prevalent, is less well documented. This pursuit of success contained two separate, though usually interrelated, facets - financial success and upward social mobility. The immoderate pursuit of wealth was often noticed by those like Thomas Carlyle (and Samuel Smiles) who condemned the idolatory of Mammon. Thus the Rev. W.K. Tweedie (Church of Scotland) stated what he contended was "obvious . . . that the spirit of our age is turned, like a sweeping rapid, in the direction of amassing riches with haste." Henry Mayhew, the investigator of London life and poverty, pointed out the other facet of success - social climbing: "It is this petty racing spirit that sets every one struggling now-a-days to get out of their own sphere and class . . . There is no such thing as contentment - all is scramble, struggle, greed, and rivalry." But Mayhew was careful to illustrate the difference between social success and financial success, for the latter was easier to achieve than the former - "see how the parvenu(e) is laughed at and despised . . ." he warned. Likewise, the Rev. William Robinson (Baptist), writing on self-education, noted that money without education was useless, for even if "success in business" was achieved, and introductions effected into "respectable society," yet the upstart's uncouth dialect would always betray their plebian origin.[16]

Sir John Kaye, historian, essayist and civil servant, attempted to soften reality and to reconcile financial success with social status by asking his contemporaries not to concentrate on the results of success, but "to honour what has won success . . . It is veneration for that type of manhood, which most nearly approaches the divine, by reason of its creative energy." Sir John then made an interesting point, remarking that not long ago success was reviled in society, but that "a healthier social philosophy is now [1860] among us," namely, it was now accepted that men who had become rich or famous "by the force of their personal characters must . . . have something in them . . ."[17] That is, that aspect of the impulse to hard work among the Victorians (the self-enforced drive to succeed), had become respectable by 1860. This raises the question of the timing of the Victorian stress on work. If, according to Sir John Kaye, the pursuit of financial and social success had become respectable by 1860 (albeit more for the promise of character revealed than for its actual results), and if the Victorian emphasis upon work is granted, when did this emphasis on work become noticeable and who were its proponents?

The question raises difficulties, because again it is necessary to distinguish between those who valued work for its own sake (this group would evidently include Sir John Kaye), and those who favoured hard work for its material rewards. As early as 1836 J.H. Newman was criticising this latter group for their "intense, sleepless, restless, never-wearied, never-satisfied, pursuit of Mammon . . ." and it is clear that the drive for financial success (although something of a permanent situation since at least the 16th Century) was a particularly obvious phenomenon by the later 18th and early 19th Centuries.[18] On the other hand, the stress upon work as a valuable pursuit in itself (whether actually believed in or not) achieved an especial prominence in the middle years of the 19th Century. In a book published in 1851 the novelist Geraldine Jewsbury has one of her characters remark that the "_prestige_ of idleness has already begun to disappear . . ." although another of her characters also comments: "It must be owned that the actual aspect of labour and of the labourer is not attractive, except to men truly religious, who work from a higher motive than that of immediate success, or personal gain and loss."[19] Likewise, another commentator, writing in 1866, seemed to consider the discredit of idleness to be firmly established by that date and gives a reason:

> Political economists have brought idlers into discredit, even among the upper classes; and it is now no uncommon thing to hear noblemen, and persons of high social station, tell audiences, at mechanics institutions, that they (the speakers) too are working men.

This should be contrasted with Henry Mayhew's pithy comment in 1860: "Society . . . seems to have had its fill of the mechanics' institute mania; the teachy-preachy fever appears to have come to a crisis . . ."[20] Mayhew was correct in thinking that mechanics' institutes had seen their day by the 1860s, but it was also clear that the upper classes were no longer quite so brazen about their claims to idleness.

If the prestige of idleness was declining, who, besides the political economists, were raising the status of work? There were at least three groups that enhanced the prestige of work around mid-century. Firstly, the upper classes redoubled their efforts to make work attractive to others; secondly, a number of Victorians, often Dissenting ministers, and thus generally spokesmen for the middle class, reacted against the image of an idle aristocracy; and thirdly, the clergy as a whole attempted to reintegrate work and religion.

Writing at mid-century, Mayhew declared:

> There is a cant abroad at the present day, that there is a special pleasure in industry, and hence we are taught to regard all those who object to work as appertaining to the class of natural vagabonds . . .

It did not take Mayhew long to find the authors of such 'cant,' noting that "it is well for fat and phlegmatic citizens to call people 'lazy scoundrels' and bid them 'go and work'; but let these gentlemen themselves try their soft hands at labour . . ." and again asking "if industry be such a supreme enjoyment, as the idle rich ever rejoice in declaring, then where is the virtue of it? . . . Let those who think work a pleasure try a week's mental or manual labour . . ."[21] Mayhew thus pointed his finger at one mid-century group, the "gentlemen" and the "idle rich," who praised the value of work, but who preferred to have someone else actually do it.

Such an attitude brought a corresponding response by a second mid-century group, those who wished to discredit the idle aristocracy and assert their own claim to social status (a response that also appealed to Smiles), for it was clear that the ideal of "the gentlemen" in the 1850s was idleness and not work, even if less openly expressed. Hence in 1850 one journal brought forward the example of Prince Albert as a working aristocrat:

> The Consort of the QUEEN, labouring day by day at the same table with the Representatives of Industry of every branch [to promote the Great Exhibition of 1851], presents a valuable lesson to those who imagine that there is something unworthy in work, and that idleness is the characteristic of a gentleman.

In 1862 the Rev. William Stevenson (Irish Presbyterian) linked the idleness of the "gentlemen" to another form of idleness, the "laziness" of scepticism, while at the same time clearly recognising the existence of a peculiarly Victorian emphasis on work, and identifying such an emphasis as a reaction both temporal and moral:

> . . . there is a healthiness about this zeal for work. As a protest against a hollow and indifferent age, an age of shams and fine gentlemen and idle, self-indulgent, shallow sceptics, an age of lazy, stereotyped and powerless beliefs, it is invaluable: and, as a reaction from last century was unavoidable, work perhaps is the safest form it could have assumed . . . It is some recognition of the meaning and dignity of life.[22]

It must have been obvious to all at mid-century that idleness was indeed a mark of social status and this situation was sufficient to account for a large measure of the chorus of reaction and praise for work in the 1850s. Such praise often came from religious Dissenters such as E.P. Hood, the popular author of some fifteen books, and a future Congregational minister, who believed that there was a new man in the 19th Century, the man of virtue, who had "extinguished the blaze of coronets, and diadems, and garters and stars . . . ," who had "torn down the veil from old collegiate establishments . . ." and had broken with the aristocratic past by "throwing sanctity around labour, and making enterprise holy . . ." This conscious rejection of the aristocratic past at mid-century was made more explicit in an article written in 1851 entitled "1801 and 1851. A Chapter of Contrasts." The article found one contrast in the new (and somewhat unconvincing) hope of what earnest labour could do, namely, to dignify humanity, for it was the manner of working, not the work itself that degraded the worker. This argument certainly implied that the work itself might be degrading, but there was plenty of praise in the 1850s for the kind of work that the middle class might undertake. Thus, the Rev. H. Dunckley (a Baptist and an Anti Corn Law League supporter) argued in 1854 that trade had finally achieved recognition and status: "Trade can be scorned no longer; it has burst forth with the splendour of heaven-made genius, and compelled the reluctant homage of all ranks . . ." However, it was probably the repeal of the Corn Laws in 1846 that gave the greatest impetus to this particular group's emphasis on the value of work:

> Much more is repealed than the old Corn-Laws. The pseudo-feudalism is abolished . . . The new laws are the index of a great social transition. They lead to the recognition, in opinion, of the nobility of industry . . .[23]

If this vision of an idle aristocracy in an age of work and progress stirred reaction in one direction, the vision of an age over-committed to material progress produced a counter-reaction in another direction, and again this occurred in the 1850s. This (third) group paradoxically emphasised the value of work by attempting to spiritualise it, thus preventing what appeared to be the secularising trend inherent in the dirve for material progress and self-enforced success. One sign of this situation occurred in the rewording of a book title that had originally appeared in 1799 and 1815 as An Enlarged Series of Extracts from the Diary & c., [of Joseph Williams of Kidderminster]. The new title for the 3rd edition of the book, printed in 1853, was The Christian Merchant: A Practical Way to make "the best of both worlds": exhibited in the life and writings of Joseph Williams of Kidderminster. That is to say, work and religion were seen as integral rather than separate - this being the central point of the group. Thus the previously cited Rev. William Stevenson complained of the "rapid growth of materialism." There was a difference between honest work and materialism, he maintained, and the difference was religion, yet this was not generally recognised:

> To work is honest enough; but prayer over and above work is treated as a courteous superfluity. Let the work be done manfully, it is preached; let it even be blundering, provided it be sincere; but as for prayer, it is somewhat a waste of energy. Or, if there be prayer, it is freely hinted, let it be kept apart . . . let it have its praying men, and give us our working men.

Stevenson did not want to be reminded of the need and dignity and sacredness of work, "the whole century is preaching that . . ." - what he wanted was to rescue work from secularism and place it back in the camp of religion: "work without prayer is as dangerous, ay, and more, than prayer without work. It is the practical ignoring of God, of a spiritual world and spiritual laws . . . It is a clear peril fo our present time."[24]

Stevenson therefore recognised the "rapid growth of materialism" and placed its "clear peril" squarely at the time of writing, 1862.

The Victorian emphasis on work had evidently reached a particular intensity in the middle years of the century, but it also continued through the century.[25] One or two examples of the continuity of the work ethic may be given. For example, an advertisement in 1889 remarked: "It is extraordinary how many men suffer now-a-days both in mind and body from a multitude of ailments resulting simply from weak nerves, consequent upon over-work, worry and other debilitating causes."[26] There was also a continuing emphasis on work by those who feared that Victorians no longer believed in the value of work for its own sake. Thus in 1879 one author complained in a familiar vein that

> when some stern moralist arises, and speaks earnestly of the dignity and honourableness of work, we yawn and murmer, 'Yes, in others.' Self-reliance has disappeared before our indolent and luxurious selfishness. This is the secret of the mania for making money by speculative companies . . . Society wishes to save itself trouble. It wants money, but does not want to work for it.

And an 1891 moralist was still offering the advice "never be ashamed of honest work . . ." It seems, therefore, that many Victorians did continue to avoid work, but also to work hard, and to preach the value of work, through the second half of the century.[27]

Its existence and duration established, the Victorian work ethic would still not be adequately explained by the attitudes so far suggested - the traditional upper class attitude; the reaction against the 'idle' aristocracy; the opposite reaction against the (theoretically) secularising trend of commerce; the enforced labour of the working classes, and the pursuit of financial and social success. For (using a wide range of 'popular' literature), it is possible to conceive of four particularly evident attitudes toward work in Victorian Britain, through which conceptual model a variety of opinions in regard to work may be explained. This conceptual model visualises these four attitudes as frequently cutting across each other and hence not operating in a mutually exclusive way. The four attitudes are: firstly, a "Traditional" attitude toward work (this does not necessarily infer paternalism, since paternalism implies responsibility, nor merely an aristocratic view, but a broader concept of work according to authoritarian and traditional guidelines); secondly, a Promethean attitude (work externalised and applied toward the control of the material world); thirdly, a Rational attitude (work seen in terms of reward or material result, and including class attitudes in regard to political and rational expectations); and fourthly, a Protean attitude (work internalised according to certain principles).

Traditional attitudes to work did encompass aristocratic attitudes, and frequently depended on religious sanctions, but even more basically, it was a question of a dichotomy of domination and subjection, of a simple matter of where authority and power rested. Thus the spread of education was feared as much as changing work roles. "I do not believe you lads would be any better," an anonymous author declared in 1857 on the subject of leisure, "for having the knowledge your Parson or your master have. That knowledge is necessary for them, but it is not necessary for you." More specifically in regard to work, the doctor to the Royal Household, John Forbes, did not doubt in 1850

> that the daily corporeal labour which is the lot of this class of men [labourers], supplies that kind of occupation which is most suited to their capacity, and which is, consequently, more productive of happiness than any other would be. I even question if the diminuation of . . . daily labour, when excessive, as, in many cases, it doubtless is, would add to their Happiness.

Such attitudes only made it necessary to describe work-roles as organised by some higher authority in order to explain them, as John Forbes explained the need to accept the condition of manual labour "with resignation, simply because the wise arrangements of the world had so decreed it: with resignation, I say, and even with contentment . . ." And from the point of view of the Church, the Rev. Tweedie appealed to his traditional authority: "God has appointed different orders in society - the high and the low, the rich and the poor - and all attempts to violate that primary law have recoiled upon their authors" [i.e. Owenites and Socialists].[28]

Traditionalists, however, had a considerable problem when they advised the working men to better their own conditions and become independent, yet at the same time remain submissive. The problem is evident in a didactic novel published in 1860, which followed the fortunes of one, Henry Birkett, in his quest for financial and moral independence. Birkett was able to remain independent of charity, and also it seems, of his shopmates, who "talked a good deal about Radicalism," and whose politics were described as "the foulest ingratitude, guised under the term independence . . ." The author obviously meant to praise not independent thinking and politics, but financial independence, for Henry Birkett's first guinea, earned by "industry, frugality, and thrift" made him a "capitalist," with a "stake in the country. He becomes somewhat conservative in his notions, and no longer wonders why a rich man should think himself somebody." The contradictions in this kind of solution were clearly spelled out at a unique London meeting in 1867, called by Anglicans and Nonconformists to discover the reasons for working class secularism. Mr. Green, a tailor, pointed out the problem:

> He did not say that it was wrong to teach a man patience under adversity, but Christianity, or rather

> the Christianity that was taught, taught a man to be perfectly satisfied with the condition in which he was placed, and to be patient under it, whilst at the same time it taught him that it was his duty and his privilege to rise to something better.[29]

Traditionalists could be found in many guises, but the overwhelming sense of mid-century 'traditional' literature was toward the society and work-roles of a hierarchical society. Some preached resignation only, as did the geologist and geographer, David Page, in 1864: "As life has its duties, and duty demands labour, so the aim [of his book] has been to inculcate submission, cheerfulness, and hope . . ." Others, such as the Rev. W. Blaikie (Free Church of Scotland), reverted again to the idea of work-roles as immutable: "The vast majority must continue to be hard workers, hewers of wood and drawers of water. This is the inexorable law of Providence and it were about as wise to change the law of gravitation . . ." Still others argued for the naked question of authority, whether it be through the birching of children to induce future obedience and virtue in whatever "condition of life . . . they may be placed . . ." or, as the Rev. John Hall (Independent; Minister of Union Chapel) desired, Church attendance to produce "subordination, rule, authority, and responsibility . . ."[30] And even the more radical popular writers, such as the Howitts (William Howitt became editor of the _People's Journal_ in 1846) took a very static attitude toward the working class. When the Positivist, Frederick Harrison, accused the Howitts of stirring up trouble through the journal, Mary Howitt replied, in a rare revelation of editorial policy: "There is no attempt to set the poor against the rich, but on the contrary, to induce them to be prudent, sober, independent; above all to be satisfied to be workers, to regard labour as a privilege rather than a penalty, which is quite our view of the case."[31]

Whatever the reasons for assigning work roles, whether through fear or selfishness or genuine belief in an immutable society, and whatever the sanctions, God or inevitability, the traditionalists in the end relied upon their own sense of authority in pointing out the work to be done, and who was to do it. This emphasis on work was caused, therefore, by an attempt to define and fix work roles, but at the same time to encourage the performance of socially desirable work. Thus the attempt to fix work roles was often accompanied by the prophecy of chaos if different work groups evaded their duty. "If servants can't be happy as servants," stated one anonymous 'traditionalist,'

> because they want to be masters, and tradesmen can't be happy as tradesmen because they want to be gentry, and gentry can't be happy as gentry because they are not nobility, why then, of course, there would be nothing but discontent.[32]

The answer was for everyone to be happy "in their own station of life." There was to be more than a hint of this 'tradition' in Smiles' thinking, even if it remained somewhat muted.

The 'traditional' attitude to work was complemented by a Promethean attitude toward work. That is, largely in order to make work more acceptable to those who worked, and particularly to the manual workers, work was given the transcendent task of conquering the material world. The often mundane drudgery of work was spiritualised by this message, and nowhere was this more obvious than in the case of the Great Exhibition of 1851.[33] Henry Mayhew felt that to working men the sight of all the products in the Exhibition would evoke thoughts of the "triumphs of labour over the elements of the whole material universe . . . [and so] cannot fail to inspire them with a sense of their position in the State, and to increase their self-respect . . ." Through the conquest of the material world, wrote another commentator on the subject of the Exhibition, the worker not only gained social status, but also fulfilled his worldly mission, namely to

> subjugate elemental nature, and confer on the Human Race that entire dominion over the earth, air, and the sea, which was enjoined in the Universal Author's first commands to man.[34]

Thus the Promethean attitude to work not only encouraged the workers by the sheer objective results of their labour, but spiritualised that labour through its triumphs over matter - the material world. Moreover, work was spiritualised in another way, as suggested in the last citation, by the representation of man's subjugation of Nature as a Divine mission. Prince Albert pointed out this ideal in a speech at the Crystal Palace:

> Man is approaching a more complete fulfillment of that great and sacred mission which he has to perform in this world. His reason being created in the image of God, he has to discover the laws by which the Almighty governs his creation, and by making these laws his standard of action, to conquer nature to his use - himself a Divine instrument.[35]

In an analagous, but more lyrical variation, the Leeds Transcendentalist and friend of Smiles', G.S. Phillips, found the myth of Prometheus explained - industry was indeed the spiritualised meaning of life. He heard "a heavenly music in the blast and terror which issue from the scrannel [thin and ugly] chimney pipes of the manufactory . . . I fancy I can read in these glorious triumphs of the soul the meaning of man's expulsion from Eden, and the significance of the beautiful allegory of Prometheus." Phillips hoped also for the regeneration of the world through knowledge, but in the meantime, "Glory to God for the blessed curse of Labour! Out of the sweat of human brows, and the toil of human hands, the uninhabitable earth has been filled with habitations . . . and made divine by the presence of human forms . . ."[36]

Perhaps the most interesting statement of Promethean labour was Carlyle's injunction to mankind to create order in the world through work. While it can be argued that there were ulterior reasons for Carlyle's emphasis on work, such as religious doubt and unsatisfactory sexual experiences, yet Carlyle's request for the Promethean worker to shape the maleable material world into order, purpose and use, was the result of his belief in the externalisation of work. Whatever virtue, faculty or energy there was in man, according to Carlyle, came out in his work, and so there was a force in man, a force for work, "giving thee no rest until thou unfold it." Carlyle's externalisation of work corresponded also to his theory of colonisation - to release and externalise the choked up "old Saxon energy" in the colonisation of "fertile untenanted Earth" - to create and conquer the Continents and Eldorados of the future.[37]

Colonisation as the expression of man's Promethean and creative energy was not unique to Carlyle. Henry Mayhew too felt that colonisation was due to the same "God-like quality in man - the great creative and heroic faculty - that changes barren plains into fertile fields, and builds up cities in the wilderness." Mayhew also pointed out a parallel quality of Promethean work - it could clear the external world of its overwhelming anonymous opposition to the hopes of the individual - not the struggle of man against man, but

> the conquest of the great host of circumstances with which we have always to battle - to the beating down of difficulties, and to the enslaving of the giant forces of the world in which we live, and making them work for the benefit of mankind . . .[38]

If the Promethean attitude toward work tried to encourage the workers by giving them a transcendent mission in the world, other Victorians preferred to remain on the more practical level of profit and reward, or the more 'Rationalised' level of the laws of political economy and nature. Joseph Bentley (a school inspector) acknowledged the general reluctance to labour, and the "scarcely concealed desire . . . to throw the burden on any other shoulders than their own," but (in a possibly self-serving argument) declared that "it is the duty of the State . . . to create in the minds of those who work, and those who employ labourers . . . that . . . wages, profits, capital, are regulated by great unchanging laws." Bentley concluded that the "utility, the honour, even dignity of labour ought also to be better understood, and more appreciated than it is."[39] In other words the situation for those who worked was undesirable, and could not be changed, but might be rationalised and explained.

Such 'Rational' attitudes to work differed from the Traditional attitude, since the latter relied upon authoritative and undefended statements rather than rational and economic explanations of the current work situation. In this context some obvious candidates are the Political Economists and Utilitarians, who generally considered work from only a practical viewpoint. John Stuart Mill's Principles of Political Economy neither externalised nor internalised work, but simply rationalised it, "labour would be devoid of its chief sweetener," he wrote, without "the thought that every effort tells perceptibly on the labourer's own interests." Mill believed that it was only necessary for the security of labour and property to be certain in order for "industry and frugality" to become pervading qualities in a people. This theory of work assumed an acquisitive man, who could only be satisfied by rationally planned work and the acquisition of wealth. Similarly Bentham felt that men laboured only for the fruits of labour, for acquisition, or for the hope of future rewards. Moreover, work and labour were seen as unpleasant, and so to

Henry Mayhew, as to Bentham and a host of others, the only inducement to labour was reward, "for work or labour is merely that which is irksome to perform, and which every man requires a certain amount of remuneration to induce him to perform."[40]

Sometimes political economists tried more complex analyses of rationalised motives to work. Nassau Senior admitted that all men hoped to obtain the greatest wealth with the least sacrifice, but there were varying reasons for the acquisition of wealth, namely, power, fame, leisure, sensual appetite, etc. Senior then launched into a class analysis of work - the poor and uneducated worked to satisfy their "appetites," meaning sensual enjoyment; the educated and wealthy upper classes worked to satisfy their vanity and desire for distinction, although unhappily their motive for accumulation was also the motive for expenditure (as in Veblen's argument); but the middle classes, although above appetite and lavish expenditure, were not above a certain vanity, which caused them to work and save but not to spend.[41] This effort at a class analysis of work by a political economist raises the question of how far the Victorian emphasis on work was motivated by class attitudes - and it is clear that to a considerable extent it was.

It has been argued, for example, that the middle class changed its attitude toward the aristocracy from one of moral superiority to one of class antagonism due to the impulse given by Benthamites and classical economists; that the working class ideal was based on the twin ideas of the labour theory of value and co-operative work; that the middle class ideal was composed partly of the concept of the productive entrepreneur, and partly of the drive for respectability among the new professional class; and that the aristocratic ideal was based not on work, but on paternal responsibility for those who did work.[42] There is in fact evidence to support a class analysis of work, for example the middle class S.D.U.K. (Society for the Diffusion of Useful Knowledge), strove to allay the passions of the machine-wrecking workers by describing machinery to them "in the light of what it produced, and the labour avoided, rather than as an object complete in itself," and in general the S.D.U.K. tried to convince working class men of the inevitability of the type of work which confronted them.[43]

Rationalised class attitudes to work certainly existed, but whether they were class attitudes first and work attitudes second, or _vice versa_, depends on the definition of 'class.' Suffice to say that there _was_ an obvious conflict between those who felt the value of work, largely the middle and working classes, and those who considered leisure and sport more estimable, mainly the upper class landed gentry. (There was also a third category, the many Victorians who needed to work but who would not or could not, and who were provided for by the Poor Laws.)[44] Theoretically a middle-working class alliance of productive workers versus aristocratic 'idlers' might have been predicted, and there was in fact a middle class attempt in this direction which failed in the 1840s. And in this context there is also evidence of a rationalised class-oriented conflict over work-roles, with the middle class attempting to mediate between the aristocracy and working classes, as in the case of the Rev. William Anderson (Congregational), who declared his intention to "check their arrogance who demand our deference in consideration of their noble ancestry . . ." but who also wished "to vindicate the dignity of humble industry . . ." And E.P. Hood asked "what great difference, then, is there, in one respect, between the nobleman who possesses these sources of revenue [coalpits and farms] and the merchant or tradesman who keeps a shop?" Hood could see no difference, and called upon both the aristocracy and the working classes "to do something useful" for he considered that "true merit consists in the correct performance of our part, whatever that may chance to be."[45] These class conscious arguments were considered necessary to counteract the irrational, and (in an industrial nation) impractical equation of leisure and gentlemanly status, as one etiquette book implied in 1865: "A true gentleman will do anything proper for him to do. He can soil his hands or use his muscles <u>when there is occasion</u>" (i.e. to carry home a market basket). This was what E.P. Hood termed "the bane of rational enterprise, [which] keeps hundreds from doing that which would be really honourable and lucrative."[46]

The rationalisation of work - whether through class attitudes, political economy, Benthamism, or simply the acknowledgement of the widespread desire to accumulate wealth - was an evident feature of the mid 19th Century. The rational relationship between work and material reward was thought to be understood and firmly fixed (without any Promethean or Traditional overtones as necessary work sanctions) and this fitting appreciation of the Utilitarian role was expressed in 1852 by E.P. Hood: "[I]n after ages," he wrote, "our railways, wreathed it may be in ivy, and the more lofty and capacious of our factories . . . will be the best practical commentary upon the books of Bentham . . ."[47]

Nevertheless, attitudes to work in Victorian Britain cannot easily be explained simply as class attitudes, or as traditional, Promethean, or rational, because another attitude often cut across those so far suggested, and yet retained a distinctive impression - the Protean attitude to work.

The Protean attitude toward work depended on the largely religious hope that work would help discipline and form the internal character, and at the same time that work would be conducted according to approved internalised principles of behaviour. Hence one book of guidance encouraged youth "to aim at the divine perfection of character and work, to be like God, who is good and to do like God . . ." The idea was for the individual to build up his character by using religious principles as a means of guiding and controlling daily activity. This effort at self-control would result in a disciplined character, which in turn would enable the individual to achieve independence from outside help. And so the Rev. T. Lynch (Nonconformist Independent) asserted flatly that "religion incites us to enterprise, and brings the man onward, so as when perfected in character, to secure circumstances as his domain and heritage."[48] But in order to recognise such perfected character, it was necessary that there be some outward sign of the internal self-control and obedience to principle. The outward sign was simply consistent conduct: "If we know such a man's principles, we may judge, with something like certainty, how he will act . . . for there is a consistency in his character." Every prudent and disciplined man would have fixed principles of action, and such consistent conduct would pay dividends, for "a steady adherence to fixed principles is the surest road to prosperity."[49]

The Rev. Lynch's mention of circumstance points up the process by which work was to be internalised into character - namely, the presence of difficulty. An author of children's tales called for the "weapons" of faith, energy and perseverance, "with which to grapple at the difficulties that it is God's law shall meet man at every stage of his life." The same sense of pre-ordained character training was developed by an anonymous author in 1852, who believed that "it is wisely ordered that this present life shall be one of discipline, and nothing brings out our latent powers, and gives such force to the character as contending with difficulties."[50] The assumption was that all individuals contained undeveloped internal powers, whose perfection into well-disciplined character was provided for by a divinely appointed series of difficulites. And of course the explanation could be reversed - since poverty and adversity were the lot of large segments of Victorian society, then the rationalisation of difficulty was simply a means of giving value and significance to unpleasant reality. Moreover, it was seen that the changing values of society presented a danger which might perhaps be countered by an emphasis on morality and character. In 1860, one unknown and fearful author claimed "there is just now great danger lest those great moral principles which are the basis of all worthy character . . . should be neglected and forgotten . . . [because] into many of the . . . halls of modern commerce, many of the Devil's cunningest imps have gone . . ."[51] This author was referring specifically to trades union strike action, but the general emphasis on internally principled work was obviously related to the feeling that the old virtues and moral values had been abandoned in favour of new and untried values.

The break with the moral values or principles of the past was noticed by several writers. Mrs. A. Hope (an upper class convert to Roman Catholicism) announced in 1843 that it was then rare to meet with "persons of active usefuleness and inflexible principle . . . [who] live up to the moral and religious precepts which their teachers have inculcated." Such a person, wrote Mrs. Hope, "cannot fail to outstrip his competitors." In the same way Sir John Kaye in 1860 called for a return to honest work and manly independence, and "to the status of our grandsires, and to give us more lowly thoughts." The reaction to this unfortunate break with the humility and dependent work of the past was indeed to re-emphasise internal morality and principle, and so the Rev. Samuel Coley scolded those who chased money and fame instead of work and duty: "Unfaithfulness in little and hidden things manifests the absence of principle in everything. Plainly, not duty, but reputation is the pole-star . . . Virtue is not in them an inward law . . ."[52] The implication was that work, duty and religion were being replaced as guidelines by a new set of instructions - success at almost any price.

This situation was distressing enough, but the Rev. Coley went on to raise an interesting question. How could internal merit or external character be judged if the traditional Christian values were reversed, as would happen if life was mde too easy by Utopians (read Socialists, radicals and trades unions) or if the acquisition of money was achieved through manipulation, rather than hard work? The Christian theory of the shaping of character through trials (difficulties) would be undermined he thought, for how could a man

> evince prudence if there exist no perils? - how show courage if there be no difficulty? - how exercise industry if there be no work? - how manifest fidelity if no one tempts? - how win victories if there be no battles?

But Coley reassured himself: "God is too wise for this: He knows comfort to be of far less importance than character . . ." E.L. Bulwer, an aristocrat and a prolific author, carried the problem one stage further, for he felt that this reversal of values had created a "crisis" in society, and he obviously considered that the attempt to "elude" obstacles rather than "conquer" them meant not only a change in attitudes toward disciplined character and persevering work, but potentially a change in social structure as well. If uncomplaining labour and patience were exchanged for education made easy and money made speculatively, then the barriers to social and financial advancement that helped to control the class structure would begin to crumble.[53]

The fears of Coley and Bulwer appeared to be justified. As the century developed the criticism of lack of principles continued, indicating the mid-century failure to internalise fixed moral and work values - for example an 1883 critique evidently linked this failure to ideological change: "If there is one character more despicable than another," wrote Joseph Johnson, "it is the vacillating changeling . . . He has no settled purpose and no settled principles." This was dangerous because a man with no settled principles was likely to adopt "every freshly-conceived notion and every new fangled fancy." And by 1897 the Rev. Horton (a Congregationalist and the first Nonconformist ever elected to a fellowship at Oxford) declared that the prevalent pursuit of success was only achieved "by the sacrifice of principle. And at the gates of society lie the slain principles which have been sacrificed . . ."[54]

A further reason for the Protean internalisation of work values was the attempt to replace the work discipline of the personalised and more easily enforced order of the old society of agriculture and small workshops with a moral self-discipline better suited to the numerically large and more distant working classes of the mid-19th Century in their factories and towns.[55] This distance between the working classes and their modes of work, and other classes in Victorian Britain, is consciously and unconsciously revealed in a preface to an 1859 book, which recounted an almost symbolic encounter with an artisan, in which a book was exchanged (presumably an R.T.S. [Religious Tract Society] tract). As the artisan reached for the book, the donor

> was struck with the strange contrast between his broad, labour-stained palm and my own slight fingers, which nearly touched his, and I experienced a feeling of peculiar and deep interest as I looked upon the working-man, with whom I was thus, for a single instance only, brought in contact . . . [and] I realised, as I had not before done, how many were the hardships of his lot . . .

This kind of contrast and separation of classes was repeated in the factory, for whereas previously the master had had "better opportunities" to study "the character of his apprentices" in the small workshop, now he was represented in the factory only by a "'code of laws for the regulation of the shop' suspended from the wall." But

> that was the age of workshops, this is the age of factories. These simple terms imply the change. Then the master was not above going through his workshop in his shirtsleeves . . .

In those days the master

> saw not only what was done, but . . . with what will it was done. Masters now drive to business at 10 or 11 o'clock, either in the showy 'trap' or on the top of an omnibus. They pay weekly wages . . . to work people whom they never see . . .[56]

If the factory "code of laws" signified the new depersonalised form of work discipline, so the Protean emphasis on internalised work values logically signified an attempt to replace the personal discipline of the structured society of the past with a moral persuasion more suited to a seemingly distant, autonomous, and less dependent working class. As J.W. Gilbart (Manager of the London and Westminster Bank) noted, the discipline of the industrial company and the discipline of the individual went together: "Fixed rules and regulations are to a public company what habits are to an individual; they insure a uniformity of conduct, and are equally essential to success."[57]

Perhaps the best summary of the Victorian work ethic would be to return to three earlier points, whose significance is attested by the vehemence of their proponents, and their frequent occurence in the literature. Firstly, the work ethic as expressed by Victorians was very often negative, emphasising the dignity of work when work was obviously not considered dignified; secondly, the work ethic was reinforced by the attempt made by the Church to re-assert its position in claiming that work was not a secular pursuit, but a religious vocation; and thirdly, the emphasis on work frequently dissolved into the search for some kind of <u>via media</u> of social structure and work roles.

The negative attitude toward work by the upper classes and the disdain with which they often held the workman and his work, aroused a reaction of something very like fear - fear that this contempt would arouse the wrong ideas among the working class. P.A. Fraser noticed with alarm the "growing disposition to view manual labour as derogatory to the dignity of the sons of respectable people, and, arising out of this feeling, the neglect of . . . parents to teach their children the duties of some industrial calling." And Joseph Bentley asked bluntly: "Why are those who manfully and dutifully do their fair share of it [work] . . . so often despised and ill-treated?" These questions were relevant, for it was recognised that those who were feared and despised generally accepted their role as the despised and "dangerous" classes. "So long as we look upon work or to it as a meanness, so long will our workers and toilers remain mean," wrote Henry Mayhew in 1851, for "if we wish to make gentlemen of our working men . . . our first step must be to assert the natural dignity of labour."

A more direct threat to the established order was also recognised - if it was the fashion among the upper classes to despise the "men of toil," then it was also the reciprocal fashion for the working men to regard those above them with "dislike" and "suspicion." The potentially dangerous result of such a continued deprecation of work was pointed out by William Unsworth in 1861: society needed "men's work" and could not "hold together" without it.[58]

Some Victorians feared, therefore, that the concept of the leisured gentleman and the parallel condemnation of work could very well pose a threat if disseminated too widely. Others, and particularly, if not exclusively, the clergy, feared another danger, that the extension of commerce was directly subversive of the old moral values (including work for its own sake) and religion itself. The danger was easily spotted by the Rev. R.T. Jeffrey:

> The mercantile spirit of the present day has grown impatient and restive under the restrictions of the moral law. The oldfashioned prescription of industry and honesty is treated as an exploded and obsolete theory for rising in the world . . . This general covetousness has led to the adoption of principles directly subversive of all Gospel morality.

Jeffrey proposed to combat the danger by linking religious devotion of worldly success, not for the purpose of heavenly salvation, as the Puritans have been accused of, but simply to keep the businessman within the pale of the Church:

> Other things being equal, ability and exertion corresponding, the probabilities of success are decidedly in favour of the devotional man. While God does not publish it as a settled principle in the economics of His providence, that He will own the prayerful activities of His people with invariable success in their secular affairs, yet we cannot think that He will leave unrewarded, even in this world, those who uniformly and systematically include Him as a party in their transactions.

And in much the same way the anonymous author of Working and Waiting (1858) produced a hero whose good fortune led him to believe that "God certainly has seen good to make me prosper abundantly . . . I owe it all to God."[59]

However, the commonest reaction was simply to state that Church and Commerce were not incompatible. The author of Success in Life (1852) declared "there is nothing incompatible between the highest morality and purest principles of true religion, and a diligent perseverence in the business of the world." The Rev. Blaikie despaired of "the rock of worldliness" but advised those who sought good situation, lucrative business, wealthy marriages, and conspicuous social positions to remember that these things were of little value compared with internal victory over greed, selfishness, ungodliness, "and the formation of a character and habits suitable to a son of God!" One clergyman even sought to bridge the gap between commerce and religion by attributing to Christianity the attractivenss of social status and the power of money - a "treasure" in its own right, although for the believing merchant the normal advice was simply the reminder that his work was done for God and not for himself, "there is no world's work to the believer, it is all the Lord's work . . ."[60]

Many Victorians felt caught, therefore, between the Scylla of secular commercialisation and the Charybdis of the leisured gentleman, a position which was complicated by the new expectations of the working classes, and particularly the 'aristocracy of labour,' the upward-striving artisans and mechanics of the Mutual Improvement Societies and Mechanics Institutes.[61] The problem was to find an ideal of work and success that was a *via media* between the *status quo* and a completely open society; between over-work and leisure; between the needs of industry, the excessive pursuit of money or social climbing, and the too ready acceptance by the working class of their disorderly, unhealthy, poverty-stricken, and potentially (for the rest of society) 'dangerous' condition.[62] Somewhat predictably this *via media* tended toward an emphasis on the value of work and character as a good in itself, quite apart from the results of such work and character, and incentives to work were presented in the shape of a variety of uneasy compromises between authoritarian directives and proposals for personal development and advance.

In his fictionalised story of the education of Benjamin Franklin (inspired perhaps by Rousseau's *Emile*), Henry Mayhew has the young Franklin ask his uncle rather plaintively:

> Is there not a medium, Josh, between the over-weening love of wealth, and the reckless disregard of it; a middle course between a despotic delight in that worldly power . . . of riches, and the servile abandonment . . . of poverty?

The medium was hard to find, but it could be achieved through moral self-control, stated Franklin's uncle. That was one answer, but Maria Edgeworth conceded that "the education of different ranks should, in some respects, be different . . . [T]heir ambition is to be directed to different objects." This was difficult in the story of 'Lazy Lawrence,' where Miss Edgeworth's "object was to excite a spirit of industry . . ." Again, care was

> taken to proportion the reward to the exertion, and to point out that people feel cheerful and happy whilst they are employed. The reward of our industrious boy, though it be money, is only money considered as the means of gratifying a benevolent wish. In a commercial nation, it is especially necessary to separate, as much as possible, the spirit of industry and avarice, and to beware lest we introduce vice under the form of virtue.[63]

How to stimulate industry for its own sake, without also stimulating a desire for money? The author of *Success in Life* relied on another solution, the possibility of honestly acquiring wealth, but, as in Wesley's solution, also dispensing that wealth in works of charity. Another compromise was sought by the Rev. J.B. Lister who saw no contradiction in finding a middle road between the excessive love of riches, or their misuse, and the comment that it was by no means despicable to contemplate making a fortune. Lister also declared that to go up in social status was to acquire habits "too expensive or too lofty . . .", but to go down was to "degrade you . . .", and so ended up by asking his readers to stay where they were, "thankful to have the opportunity of taking an honourable part in the struggle for life . . ." E.P. Hood took a similarly equivocal position, declaring that time and space would prevent a catalogue of those who had ascended to places of eminence from the most lowly situations. But he warned the reader not to confuse in his mind splendid living with real dignity and worth. Hood's solution was truly an open-ended one, for while claiming that people should remain in their sphere of life, he described man's sphere of life as that "in which he is born, or which he makes for himself."[64]

Other attempts to find a *via media* concentrated on allowing limited social mobility. William Unsworth thought that thousands of poor men might not become statesmen or field marshals, but that they might become masters, managers, foremen, "or at the very least, sensible and intelligent workmen." And the hero of an 1860 novel, Mark Gibson, announced his limited hopes: "I may not be great, I may not be rich, I care not to be either; but I feel determined to get a few steps up the ladder and am longing to climb." Another novel, Mrs. Craik's *John Halifax, Gentleman* (1856), presented the ideal of the self-made man with a fairly common restraining twist - the hero, unknown to all, had been born a gentleman and so his elevation posed no threat to the established order. However, a clearer sign of uneasiness occurred in an 1870 novel in which one spokesman complained of "the horror of this rapid money making" and felt it "worse to have too much money than too little." But in the end his ideal was to find a *via media* between "the equally balanced evils of TOO MUCH AND TOO LITTLE MONEY."[65] There were many attempts, therefore, to find a middle way for those eager to improve themselves - a middle way which would not encourage too much social mobility nor too much devotion to business - and at least the Rev. Blaikie was confident that a *via media* was there to be found: "difficult though it be to find the middle channel between Scylla and Charybdis, between waste and worldliness, it does exist and may be found."

It remains to suggest that another *via media* between the principles of authority and personal development was canvassed in Victorian Britain, namely, the ideal of self-help[66] as expressed by Samuel Smiles. This enormously popular author came to be seen both by his contemporaries and his future critics as the outstanding exponent of the Victorian emphasis on individualistic work and thrift. The story of Smiles' intellectual origins, life and many books was more complex than that assessment, but his ideal of self-help did touch the hopes and aspirations of great numbers of Victorians, and his advice on work and labour was a microcosm in many ways of the attitudes of a hard working society. Hence the study of Samuel Smiles and his message will be able to provide, through the understanding of one prominent and representative expression of the work ethic, a detailed insight into the Victorian preoccupation with the subject of work.

## Samuel Smiles: Introduction and Chronology.

Samuel Smiles was born in 1812 and lived into the 20th Century, dying in 1904. His life therefore spanned almost the entire 19th Century, but he did not achieve a literary reputation until the publication of Self-Help in 1859, at the age of 47. Yet his life before 1859 was full of politics and literary work, as well as a medical practice and railway work. In fact Smiles' life is striking for its duality - writing articles and books in his spare time, and pursuing a regular occupation during the day. In the context of Victorian literature this was perhaps not so unusual, witness Matthew Arnold and, for a considerable time at least, James and John Stuart Mill. But Smiles' relentless authorship in the idle moments of time revealed either extraordinary energy or an impressive conscience, and this dual career continued after his literary success in 1859, until an almost inevitable stroke in 1871 ended his regular occupation once and for all, although he continued to write. Smiles' last book, a life of Josiah Wedgewood, was published in 1894, for he had stopped writing his Autobiography (edited by Thomas Mackay and published in 1905) in his 78th year, 1890.

Smiles was the eldest of a large family of eleven children, born in Scotland to a Haddington couple, whose income came from a general merchant's store. At the age of 14 (1826) Smiles was apprenticed to a doctor in Haddington, in which position he read widely, including the novels of Fielding, Richardson and Smollett. (It was another striking contrast in Smiles' life, that although he himself was well educated and obviously continued to read voraciously, his 'self-help' books stressed that the best and truest education was to be learnt in daily life, and not through reading or in formal education.) Smiles moved to Leith in 1829, and matriculated at Edinburgh University in November 1829, in order to attend medical classes.

Smiles' life in Edinburgh is obscure, but it appears that he was keenly aware of the phrenology taught by George Combe, and he also seems to have found Dr. Fletcher's lectures on physiology the most memorable of those he attended. Smiles implies that he was influenced, also, by the Reform movement in politics, from 1830 on, and it is true that he began to write for the Edinburgh Weekly Chronicle sometime in the mid-1830s, a paper that has been described as a Dissenter's paper, whose editor, Dr. Thomas Murray, was a moderate reformer, 'though "erst a friend of Chartists."[67] In any case Smiles graduated from Edinburgh as a surgeon in November, 1832, only a few days before his 20th birthday. Unfortunately, Smiles could not find a medical practice, there being already too many army and navy surgeons discharged after the Napoleonic wars. However, Smiles did practice medicine fitfully in Haddington, and to fill in his spare time delivered lectures on scientific and medical subjects, learnt French, studied music, and wrote a book entitled Physical Education (1838). The book was not a success, but it is important as a source of Smiles' early ideas on the physiology and learning processes of man - an essential starting point for the study of his ideal of self-help.

After a visit to Holland to acquire another medical degree from Leyden (1838) Smiles was offered a post as editor of the Leeds Times, which he accepted and which he pursued for the next four years (1839-1842). This political and literary period is dealt with in Chapter II, but suffice to say that Smiles (like Dr. Thomas Murray) pursued a middle course as editor, between the Chartist Northern Star and the Whig Leeds Mercury, although initially leaning toward a radical position. Smiles left the Leeds Times at the beginning of 1843, partly to earn more money, since he was contemplating marriage, and partly because, in Carlyle's phrase, the perpetual "threshing of straw that had been a thousand times threshed" had begun to pall - four years of editorial writing as a political reformer had led to repetition and staleness.[68] During 1843 Smiles again practiced as a surgeon, wrote an undistinguished History of Ireland (1844) and in December, married Sarah Anne Dixon, daughter of a plumbing contractor.[69]

Smiles abandoned medicine for the assistant secretaryship of the Leeds and Thirsk Railway in 1845, a post he held until 1854, when he transferred to the South-Eastern Railway as secretary, and left the North of England for ever. The 1840s in Leeds had been active years for Smiles, not merely occupationally, but as a speaker, for he lectured widely, on subjects from "Animal Magnetism" (for the Leeds Mechanics Institution and Literary Society), to "Comparative Anatomy, [the] Natural History of beasts, birds, fishes, and insects . . . occasionally on Geography and its kindred subjects . . . and . . . biblical lessons . . ." (for the Zion Sunday School), to more political subjects such as the Corn Laws or the Suffrage question (at city-wide meetings).[70] During the 1840s Smiles also wrote for a number of reform journals, including Eliza Cook's Journal, but he discontinued this in 1853, and thereafter wrote articles only for the more conservative magazines, the Quarterly Review and Good Words.

Indeed the 1850s was a time of change for Smiles, not only geographically, but politically, and Self-Help, despite its roots in the 1830-1859 period, also owed something to this change, for the book represented a move away from the more radical days of, for example, 1839, and even from the less radical, but still reforming, days of the 1840s. With the publication of Self-Help (1859), Smiles' reputation was made, and while he continued the 'self-help' series - Character (1871), Thrift (1875), Duty (1880), Life and Labour (1887)[71] - he also wrote a great many other books of biography and industry, chiefly the four volume Lives of the Engineers (1861-62). Strangely enough, despite the popularity of his books and their high rate of sales, Smiles appeared to have felt criticised and misunderstood by his contemporaries (as indeed he was), who accused him of writing selfish success stories. In contrast, Smiles found a much greater social acceptance on the Continent than in England, and frequently remarked on both situations, besides giving lengthy descriptions in his Autobiography of his reception into the upper reaches of Italian society. Certainly Smiles' books were translated into at least 23 languages, and in Italy alone Self-Help had gone through 18 editions and 75,000 copies by 1889.[72] In this regard, the success of Self-Help in Japan, although most remarkable, is just one instance of the popularity of Smiles' books around the world.

Self-Help was enthusiastically received in Japan in the 1880s through the translation of Keiu. Its acceptance was signified at the turn of the century, for when thirty eminent Japanese were asked to name for modern youth a work of spiritual sustenance, "equivalent to the Bible for Christians," half of them suggested Self-Help. The editor of the Japanese "Success" magazine Saiko (1902) claimed Smiles as his forerunner, believing that only the Smiles tradition was capable of opposing the organisation man of "no fixed principles" and replacing him with the man of character, who lived by his own abilities, while respecting the lives of others.[73] Smiles' books were, of course, also well-received in Britain, besides their success abroad. Apart from the sheer numbers of books sold (up to the beginning of 1905, for example, some 258,000 copies of Self-Help had been printed), Self-Help also received the accolade of being included in Sir John Lubbock's list of the 100 Best Books, and several of Smiles' other books received the imprimatur of the Times Book Club selected list, and various other guides to good reading.[74]

Moreover Smiles himself acknowledged that one at least of his books was used as a school text book, and from the point of view of influence, it is also the case that the publication of Thrift led to the establishment of the National Thrift Society.[75] The mention of school text books raises the problem of who actually did or did not read Smiles' books. The former category would include schoolboys, for apart from use as text books, Smiles' works were given as school prizes, or simply as parental gifts. The latter category included many of the working class, who were illiterate at mid-19th Century, while those that *were* literate often preferred other fare. As Smiles once noted on learning of the failure of his cheap edition of the life of George Stephenson, "Cheap books won't do. The glorious working man doesn't read. He prefers spending his money on beer. Hence the failure of my 3/6 Stephenson." However, judging from the testinony of certain readers of Self-Help, and from one author who accused readers of turning to Self-Help, Practical Treatises upon Business, and Young Men's Manuals in search of a magic way to make a fortune, it appears that both the self-educated working class and the middle class were readers, using Smiles' books as a source of encouragement, and as manuals for rising in the world. But lastly, a comment by Sir John Kaye indicates a wider audience: "Have we not all been reading lately about 'Self-Help,' and what has charmed us so much?", he asked in 1860.[76]

With such slight evidence it would be difficult to arrive at a firm conclusion. However, it seems likely that although Smiles' books must have had a fairly wide audience, the largest group of readers would logically have come from the "middling class" (the artisans and mechanics of the "aristocracy of labour," and the lower middle class) for these were the groups that had the most to gain from the encouragement of the ideal of self-help. Moreover, these were the very groups that Smiles had addressed in Leeds in the 1840s, with his earlier versions of self-help and self-education - groups belonging to Mutual Improvement Societies, Mechanics Institutes, Church organisations and Temperance Societies. Furthermore Smiles claimed that his talks to these organisations were received with "enthusiasm" and had had a "rousing effect,"[77] although it can be counter-argued that the message they took away was not the one that Smiles intended to convey, even if Smiles appears more than pleased in his Autobiography with the letters he received from anxious and persevering readers. Some of these questions will be approached in the following chapters, but for the moment a description by George Gissing of a humble admirer of Smiles' message neatly expresses the hopes and optimism engendered by Smiles' books:

> for years he had sat at the feet of Dr. Smiles, whose popular volumes he possessed and cherished. He had long practised thrift and self-help; all manner of admirable axioms nested in his cheery little soul . . . His ambition was to be a Man.[78]

Smiles had moved south in 1854 to work for the South Eastern Railway and he continued in the same position until 1866, when overwork, worry and dissatisfaction caused him to leave and begin work for the National Provident Assurance Company, where it seems that Smiles was not "an outstanding success and apparently . . . found the work too much for him . . ." Smiles implicitly denies this in his Autobiography claiming that the work "was of a comparatively easy sort." Be that as it may,

Smiles did suffer from a stroke, as previously noted, and retired from business in 1871.[79] That Smiles became ill from overwork was typical, yet curious also, for he could well have existed by his pen alone, having enough literary offers by the 1860s to keep him and his family. But by then he had an ingrained aversion to relying on literature, possibly because it had earlier "failed" him, but more likely because he felt a (psychological) need "in spirit and in fact" to work at a regular employment.[80] Ironically Smiles found it necessary to cultivate idleness after his illness, and probably to cultivate optimism too, for in the 1860s and 1870s his letters often dwelt on the possibility of death. "My time is nearly over," he wrote in 1870, some 34 years before his actual demise.[81]

In 1877 Smiles continued to believe that death was near, lamenting

> And yet how little I have done. How little use I have made of my time. I have no end of things to do, but I know that I shall never do them.

Smiles' despair over the passage of time has a Calvinist ring about it, and certainly he seems to have felt the need to justify his time on earth, for his Autobiography, like the autobiographies of so many other Victorians, does work up to a considerable amount of self-examination, and contains an inordinate number of letters, addresses, and interviews praising the value of his work. In this regard Smiles was strikingly deprecative of his own literary work, writing privately that it was done merely as "an adjunct and as an amusement . . . working up the little bits of time that are vacant . . ." and again referring to Thrift and Self-Help as made up "for the most part of old scraps . . ."[82] For in the end Smiles' Autobiography and private correspondence reflect not the outward confidence of his published work, but a considerable measure of private anxiety and social insecurity.[83]

The preceding discussion of the Victorian work ethic and Smiles' own background provides a base on which to build the following chapters as they deal with Smiles' own concepts of work and self-help, and their development within the context of the Victorian emphasis on work. Some of the themes already noted will reoccur in Smiles' attitude toward work, and others will help to place his ideas against the wider background of the Victorian work ethic.

## Chapter I - Footnotes

[1]See Appendix A for definition of 'work'.

[2]Edward Heath, "Preface," Fair Deal at Work: The Conservative approach to modern industrial relations (London, 1968), p. 5.

[3]The foregoing discussion of work and labour in history has been based on Sebastian de Grazia, Of Time, Work, and Leisure (Anchor Books edition; New York, 1964), Chapters 1 and 2; Hannah Arendt, The Human Condition (Anchor Books edition; New York, 1959), passim; and Michael Harrington, The Accidental Century (Penguin Books edition; Baltimore, 1967), Chapter 8.

[4]Locke goes on: "Whatsoever, then, he removes out of the state that Nature hath provided and left it in, he hath mixed his labour with it, and joined to it something that is his own, and thereby makes it his property.", Maurice Cranston, ed., Locke on Politics, Religion and Education, (Collier Books edition; New York, 1965), p. 29.

[5]Darton's Children's Favourite Reward Books (London, 1857), p. 4. Maria Edgeworth, Fireside Stories (London, 1860), p. 23.

[6]Karl Löwith, From Hegel to Nietzsche; the Revolution in Nineteenth Century Thought, tr. David E. Green (Anchor Books edition; New York, 1967), p. 261.

[7]E.J. Hobsbawm, Industry and Empire: An Economic History of Britain since 1750 (London, 1968), p. 68.

[8]For example, J. Marlowe, The Puritan Tradition in English Life (London, 1956), p. 83; J.F.C. Harrison, Learning and Living, 1790-1960: A Study in the History of the English Adult Education Movement (London, 1961), p. 210; Walter Houghton, The Victorian Frame of Mind, 1830-1870 (New Haven, 1957), pp. 242-62 for the study of work attitudes through the medium

of such figures as Carlyle and Charles Kingsley. More recently, John Burnett (ed.), Useful Toil: Autobiographies of Working People from the 1820's to the 1920's (London, 1974) has revealed attitudes to work by those who actually did the work.

[9] R.H. Tawney, Religion and the Rise of Capitalism (Mentor edition; New York, 1947), pp. 226, 188, and cf. p. 226 where Tawney seems to ascribe a more causative role to Puritanism. Max Weber, The Protestant Ethic and the Spirit of Capitalism, tr. Talcott Parsons (Scribner Library edition; New York, 1958), pp. 180, 91, and cf. p. 174 where Weber, like Tawney, appears to offer a more strongly causative approach.

[10] Ibid., p. 115; Tawney, Religion, p. 210.

[11] Michael Walzer, The Revolution of the Saints (London, 1966), pp. 209, 210. Walzer also argues that the four main problems confronting the Puritans were rural depopulation, rapid urbanisation, social disorganisation, and the creation of a religious vacuum, pp. 201 ff.

[12] Work and Pray (London, 1853), p. 3. William Unsworth, Self-Culture and Self-Reliance: or, the Poor Man's Help to Elevation on Earth and in Heaven (London and Alford, 1861), p. 23. Rev. W.F. Stevenson, Praying and Working. Being an Account of what Men can do when in Earnest (London, 1862), p. 1.

[13] Rev. J. Kennedy, Work and Conflict; or, the Divine Life in its Progress (London, 1860), p. 100.

[14] "Effects of Over-Confinement to Business," The Journal of Health, (New Series; London), June, 1853, vol. II, p. 222. "Rest-Day Doctrines," The Working Man (London), June 2, 1866, vol. I, p. 344.

[15] How to Get Money Quickly; or, Thirty Ways of Making a Fortune (London, 1866), p. 3.

[16] F. Engels, The Condition of the Working-Class in England in 1844 tr. F.K. Wischnewetzky (Paperback edition; George Allen and Unwin Ltd., London, 1968), pp. 155 ff. For long hours of work by store clerks, George Dawson, Lecture on the Late Hour System (Manchester, 1846); and for domestic servants' hours, Mrs. Beeton, The Book of Household Management (New edition; London, 1888), pp. 1478-1483, where, for example, the summer duties of the housemaid were supposed to begin at 6 a.m. and conclude only when the rest of the house had retired. Rev. W.K. Tweedie, Man and his Money: its Use and Abuse (London, 1855), p. 30. Henry Mayhew, Young Benjamin Franklin (London, 1870), p. 468. William Robinson, Self-Education; or, the value of mental culture with the practicability of its attainment under disadvantages (Second edition; London, 1845), p. 47.

[17] [Sir John Kaye], "Success," Cornhill Magazine (London), Dec. 1860, vol. II, p. 729.

[18] J.H. Newman, "Doing Glory to God in pursuits of the World," sermon preached Nov. 1, 1836, in J.H. Newman, Parochial and Plain Sermons (New edition; London, 1891), vol. VIII, p. 160. The pursuit of wealth and status from before the Reformation onward is summarised in Harold Perkin, The Origins of Modern English Society, 1780-1880 (London and Toronto, 1969), pp. 56-62 and Chapters III, IV and VII. A case study of economic growth in Leeds between 1760 and 1844 concentrates on the early 19th Century - 1805 ff. - as especially favourable to capital accumulation and financial gain, C.M. Elliott, "The Ideology of Economic Growth: A Case Study," in E.L. Jones and G.E. Mingay (eds.), Land, Labour, and Population in the Industrial Revolution (London, 1967), p. 92 and pp. 76-99 generally.

[19] Geraldine Jewsbury, Marian Withers (3 vols.; London, 1851), vol. II, p. 29 and vol. III, pp. 113-14. Another novelist, Mrs. Craik, had one of

her characters declare "even I . . . have lived to see so great a change in manners and morals that intemperance, instead of being the usual characteristic of a "gentleman" has become a rare failing, a universally contemned disgrace," Mrs. Craik, John Halifax Gentleman (3 vols.; London, 1856), vol. II, pp. 208-209. Where temperance led, industry and thrift could not be far behind.

[20]"Diversity of the Working Classes," The Working Man, Jan. 13, 1866, vol. I, p. 24. Mayhew, Benjamin Franklin, p. viii.

[21]Henry Mayhew, London Labour and the London Poor; a Cyclopaedia of the Condition and Earnings of Those that will Work, Those that cannot Work, and Those that will not Work (4 vols.; New edition; London, 1861-62), vol. II, p. 5. Henry Mayhew, 1851; or, the Adventures of Mr. and Mrs. Cursty Sandboys (London, 1851), pp. 154-155.

[22]"Prince Albert," The Journal of the Great Exhbition of 1851. Its Origin, History and Progress (London, 1851), Nov. 9, 1850, vol. I, no. 1. Stevenson, Praying and working, p. 2.

[23]E.P. Hood, Moral Manhood (London, 1852), pp. 58, 56, 57. "1801 and 1851. A Chapter of Contrasts," The Journal of Industry (London, 1850-51), Jan. 11, 1851, vol. I, p. 55. (E.P. Hood gave the same excuse for the degradation of factory work - it was not the actual employment, but the motive and object that gave work its real dignity, E.P. Hood, Self-Formation (London, 1858), p. 247.) Rev. H. Dunckley, Charter of the Nations (London and Manchester, 1854), p. 25. The Daily News, June 26, 1846, cited in N. McCord, The Anti Corn Law League, 1838-1846 (London, 1958), p. 215.

[24]B. Hanbury, The Christian Merchant: A practical way to make "the best of both worlds": exhibited in the life and writings of Joseph

Williams of Kidderminster (3rd edition; London, 1853), p. xix; Hanbury also noted the difference between the "gross profanity and wide-spread ignorance" of his youth (1780s) and the diffusion of knowledge and marvels of science of "these later times" (1853), p. xxiii. Stevenson, Praying and Working, pp. 3, 6.

[25]See Appendix B.

[26]The advertisement was for electropathic belts (which commenced their healing career in 1864) in Work: An Illustrated Magazine of Practice and Theory (London), Oct. 5, 1889, vol. I, p. 464.

[27]W.H. Davenport Adams, The Secret of Success; or, How to get on in the world (London, 1879), p. 123. Ruth Lamb, Work, Wait, Win (London, 1891), p. 291. S.G. Checkland has remarked that the "second half of the century may well have seen in Britain a greater emphasis upon the virtues of disciplined work and thrift" than the first half of the century, S.G. Checkland, The Rise of Industrial Society in England, 1815-1885 (New York, 1964), p. 299.

[28]A few plain Words to Labouring Lads about their leisure Time (London, 1857), p. 5. John Forbes (M.D.), Happiness in its Relations to Work and Knowledge (London, 1850), pp. 30, 35. Forbes' book was originally delivered as lectures to a mechanics institute, and it is interesting to note that the second quote was not included in the lectures - even he did not have the nerve to spell out his rationale for labour in the lecture. Tweedie, Man and his Money, p. 109.

[29]Henry Birkett; the story of a man who helped himself (London, 1860), pp. 261, 262, 288. Working Men and Religious Institutions. Report of the Speeches at the Conference at the London Coffee House, Jan. 21, 1867 (London, 1867), p. 18. So also William Unsworth asked the working classes

to educate themselves, but warned "let the labouring classes carefully avoid unbecoming demeanour toward their superiors, . . ." Unsworth, Self-Culture, p. 31.

[30]David Page (ed.), Songs of Life and Labour (Edinburgh, 1864), p. vi. Rev. W. Blaikie, Better Days for Working People (London, 1863), p. 85. R.W. Fraser, Head and Hand, or Thought and Action in reference to Success and Happiness (New edition; London and Edinburgh, 1865), pp. 253, 257, 263. Rev. John Hall, The sons of Toil and the Crystal Palace (London, 1853), p. 37 (Hall incidentally claimed that atheism would lead inevitably to anarchy, p. 38).

[31]Mary Howitt to the Harrisons, no date, but presumably between 1846 and 1847 when the People's Journal ceased publication, cited in Amice Lee, Laurels and Rosemary. The Life of William and Mary Howitt (Oxford, 1955), p. 172.

[32]Working and Waiting (London, 1858), pp. 269-70.

[33]One evangelical clergyman, the Rev. Henry Birch, actually wrote a book called The "Great Exhibition" Spiritualised (London, 1851), in which he called for the spread of commerce and civilisation over the world, as a result of which mission the downfall of heathens, Mohammedans and Jews would occur, p. 7. Y. Ffrench comes to a somewhat similar conclusion in The Great Exhbition, 1851 (London, 1950), p. 222.

[34]Mayhew, 1851, p. 132. Charles Vickerman (Huddersfield woollen spinner), "The Olympiad of Labour," The Working Man's Friend and Family Instructor (London), Supplement for Nov. 1850, p. 2.

[35]Reported in The Working Man's Friend 1853, vol. III, p. 143.

[36]G.S. Phillips, Chapters in the History of a Life (London and Leeds, 1849), pp. 168, 171.

[37]Thomas Carlyle, On Heroes, Hero-Worship, and the Heroic in History (London, 1846), p. 319. Thomas Carlyle, "Past and Present" in Works (26 vols.; Centennial Memorial edition; Boston 1897), vol. XIX, p. 154. Thomas Carlyle, "Characteristics," ibid., vol. XVI, pp. 380-83.

[38]Mayhew, Benjamin Franklin, pp. 79, 470.

[39]Joseph Bentley, The Best Uninspired Book for teaching Children how to become "well-off" in this World, and happy in the next (London, 1864), pp. 172, 176, 187. For an explanation of the limited distribution of wealth as "a positive secondary law," see Rev. T. Milner, The Elevation of the People, Moral, Instructional and Social (London, 1846), p. 85.

[40]John Robson (ed.), Collected Works of John Stuart Mill, The Principles of Political Economy (2 vols.; Annotated 1848 edition; University of Toronto, 1965), vol. II, pp. 978 (note), 707. Jeremy Bentham claimed that "Aversion, - not desire, - is the emotion - which labour, taken by itself, is qualified to produce," Bentham, Economic Writings, ed. W. Stark (3 vols.; London, 1954), vol. III, p. 428. Mayhew, London Labour, vol. II, p. 5. The idea of work and reward was somewhat naturally a very widespread source of encouragement for the working classes (and indeed all classes), e.g. John Wade, History of the Middle and working Classes (London, 1835), p. 179, and especially among the proponents of the labour theory of value, the Ricardian Socialists, e.g. John Francis Bray, Labour's Wrongs and Labour's Remedy (Leeds, 1839) pp. 83, 183; Thomas Hodgskin, Popular Political Economy (Reprinted Economic Classics; New York, 1966), p. x.

[41]Nassau Senior, Industrial Efficiency and Social Economy, ed. Leon Levy (2 vols.; London, 1928), vol. I, pp. 65-69. Senior also made a

distinction between indolence (the dislike of labour) and idleness (the desire for amusement), vol. I, p. 66.

[42]Perkin, Origins of Modern English Society, Chapter VII.

[43]Monica Grobel, "The Society for the Diffusion of Useful Knowledge, 1826-1845" (4 vols.; unpublished Master's thesis, University College, London, 1933), vol. III, pp. 812, 814. Charles Knight, the S.D.U.K. (Society for the Diffusion of Useful Knowledge) publisher, wanted the working classes to see that the good was "in the results of the labour" and not "as too many think even now, that the good was in the labour" itself, Charles Knight, Knowledge is Power: A view of the Productive Forces of Modern Society, and the Results of Labour, Capital and Skill (London, 1855), p. 101.

[44]The sub-title of Henry Mayhew's investigation of London's workers and poor is enlightening - a Cyclopaedia of the Condition and Earnings of Those that will Work, Those that cannot Work, and Those that will not Work. Mayhew did not find it necessary to investigate a fourth category, those that need not work.

[45]Rev. William Anderson, Self-Made Men (London, 1861), p. 295. E.P. Hood, Common Sense (London, 1852), p. 43.

[46]How to Behave: A Pocket Manual of Etiquette and Guide to Correct Personal Habits (Glasgow, 1865), pp. 112-13 (emphasis mine). Hood, Common Sense, p. 43.

[47]Hood, Moral Manhood, p. 153.

[48]How to Live; or, Youth's Gospel (Edinburgh, 1862), p. 39. Rev. T.T. Lynch, Lectures in aid of self-improvement (London, 1853), p. 150.

[49]Self-Reliance; A Book for Young Men: being brief Biographic Sketches of men who have risen to Independence and Usefulness by

Perseverence and Energy (London, 1852), p. ix. J.W. Gilbart, The Moral and Religious Duties of Public Companies (London, 1856), pp. 36, 18.

[50] C.E. Bowen, Jack the Conquerer; or, Difficulties Overcome (London, 1868), p. 119 - the moral of this particular tale being that the artificial removal of Jack's difficulties would also remove his motive to exertion. Self-Reliance, p. xi. Rev. J.B. Lister, How to Succeed in Life: A Guide to the Young (London, 1855), p. 32 gave an almost identical explanation of the uses of difficulty.

[51] Words of Wisdom for the Sons of Toil (London and Leeds, 1860), p. 62.

[52] Mrs. Hope, On Self-Education and the Formation of Character (London, 1843), p. 4. [Sir John Kaye], "Work," Cornhill Magazine, 1860, vol. II, p. 601. Rev. Samuel Coley, "The Blessed Life," Lectures delivered before the Y.M.C.A. (Young Men's Christian Association) in Exeter Hall, from Nov. 1860 to Feb. 1861 (London, 1861), p. 336.

[53] Rev. Samuel Coley, "The Blessed Life," Lectures delivered before the Y.M.C.A., pp. 339, 338, 337. E.L. Bulwer, Lucretia; or the Children of the Night (London, 1853), pp. vii-viii. Since Bulwer sets out his reaction to changing attitudes toward work and other moral values so clearly, it is incorporated in Appendix C.

[54] Joseph Johnson, Self-Effort, or the true method of attaining success in Life (London, 1883), p. 380. Rev. Robert F. Horton, Success and Failure (London, 1897), p. 48.

[55] The new work discipline of the 19th Century was remarked by one author in 1875, who complained that the locally organised work of the past had been replaced by the present separation of home and work place, "nowadays such different things, so far distant from each other that they

really have no connection . . ." This led to alienation, a "hardness, indifference, and lack of sympathy" to those at work, H.A. Page [A.H. Japp], Noble Workers: A Book of Examples for Young Men (London, 1875), p. 393.

[56]C.L. Brightwell, Heroes of the Laboratory and the Workshop (London, 1859), p. v. Henry Birkett, pp. 319-20.

[57]Gilbart, Moral and Religious Duties, p. 18.

[58]P.A. Fraser, On Some of the Causes which at present retard the Moral and Intellectual Progress of the Working Classes (Edinburgh, 1857), p. 15. Bentley, The Best Uninspired Book, p. 165. Mayhew, 1851, pp. 155-56. "Letters to Working Men," The Working Man's Friend, Oct. 2, 1852, vol. III, p. 9. Unsworth, Self-Culture, p. 29.

[59]Rev. R.T. Jeffrey, "Commerce Christianised," Lectures delivered before the Y.M.C.A., pp. 303, 298. Working and Waiting, p. 307.

[60]Success in Life, A Book for Young Men (London, 1852), p. iv. Blaikie, Better Days, pp. 107, 235, 205. Lister, How to Succeed in Life, pp. 76-77, 84. 92. M.M. Brewster, Work, or Plenty to do and how to do it (Edinburgh, 1858), p. 12. Brewster's was also one of the few books consulted that advocated work as a solution to doubt and scepticism, p. 57. The Rev. F. Paget, The Hallowing of Work (London, 1888), p. 24 and footnote, p. 24, where Paget also saw worldliness rather than rationalism as the danger. And cf. Religion in its Relation to Commerce (London, 1852), p. 20 where speculation is cautiously accepted.

[61]For the aristocracy of labour see E.J. Hobsbawm, Labouring Men (Anchor Books edition; New York, 1967), pp. 321-370. Perhaps this category of 'upward striving' should include what one etiquette book described as "that immense substratum of lower middle-class which interposes between the

middle and working classes . . ." Countess of . . ., Good Society (London and New York, 1869), pp. vii-viii. Mutual Improvement Societies have not often been studied, but in Manchester one such society moved from being an exclusively Church-oriented group in 1843, studying such subjects as "Proofs for the existence of God," to a more commercially minded approach in 1858, "How far will a Christian course of conduct in young men conduce to their secular interests in commercial towns" and in 1861, to preparation of youth "for life, real active life." The Bennet Street Mutual Improvement Class (3 vols.; MS M38, Manchester Public Library, n.d.), vols. I and III, no page nos.

[62] For example, the Rev. W. Tuckniss' description of the "non-Workers" as the "Dangerous Classes" in Mayhew, London Labour, vol. IV, p. v.

[63] Mayhew, Benjamin Franklin, pp. 142-43, 137. Maria Edgeworth, The Parent's Assistant; or Stories for Children (London, 1854), pp. viii-ix. (This preface remained the same in the editions of 1864, 1885, and 1897.)

[64] Success in Life, p. 307. Lister, How to Succeed, pp. 73, 32, 62, 72. E.P. Hood, The Peerage of Poverty, or Learners and Workers in Fields, Farms and Factories (3rd edition; London, 1859), p. 67; Hood, Common Sense, p. 87.

[65] Unsworth, Self-Culture, p. 37. Henry Birkett, p. 175. Craik, John Halifax, vol. III, p. 31, vol. II, pp. 145, 205. Too Much and Too Little Money (2 vols.; London, 1870), vol. I, p. 60, vol. II, p. 235.

[66] Blaikie, Better Days, p. 108. That the ideal of self-help was a middle solution to the condition and aspirations of the lower middle and working classes will be argued, but in the meantime the following quote may show how the via media was handled in one particular instance: in an S.P.C.K. (Society for the Promotion of Christian Knowledge) story two

children were given advice by their parents, "they told us to be ourselves, but not to trust in ourselves . . ." The village Beech-Tree; or, Work and Trust (S.P.C.K.; London, 1872), p. 33 (emphasis mine).

[67]R.M.W. Cowan, The Newspaper in Scotland: A study of its first expansion, 1815-1860 (Glasgow, 1946), p. 137. The information on Smiles comes from the early chapters of his Autobiography, ed. T. Mackay (London, 1905).

[68]It has been suggested that Smiles lacked endurance and application in leaving the Leeds Times, Donald Read, Press and People, 1790-1850 (London, 1961), p. 94, but the two reasons given above seem an adequate explanation. Smiles, Autobiography, p. 126. Carlyle's phrase is actually threshing straw "a hundred times without wheat," Carlyle, "Sir Walter Scott" in Works, vol. XVII, p. 460.

[69]A letter from one H. Askew in the Yorkshire Evening Post, c. June, 1929, contended that Smiles had married "a lady of fortune," Alf Mattison Papers (MSS Folders 33 and 34; Leeds Public Library), Folder 34. However, this is not borne out by Smiles' subsequent career, nor by his decision to earn more money as a surgeon in preparation for marriage. Although the editor of Smiles' Autobiography, p. 128, gives Smiles' wife's maiden name as Holmes, it appears as Dixon in the marriage certificate, in Smiles Collection (Archives, Leeds Public Library) (hereinafter Smiles Correspondence), SS/B/66.

[70]Report of the Committee of the Leeds Mechanics Institution and Literary Society (Leeds, Jan. 1844), p. 12 (copy British Museum); animal magnetism formed part of the health movement associated with Physical Puritanism. B.A. Kilburne, Annals of Zion Sunday Schools, New Wortley (Leeds University Library), MS 116, p. 214. Smiles to Leeds Literary

Institute, c. 1840, in Miscellaneous Smiles Correspondence (Leeds Public Library), for his activity as an Anti Corn Law speaker.

[71]Curiously, this last 'self-help' volume, Life and Labour, or Characteristics of Men of Industry, Culture and Genius (London, 1887) is usually omitted from discussion of the self-help series, e.g. Asa Briggs, Victorian People (Harper Colophon edition; New York, 1963), p. 123; Harrison, Learning and Living, p. 203, footnote 1.

[72]Smiles, Autobiography, pp. 294, 410, 336-38, particularly Chapters XXI and XXIII ('Appreciation from Foreignors'), and for Italian sales, p. 409.

[73]R.P. Dore (ed.), Aspects of Social Change in Modern Japan (Princeton, 1967), pp. 130-34. The impact of self-help in Japan is thoroughly evaluated in Earl Kinmouth, "Nakamura Keiu and Samuel Smiles," American Historical Review, 1980, vol. 85, no. 3, pp. 535-556.

[74]Smiles, Autobiography, p. 223, note by editor. Sir John Lubbock, The Best 100 Books (first drawn up in 1885-86; New York, 1887), p. 60; and a report from Birmingham also showed that the city library lent out Character 44 times (presumably in 1886) compared with 181 borrowings of Adam Bede and 389 of Pickwick, ibid., p. 61. The Times Book Club Selected List of the Best Books (6th edition; London, 1913), p. 39, where Lives of the Engineers was recommended. Similarly, Lives of the Engineers, together with Nasmyth and the Life of Thomas Edward were recommended by E.B. Sargant and B. Whishaw (eds.), A Guide Book to Books (London, 1891), pp. 95, 96, 315. And John Robertson of the Rationalist Press referred to Smiles' History of Ireland, Huguenots, Nasmyth and Lives of the Engineers in his edited Courses of Study (London, 1904), pp. 298, 388, 401.

[75]Smiles to G. Bell, Feb. 22, 1877 (MS letter owned by G. Bell Ltd., Publishers, London). T. Bowden Green (ed.), Portraits of Dr. Samuel Smiles at Different Periods of His Life (London, 1904), p. 68.

[76]On school boys, Smiles, Autobiography, p. 326; and a personal interview at the British Museum, Jan. 12, 1969, with a Mr. Rose whose father pressed Self-Help on him as a schoolboy at the turn of the century; Smiles to Janet Hartree, Nov. 11, 1881, Smiles Correspondence, SS/AI/128a. On working class illiteracy, see diagram in Hobsbawm, Industry and Empire, p. 20 (back section); Smiles to Janet Hartree, Nov. 11, 1881, Smiles Correspondence, SS/AI/128a. For Self-Help as a source of encouragement and mobility, Smiles, Autobiography, pp. 224, 228, 331, 341, 388-389, 392; Davenport Adams, The Secret of Success, p. 351. [Sir John Kaye], "Success," Cornhill Magazine, Dec. 1860, vol. II, p. 729.

[77]R.S. Neale finds this "middling class" to be a socially mobile class mid-way between the middle and working classes, R.S. Neale, "Class and Class-Consciousness in early 19th Century England: Three Classes or Five?" Victorian Studies, Sept. 1968, vol. XII, p. 23. Smiles, Autobiography, pp. 127, 131, 134. Smiles, "A Work that Prospered," Good Words for the Young of all Ages (London), 1877, vol. XVIII, p. 387.

[78]Smiles, Autobiography, p. 133. George Gissing, "Under an Umbrella" (1893), in George Gissing Stories and Sketches (London, 1938), p. 117 - a little later in the story, when the hero is faced with a challenge: "Courage and Dr. Smiles to the rescue!", p. 121.

[79]Stanley Hazell, A Record of the First Hundred Years of the National Provident Institution, 1835-1935 (Cambridge, 1935), p. 48. Smiles, Autobiography, p. 264.

[80]Ibid., pp. 262, 129, 130.

[81]Smiles to Farquharson, 20 Jan. 1870 (MS 966, National Library of Scotland), ff. 323-324; and similarly, Smiles to Rev. E.R. Larkin, 18 April 1868, *ibid.*, ff. 321-322.

[82]Smiles to Janet Hartree, Oct. 19, 1877, *Smiles Correspondence*, SS/AI/80a; Smiles to Billio, Oct. 30, 1868, *ibid.*, SS/AII/15; Smiles to Willie, Nov. 5, 1875, *ibid.*, SS/AII/67. A discussion of Victorian autobiography occurs in J.H. Buckley, *The Triumph of Time* (Cambridge, Mass., 1967), p. 99. Smiles' self-examination occurs, for example, in his *Autobiography*, p. 384: "I wish I had the power to retouch my life . . ." In regard to Smiles' depreciation of his own work, it is surprising how diligently he researched some of his books and articles, e.g. two months for one article, Smiles to R. Harrison, June 22, 1860 (MSS Collection of Autograph Letters, University of London), AL 108.

[83]This social insecurity is revealed in Smiles' criticism of the middle class usage of family crests, Smiles, *Thrift* (New York, 1876), p. 108, yet his own notepaper displays a crest from the late 1860s on. His insignia (a hand clutching a quarter moon, surrounded by a metal belt) is inscribed "*Industria Virtus et Fortitudo*." Labour provides its own social status.

## CHAPTER II

## SAMUEL SMILES AND THE ORIGINS OF THE CONCEPT OF SELF-HELP: THE MORALITY OF WORK AND MAN'S PLACE IN SOCIETY, 1830-1859.[1]

There has grown up around Smiles a double myth. Firstly, that Smiles produced a myth of his own--the myth of the self-made man--and secondly that the message he wanted to put over was the gospel of success.

For example, one historian considers Smiles' book _Self-Help_ (1859) as a "piece of success literature," and an effort to elevate "the self-made man into an almost mystical figure." To support the theory that Smiles was an advocate of the idea of success, a quotation from _Self-Help_ is used: "What some men are, all without difficulty might be. Employ the same means, and the same results will follow." Perhaps the quotation should have been continued: "That there should be a class of men who live by their daily labour in every state is the ordinance of God, and doubtless is a wise and righteous one; but that this class should be otherwise than frugal, contented, intelligent, and happy, is not the design of Providence . . ." Here Smiles is evidently referring not to success but to a state of relative contentment. Most recently another critic advanced the same argument: "As Samuel Smiles was to put it in _Self-Help_, 'What some men are, all without difficulty might be. Employ the same means, and the same results will follow.'" Again the quotation is not continued, and the conclusion drawn that Smiles was putting forward the myth of the self-made man.[2] While it can be said that those who wanted to advance economically and socially did find encouragement in Smiles' books and articles, and although it is true that Smiles was often accepted by his contemporaries as proposing such a philosophy, it is also true that the main thrust of his philosophy was aimed at other motives and other values.

In order to reconsider the myths of success and the self-made man in Smiles' thought, and in order to understand his ideas on work and society as a unified whole, it is necessary to start from the last years of the 18th Century, for Smiles was in part a man of that century. A religious historian has noted that

> It was amongst the nonconformists that the cult of liberty, both in theology and in politics, found fullest scope. In their case, rationalism often passed over into untarianism. Their more advanced representatives followed Bentham and the utilitarians in ethics, Adam Smith in economics, David Hartley in psychology, and Charles James Fox . . . in politics.[3]

Apart from the reference to C.J. Fox[4] this description applies particularly well to Smiles, for these five areas were the intellectual starting points which led on to his philosophy of self-help and his concept of work. Later on, the events of the 1840s were to shift his focus slightly, but in the 1830s, and during his medical studies at Edinburgh (1829-1832), Smiles formed most of his basic ideas. The following sections will therefore concentrate on the five areas of religion, ethics, psychology, economics and politics and will conclude with a section on the more immediate reasons for the writing of Self-Help. In general, the first three sections will reassess the myth of success, and the last three will approach the ideal of self-help from differing viewpoints.

## Religion, Unitarianism and the Structure of Society

Smiles' parents were of small means, his father being a general merchant in Haddington, near Edinburgh. When Smiles left home in 1829 for Edinburgh University medical school, his parents gave him a letter, containing much advice, including the promise that "nothing shall be wanting on our part for your good, you will be provided with the meins [sic] of making you respectable in the worald [sic] . . ." According to Robert, one of Smiles' eleven brothers, their parents "were worthy people of the middle class, of untiring industry, and possessed of the praiseworthy ambition to educate and train their children for a higher rank and position than their own." It is clear that Smiles inherited a positive attitude toward hard work and education from his parents, and as he said himself, his parents set before him two specific goals: education and "industry - more important even than knowledge."[5]

Smiles' parents also brought up their sons in a particularly strict form of Calvinism. Smiles remembered that his Sundays were filled with

> prayers an ell long, with the psalms and . . . 'kirk' three times a day . . . no 'novells' (only 'guid' books) - and a great deal that was narrow, sectarian, rigid, and (as I now think) unchristian . . . I remember being one of a party when a child - to go to a field preaching sixteen miles distant - going in the morning and returning at night; - it was the sort of Holy Fair you will find in Burns . . .[6]

Smiles' ancestors and grandfather were Cameronians, and his father an Anti-Burgher--"a sort of Quaker Presbyterian." The Anti-Burghers were a part of the Secession Church of Scotland, who rejected any interference from the State (the Burgess Oath) and who clung to a strict Calvinism based upon the Westminster Confession of 1643-44.[7] Smiles was raised, it seems likely, in his father's church, where, as he said, the preacher taught "the narrowest Calvinism . . . there was far more fear than love in his sermons." Sundays were spent in a continual round of sermons, prayers, catechism, paraphrasing, Bible reading, and studying of Evangelical sermons or the Secession Magazine. Smiles rebelled from all this in his adult years but it had its effect, for he remained a deeply religious person, with a strong sense of moral responsibility toward life's activities.[8]

Calvinism also contained some lessons that could be applied to the value of work and the place of man in society. What were they? Specifically, Calvinism taught that the individual could safely rely upon his own judgment in making a Covenant with God, in interpreting the Scriptures, and in following the dictates of his conscience in the religious duties of life.[9] This Calvinistic emphasis upon the individual covenant and the self-reliance of the individual in religious matters, was to pass over into a secular self-reliance in all Smiles' books. An apt illustration of the theme comes from Dr. Thomas Murray, one of Smiles' mentors in Edinburgh, and himself a Calvinist, when he wrote: "Let every man depend on himself. Self-reliance, combined with integrity and perseverance, is independent of all patronage, and is the most secure foundation of respectability and happiness."[10] Smiles could also learn from Calvinism that God had called man to his vocation in a particular sphere of life, from which sphere one should not move without just cause; that God had ordered society so that men should be mutually responsible to each other; and that God directed society and the world according to Providence, so that neither chance nor accident occurred, either in regard to reward and punishment, or in any sphere of life.[11] It may also be that Smiles' favourite phrase, "heaven helps those who help themselves" stemmed from the feeling among Calvinists that while one's prosperity on earth did not necessarily mean that one was of the elect, yet it was a favourable sign. Calvinism also stressed a constant and systematic self-control, and the formation of a disciplined character, as against the irrational impulses of man's lower nature.[12]

Having put forward those areas of Calvinism which tend to reappear in Smiles' writings, it is possible to turn to another religious source of Smiles' thought. Those Calvinists who rejected the austerity of Calvinism often turned to a religion that combined reason and a milder faith--namely, Unitarianism. Although Smiles was careful never to reveal his religious allegiance in print, presumably because of his dislike of sectarianism, a great deal of evidence points towards his sympathy and agreement with the Unitarians.

In the early 1830s, Smiles approached the same materialistic and necessitarian position[13] as an earlier Unitarian, who had also been brought up as a Calvinist, and had also turned to writing and scientific pursuits, Joseph Priestley. But while Priestley remained a materialist and a determinist (although retaining a basic element of individual moral responsibility)[14] Smiles did not in the end supplant his belief in a body-soul dualism and in the freedom of the individual will. Nevertheless, Smiles did emerge from this crisis of faith with a set of attitudes to religious, social and moral problems which could accommodate both his stern upbringing and his rational, scientific education, and which turned out to be similar and compatible with, if not identical to, the Unitarian ethos. In the early 19th Century many who were well-educated were also Unitarians, and were able to combine the somewhat stern, emotionless and calculating individualism of their religion (added to a certain necessitarianism via Priestley) with an allegiance to social reform and to Utilitarianism. In the 1830s, following a similar pattern, Smiles subscribed both to the leading Unitarian journal, the Monthly Repository whose work he particularly admired, Mary Leman Gillies. He also met other Unitarians in London, including the Utilitarian-Unitarians, Dr. Bowring and Dr. Southwood

Smith.[16] In Leeds, Smiles allied with two well-known Unitarians, Hamer Stansfeld and J.G. Marshall, in founding and supporting the Household Suffrage Association.[17] Smiles also taught for some time at the Zion Sunday School in New Wortley, Leeds, which was thought of as a Unitarian school, "and for many year [sic] after, the school was looked upon [by malcontents] . . . as being . . . calculated to degrade the morals and religious sentiments of all . . . within its walls."[18] Smiles and the publisher of the Leeds Times, Hobson, printed a sermon in 1841 by the Unitarian minister of Leeds, the Rev. Wicksteed, attacking the Anglican Minister, Dr. Hook. Smiles also had close political connections with the Rev. Wicksteed, since the leader of the Anti Corn Law League, Cobden, on one occasion sent him (Smiles) a special message about Wicksteed. When Smiles assumed the lead in promoting the Woodhouse Mechanics Institute in Leeds, he delivered the opening address, and Wicksteed was selected to deliver the address at the following meeting of the Institute, and years later, in 1883, Smiles mentions that he lunched with Wicksteed.[19] Smiles' wife, Sarah Dixon, had been educated at a Unitarian school in Liverpool, run by Miss Martineau, sister of the Unitarian leader, Dr. James Martineau, and in later life Smiles attended the sermons of the Unitarian, Stopford Brooke. Finally, Smiles made very frequent and admiring references to the Boston Unitarian, W.E. Channing, whose philosophy bore some close similarities to Smiles' own ideas.[20]

The foregoing is an attempt to show Smiles' agreement and sympathy with Unitarianism, rather than an effort to reveal him as a committed church-going Unitarian.[21] The signficance of this relationship in terms of Smiles' concept of work and self-help can best be illustrated by referring to two specific examples of interaction between Smiles and Unitarianism: the Monthly Repository and W.E. Channing.

Smiles subscribed to the Monthly Repository during the 1830s, when W.J. Fox was the editor. Fox, who had also retreated from an earlier Calvinism, was representative of the progressive wing of the Unitarians. He believed in a society in which every man was placed according to his ability, and rewarded according to his work, and in which none would be idle. More specifically, Fox suggested that schools and savings banks should replace private charity, that the Corn Laws be abolished, and that labour should be freed from all restrictions, since distress was caused by "apprenticeship, the interference of corporations, and the combinations of the workmen . . . Labour, like water, would find its level." Here, in 1833, is the same emphasis on education, saving and Free Trade which Smiles was later to expound, and in particular (because of the "laws" of supply and demand) the same blind spot in regard to the effectiveness of Trades Unions.[22]

Another contributor to the Monthly Repository was Mary Leman Gillies, afterwards Mrs. Grimstone. Smiles found her articles so worthwhile that he "had read and re-read" them. What did Smiles find that was so interesting? He discovered a compatible viewpoint which saw man as impelled "by natural wants and inherent energies . . . ," and fuelled by "the burning energy of innate power, which cultivation may increase, but cannot create." Smiles too considered that man contained within himself a natural drive to work, prompted by "our natural wants and our manifold needs."[23] Mary Leman Gillies went on to envision a Utopia, created through the perfectible quality of man and the divinely ordained path of progress. Man was in fact "hastening toward a high and happy state, and [would] attain it by the working out of the principle of progression implanted in him. The work of the Supreme has its course." Smiles also thought that man had within him dormant or otherwise the desire to progress. The competitive spirit was "deeply rooted in man, leading him to . . . endeavour to realise something better and higher than he has yet attained." Man "feels within himself all those noble aspirations which the Creator has implanted in the bosom alike of the meanest and mightiest . . ."[24]

Mary Leman Gillies outlined what she meant by progress. Man was a progressive being, but "only in proportion as he advances to the harmonious development and happy exercise of all his powers that he is really admirable." The powers of men were those "which God has given to each individual, and which, by right exercise, and indefatigable cultivation, that individual has proved to the utmost." Smiles paralleled this view too--education should lead to "the development of man's whole constitution; physical, moral, and intellectual . . . to be the best enabled to raise himself on earth, to the very summit of his nature."[24] The tendency in this direction of thought was to turn the individual upon his own resources, and so when Mary Leman Gillies went on to write for the same magazine as Smiles in the mid 1840s, the People's Journal, she used Smiles' own phrasing: "It is true those only will be helped who can help themselves." What could be closer to Smiles' later concept of self-help than Mary Leman Gillies' statement in 1835: "It cannot be too continually and forcible impressed upon a people, that the work of their improvement, independence, and happiness, depends upon themselves?"[26]

Nevertheless, there was also a tendency in Unitarian thought, following Priestley, to see society as somewhat deterministically fixed within a static framework of natural law and a divinely ordered hierarchy of existence. Such an opinion conflicted with the Unitarian (and 19th Century) emphasis on the importance and perfectibility of the individual, and so while reason and experience made Mary Leman Gillies "perceive and acknowledge the inextricable, unalienable, universal, and eternal linking of the whole chain of being--[yet] I feel so strongly within me the principle of independence, the sense of oneness . . ." Smiles felt this same conflict, but perhaps because of his early Calvinism, stressed two points--the eternal Providence of God, and the need for man to work out his vocation <u>within</u> the sphere appointed by God. Smiles believed that "human societies . . . have a fixed, a definite tendency. God rules this . . . world, not by chance and for time, but by providence and law."[27] Man "must have faith in the completeness of the design which our little individual lives form a part. We have each to do our duty in that sphere of life in which we have been placed." Each man "can do his duty in that sphere in which Providence had placed him."[28]

The theme of self-culture and work within the sphere in which the individual had been called, had a corollary, which Mary Leman Gillies pointed out. She rejected "<u>aspiration</u>--the desire of rising . . ." as an unworthy desire for pelf and place.[29] Smiles too was uncomfortable with the idea of individuals rising out of their class. Although not actively opposed to the process when achieved as a by-product of honest endeavour, Smiles never viewed the attainment of wealth and social status as worthy aims of life. Education, for example, was to be seen "not as a means of raising up a few clever and talented men into a higher rank of life--but of <u>elevating and improving the whole class</u>--of elevating the entire condition of the working man."[30] What was to be elevated was the "condition" and not the "rank."

This was, in fact, a fairly common sentiment in the 1840s and earlier. For example, the Rev. Thomas Milner, a writer for the Religious Tract Society, believed that the object of education was

> not to raise the manual labour classes above their condition, but to raise the condition itself. There have been striking examples, indeed, of individuals ascending from the depths of society to stations of ease and affluence by the cultivation of their native powers of mind; but it is false philanthropy to parade such examples before . . . the poor, to awaken aspiration and expectancey . . . [for] while one succeeds, the thousands must necessarily fail, and is the way to foster discontent.[31]

Smiles himself was not disturbed by the idea that education bred discontent. In fact, he seemed to think that "the general diffusion of intelligence and education amongst the working man, must be productive of the most beneficial results."[32] Smiles hoped that self-education and self-culture might lead to a general spirit of self-help, and thus to the moral regeneration of the whole working-class. Smiles was thinking therefore in terms of a society which was largely static in regard to individual social mobility, but which was open to the mental and moral advance of the entire working class. Thus the adoption of the spirit of self-help by the working class "more than any other measure [would] serve to raise them as a class, and this, not by pulling down others, but by levelling them up to a higher and still advancing standard of religion, intelligence, and virtue." However, the <u>social</u> mobility of the working class as a whole was limited by the naturally (and divinely) ordered human condition. "The great majority of men, in all times, however enlightened, must necessarily be engaged in the ordinary advocations of industry; and no degree of culture which can be conferred upon the community will ever enable them--even were it desirable, which it is not--to get rid of the daily work of society, which must be done."[33] Smiles, therefore, (although never totally consistent) did fundamentally consider that man should pursue self-culture, self-perfection, and the development of the work or vocation in which he was engaged, but not social mobility.

Smiles' ideas on work and society were reinforced by the lectures of Dr. John Fletcher, which he attended as a medical student at Edinburgh.[34] Fletcher's lectures were significant because they presented to Smiles the traditional picture of nature as a stable framework of structures fitted for the activities of man. Fletcher believed that because of the harmony of the laws of nature under the design of God, each species reached its appointed place in the great chain of being, after passing through the various stages of the species beneath it as it matured. Further, man was intelligent and hence perfectible: "Of all animals, Man, who has the largest and most complicated Brain, is the most improveable. He is the most capable of advancing from what he does know, to what he does not--from what he can do, to what he cannot . . ."[35] Smiles was thus educated to think in terms of a static framework (either of nature or of a social class structure) within which man actively went about the business of improving himself and his condition, and thereby his society, but was not encouraged to move outside his "sphere" of life.

This "sphere" of life thinking comes out in Smiles' earliest book, published in 1838. Smiles thought every child should be educated to a knowledge of "his relations to his fellow-beings and thus fitted [sic] for his sphere of usefulness in society." More specifically, Smiles used a 'Providential' terminology when stating several times in Self-Help that man should be satisfied to work on in that sphere of life which God had allotted to him. The chief object of culture was "to enlarge our individual intelligence, and render us more useful and efficient workers in the sphere of life to which we may be called." The benefactors of England were those who were "content simply to do the work they have been appointed to do . . ." Respectability was not outward show, but simply going "patiently onward in the condition of life in which it has pleased God to call us . . ."[36]

Another example of Smiles' "static" view of society is in his use of the world 'scale.' Smiles may have been deliberately vague when proposing permissible objectives of work and endeavour, but it is more likely that his use of 'scale' originated from the 'chain of being' terminology in Fletcher's lectures and still current as a widely held theory in the 1830s. So, in discussing the desire for knowledge among the working classes, Smiles wrote that it was "a manly desire to elevate themselves in the <u>scale</u> of civilised being--to live, in fact, for purposes far beyond those of mere animal existence." What Smiles wanted for the working classes was "their elevation in the <u>scale</u> of society as a fulfillment . . . of the end of their being--self-improvement and elevation of moral and intellectual character." The Chartist movement was the simple desire of the "working men of this country to elevate themselves in the social <u>scale</u> . . ." The 'scale' of being could even be applied to nations, for it seemed that Britain occupied a particular "position in the <u>scale</u> of nations . . ."[37]

Scales of civilised being, of society, of moral and social life, of nations--what did they mean to Smiles? The implication seemed to be that man found himself framed against a series of imaginary scales on different social and moral levels, and that by diligent work and activitiy, man might raise himself a few imaginary and invisible notches within each particular scale. The very vagueness of the aims to be pursued and the route to be followed, suggests that Smiles wanted to emphasise work and activity, rather than any defined purpose, and that the "chain of being" concept inhibited him from advocating a restructuring of society. Instead, Smiles though of society as an integrated whole, as a series of interacting circles, which required the appropriate response by each individual for the well-being of the whole: "The life of each man tells upon the whole life of society. Each man has his own special duty to perform--his own work to do. If he does it not, he himself suffers, and others suffer through him." In fact, the sense of inter-related organic unity referred to the whole universe, "no individual in the universe stands alone; he is a component part of a system of mutual dependencies . . ."[38]

Just as the theory of evolution was delayed by a belief in a rigid chain of being and the divinely ordered structure of nature, so Smiles' religious background and medical education led him to think of a largely static society, based upon divinely ordered purpose and placed against the reliable framework of nature. And just as Darwin was able to overcome this inertia, so too did Smiles. But when Smiles discussed the idea of development, it did not lead to an emphasis on social mobility, rather he emphasised self-culture and self-education, which was not "a means of getting past others in the world" but "a power to elevate the character and expand the spiritual nature . . ."[39] Again, this did not mean that Smiles actively opposed the social elevation or financial success of any individual, but merely that there were other more important matters to consider, namely the cultivation and education of the powers and faculties of every individual; the elevation of the condition of the entire working class rather than the elevation of exceptional individuals; and, as a final brake on the concept of social mobility, the ever present need for the work and labour of society to be done by a large and permanent working class.[40]

The purpose of this section has been to show that, through his Calvinist upbringing, medical education, and sympathy with Unitarian literature and people, Smiles retained a sense of the divine providence, moral purpose, and preordained structure of life and society. What was essential was the work and not the success that might follow the results of that work, for Smiles was "impressed with the conviction that every human being is sent into this world to do work of one kind or another . . ."[41] Further reinforcement for this direction of thought came from another Unitarian source, the writings of the Boston Unitarian, W.E. Channing.

Towards the end of 1838, Smiles read Channing's lecture on Self-Culture, and devoted two columns of the Leeds Times to quotations from the lecture. Channing was a New England Unitarian, whose reaction from Calvinism, and subsequent acceptance of the rationalism of the Enlightenment, belief in progress, and the need for individual self-reliance, obviously appealed to Smiles.[42] Like Smiles, Channing felt that Labour and Culture could and should be united; that books, schools, and learning were not absolutely essential; that moral worth was more important than wealth; and that man and the world had been created for an intelligible purpose. As Channing said, man "has made life a struggle for money, not a state for moral and mental happiness as it should be. Hence the inequalities of condition in society . . . the wealth, the idleness . . .[43]

Some time later Smiles inserted another excerpt from Channing in the Leeds Times, this time from his lecture On the Elevation of the Labouring Portion of the Community (see left hand quote below). This may be compared with paragraphs from Smiles' own Self-Help (see right hand quote below):

| | |
|---|---|
| Man owes his growth, his energy, chiefly to that striving of the will, | Nothing that is of real worth can be achieved without coura- |

| | |
|---|---|
| that conflict with difficulty we call effort. Easy, pleasant work does not . . . give a consciousness of their powers, does not train them to endurance, to perseverence, to steady force of will; that force without which all other acquisitions avail nothing. Manual labour is a school, in which men are placed to get energy of purpose and character, a vastly more important endowment than all the learning of all other schools.[44] | geous working. Man owes his growth chiefly to that active striving of the will, that encounter with difficulty, which we call effort . . .[45]<br><br>An easy and luxurious existence does not train men to effort or encounter with difficulty; nor does it awaken that consciousness of power which is so necessary for energetic and effective action in life.[46] |

Various other parallels can be drawn, as, for example, when Channing and Smiles emphasise the need for internal freedom (self-control) before external freedom (political liberty), or when Channing and Smiles both condemn the over-working of the poorer classes, and suggest that all classes would benefit from an education in manual labour.[47] In his talk on the elevation of the labouring classes, Channing also recommended that books be written on the subject of the useful arts and their inventors, and that lectures be delivered on the important trades, their use, and their inventors. This would "introduce them [the inventors] to men whom they may well make their models." Whether Smiles found his inspiration in Channing's recommendation or not, he did deliver such a lecture, and published it in 1844.[48]

Smiles' 1844 lecture contained several echoes of Channing, once quoting him on the possibility of progress in every condition of life, twice warning that culture and education were not to be pursued for the purpose of individual advancement to a higher rank of life (Channing too was very clear that he wanted "inward" change, not "new titles and an artificial rank"), and paraphrasing Channing on the dignity of labour and the need for all to work.[49] Of course, there were differences between Smiles and Channing--Smiles was more radical politically, and had the

English aristocracy and the suffrage problem to contend with--but the similarities were more striking. For both Smiles and Channing work and privation were essential, not only because work provided the necessities of life, but because it helped to perfect the character and virtues of man. Smiles inserted a further selection from Channing to this effect in the Leeds Times of July 1841:

> The material world does much for the mind by its beauty and order; but it does more by the pains and inflicts--by its obstinate resistance, which nothing but toil can overcome--by its vast forces, which nothing but unremitting skill and effort can turn to our use . . .[50]

The Calvinistic concept of the uses of suffering and difficulty remained central to the thinking of both Smiles and Channing. As Smiles wrote in Duty: "Are not difficulty and suffering necessary to evoke the highest forms of character, energy and genius? Effort and endurance, striving and submitting, energy and patience, enter into every destiny."[51]

Perhaps the most evident effect that Channing had on Smiles was the idea of the importance of man and his God-given powers or faculties. Smiles thought Channing's message was that "man is worth more than wealth or show . . . ," that the important thing was not rank or class, but

> the common nature that lies below there; and we are beginning to learn that every being . . . has noble powers to cultivate . . . The grand idea of humanity, of the importance of man as man, is spreading . . . [T]hat every human being should have the means of self-culture, of progress in knowledge and virtue . . . of exercising the powers and affections . . .--this is slowly taking its place, as the highest social truth.[52]

Smiles therefore blamed society for setting "too small a value . . . upon Man . . . [H]is noble and better nature has been too little cherished . . ." and counselled the poor man to "feel that he is not a degraded being, but one of God's creatures, endowed with all the noble attributes of a rational and intelligent being."[53] Smiles meant that every individual contained within himself the possibility of improvement and that every man should work resolutely at the "energetic development and exercise of faculties, the germs of which at least are in every human heart."[54] Here, Smiles followed Channing in thinking of work in terms of self-culture and the exercise of the faculties. This idea of self-culture and self-education was to play an extremely important role in Smiles' thought, for his concept of self-help was permeated with the belief that every individual was capable of improving himself, and should be encouraged to do so, because every individual contained within himself the divinely granted power of his faculties. Nevertheless, the effect of this progressive Unitarian emphasis on self-culture had a reverse side too, for it placed the stress once more on the internal reform of the individual, rather than improvement through institutional or government help, and it de-emphasised the possibility of the working class improving their lot through social mobility or financial gain. In other words, personal improvement through self-culture preceded social and political advance.[55]

On the death of Channing in 1842, Smiles wrote an obituary picking out the three lectures which he had appreciated most, and went on to summarise Channing's achievements: "He proclaimed the dignity of labour, the supremacy of mind and virtue, and the true nobility of manhood." Channing had also been correct, thought Smiles, in opposing the money-getting spirit and selfishness of the age.[56] Together with three other reformers, Channing had advanced the idea that "every human being is of worth, and is to [be] valued, because of himself, as well as because of the Creator that called him into being." There was a "new idea in society--namely, that Man is above Money, and the immortal mind more valuable than perishing lucre."[57]

A similar message was put over by the (Unitarian) Zion Sunday School in Leeds, where Smiles had taught in the late 1840s. At the anniversary celebration in 1851, an elegy on the death of Channing was delivered, and another piece presented, entitled All Have Got their Work to do:

> Life is but a scene of labour
> Everyone's his task afsigned,
> ............................
> We must strive by Education
> Man's condition to improve
> And bind men of every station
> In a bond of mutual love.
> All must then be up and stirring . . .

Again the concept of a rather static society is presented, with the emphasis on education improving the condition rather than the social status of man, and the hope that society would become united. In about 1860, the message from the Zion Sunday School was much the same, but there was a subtle shift away from education and assigned tasks toward a slightly more activist role for the individual - a shift that Smiles himself reflected between the late 1840s and 1859. In a piece entitled Who are the great?, the unknown author attacked those who

> Sit at home, in useless ease,
> Forgetting they've a God to please,
> Who unto them hath talents lent
> That should in usefulness be spent.

And posterity revealed that

> The self-enobled man's the great
> Not he who owns the most estate.[58]

Perhaps these two simple poems, composed by young artisans, catch more of the Unitarian spirit of divine providence, individual moral purpose, self-culture and self-education, than all the articles in the Monthly Repository and all the lectures of W.E. Channing.[59] It was this Unitarian background - the Zion Sunday School, the articles of Mary Leman Gillies, the lectures of W.E. Channing - and Smiles' own Calvinist youth, parental influence and medical education which helped to shape his ideas on work and society. Work should be undertaken for its own sake; wealth and status should be rejected for activity within the sphere in which man found himself; each and every man had his own special work and duties to perform; each and every man was an important individual in the eyes of God, with divinely endowed faculties, which he should strive himself to develop to their utmost; each and every man was perfectible and so could and should help himself; but at the same time there was a divine order of nature and society to which man should adapt. Work and self-help, striving and character formation, education and self-improvement - these were important activities in themselves and required no further aims such as the 'success' of higher social status or increased wealth.

## Ethics and the Philosophy of History

Smiles had some difficulty in finding and pursuing a consistent system of ethics. Attracted initially to Benthamism, and believing in a Utilitarian concept of society, Smiles also was influenced by 18th Century concepts of a mechanical universe, operating according to a series of understandable but unchangeable laws. Smiles' idea of progress in history fitted into this pattern, for he thought that man should understand and adapt to the inexorable advance of civilisation. Smiles' ethics of work and behaviour were therefore conditioned by a certain determinism, although he also wanted to express the initiative and will power of the individual.

Smiles followed Bentham to a certain extent in his ethics, but much further in his politics. In regard to legislation and government, Smiles was clear that the "grand touchstone of utility" should be applied, and that the "democratic" or "greatest happiness principle" should be "the rule for all legislation." And in the Leeds Times of 1841, Smiles ran a series of articles entitled "The 'Greatest Happiness' Principle."[60] Smiles admired Bentham enough to say in 1842 that "Bentham was, and still is, the teacher of our time," although he went on to restrict Bentham's contribution to two areas - socially-useful destructive criticism and an opposition to class interests.[61] It is true also that Smiles' ethics were similar to Bentham's in certain respects: for example, in the belief that each individual was the best judge of his own interests; that private and public interest should coincide; and that human nature (at least in the Anglo-Saxon race) was essentially similar. In his early writings, too, Smiles sometimes sounded very like Bentham:

> Like labour of the body, labour of the mind is useless or hurtful to the youth unless the object for which it is undertaken presents to him some interest or gratification.

Or

> This is the age of utility. Let us apply the principle here as elsewhere. Let us, in short, make the most of woman [as educators of children, so] . . . as to increase the amount of general happiness.[62]

Nevertheless, Smiles did differ from Bentham in many respects, one being that he believed, in contradiction to Bentham's test of the law through the application of the principle of utility, that laws were the natural moral expression of the community. Other, more pertinent differences were that Smiles never did admit the hedonistic pleasure-pain principle as a rule for the conduct of life, and he also did not approve of Bentham's devaluation of the dignity of labour through the work and reward symbiosis. As Bentham once wrote, the "desire of labour for the sake of labour . . . is a sort of desire that seems scarcely to have place in the human breast . . . [D]isguised under the name of desire of labour, the desire of wealth has been, in some measure, preserved . . ."[63]

Perhaps the most surprising aspect of Smiles' attitude toward the ethics of work and society, in view of his reputation as an advocate of success and the self-made man, is his rejection of the Benthamite work and reward symbiosis - the "cash-nexus" form of society. Stimulated by Channing's views on man and money, acquainted with the writings of Carlyle, and conscious of his own relative poverty as editor of the Leeds Times, Smiles launched into a violent attack on "the doctrine of the money-getting millions." There was only one test of man in society:

> Is he rich? That is the grand test of his "respectability" and social importance. If the man be poor, he is nil!
>
> The same spirit runs through the entire system of society. It is characteristic of the age we live in. Pelf is the god which the nation worships; cash payment is the principal bond which now links men together. The prevailing principle is self - self in all its intenseness. It prevails among all classes, and manifests itself in the spirit of competition which now tears society asunder. All are eager to be first - not first in moral worth and excellence, but in Money. Thus brothers struggle against brothers, heart-burnings are engendered between families, classes war against classes, and all suspect, despise, and fight against each other. There is scarcely one solitary spot in the social system, which this intense money-getting spirit has not invaded and polluted.

Religion also was to blame for it was "merely a cold and heartless worship of Mammon, which . . . nourishes . . . an avarice so intense as to brave the fear neither of shame, disgrace, nor punishment."[64] Smiles was free with his predictions of social disaster, "the encroaching spirit of PELF . . . threatens to engulph everything that is fair and beatiful in our land," he wrote, and again: "The inordinate desire for selfish aggrandisement and for mere grovelling lucre-making, is a moral cancer which is now eating into the very heart of the community. It threatens to break up the entire social system . . ." The desire for gain also had many side-effects, for the "love of MONEY . . . when set above all others, and made the main business of life, involves a horrid tear and wear of the human heart, is withering to all social enjoyments, and inflicts on society . . . the most deadly mischiefs and calamities." It is very clear that for Smiles the spirit of acquisition was not desirable, and that the attainment of wealth was not evidence of moral worth.[65]

Having disposed of social mobility and the acquisition of wealth (including the Benthamite work and reward symbiosis) as legitimate aims in the conduct of life, it was necessary for Smiles to propose a number of alternative sanctions for the daily work of society. These included Divine command, the need for adaptation to the laws of nature, a moderated self-interest, and the promptings of the intuitive moral conscience.

Characteristic of all Smiles' writings is a belief in a controlled self-interest, opposed to the indiscriminate pursuit of pelf, but emphasising individual initiative and will-power. This stemmed partly from his religious background and affiliations, and partly from his acceptance of Adam Smith's identification of public and private interests, which found expression in an individualistic concept of society, neatly summarised in John Stuart Mill's statement: "The worth of a State, in the long run, is the worth of the individuals composing it." Smiles placed this sentiment at the head of the first chapter of Self-Help, but he had himself consistently expressed the same belief: "Society being made up of units, will be happy and prosperous, or the reverse, exactly in the same degree that the individuals which compose it are."[66]

The successful working of this concept of the individual within the state requires that the activity of each person automatically contributes to the welfare of the nation. Smiles was not aware of the potential contradictions in this concept because of his subconscious belief that the world was rationally and beneficially ordered. Like another lapsed Calvinist, Carlyle, he assumed that each individual's work and duty would be intuitively evident to him, each man would be able to recognise and "do his duty in that sphere in which Providence has placed him . . ." Such intuition was obviously based on the conscience of the individual, although Smiles also thought that conscience and intuition were the result of the "school of life," namely wordly experience: "It is there that we find our chief sphere of duty, that we learn the discipline of work . . ."[67] If it was not difficult to discover the "right thing" to do, the determination to do it was sometimes more difficult: "We must cultivate the disposition and resolution to do the right thing, and when the determination is formed, set vigorously about doing it." Similarly a less than earnest attitude to life would mean a regrettable tendency toward "stopping short of the right thing."[68] The inclination in Smiles' ethics was for the individual to rationalise his particular vocation in society and adapt as best he could to the environment. This attitude could and did include the right of the individual to self-culture and mental self-improvement. But might there not arise some conflict between the role of the free individual - using his cultivated mental faculties and will power in pursuing his own rational self-interest - and the existence of a pre-ordained "order" to which man should conform? Smiles did not feel it necessary to defend this potential contradiction until challenged by radical ideas in the 1880s, but when so challenged, he came down heavily in favour of the divine and unalterable order of society:

> We must believe that the universe is wisely ordained, and that every man must conform to the order which he cannot change; that whatever the Deity has done is good . . .[69]

However, there was another source of Smiles' thought in the 1830s which also tended to combine rationalism, self-culture, and the need for adaptation to a pre-ordained "order," and this was the faculty psychology of the current common sense school of Scottish philosophy, allied to an 18th Century reliance on rationalism and naturalism.[70] Smiles must have come into contact with this tradition at Edinburgh, but the particular blend of rationalism, self-culture, faculty psychology, and naturalism, came to his attention through the work of two brothers from Edinburgh, Andrew and George Combe. Andrew Combe (1797-1847) was a medical doctor whose books on physiology and health were admired by Smiles; while George Combe (1788-1858) was a self-educated writer on moral philosphy and phrenology, a friend and correspondent of Channing's, and a Theist, if not a Unitarian.[71] Samuel Smiles' initial contact with George Combe most probably occurred in April 1832, when Combe lectured to Dr. Macintosh's medical class at Edinburgh - the very class in which Smiles was himself enrolled during the same spring of 1832.[72] In any case, on completing his first book, Physical Education, in 1837, Smiles sent it to George Combe and asked for his opinion, stressing in particular his agreement with the "physiological principles" advanced by Combe, and affirming his faith in principle and reason as the ultimate guide to social and physical problems. Smiles complained to Combe that

> reason and principle with the mass of mankind, are, and mainly will remain, in abeyance to feelings of an

> evanescent nature, - to fancy, to passion, or perhaps prejudice.[73]

In reply, Combe withheld his opinion on Smiles' book and stated his views on progress via reason:

> I think that as man is in his nature _rational_, he _will_ come to act in harmony with the dictates of reason after _he_ _knows_ _them_. At present he _does_ _not_ _know_ _them_.[74]

This combination of reason and adaptation had been advanced earlier by George Combe in his _Constitution of Man_ (2nd edition; Edinburgh, 1835), and also in his _Moral Philosophy_, which had originally been delivered as lectures to the Edinburgh Philosophical Association, and reported in the _Edinburgh Weekly Chronicle_ during 1835 and 1836. This was something of a coincidence, for Smiles himself had been writing editorials for the _Edinburgh Weekly Chronicle_ at approximately the same time (1836-1837) and it would have been strange had he not read Combe.[75] The ethics that Combe espoused saw man as divided into three areas of motivation - the feelings (animal and physical); the sentiments (what might be termed the moral faculties or instincts); and the intellectual faculties (these included the senses, the intellect and the reflective intellect). Further, the world operated according to moral and intellectual laws, as well as physical and organic laws. The object of life, therefore, was to discover what these laws were, and then adapt to them. This could be done by relying on the intellect, harmonising the moral and intellectual faculties, and controlling the animal propensities. The virtue of an action, therefore, lay "in its being in harmony with the dictates of enlightened intellect and of all the moral faculties acting in combination." However, the faculties were not given full-grown, but had to be exercised and cultivated in order to perform their true mission of adaptation to the laws of nature and the achievement of internal harmony.[76] Hence Combe's democratic pronouncements that even "labourers have faculties capable of far higher aims . . . ," that their life of labour did not "afford scope for the exercise of their noblest and best gifts," and that this did not "favour their steady advance in the scale of moral religious, and intellectual existence."[77]

Smiles too relied on the existence of law in all areas of life, and on the need for the necessary balance of faculties. He adopted, also, a similar tripartite division of man. But before turning to Smiles' discussion of the physiology of man, it will be useful to look at his somewhat deterministic use of the naturalistic tradition.[78] Smiles tended to confuse the laws of science with the traditional religious idea of Natural Law advanced by such exponents as Thomas Aquinas and Richard Hooker. Perhaps some of his confusion stemmed from Andrew Combe, whose work Smiles had found "of great use . . ." and who retained "a strong belief that the laws of nature were the expression of divine wisdom."[79] In any case, in order to explain the social order, and man's place and work in it, Smiles often appealed to the beneficence of God, who, for example, created children "in admirable adaptation to external nature . . ." or who had made the earth naturally plentiful, since it was only man's selfish legislation that stood "between the human family and the Divine bounty . . ."[80] At other times Smiles seemed to invest an almost overwhelming power in natural law: "The laws that regulate and govern living beings or organised nature, are as invariable as those which regulate the physical or material world . . ."[81] Later on, Smiles was to use a variation of the same argument to counsel patience: "There are many who murmur and complain at the law of labour under which we live, without reflecting that obediance to it is not only in conformity with the Divine

Will, but also necessary for the development of our intelligence and for the thorough enjoyment of our common nature."[82]

The existence of law in every sphere of life was supported by scientific research: "Few things that happen in the world are the results of accident. Law governs all; there is even a law of Chance and Probabilities, which has been elaborated by Laplace, Quetelet and others . . ." In fact, "man lives and dies in conformity to a law."[83] The conclusions to be drawn from Smiles' use of the concept of law were, firstly, that man could discover and then work in conformity with the laws of nature; secondly, that personal or national failure could be traced either to ignorance of the laws of nature or unwillingness to adapt to them; and thirdly, that the continuous operation of these laws of nature called for a reliable chain of cause and effect which would eliminate such unnatural things as 'chance' or 'accident' in man's work and effort in life.

Indeed, Smiles did make these assumptions. Social evils, he claimed, could not be blamed on competition, since such an ill-founded accusation merely reflected "our inability in most cases to trace the chain of causation to its right source. It saves the problem of searching." Moreover, the great discoveries of the past by scientists could not be attributed to accident, as very often was done; "nothing can be more unfounded . . . [because] their discoveries were invariably the result of patient labour, of long study, and of earnest investigation . . ." Logically, therefore, no one need falter in the work of life - man must "try hard, try often, and he cannot fail ultimately to succeed."[84] Smiles was able to extend this principle to all areas of life, for "failure" (poverty, ignorance, financial dependence, loss of self-respect) and "success" (self-culture, self-respect, manly defeat of difficulties, financial independence) could be linked to personal qualities and personal responsibility, since nature was bountiful,[85] and neither chance nor accident existed. Thus, Smiles could state dogmatically that "diligence and patience will invariably be rewarded," and that "there has long been a popular belief in 'good luck'; but, like many other popular notions, it is gradually giving way. The conviction is now extending that diligence is the mother of good luck . . ." And so when Smiles reviewed the life of the artists Gibson and Thorburn, he came to the conclusion that their achievements came not "by 'luck,' 'good fortune,' or anything else but . . . [by] sheer industry, application and hard work."[86]

The necessary linkage of cause and effect, therefore, operated as much in the field of work and labour as it did through the action of the laws of nature. Indeed, the process could be applied back into history, or forward into the future; for as Smiles said, "every man should grasp the idea that he is but a link in the chain of creation . . ."[87] Man's work and activities assumed an awesome dignity and responsibility in Smiles' synthesis of the laws of history and mechanical causation:

> Every act has its influence upon the destinies of man . . . every life . . . bears with it a long train of consequences, extending through generations unborn . . . Let them be worthy of man and improvement.

Smiles was fond of this thought and repeated it a number of times:

> There is something solemn and awful in the thought that there is not an act nor thought in the life of a human being but carries with it a train of consequences, the end of which we may never trace.[88]

Smiles' theory of history was evidently influenced by the historicism epitomised since the 1770s by Herder and the German sense of historical continuity. Smiles conceived of British history as one continuous organic whole - the past and the future bound firmly together by the work and activity of each generation:

> As the present is rooted in the past, and the lives and examples of our forefathers still to a great extent influence us, so are we by our daily acts contributing to form the condition and character of the future. The living man is a fruit formed and ripened by the culture of all the foregoing cultures. Generations six thousand years deep stand behind us, each laying its hands upon its successor's shoulders, and the living generation continues the magnetic current of action and example destined to bind the remotest past with the most distant future.[89]

This passage paradoxically implies both a certain historicist determinism and a considerable significance for the work and activity of every individual. In fact, Smiles was careful to point out the crucial role of the individual: "the living, active man is the link that binds the two ages together - the age that is coming, with the age that is passing away."[90]

Smiles' other references to history have a similarly equivocal application for his code of ethical behaviour - man's work on earth was to a great extent determined by his predecessors, but just because of this fact man's work assumed a considerable significance for those that were to follow him. Hence Smiles' view of history is teleological and even Marxian:

> The march of civilisation is steady and majestic. Beginning with the few [the upper class nobility and intellectuals] . . . it proceeds grandly onward, the ranks of its great army every swelling as it proceeds along the path of ages . . . [C]ommerce is freed, and the great middle class body, containing in themselves the elements of the highest social activity, and the best practical morality, press on to the front of the movement . . . [R]ecruits are gained at every step, and the triumphant march is still onward. The elevation of the working classes next gains attention . . . Such is the march of improvement in our own day. One by one, the depressed classes are emancipated, raised and admitted members of the grand

> allied army of civilisation - marching across the world, conquering and to conquer.[91]

Smiles saw no contradiction between the overall plan of history - the pre-determined march of each of the three classes to civilisation - and the 'free' activity of the individuals concerned.

Indeed, Smiles laid considerable emphasis on the need for discipline and submission to authority in the progress of history - the very opposite of a free activity in search of individual success - "Drill means discipline, training, education . . . It has been the first education of all nations. The duty of obediance is thus taught on a large scale; submission to authority; united action under a common head. Barbarism is thus organised; nations are disciplined and prepared for better things . . ." And as nations grow older, they "adopt other methods of discipline. The drill becomes Industrial. Conquest and destruction give place to production . . ." As an example, Smiles referred somewhat condescendingly to the drilling of the Russian hordes by Tsar Peter, a process that "may, in the order of Providence, be the appointed way by which the nations of the East are yet to be led towards higher civilisation and freedom."[92]

Smiles' idea of progress in history was a two-stage process that would eventually embrace all men. The first stage was simply to join the ranks of the civilised - to reach a certain level of education, activity and conduct in life. This stage was easily recognised, for "it is the great distinctive characteristic of man in a civilised state, that he is ever aiming at progress." And conversely, Smiles pointed out that the degradations of savage life were caused by a lack of desire for progress, just as the Baptist minister, William Robinson, noticed that the "aversion to labour" of savages "bears an exact proportion to their ignorance: and national indolence has invariably been found to give way . . . to the advancement of knowledge and civilisation."[93] Smiles believed that the upper and middle classes had already reached this first stage. The second stage had no specific goal or Utopia, but consisted of the eternal onward march of civilisation and education. Before considering this final stage, it will be useful to see how the first stage could be reached.

The first stage of progress in history was reached through various means. Sometimes the process was seen as simply teleological. For example, the serfs of the Middle Ages, although legally bound to their masters, showed "a great deal of self-dependence, the men were in training for better things."[94] Sometimes Smiles considered the history of England to be largely the record of a struggle between two races - the Normans and the Saxons. Both races contributed, however, to England's future civilisation, the Normans introducing power, fighting ability and aristocratic institutions, while the Saxons maintained an independent, manly and industrious undercurrent of life.[95] Hence the Saxons contributed "that patient toil and energetic spirit of self-help, which is so peculiar a feature of the Saxon races." The framework of British racial history was completed by the influx of Protestant refugees at various times: "To the country of the Britons, the Saxons brought their industry, the Northmen their energy, and the Flemings and the French their skill and spirit of liberty . . ." At other times, Smiles saw particular groups as representing the force of civilisation. Thus the monks of the mediaeval church had originally "represented the moral will and intelligence of society . . ."[96]

Over and above these suggestions, however, was one particular strategy by which the first stage of civilisation had been reached by the feudal aristocracy and the middle classes. This was through the method of association or combination. But whereas the feudal aristocracy had used combination and naked force to rise from barbarism, the middle classes had used combination and industry. And the working classes should realise that they must imitate the middle class example, for the "secret of social development is to be found in co-operation . . ." And ever since the middle classes had used association, they had proved its worth, because no "class has risen so rapidly, or done more by their energy and industry . . ."[97] At a deeper and more psychological level, Smiles followed the previously cited William Robinson (and John Stuart Mill) in thinking that the progress and advance of civilisation also depended on the spread of knowledge and the arousal of discontent among the degraded. The tendency of civilisation, wrote Smiles,

> is to awaken appetites . . . Thus, knowledge conferred upon the lower portions of the community, by revealing to them their utterly degraded position in society, will necessarily inspire them with a desire to elevate themselves. They must first be made to feel the lowness of their position, and to become actually discontented with it, ere they can experience any desire to elevate themselves above it. The discontent is a first symptom of an awakened appetite for self-betterment - for elevation in the scale of rational being. Contentment with too little is the cause of the degradations of savage life . . .[98]

Once knowledge had of necessity awakened the appetite for improvement, and association had provided the lever for economic advance, the working classes were ready to move grandly along the second stage of civilisation.

The on-going process of the second stage referred less to chosen groups and predetermined progess, than to advances which linked material growth and technology to social democracy. This process was most visible in two areas of life: the new railways and the growth of towns. Smiles saw the railway as part of a great social revolution, one of "the levelling tendencies of the age." It put an end to that distinction of rank in travelling which "was one of the few things left by which the nobleman could be distinguished from the Manchester manufacturer and bagman." Moreover, the railway brought town and country together, rescuing the one from over-worked squalor and the other from idle ignorance.[99] Smiles also thought that the railways would eliminate the problems of distance and time, and would "make the whole kingdom as one great city." The growth of the railways had occurred at the same time as the development of the large industrial towns, and the towns had performed their civilising and democratic role by becoming the centres of "social and political life and movement" - in fact they were, in a rather unhappy phrase, "great accumulated deposits of civilisation." Even London, which dismayed Smiles by its size and confusion, was pleasingly democratic to the capable workman: "There is indeed a wonderful impartiality about London. There the capable person usually finds his place. When work of importance is required, nobody cares to ask where the man who can do it best comes from . . . but what he is, and what he can do."[100]

The essence behind the two stages of civilisation was work - nothing could be achieved without work - as demonstrated in the life of George Stephenson, whose hard work in overcoming the technical difficulties of the steam locomotive had contributed to the "great civilising power" of the railways.[101] Thus the work of the individual, the mingling of races, the agencies of combination and association, and the deterministic march of progress - all these contributed in pushing the country along the path of civilisation. Yet for all Smiles' optimism, and the ideas of development and progression contained in his historicism, he was curiously lacking in a vision of the future. In fact, if Smiles' march of civilisation was forward-looking, it was evident that his society of the future was supposed to operate with the values and morality of the past. And conversely, to project a little, the late Victorian Socialists such as William Morris took their ideal societies from the mythical mediaeval past, but endowed them with the values of a future-orientated Utopia.

Smiles' historicism was also consistent in explaining colonisation in terms of the power of the traditional values allied to a sense of destiny. Smiles believed that Britain in particular, and the Caucasian race in general, had been endowed with unique resources in order to accomplish their work and destiny: following the racial theorist Blumenbach, Smiles claimed that the Caucasians had a "superior capacity for civilisation. Nearly all the great men who have ever lived, belonged to this variety of the race. The great empires of the earth have been founded by them . . ." Smiles continued by explaining why the whites were superior civilisers, and rationalised the process by giving it an air of Darwinian inevitability:

> White people have distinguished themselves in all climates. They are intelligent, enterprising, hardy, and industrious. It seems to be their destiny to occupy the world and subdue it; for they are, year by year, spreading themselves rapidly in all the quarters of the earth, planting the germs of future empires; and the weaker races degenerate and finally disappear wherever they go.[102]

Once again, the implication for Smiles' ethics was that history had a general on-going purpose, that man (especially the Caucasian) should discover what it was, and should then work to fulfill it.

The whole tendency of Smiles' ethics, his use of the laws of nature and his view of man's work in history and society, was, in fact, toward the establishment of an objective, ultimately God-given, standard to which man must conform or suffer. Despite appeals to the self-interest of the individual, Smiles actually placed man within the framework of nature - a framework which had much to do with work and cultivation of character and little to do with success or social mobility. The improvement of humanity could only come through an understanding of history and the laws of nature, and a recognition of the agencies of progress. Nevertheless, Smiles' determinism did allow the individual to make an impact by doing his work in the world, and particularly through the process of self-improvement.

However, self-improvement implied a knowledge of the physiology of man and his possibilities - a knowledge that Smiles had attained as a medical student, and which he used in discussing the anthropology and psychology of man in regard to his ideal of work and self-help.

## Anthropology, Psychology and the Formation of Character

Smiles was educated, as his earliest book, Physical Education (1838), makes clear, to follow a Lockean and sensationalist psychology. Moreover, he thought that man's moral faculties developed earlier than the intellectual faculties, and hence required an authoritative training in the home. However, Smiles began to realise the deterministic aspects of his sensationalist psychology and stress on early training, and so tried to supplement this with a consideration of the free will-power and energy of the individual. The result was a confusion in Smiles' attitude toward the formation of such habits as industry and perseverence in the character of the individual - a confusion that stemmed from the problem of free will and determinism. Nevertheless, character and right conduct rather than 'success' remained the most important element in Smiles' evaluation of the worth of man.

Smiles' view of the structure of man followed the current faculty psychology then in use by most individuals and schools of thought, including the Combe brothers and Scottish common sense philosophy. Smiles' psychology proposed the tripartite division of man into a "mental, moral and physical being," sometimes substituting 'intellectual' for 'mental.'[103] This division was important for Smiles' thought because it gave to man an area - the moral faculties - which were crucial for the development of the kind of person Smiles wanted the working class to become. It was the moral faculties which forged the character, learnt the virtues, and developed the habits of industry, diligence and perseverence.

How did this situation come about? The basis of Smiles' psychology was evidently Lockean, but derived partly from Rousseau's Emile. Smiles followed Rousseau in claiming that everything entered the understanding through the senses: "It is only after the senses have been in so far cultivated, that the mind can be said to exist, as it is through this avenue all its first ideas are acquired." Furthermore, Smiles believed Rousseau was correct in thinking that the "last part of the constitution of man that is developed is the intellectual . . ."[104] This situation resulted in an educational time-table that emphasised first the early exercise of the moral faculties (and also the physical faculties) but delayed cultivation of the mental faculties until late in childhood, and possibly not even until manhood. Thus Smiles declared that the "main object of early education should be to direct the sentiments and emotions, and implant in the mind the germs of virtuous principles." On the other hand, "it is only in advanced manhood that the reasoning faculties have become fairly developed, grow strong by practice, and full by application."[105]

In consequence Smiles de-emphasised the role of schools and schooling in favour of later adult self-culture via diligent application - a lesson that fitted in with Smiles' stress on the early and primary role of the moral virtues (which benefitted little from school), and could also apply to the situation of the largely unschooled working class. "The highest culture," wrote Smiles, "is not obtained from teachers when at school or college, so much as by our own diligent self-education when we have become men."[106] Sensationalist psychology also led Smiles, like Rousseau, to believe in the importance of the environment, as opposed to organised schooling, as an educational factor. Rousseau's Emile contained the advice: "I cannot repeat it too often: Let your lessons to youth consist in action rather than words; they must learn nothing from books which may be taught by experience." Smiles' own advice was similar: "A man perfects himself by work much more than by reading, - that it is life rather than literature, action rather than study, and character rather than biography, that tends perpetually to renovate mankind."[107]

For Smiles, therefore, as for Rousseau, the education of the moral faculties occurred first, and that of the intellectual faculties last. Moreover, the environment contained its own educational facilities for adult life. The result was an extraordinary (and almost Freudian) emphasis on the impact of early impressions and instruction on the future moral behaviour of the infant. Smiles believed that

> the impressions made at [infancy] . . . are never effaced: they endure throughout the entire future life. It is then that the germs of vices and virtues are first sown, and that the feelings and sentiments are first developed, which give a character to the future man or woman. In early years impressions are easily made, because then all the materials of which the human being is composed, are soft and ductile. Those impulses to conduct, which last the longest, and are rooted the deepest, always have their origin near our birth; the principles then implanted in our mind generally cleaving to the soil, through good and through evil, during life.

Smiles believed, therefore, that the moral sense or faculty existed at birth, but only as an empty or blank receptacle, which should be judiciously filled both by the child's mother and by an early and careful moral education. These early influences guided man's habits of work and character for industry or idleness to the end of his life, and could only be altered with difficulty.[108] The habits of work, diligence and perseverence were thus not inherent, but had to be assimilated in early youth.

The training of the moral virtues and character of each child was vital for the development of society and the attainment of the first stage of civilisation, because "all experience serves to prove that the worth and strength of a state depends far less upon the form of its institutions than upon the character of its men. For the nation is only the aggregate of individual conditions, and civilisation itself is but a question of personal improvement." This Utilitarian concept of society as an aggregate of individuals meant that progress "resolves itself into a question of _individual training_."[109] Furthermore, government legislation could not affect the moral vices and virtues - this was simply a truism for Smiles. No government could alter adult behaviour - could make "the idle and slovenly industrious, the improvident careful, the drunken sober, the lewd virtuous. No! These are reforms which must spring from the people themselves."[110] And internal moral improvement was essential because "mere intellect will raise neither individuals nor nations to greatness and happiness. It is not mental but moral power which makes a people great."[111] These two viewpoints taken together (the individualistic concept of society and the importance of the moral faculties) could only lead to an emphasis on individual moral improvement as the _sine qua non_ of social and national progress. Civilisation and social development, therefore, could not be achieved without the proper education of the individual in virtue and character.

The performance of this necessary education was accomplished, as we have seen, by the early application of correct impressions upon the "soft and ductile" materials of the child.[112] Smiles seemed uncertain as to the exact physiology of the child in this Lockean process, often referring to a soft and plastic "mind," but sometimes including the "nervous system" or more generally all the "materials" of which the child was composed. In any case, the process itself was evident: the young were "always ready to take the first impressions stamped upon them . . ."[113] Since the moral virtues were not innate, but had to be learnt, and since the blank moral faculty existed in infancy, Smiles, like Rousseau, turned somewhat naturally to the influence of mothers over the young. The mothers of the nation should set good examples because "the character of man mainly depends on the character of their mothers . . ." and "when the character is forming, every little circumstance exercises its proper influence . . . If we would have fine character, therefore, we must set before childhood fine models . . ."[114]

At this point, in order to understand the transfer of circumstance, training and example into moral virtue and fine character - of impressionable children into men of steady industry - it is necessary to turn to Smiles' use of visual domestic example. Smiles thought that "whatever is seen in fact, makes far deeper impressions than anything that is read or heard . . . [I]n early youth . . . the eye is the chief inlet of knowledge. Whatever children see, they unconsciously imitate; and they insensibly become like to those who are about them . . ." Hence the immense value of domestic training, for "the characters of parents are thus constantly repeated in their children; and the acts of affection, discipline, industry, and self-control, which they daily exemplify, live and act when all else which they may have learned through the ear has long been forgotten."[115]

Once the virtuous act was seen and imitated, and then repeated, it became easier and easier until it was formed into a habit, which "binds as with a chain of iron." However, Smiles was forced by his position to admit a rather extensive determinism: "Self-respect, self-help, application, industry, integrity - all are of the nature of habits, not beliefs[116] . . . It thus happens that as we grow older, a portion of our free activity and individuality becomes suspended in habit; our actions become of the nature of fate . . ."[117] The importance of early influence in determining later moral behaviour was constantly reiterated by Smiles. The

> infant mind, when it first appears, is a thing of mere bias, and like the pliant sapling takes the direction her [mother's] influence gives it. It inclines before every feeling - yields to every impulse; and as these more or less prevail, it becomes confirmed under their sway, 'till it gradually assumes its peculiar confirmation - like the full-grown oak of the forest, to be abiding and almost unchangeable.[118]

The dichotomy between determinism and freedom of action that persists throughout Smiles' writing is very obvious here, for if man's early training was so important for his later life, one could hardly blame the untrained or badly trained individual for his later actions, and yet Smiles readily does so, particularly in the later books of the 'self-help' series.[119]

Smiles was caught in the difficult statement that character was formed both for and by the individual. The problem was that Smiles had inherited the Lockean psychology and implicit determinism of the 18th Century, which considered the mind and character to be built up by the influence of external circumstances,[120] and in Smiles' case this referred especially to the development of the moral behaviour of the individual. Logically Smiles could have gone on to Priestley's necessitarian form of ethics, and as we have seen he originally toyed with the idea. But the individualism of his early Calvinism; his respect for the 'self-help' articles of Mary Leman Gillies; the acknowledged influence of Channing's views of the high dignity of man; and the emphasis on the individual character and will-power that he felt so strongly about, and that was later reinforced in reading Carlyle, Emerson and others[121] - all helped to move Smiles toward an uneasy position half-way between acknowledging the power of circumstances, and at the same time upholding the free activity of the individual.

The change is significant, because on the one side a sensationalist psychology could lead to a Utilitarian concept of work, based on a rational evaluation of external impressions and the hedonistic satisfaction of individual wants and desires (involving the intellectual faculties in rational pursuit of the work and reward symbiosis) - and on the other side a moral sense philosophy could lead to the Carlylean vision of work and heroic conflict with the environment (based on the use of the innate moral faculties, such as energy, perseverence and will-power, in pursuit of an intuitively known purpose).

Smiles was facing much the same problem as John Stuart Mill in his retreat from a stricly rational and sensationalist psychology. J.S. Mill wrote in his Autobiography that he had been made to feel "the helpless slave of antecedent circumstances; as if my character and that of all others had been formed for us by agencies beyond our control, and was wholly out of our own power." However, like Smiles, Mill recovered some freedom of action:

> I saw that though our character is formed by circumstances, our own desires can do much to shape those circumstances; and that . . . we have real power over the formation of our own character; that our will, by influencing some of our circumstances, can modify our future habits or capabilities of willing.[122]

Smiles too felt that

> Every man possesses a free activity in himself, he has a power of will, innate energy and means of action, which enable him in a great measure to act the part of his own educator, his own emancipator. We are not the mere slaves of circumstances . . . but are . . . endowed with power to battle and contend with adverse circumstances; and by dint of perseverence, and strong valour, to overcome them . . .[123]

Smiles also fell into a similar problem of determinism and free will in relation to the doctrine of the association of ideas[124] - a doctrine which John Stuart Mill too had been trained in. Smiles believed that if the mind was properly cultivated, it would associate ideas regarding sense objects; understand the general laws they (the sense objects) obeyed; and trace causes and sequences (cause and effect) in all their relations.[125] The conclusion to be drawn was that man could understand and perhaps control the environment, and that the intellect could legitimately direct man's work and activity. Indeed it was the intellect which "makes him [man] toil up the steep of ambition, thread the rough and crooked paths of worldliness, or labour with untiring zeal in the great cause of humanity."[126] Nevertheless, while the association of ideas helped to re-establish control over the cause and effect relationship destroyed by Hume, it also led to the kind of conditioned thinking envisaged by Samuel Bailey, the Sheffield philosopher, whom Smiles admired:

> Before we have well emerged from infancy, our moral and intellectual constitution has been so far formed, that certain ideas or circumstances awaken peculiar emotions in the breast, with almost the same precision as the touch of the finger elicits from the keys of a harpsichord their respective musical notes.[127]

The association of ideas could also therefore be considered as a vital stage in the formation of habits and character <u>for</u> the individual and not <u>by</u> the individual. Hartley had stated in 1749 that a series of sensations, ABC, impressed on the mind, would arouse ideas ABC, but that after repetition, A, coming by itself, would arouse ideas BC. Hence one could visualise the early formation, for example, of the habit of work, because by constant repetition, the practice of the habit of work would short-circuit the sense process originally required to give it validity, and the stimulus A (visual perception of an example or model, or of a task previously and repeatedly accomplished) would automatically bring about ideas BC (impulses to activity). Thus the desire to work at a particular task or not would soon become a habit, a reflex action, requiring no rational reflection of judgement, and indeed would join the category of impulses which Smiles catalogued as moral faculties or instincts. While Smiles did not spell out these conclusions to his association theory, the constant stress on the formation of habits and virtues through example, imitation and repetition certainly imply it.

Smiles' whole problem with the question of determinism, free-will, and character formation had arisen, as this section tries to make clear, because of his sensationalist psychology and through his distinction between man's intellectual nature, which developed late, and was open to modification throughout life, and man's moral nature, which matured early and whose feelings, sentiments and impulses to conduct usually remained unchanged. The intellectual nature of man was both the passive recipient of external impressions and also the active judge of those impressions, for "the life of man is made up of a continual succession of experiences. Climate, the seasons, passing events, passions and desires, age, the opinion of others, all modify his principles and his opinions from birth until death."[128] And yet the developed intellectual nature contained the faculties of judgement, reason, reflection, and intellect, and was "not a mere recipient of impressions derived from others, but possessed . . . an inherent power of judging and deciding for itself . . ."[129] This should be contrasted again with the moral faculty, whose learning powers were alsmost entirely passive from an early age, not only through the sensationalist idea of a "soft and ductile" impressionable moral faculty, but also through a process of unconscious imitation: "His [the child's] imitative powers become excited; he insensibly imitates the motions and gestures of those around him . . ."[130]

What Smiles had done, therefore, was to set up a two-tier psychology, in which the moral side of man was determined to a very considerable extent by early impressions, while the rational or intellectual side of man retained a freedom to judge for itself, although it, too, owed its being to sense-experience. Smiles found this psychology convenient because, in line with his Scottish Calvinist and Unitarian associations, he remained morally conservative; but in line with his education, and position as a rational Dissenter, he became intellectually, politically, and doctrinally more open. He wanted men to think for themselves, because "it is the monster evil of our present system of mental training, that the heavy hand of proscription is laid on the human mind . . . The young mind is compelled to walk in the darkness of dogmatism . . . that to doubt is to be ruined, and to dissent from established forms of opinion . . . is to incur certain infamy and degradation."[131]

Part of the significance of Smiles' psychology from the point of view of work and labour was that because he separated the moral faculty and moral conduct (industry, diligence, perseverence, etc.) from the intellectual side of man, to the end of his life he was never able to reconsider the efficiency and value of the simple, traditional moral virtues in an increasingly complex and changing society.[132] Furthermore, in addressing the problems of society and the individual, Smiles usually proposed as a solution the training of the individual character through the improvement of the moral faculties (i.e. moral virtues). Indeed, the emphasis that Smiles laid on character was so persistent that the remainder of this section will be largely concerned with variations on the theme of character formation.

When Smiles came to consider the formation of character in relation to the tripartite nature of man (Moral, Intellectual and Physical), he ostensibly followed George Combe and the Scottish common sense school of philosophy in advocating a harmonious balance. Smiles never resolved the problem of how such a harmonious balance might be maintained except to recommend in a general way

> The education or training of all parts of a man's nature; the physical and moral, as well as the intellectual. Each must be developed, and yet each must yield something to satisfy the claims of the others . . . It is only by wisely training all three together that the complete man can be found.[133]

However, Smiles now introduced another element into his already confusing account of the making of the complete man, and this was the ideal of consistent conduct. Consistent conduct revealed to the outside world the presence of a finely moulded character, and also the presence of the underlying principles that guided the character. The way in which Smiles viewed the appearance and function of 'principles' underlies his insistence on the formation of character, and also raises again from another angle the question of free will and determinism.

Smiles considered that 'principle' operated on a deeper level than the habits and virtues, and thus served as a more certain guide to action and moral conduct. Smiles saw the habits of perseverence and industry, for example, as capable of being defended on two levels, firstly as automatic habits, and secondly as based on principle:

> It is in the outworks of the habits formed in early life that the real strength of the defence [against the temptations of vice] must lie; for it has been wisely ordained, that the machinery of moral existence should be carried on principally through the medium of the habits, so as to save the wear and tear of the great principles within.[134]

In his earliest book, Physical Education (1838), Smiles made a subtle distinction between the acquisition of "good principles" and the existence of "intuitive principle," For Smiles, "intuitive principle" formed part of the moral faculty, consisting of the emotions and the sentiments, without any power at birth, but growing naturally with the child. Intuitive principle was, however, weaker than domestic example: "The influence of example and early habit accounts more for the behaviour of a child than intuitive principles . . ." Hence Smiles went on to stress the need for "implanting early the seeds of good principles in the young mind . . ."[135] "Good principles" were thus implanted through example, habit, and instruction, and were both supplementary to, and more powerful than, the naturally acquired "intuitive principle."

This distinction between two forms of principles - one learnt and one acquired naturally - serves only to increase the difficulty between Smiles' determinism and free will in regard to the conduct of life. "Good principles" were instilled authoritatively in the child and even in the adult, but "intuitive principles," the moral emotions and sentiments, were still the private enclave of each individual, and could be matured by the individual acting on his own initiative. Thus, young men could have the "true principles of judgement and action" implanted in their minds, but self-education was also a continuous process during life, when "principles have to be acquired, or at least mature . . ."[136] evidently by the individual himself. The individual retained, therefore, an area which still required a self-helping process, and indeed in the case of his own daughter, Smiles seemed to place as much emphasis on adult self-development as upon the early example of home and the authority of assimilated principles:

> You are quite right to be impressed with a sense of responsibility, and of duty; for you have now to depend upon your own judgement and principles as a defence against frivolity, temptations, and the vices which flesh is heir to; and though the example which you have seen at home will, I hope, always be valuable to you throughout life, you yourself have to act, and think, and work, for your own improvement of mind and heart and character.[137]

The sequence of character formation therefore consisted of three stages. First, the development of the two forms of principle. Second, the acquisition of virtuous habits on the basis of principle. Third, the formation of a consistent character on the basis of the virtuous habits. Moreover, while the underlying principles were seen as trustworthy, the formation of character actually required constant self-discipline, self-control and self-denial, both because vices might creep in and subvert the habits, and because it simply took time to build up the necessary habits on the basis of the underlying principles. So the formation of a consistent character, and the constant self-control required to keep the character functioning correctly, was, as with the Calvinists, the occupation of a life time.[138]

The desire for consistent character and conduct, as decided by principle, was a favourite theme of other Victorian moralists besides Smiles: "It is not the impulse of a moment, it is deliberate action, that decides character. That alone can indicate deep-seated motive, . . ." wrote the Rev. Tweedie. And James Alexander in The Young Man in Business, called for "PRINCIPLE" - one who acts from "a heart spring of perennnial conviction as to duty. He is principled by intelligent conscientiousness. He works by rule. He carries within a little chart and compass of right and wrong." J.W. Gilbart compared men and companies: "Fixed rules and regulations are to a public company what habits are to an individual; they insure a uniformity of conduct."[139] The emphasis on principle and character in Victorian England had much to do with what was considered to be crumbling standards of morality, and Smiles certainly shared the concern of these three authors. "Principle of all sorts," he complained, "are at a woeful discount . . . Everything like energy, decision, self-dependence has melted away. The admiration of the great, the noble, the beautiful . . . the love of principle and dependence on them, - mark not the character of the present generation."[140] Smiles was referring not only to the passing away of a set of moral values, but to the lack of any kind of standard at all, good or bad. In this context, it is interesting to read of a parallel attempt by the Congregational minister, Robert Vaughan, to reintroduce a standard of conduct based, like Smiles' moral education, upon principle and authority. Vaughan reflected that feudalism and its ethics had been replaced by modern society and the idea of "the moral": "Under this new influence, men will be less governed by passion," he wrote hopefully, "but they will be more obedient to principle." The new morality would not be daring or brilliant, thought Vaughan, but it would be honest, orderly, laborious and useful.[141]

Finally, Smiles put forward one other method by which character could be guided - and this was (in the style of Channing, William Paley, and Calvinism)[141] the perfection of character through difficulty, obstacles, poverty and suffering.[143] These stimulii tended, of necessity, to evoke such virtues as patience, perseverence and industry. This argument raises the suspicion that what Smiles really valued was the actual exercise of the traditional virtues (hopefully turned into habits) as an end in themselves. While the formation of character was seen as the ultimate aim, in the meantime the virtues of work, perseverence, duty, energetic purpose, etc., were themselves acceptable aims in life, since in any case, as Smiles said, the business of character formation required constant self-discipline. Smiles reasoned that without difficulty there would be no need for effort and virtue, and so pointed out the need for difficulty as the source of "strength, discipline, and virtue."[144]

In a similar way, the value of obstacles and difficulties was not merely that they stimulated the virtues and helped to form the character, but that they stimulated exertion "which is so essential to sound discipline." Equally, the school of Difficulty was "the best school of moral discipline . . ." and even learning to play the violin "disciplines in patience, - it practically teaches the grand lesson that difficulty is to be overcome by perseverence . . ."[145] It is here that the authoritarian side of Smiles emerges in his consideration of the physical nature of man - and its place in character formation. Although not so evident as an attitude in Physical Education (1838), Smiles knew the power of the sensual appetites, especially when the labouring class was encouraged by poverty to "low desires, evil passions, and criminal tendencies . . . a sacrifice to the temptations of his appetites . . ." While in the late 1830s Smiles had advocated the satisfaction of the animal appetites through the eradication of poverty and hunger,[146] by the 1850s he was less sanguine and conceived the problem to be widespread. Man "must drill his desires, and keep them under subjection, - they must obey the word of command, otherwise he is the sport of passion and impulse." The answer was to subject the individual to strong training. The first "drilling-place of every human being, and the best, is the Home; the next is the School; the third is the Workshop. Here we have the moral, the intellectual, and the industrial discipline of the human being provided for."[147] Work therefore fitted into the slot of disciplining the physical (industrial) side of man, and so could be seen as a useful exercise in character formation: "Work is one of the best educators of practical character. It evokes and disciplines obediance, self-control, attention, application and perseverence . . ." And once the character had been educated, it still required constant surveillance, for Smiles considered that "the true Gentleman is under strict self-control."[148]

In whatever way the character was formed, Smiles considered it to be the chief object of endeavour in life. Consequently character counted for more than success: "The truest test of success in life is Character. Has a man built up not a fortune, but a well-disciplined, well-regulated character? Has he acquired, not mere gold or acres, but virtue, benevolence and wisdom? . . . That is the only true test of a man."[149] Smiles enlarged on the true object of life:

> The highest object of life we take to be to form a manly character, and to work out the best development possible, of body and spirit - of mind, conscience, heart and soul. This is the end: All else ought to be regarded but as the means. Accordingly, that is not the most successful life in which a man gets the most pleasure, the most money, the most power or place, honour or fame, but that in which a man gets the most manhood, and performs the greatest amounts of useful work and of human duty.[150]

And in writing his self-help stories it was ultimately character that interested Smiles. While working on a brief biography of James Watt, he wrote to a friend: "What appears to persons who are intimate with distinguished men, to be _trifles_, really, when properly interwoven with the narration of such men's lives, constitute one of the charms of biography. For trifles often indicate _character_, which is the main thing to be delineated."[151]

Why was character formation so important to Smiles? It was partly an authoritarian principle. The progress of individuals and nations, and the defence of life, liberty, and property, were dependent on the observance of an established moral order, and the subordination of the individual to that order. "Character is human nature in its best form," Smiles noted. "It is moral order embodied in the individual." Further, "the strength, the industry, and the civilisation of nations, - all depend upon individual character; and the very foundations of civil security rest upon it. Laws and institutions are but its outgrowth."[152] Smiles' list of noble and virtuous individuals were models chosen to reveal not the achievement of wealth, status or public adulation, but the visible expression of this moral order through their practice of such traditional virtues as industry and perseverence. Smiles was not so naive as to expect the average working class man to achieve extraordinary intellectual and inventive results, rather he wanted to point out the values which he considered necessary for the right functioning of society. Smiles also emphasised character formation because he was proposing a set of values that were supposed to undercut the aristocratic ideal. Consequently the other (non-authoritarian) side of his thought emphasised the development of society and the individual through the new dignity that the working class would achieve by self-respect, self-help, application, integrity, industry - and the effort at self-culture - for "every human being has in him the seeds of good- has capabilities, which if duly exercised, would render him useful, respected, intelligent, and happy . . ."[152]

The conclusion of this section on anthropology and psychology is that Smiles started with a Lockean sensationalist view of man, but by following Rousseau and the current faculty psychology of George Combe and others he gave to man an area - the moral faculties - which could and should be trained in a very authoritarian way at an early age, but which nevertheless reqired development and self-control by the individual concerned. Smiles' stress on the training of the moral faculties was important, because it was the moral faculties which controlled the individual's habits of work and industry or of idleness and dissipation. The intellectual faculties were de-emphasised, despite the theory of the association of ideas which allowed man the possibility of rationally understanding and controlling the environment. Because of the importance of the moral faculties in the formation of character, Smiles dwelt on the technique of acquiring principles and habits, and in the process revealed a substantial contradiction between character that was formed _for_ the individual, and the portion that could be formed _by_ the individual. The reasons for Smiles' stress on character revealed both an authoritarian and a developmental content, and further, since character formation was an end in itself, and since the habit of work played an important part in the formation of character, then constant self-disciplined work could also be seen as an end in itself.

Support for Smiles' use of the virtues of work and perseverence in the formation of character came from the Lockean labour theory of value. Smiles often referred to labour-value in discussing not only material property, but self-education: "Knowledge conquered by labour becomes a possession - a property entirely our own;" and criticised labour-saving devices in education, stating baldly: "Labour is still and ever will be, the inevitable price set upon everything which is valuable."[154] Nevertheless, Smiles gave labour another essential function, that of national progress. But for the elucidation of this it will be necessary to turn to the next section.

## Economics and the Industrial System

Smiles believed that the object of Political Economy was to suggest the means of creating and increasing the wealth of nations. He also believed that the wealth of a nation was roughly synonymous with civilisation, well-being and prosperity. The chief agent in the creation of wealth was labour, allied to individual saving, for labour was able to provide both subsistence and the conserved result of labour, namely fixed and circulating capital. Capital in turn engendered the growth of trade and commerce, which eventually produced the basis for a prosperous civilisation. From this basic chain of cause and effect Smiles deduced that labour, and the saving of the results of labour to create capital, were two of the most important duties of economic man, since Smiles assumed that economic expansion inevitably brought benefits to all.[155] However,

Smiles did not formulate these ideas on Political and Private Economy in print until the publication of Thrift in 1875, and prior to that his statements on economics emerged piecemeal. One thing that was certain was the veneration with which Smiles, like other middle class inheritors of the Dissenting tradition, viewed the possibilities of trade and industry. So, for example, in describing the industrialisation of the Potteries district under the leadership of Josiah Wedgewood, Smiles rejoiced at the way in which "a half-savage, thinly peopled district of some 7,000 persons in 1760, partially employed and ill-remunerated . . . increases, in the course of 25 years, to about treble the population, abundantly employed, prosperous and comfortable."[156]

The genesis of Smiles' ideas on economics apparently derived from Adam Smith, whose analysis of economic growth he admired,[157] and whom he appeared to follow in regard to the basic ideas of division of labour, Free Trade, labour value, capital accumulation, and the ultimate benefits of competition and economic expansion. Smiles also rejected (as did Adam Smith) the idea that population growth necessarily pressed on supply and kept the poor at subsistence levels, although in this case Smiles was not so much expressing any classical analysis as attacking Malthus and like-minded clergy and political economists for their relegation of the poor to eternal poverty. On the other hand, while Adam Smith felt that wages depended on the size of the 'wage-fund' and 'the general circumstances' of the economy, Smiles took the slightly more stringent position that wages depended "almost entirely" on the demand for labour.[158] Smiles therefore opted for a constantly expanding economy and, as it transpired, a rigid "law" of supply and demand for the explanation of wage rates, while Adam Smith, though requiring economic growth, related wages and employment to the size of the non-wage share of income (profits and rent) available for further investment, and hence higher generation of profits, wage-fund and employment.

However, it is possible that Smiles learnt the practical application of his economics from Dr. Thomas Murray (who lectured on the subject in Edinburgh at the behest of George Combe) and who printed the lectures in the Edinburgh Weekly Chronicle during 1836 and 1837, at approximately the time Smiles was writing for the same newspaper. Certainly Murray's lectures struck the same note as Smiles' later writings in regard to the belief that civilisation began with labour and individual saving, and in Murray's general attack on the evils of the Corn Laws, on government interference with industry, and on the folly of workers' combinations attempting to raise wages.[159]

It has been claimed that Smiles represented (among others) the middle class entrepreneural ideal in Victorian England, an ideal that rested principally on three starting points - active capital investment, free competition, and socially beneficial results. The propaganda to sustain this entrepreneural ideal was the myth of the self-made man as the ideal capital accumulator and productive entrepreneur.[160] In order to approach an estimate of this claim, and at the same time to understand the relations between Smiles' economics and his attitude toward work and self-help, it will be useful to look briefly at firstly his ideas on labour-value and the use of capital; secondly, Free Trade; and lastly, Competition. Then it will be useful to discover the assumptions underlying Smiles' views; and finally to ascertain how Smiles' economics contributed to the ideal of self-help.

Smiles believed that labour did, in some old-fashioned way, confer value on commodities, and (with Locke) that the property of the working classes was their labour power: "Their Labour is their property - their ALL - just as much as the rich man's estate is to him . . ." However, in the 1830s and '40s Smiles was not thinking of capital accumulation by the worker, but rather that the only thing between the worker and starvation was his labour, and that therefore capital required security in order to generate profit and thus employ the working class. Smiles was less certain about the measurement of commodity labour value, and in fact rarely mentioned the subject except in vague terms: "Commodities may, in proportion to the ease with which they are obtained, lose at once both their external value and their intrinsic merit," or: "Labour and skill applied to the vulgarest things invest them at once with precious value." In fact, Smiles' statement that "labour is the price set upon everything valuable" meant not that labour conferred some measurable value on a commodity, but that in Smiles' value system there existed an unwritten and ultimately God-given law, which required labour to come before reward. Hence Smiles' attack on the young generation: "Our young men are still eager to arrive at great results without the drudgery of labour."[161] For Smiles, work and labour had a value that transcended economics.

The investment of capital, following its accumulation, was of course a fundamental activity of the middle class Victorian entrepreneur. Smiles considered it a truism that labour without capital was useless, and that capital accumulation and investment was essential for national progress. Smiles thought, for example, that Ireland had once achieved a golden age in the late 18th Century, when capital and labour combined so that "wealth multiplied apace. Peace and Order overspread the land . . . only the sounds of busy industry were to be heard."[162] However, when Smiles discussed the role of capital in regard to the working classes, he usually referred to it in two ways - first as an agency for employing the unemployed, and secondly as an intangible and "inherited" property in the form of skill and working ability, which was handed down from generation to generation.

These two attitudes occur frequently in Smiles' Lives of the Engineers (1861-62) and will be treated in Chapter IV. The point to be made here is that Smiles made a distinction between what the working class man could do (either work, invent or use his "inherited' skill) and what the merchants and traders could do in promoting these inventions and skills (produce the necessary capital and employ the workers).[163] Hence Smiles claimed that the "mere material wealth bequeathed to us by our forefathers forms but an insignificant item in the sum of our inheritance." Smiles really wanted to advance the cooperation of labour and capital, in which the working class produced the labour and the wealthy produced the capital to employ the labour. Moreover, for the smooth functioning of the economic process, Smiles wanted to stress private economy (which would keep the working class able to work, and clear of poverty and charity) and not political economy (which was involved with the much more difficult question of the accumulation of capital and the distribution of wealth). The accumulation of capital had been a central feature of political economy since Ricardo, but it is striking that Smiles' writings had little to say about capital accumulation until 1875, yet had much to say on the subject of saving as a means of individual independence. Money was to be saved for a more modest cause than capital accumulation, "not merely [for] the immediate supply of nature's wants, but the reserve in addition . . . [for] the evening of existence." The chief reason to save, then, was "for the purpose of being independent . . . ," but not for the creation of entrepreneurs or of capital for investment.[164]

Nevertheless Smiles was aware that it was capital which set machines and factories to work, and that this capital had to come from somewhere. It did not come from the combined result of the savings of each workman, but from the resources of the middle class merchants and traders who had accumulated this capital in the distant past. The entrepreneurs were those who were already wealthy middle class men, willing to invest, and not the self-made men of the present age.[165] To set the record straight, it should also be admitted that the London Builders Strike of 1859 produced a reaction from Smiles in the shape of an article for the conservative Quarterly Review attempting to undercut the rationale of striking. In the article Smiles introduced the "law" of supply and demand and denied the validity of attempts to raise wages - labour could not earn more than supply and demand allowed, a fact which was as certain as "the law of gravitation." Indeed "there is a natural law of remuneration for every kind of labour which the power of all trades' unions cannot alter." This did not allow the workman much leeway in accumulating capital, but on the other hand Smiles tried to also undercut the strike by encouraging the workmen with tales of the past: "The most successful accumulators of capital have in all times risen from the ranks of labour itself . . ."[166] A debateable conclusion, but in any case Smiles' attitude in this article was aimed more at the prevention of strikes than at any genuine encouragement of working class entrepreneurs. Smiles' basic approach remained the same - work and thrifty saving gave the worker security, not capital.

The next principle to be considered is that of Free Trade. Closely linked to Free Trade were the somewhat synonymous principles of laissez-faire and competition, although laissez-faire could be used in a wider context than Free Trade, while competition pertained more to the idea of economic progress through rivalry and conflict. Prior to the repeal of the Corn Laws in 1846 Smiles saw Free Trade simply in terms of the iniquitous corn Laws. By their nature the Corn Laws represented a monopoly since "the avenues of trade have been closed up by the landlords . . ." Smiles angrily charged that "the hereditary land class [had] doomed the hereditary slave class of our country to poverty . . ." The solution was simple: "Let industry but be relieved of its aristocratic incubus, and the rights of labour be respected and honoured as they deserve, and there is no limit to the advancement of our country in knowledge, wealth, and civilisation."[167] Here Smiles showed both his opposition to the monopoly tactics of the aristocracy (though not to the aristocracy as an institution) and his sublime faith in the power of industry to achieve widespread results over and above economic growth.

Perhaps a more revealing sign of Smiles' approach to Free Trade was his difficulty over the question of Short Time in factories and the limits of government interference in industry. In 1839 Smiles opposed factory legislation and blamed the Corn Laws for long hours, low wages and unemployment, although qualifying his position: "Provided labour has a free market, and free and equal exchanges, the meddling of legislators can result only in injury to the labouring population." This was certainly Adam Smith's paradigm of the free market and the benefit of Free Trade. Smiles continued to blame the Corn Laws (and to a lesser extent the introduction of machinery) for the problems of the labouring classes,[168] and by February 1841 was attacking legislation of all sorts - Corn Laws, Poor Laws and Factory Laws. Smiles picked out Factory Laws for especial criticism, partly because they had been concocted by the Landlord, and partly because they denied the workman full opportunity to earn his expensive bread.[169]

By the beginning of 1842 the Ten Hour Movement was gathering strength, and Smiles adopted the classic middle class response that "short time" was an obvious plot by the landed Tories to undermine the manufacturing class. At this stage (January 29, 1842) Smiles was accused by the Chartist newspaper in Leeds, the Northern Star, of being bought up by two of the Leeds factory lords (presumably Marshall and Gott) and he expediently retreated a short distance: "We have always advocated the shortening of the hours of labour . . ." But the next week Smiles stood by his old position: "The great desideratum is to extend and open up new sources of employment for the labouring classes, instead of restricting and shutting up the old ones." He agreed that misery existed, especially of a "moral and physical kind," but felt that industry was not to be lightly tampered with, and that the best policy was "to extend the sphere of industry" by taking off the "unnatural restrictions upon trade and commerce . . ."[170] Smiles' position evidently depended on the law of supply and demand - wages would find their own level automatically since "their rate depends almost entirely on the demand for labour."[171] Therefore the way to raise wages and employment was simply to create more industries which would demand more labour and so place the workers on the favourable end of the supply and demand equation. To restrict the hours of labour was not, in the long run, going to raise wages or create new jobs.

The Ten Hours Bill finally passed in 1847 with large majorities, and by this time too Smiles had come to favour the Short Time question. Factory conditions now seemed more degrading to Smiles, and he had become increasingly worried by the split between masters and workers, "the only bond of connection between them being that of hire, or weekly wages."[172] Sympathy between classes was lacking, and at the same time the working class did not seem to be advancing in moral elevation at all. Interestingly enough, in an article in 1847, Smiles was able to distinguish between the protectionist Ferrand and other "abettors of monopoly" (whom he still generally opposed, though not on the question of Short Time); and those like Cobden (whom he normally supported) but who had fallen into some disfavour with him by continuing to fight against the Short Time question. Smiles now approved of Short Time, since the labouring people needed "time for the improvement and sustenance of their moral and intellectual nature."[173] Smiles was still in favour of Free Trade and in opposition to "monopoly" but now it seemed that the moral and cultural improvement of the workers was of such importance that it could breach the Free Trade 'law." The question of wages and employment had largely dropped out of the situation because an ecomomic solution based on Free Trade was beyond human manipulation, and Smiles was therefore concentrating on other answers to the growing demands of the working classes, voiced principally through the Chartist movement.

In 1842 Smiles had discussed the views of Fourier, the French Socialist, on association, and had concluded that association and voluntary labour <u>were</u> compatible, since physiology taught that men would be compelled to labour as a means of "keeping in health." Of course, excessive labour was harmful, but the powers of machinery were sufficiently advanced to dispel that fear. Smiles closed his review of the "phalanstery" sceme by praising Fourier for trying to develop "the physical, the intellectual, and the moral powers of every human being . . ." And two years earlier Smiles had urged the workers to grow their own food through some form of cooperation, and thus become "self-supporting and self-dependence."[174] After the repeal of the Corn Laws in 1846 Smiles turned his attention more seriously to the principle of cooperation as likely to realise the emancipation of the working classes. Although condemning strikes and combinations as cooperation's most imperfect form, Smiles particularly praised the work of the Leeds Redemption Society (a communitarian project that operated a farm among other activities), which aimed at the "reconciliation of labour with capital, and the constantaneous advancement of human happiness with the progress of the industrial acts."[175]

Smiles' involvement with this cooperative project in 1847 and his hopes for its useful results may be gauged from a speech given by William Howitt, the reformer and author, at the first soirée of the Leeds Redemption Society, in which he stated that he was gratified to be "seconding the efforts of that worthy man, Dr. Smiles (hear, hear), to bring before them the . . . essentially useful and important principles of co-operation . . ."[176] In effect Smiles and other proponents of the Redemption Society were willing to go beyond the system of laissez-faire in an attempt to improve the condition of the working classes, but were still insistent that the workers rely upon themselves in organising cooperation, and particularly that the workers should not apply to government reform. The suspicion arises that the promoters of the Redemption Society were not above an attempt to undercut the Chartist movement, as various articles in the Herald of Redemption seemed to indicate. One, for example, entitled in

Smilesian language "God helps those who help themselves," advised "the people to put little value upon agitation for mere legislative reform" since "agitation by the working class has ever failed in obtaining the smallest concession to humanity or justice." Be that as it may, the article also went beyond laissez-faire by calling for legislative interference in the cause of Education and Sanitary Reform.[177] The attitude was that in matters of earning a living the working class should rely on self-help, even in the form of cooperative self-help, but that for the removal of certain evils, the government could theoretically break the laissez-faire deadlock.

This was also Smiles' basic attitude. Where economic self-help was concerned Smiles was anxious to let alone, but where the evils of society could be removed, he was willing to consider government intervention. Starting somewhat cautiously on this tack in 1847, and following his support for short Time and Association, Smiles justified his breach of Free Trade "law" by calling for a wider definition of the phrase. This meant that Free Trade was "only part of a struggle for a still larger freedom," what Smiles called 'social economy' - "how the means of happiness are to be the most equitably distributed for the well-being of those who produce them."[178] By 1852 Smiles was able boldly to criticise the "mania" for Free Trade, "to the extent of doing nothing for nobody, but letting everybody do everything for themselves. We were to let everything alone. To leave towns uncleansed, streets unsewered, children uneducated, criminals unreformed, paupers unfed, letters uncarried . . ." However, Smiles qualified this strong position by generally applying the phrase Free Trade to only one area - "Not so long ago Free Trade was the great question; and Free Trade became the law."[179] For Smiles, therefore, Free Trade referred specifically to the Corn Laws, and to those acts of monopoly which did not benefit the well-being of the people. Smiles tried thereafter to steer a moderate course which rejected total laissez-faire, the "free-trade idea run mad,"[180] and which permitted government removal of evils, including monopoly, in the interests of economic self-help.

In regard to competition, Smiles was aware of the criticisms levelled at it for creating poverty, unemployment and the lack of sympathy in society. But he believed that "though mixed with necessary evil, there will be the ultimate beneficial results of Competition." These benefits included the stimulation of the character, qualities and culture of men, and the development of the country's resources, invention and industry. By 1852 Smiles had lost faith in cooperation as the ideal or only solution (the Leeds Redemption Society was fading away on a barren farm in Wales) and he saw competition as one of the necessary stimulii to material progress. The competitive spirit was in any case instinctual with man, and the lack of competition would only aid the indolent and stupid, and would certainly not increase employment in the over-employed trades. Unemployment was due not to competition, but to the "character of the workman" and his unthinking refusal to change trades - a "man fails because he wants merit, or he wants industry . . ."[181] Smiles' somewhat narrow attitude toward unemployment and poverty reflected a faith in the economic system which had become crystallised by this time, 1852.

This faith did not need to refer to intricate arguments over Political Economy, Free Trade, laissez-faire, etc., but simply to a belief that with the removal of social, economic and political evils, a man could fit into the economic system, and work his way to independence and respectability, whatever the difficulties. By mid-century, English society and the class structure had evolved some kind of *modus vivendi*;[182] Free Trade had been obtained in 1846; the standard of living was rising generally, if slowly; the Chartist movement had passed away; the Great Exhibition had given visible signs of material progress and the Factory Acts were believed to curtail the worst abuses of industrialism. Smiles seemed to reflect this new national confidence in his uncritical acceptance of the viable *economic* possibilities of the working class. Despite his criticism of the evils that still existed, Smiles felt optimistic enough to blame the existing privation on the want of character, foresight and working ability of the individual. Smiles' earliest editorials in the *Leeds Times* had stressed the need for self-help, but nevertheless, his position in the early 1850s showed a remarkable change from his more critical and troubled stance in 1839. Thus in March 1839 Smiles wrote that the causes of crime were not due to individual failings, but "bad government, bad legislation, and bad social arrangements . . ." and in October 1839 that poverty was not due to "improvidence, idleness, imprudent marriages, and bad domestic management" but to "bad social and political institutions."[183]

However, by 1852 Smiles evidently believed that the advantages of economic competition outweighed the need for radical criticism of the system and its institutions, and that there were no viable alternatives to the competitive system. Yet Smiles was aware of the evils mixed in with competition, and his dislike of money grubbing and mammon worship remained with him to the end of his life, so that it cannot be said Smiles was a totally enthusiastic supporter of competition. To remove competition would not improve the situation, he thought, whereas the existence of competition at least acted as a spur to economic growth.

From this discussion of labour value, capital investment, Free Trade and competition, it may be concluded that Smiles did support, with qualifications, an entrepreneurial and industrial society as a necessary and useful menas of economic and hence social advance, but that he did not attempt to produce the myth of the self-made man as the ideal productive entrepreneur (with the possible exception of his Quarterly Review article). Rather, Smiles was concerned with the way in which the working class could avoid poverty, unemployment, and physical and moral degradation - a problem which concerned him throughout the 'self-help' series of books. Nevertheless, Smiles did accept some form of competitive system, and often visualised industrialisation as a necessary (and potentially unlimited) source of social benefit if left to expand without unnecessary restrictions. Why was this? There were perhaps two major assumptions.

The first reason related to Smiles' *à priori* assumption in regard to the bounty of Nature. Smiles was convinced that over-population and starvation were totally unnecessary: "There is no such thing as a surplus population," he wrote in 1842. "There never is, and there never has been. The earth is rich enough, and fertile enough for us all. Nature's resources have never yet been gauged; there is no possibility of exhausting them. The earth teems with abundance of food for man and beast." Why then did suffering exist? "has the Creator blasted the earth with sterility? . . . No! No! But man has cursed the earth with his villainous legislation: his selfishness has raised a barrier between the human family and the Divine bounty . . ." It was evident that the Corn Laws were at fault, for abolition of them would open the way to physical comfort, which "every man is able to attain . . . in this abundant and plenteous country, rich in all the wealth which nature yields."[184]

Smiles' faith in the abundance of a Divinely created Nature did not stop there, but also embraced the idea that Nature would, in some self-acting way, reconcile itself to industry in a mutually beneficial form. Thus Smiles was able to criticise the landlords' Corn Laws, and yet justify the enslavement of man by machinery. Smiles assumed, in a leap of faith, that mechanism and nature would finally accommodate themselves to each other, and enable the labouring classes" to obtain the physical comforts of life . . ."[185] On the other hand, Corn Laws and aristocratic legislation could not be accommodated to Nature. This was because they interfered with the system of production, a system which was capable of altering a district in which "a few half-starved labourers lived, in comfortless hovels . . . [into] towns and cities, crowded with a skilled, industrious, artizan population." Smiles came to the conclusion therefore that suffering was caused "chiefly from the interference of the legislature with the laws of nature and of society."[186] In other words, a system of machine production could be imposed upon Nature, and having revealed its benefits to society, could be elevated to the same status as Nature in the sense that it too operated according to absolute laws and could not be disturbed without harmful results. The system of production had become a "law of society" in a way which Corn Laws and aristocratic rule could not duplicate, because of the two, only the system of production appeared to be as ultimately beneficial and permanent as Nature was.

This was an _aperçu_ that Smiles could not have made from direct observation (the introduction of machinery actually caused much distress to the handloom weavers, among many others) but only through his belief in the fertility of Nature's resources, and in his conviction that 'law-creating' absolutes operated best when left alone. Indeed, it is possible to see the source of Smiles' ideas on the inviolability of Nature and the industrial system as originating from his training as a doctor. The practice of a doctor should be similar to that of a social reformer or of the government - simply to offer assistance where possible by removing obstacles to sound economic or bodily growth, but in general to leave well alone. Just as Smiles called for the removal of the causes of poverty in order to "afford the industrious the means of self-dependence . . ." or for the removal of "unnatural" restrictions on trade and commerce,[187] so he called for the physician "to remove obstructions to her [Nature's] peaceful and healthy action." The physician should regulate and assist Nature only in repairing derangements [evils], since the major part of his duty was to know and be guided by the "certain laws" of Nature: "Proper management is thus merely an effectual co-operation with nature." Equally, child management "chiefly consists in non-interference with the natural processes . . ."[188] The negative side of Smiles' ideal as a doctor can also be related to his concept of self-help. Smiles actually emphasised medical and sanitary prevention rather than cure, and in helping patients to help themselves. It was easier to preserve the healthy action of the system when sound, considered Smiles, than to repair it after debilitation - diseases should be avoided rather than cured. Similarly the object of the nurse should be "to aid Nature, and imitate her in her efforts at self-relief." Finally, the individual should learn that the preservation of his life and health was in "so great a measure the result of his own care and watchfulness."[189] Smiles' training and practice as a doctor was, therefore, consistent with the concept of economic self-help and appears to have contributed to the formation of that concept. Perhaps it would be more accurate to say that Smiles' medical training supplemented his faith in Nature, which however pre-dated his Edinburgh education and originated in his religious background and concepts of a beneficially ordered world. In any case, a strong element of his insistence on the moral duty of work and self-help must have been based on a trust in Nature which flowed over into trust in the economic system.

The second assumption, or series of related assumptions, behind Smiles' belief in the potential of economic progress (and another reason for his insistence upon the value of the work of the individual) was derived from the influence of Newtonian physics. According to Newton's third Law of Motion every action has an opposite and equal reaction. This could be construed to mean, as Charles Babbage put it: "No motion impressed by natural causes, or by human agency, is every obliterated." Smiles quoted a long section from Babbage in Self-Help, including this sentence, and gave it his own interpretation: "The civilisation we enjoy is but the sum of the useful efforts of labour during the past centuries . . . For no human labour is altogether lost; some remnant of useful effect surviving for the benefit of the race, if not of the individual." Smiles was impressed by the idea that a man's labours "are not lost - they are propagated through all time . . ."[190] This concept seems to have been reasonably widespread, and was mentioned by at least one other popular author, who was also a friend of Smiles', Sir Arthur Helps. Helps wrote that "the result of any endeavour, however small in itself, may be of infinite extent in the future. Nothing is lost."[191]

If the results of human labour were capable of conservation and aggregation, then the progress of civilisation could be seen in a very optimistic light. In the first place, it was evidently linear. Smiles' teacher in Edinburgh, Dr. Fletcher, phrased it from the point of view of intellectual progress, but there was no reason why it could not be applied economically as well. "Man," declaimed Fletcher, "being capable of leaving behind him records of his attainments, so that his successors may begin where he leaves off, he is capable likewise of progressive civilisation."[192] In the second place, civilisation and economic growth could be seen as cumulative. All that was required was the constant piling up of acts of useful labour, one on top of the other. The progress of the nation, therefore, might be resolved into a simple Utilitarian calculus, a sum of addition, just as regress might be a question of subtraction. Smiles put forward just such a sense of accumulation and subtraction when he wrote that man "by his several acts . . . either increases or diminishes the sum of human good now and forever." And "national progress is the sum of individual industry, energy, and uprightness, as national decay is of individual idleness, selfishness, and vice."[193] The analogy of addition and subtraction can be carried too far, but it is logical that Smiles should be at one with the atomistic concept of society and economics generally held in Victorian England before the advent of Herbert Spencer and Charles Darwin.

If there was one striking motif in Smiles' concept of economic progress, it was the way in which he firmly linked the industry and thrift of each individual to the progress of the nation. An opposite image would be that of a community involved in constructing a house. All worked together, "one generation carrying forward the labours of another, building up the character of the country, and establishing its prosperity on solid foundations." Everyone contributed, since the action of the "least significant person" added to the "general result."[194] If the individual did not contribute, then there was a chance of regress, for as Smiles noted later, countries that were idle and luxurious "must inevitably die out, and laborious, energetic nations take their place." But Smiles was happy to note the example of the heroic troops at the seige of Sebastopol which showed that "our countrymen are as yet an undegenerate race."[195]

Indeed Smiles borrowed another metaphor from the sciences to describe the way in which individual efforts, combined together, determined the state of national growth. This was the idea of the proportionality of all energy processes - a proportionality which prevented an effect greater than its cause, or the emergence of something out of nothing - and which later in the 19th Century became the second law of thermo-dynamics. Using this metaphor Smiles visualised society rather as a self-adjusting body of water (character replacing the concept of energy) with the resulting cause and effect determining the level. "In the order of nature," Smiles noted, "the collective character of a nation will surely find its befitting results in its law and its government, [or in industry and material growth he might have added] as water finds its own level." Since industry and civilisation depended on individual character, so it was that "in the just balance of nature, individuals, and nations, and races, will obtain just so much as they deserve, and no more. And as effect finds its cause, so surely does quality of character . . . produce its befitting results."[196] Nature was neutral but just, and people got what they deserved. An individual suffering from poverty or unemployment could be condemned for personal failure, since his problems could not be blamed on Nature or society - and thus the only answer was self-help.

Finally it might be argued that Smiles' constant references to the work and struggles of past generations in the building up of a country's resources and civilisation may well have dispensed with any understanding of political economy, and instead have represented feelings of guilt toward his own parents, and particularly his mother. When his father died of cholera, Smiles was at medical school, and was persuaded by his mother to continue, although the cost and difficulties must have been hard for her to bear, especially as an independent debt of some £270 had to be paid at approximately the same time. (It is also curious that soon after this event Smiles read a book by the French author, Aimé-Martin, which apparently convinced him of the power of women in the world - perhaps a reflection of his debt to his mother.)[197] Whatever the origin of Smiles' sense of obligation to his parents and past generations, he often dwelt on the subject of parent-child relationships, once remarking that "duty [of parents and children] is a thing that is due, and must be paid by every man who would avoid present discredit and eventual moral insolvency. It is an obligation . . ." And at another time urging young men "to cherish profound gratitude" for their parents, who represented "centuries of labour and good conduct . . . The virtues of their generous labours are an image of the dead . . . it is steadfast perseverence which keeps their honour bright."[198]

The point is that Smiles' emphasis on hard work and thrift was not just a function of Private or Political Economy, but a result of some sense of debt that he felt the present generation owed the past. The repression of present enjoyment for self-denial, saving, and work, was sanctioned by Smiles in terms of "Duty" or "Conscience," but it was a debt that had to be paid to society, on behalf of the labours of the past generations, just as a sum of money (acquired but not earned) would also have to be repaid, or just as Time, freely given by God and therefore unearned, would have to be repaid through the careful accounting for and use of every hour. Smiles therefore is able to make the unsupported statement that because man's birthright consisted of the [unearned] "labours of our forefathers . . . we can not enjoy them unless we ourselves take part in the work."[199]

And reverting to an earlier point, Smiles makes an interesting observation on the value of labour, clearly transcending any meaning of economics or theory of labour-value: "The present age being so decidedly mechanical - our leading inventions resulting in the triumph of science at the expense of labour, - there is a strong tendency and desire to arrive at results suddenly, without undergoing the dull plodding which our laborious ancestors were willing and obliged to confront." This passage is reminiscent of Carlyle's 1829 attack on mechanism as the cause of a loss of "faith in individual endeavour," although there is an even closer resemblance to E.L. Bulwer's fears that the "diseased" symptom of the times was the attempt by all and sundry to evade the benefits of obstacles, labour and toil.[200] Similarly, Smiles was dismayed by the change in the "rules" of life - by the way in which inventions and various trends in society were encouraging man to evade the God-given "laws" of society - namely, 'In the sweat of thy brow shalt thou earn bread,' and the subsequent equation which required cause (labour) before effect (results). Smiles must have felt that man was breaking faith with the toil and suffering of past generations by refusing to repay the debt in the same kind of currency.

The conclusion of this section is that while Smiles did not reveal a coherent economic theory, it is plain that he did favour some form of competitive system, by means of which the country could be spurred toward an ultimate civilisation. Yet Smiles did not speak to the ideal of the self-made man in the sense of encouraging every working man to achieve entrepreneurial status. Rather Smiles conceived of an atomistic society, advancing as a stream of water would advance, each molecule playing its working part and none retarding the total advance by subtracting from the work or financial resources of the whole. At the same time Smiles was committed to the improvement of working class conditions, and although his impulses toward self-help and the value of labour (coupled with his faith in the natural bounty and the benefits of industry) steered him toward a laissez-faire economics, he did try to broaden the concept of Free Trade to allow reform in several areas. Moreover by 1847 he did support both Short Time and different varieties of association and cooperation. In fact, like his Redemption Society friend, James Hole,[201] Smiles was in a muddled way trying to steer a middle course between an authoritarian form of paternalism or legislation and complete laissez-faire. Chronologically, this middle position had been reached after some quite radical changes of mind. While in 1839 Smiles was inclined to a strong laissez-faire position in reaction to the landed aristocracy, entailing an opposition to Short Time, but coupled with some harsh criticisms of the social system rather than the individual, by the early 1850s Smiles was somewhat less opposed in principle to government intervention, had changed to support of Short Time, and was inclined to blame social problems on the individual. Not a particularly consistent position, but with Free Trade realised, the limits of cooperation revealed, Chartism, Socialism and nearly all forms of government intervention rejected, and with the faults of total laissez-faire apparent, Smiles was driven back on to the only solution he could think of, an individualistic self-help of work, saving and economic independence. And self-help was important because with Smiles' identification of material progress and national well-being, of individuals with the nation, it was absolutely essential that each productive member of society played his part in advancing the progress of the nation as a whole.

If Smiles' economics aimed at individual thrift and industry as the sine qua non of national progress and civlisation, it was also apparent that commerce had a political role to play. Writing in 1844, Smiles contended that

> Liberty invariably follows in its [Commerce's] steps; together with knowledge, religion, and happiness. It breaks down in time the despotism of the mightiest tyrants. The spirit of commercial enterprise has, at all times, been opposed to the spirit of barbarism, and is destructive of feudal legislation. It is hostile to monopoly, and to all exclusive rights and privileges. Without commerce, indeed, no nation has ever made distinguished progress in the higher stages of human civilisation.[202]

This passage gives some of the flavour of Smiles' strong opposition to aristocratic privilege - an opposition that gave self-help whatever moral fervour it possessed; namely, as a crusade designed to help the working classes undercut the educational, political and economic advantages of the 'idle' rich. This will be the concern of the next section.

## Politics, Government and Class Conflict

One of Smiles' earliest recorded impressions in life was to result in a lasting sense of the injustice of the power of money and the exclusiveness of the class structure. His first teacher (or dominie), Smiles recalled, used to favour the sons of provosts, bailies, town councillors, or the children of well-to-do men, and he acknowledged that "I was the son of none of these distinguished personages and not a favourite." Moreover, his teacher, having once been a Dissenter and having deserted the cause, reserved his hatred for those that still were Dissenters. (The renunciation of Dissent in 19th Century Britain was a sure sign of an attempt at social climbing.) In a letter to his daughter Smiles recalled what must have been a difficult experience for a young schoolboy, and at the same time reveals how the experience helped to shape his ideas on work and self-help as a means of overcoming the advantages of those who were socially and financially favoured. His old schoolmaster, wrote Smiles

> was a brute, and had no sympathy with boys willing to work. Besides he was a man who had favourites - swells and sons of rich men. He had many prizes [prize pupils], but in life they all disappeared. It was really the dunces who made the best figure. Given the proper beginning everything else depends upon habit and perseverence.

Smiles' bitterness over his own poor showing at school comes out in several statements; for example that early cleverness was no test of the height to which grown men might reach, for "precocity is quite as often a symptom of disease as an indication of intellectual vigour in youth."[203] Even in 1891, some seventy years after his school days, Smiles remembered that he was thought of as one of the dunces, "only fit to sweep the street of my native borough," so that his teacher had "threatened to dash my brains against the wall. This was his ordinary way of speaking to those who were not his favourites."[204]

It did not take Smiles long to retaliate against the "favourites" of political and social life, the aristocracy, and to draw his own conclusions. In Smiles' very first article for the <u>Leeds Times</u> in January 1839, he derided the House of Peers as "that rotten and most corrupt of all corporations" and as "that Lazaar-house of Incurables," while the Court revealed only "a caterpillar influence" (i.e. useless and parasitical) and the youthful Queen herself represented merely the "puppetry of thrones." Smiles' conclusion was that improvement lay only "in the people themselves . . . To themselves alone must they look for the means of progression."[205] So it was that at the very beginning of his foray into public life that Smiles set down his credo of self-help in politics - a political credo born of personal experience and pragmatism. Smiles' whole approach to politics reflected his ideals of work and self-help, and particularly in reference to three problems: the function of the three classes in society; the nature of the class structure; and the changing role he envisaged for the government.

Smiles thought that the aristocracy were guilty of three counts against the public interest: they bred a false spirit of rank and wealth, they performed a positive evil in that they obstructed the industrial, social and political freedoms of the country, and they refused to perform any useful function - indeed they were idle and perforce lived on the work of others.

The aristocracy fostered a class spirit that affected all ranks of society, and especially the middle class, whom Smiles sometimes despaired of: "The middle class of this country is thoroughly aristocratic in its spirit. It worships and adulates rank and fashion: it is deeply tainted with the beggarly pride of caste." Besides fostering a false respectability and worship of rank and wealth (external show instead of internal merit), class spirit also divided the country, and worse than that, the functions of the people: "The progress of class selfishness has elevated the one [the Court or aristocracy] to the abasement of the other [the People] - the idle few at the expense of the labouring many . . ."[206]

The result of this spirit of class was, as Smiles intimates, the devaluation of the dignity of labour and the devaluation of the dignity of man. The "aristocratic spirit" had allowed the individual to be "despised because of his want of some adventitious circumstances of rank or wealth.

The MAN is overlooked for the puppet . . ." Moreover, if labour was to regain its proper position there must be a de-emphasis of class: "The anti-social, sectarian, and class spirit, so distinctive of all classes in this country, must be broken down . . . We must recognise the dignity of labour for all . . ."[207] And as a corollary to this criticism Smiles rejected the "spirit of aristocratic self-aggrandisement," the single minded effort by the aristocracy to gain wealth at the expense of labour, to the detriment of the "social and moral elevation of the great mass of the people . . ."[208] The shameful fact was that the aristocracy taught the people (especially women) "to value things by their externals, and their externals only." Therefore, the aristocracy were not valued for any internal merit, and Smiles listed the qualities he evidently thought the aristocracy lacked - moral wealth; mental greatness; industry; prudence or economy; foresight, knowledge, attainments, experience, or character - and concluded that the aristocracy were valued only for their "rank, wealth and fashion."[209]

Smiles' chief complaint against the positive evil of the aristocracy was, of course, their opposition to the repeal of the Corn Laws, and his criticism usually ran in the form of clear-cut alternatives of good and evil. In April 1840, for example, his article on the Corn Laws stated that "it is Aristocracy against Industry - Possessions against People - Monopoly and Restrictions against Commerce and Freedom." Sometimes Smiles saw the evil of the aristocracy as pauperising the country through a kind of law of action and reaction, of cause and effect: <u>because</u> the landed aristocracy had accumulated vast property by controlling the laws of primogeniture and entail, <u>therefore</u> thousands had been made poor, and <u>because</u> one man had accumulated £100,000 a year, therefore 100,000 people were wasting their lives in incessant toil and living on half rations.[210]

Smiles was particularly concerned with Adam Smith's influential division of the population into producers and non-producers. It was clear to Smiles that there was an organised plan by the privileged few to maintain themselves "at the expense of the Industrious Many." There was in existence an actual system of "depredation upon the labour, the industry, and the property of the public." The aristocracy exacted industry from others for obvious reasons - so that they might live well, enjoy their vices, and "set aside the command of god, 'He that will not work, shall not eat.'" Apart from forcing misery on others and enjoying their vices (which idleness normally fostered) Smiles was also incensed by the fact that the aristocratic idlers were living on public taxes - taxes which Smiles himself had to pay.[211] The aristocracy through their idleness were not just a passive evil, therefore, but a positive one, for, as Smiles put it, "if a man do not manage honestly to live within his own means, he must necessarily be living dishonestly upon the means of somebody else."[212]

Smiles seemed to have ambivalent feelings when he considered what the function of the aristocracy should actually be, and his excoriation of the aristocracy, while often vituperative, fell curiously short of any practical measures. It has been said that Calvinism, while critical of those that did not work, failed to conceive clearly any indebtedness of the rich to the poor, and equally did not press a strong criticism of ownership. In view of Smiles' early Calvinism, it is interesting to note that his criticism did not involve either of these two points, and was often completely negative. Thus in 1841 Smiles somewhat meekly requested:

"Let the landlords be content with their estates; only let the people enjoy the full freedom of living by their daily labour."[213]

The furthest extent of Smiles' criticism of the function of the aristocracy was the demand that they work and thereby add something to the wealth of the country instead of existing on that wealth, particularly in times of recession:

> While bankruptcy and ruin are overtaking all the classes who labour for their subsistence, affluence and luxury still surround the classes who neither toil nor spin, and who have never added the value of one farthing to the wealth and property of the community. Millions must be content, it seems, with working harder and faring worse, that men of aristocratic "station" may not be reduced in the means of luxurious idleness and extravangance.[214]

Yet Smiles does not question the right of the aristocracy to withhold all their wealth in times of hunger and unemployment, nor does he formulate any specific plans, but only suggests that if the aristocracy were to work, then the millions would not have to supprt them, and so would be in a happier position themselves. In fact, Smiles usually advanced to the attack in terms of Calvinist morality - the distinction between work and idleness. The aristocracy "do not need to work. They have no call to be industrious. They are profitless, and worse than profitless existences. They are almost wholly occupied in amusement . . ."[215]

The most striking aspect of Smiles' attitude toward the function of the aristocracy was that the aristocracy simply did not have a leadership role to fulfill. In view of the situation in the 1840s perhaps this was understandable - the aristocracy were seen in negative terms as an obstructive and avaricious enemy that could be dispensed with.[216] If this was the case, Smiles was then forced to make a choice among other sections of the community for the role of moral and social leadership.

Interestingly enough Smiles found this a hard choice during his editorship of the Leeds Times, 1839-1842 (and afterwards), as his vacillation between support for Complete Suffrage (meaning his hope for the union of middle and working classes) and Household Suffrage (middle class only) showed. At one stage (January 1841) Smiles thought that there were only two interests in society - "those who live upon their own labour, and those who live upon the labour of others. The working and middle classes constitute the former, the Aristocracy constitute the latter, interest."[217]

However, the 'physical force' Chartist attacks on property in 1842 worried Smiles and he began to "assign" more favourable roles to the middle classes. While acknowledging in December 1842 that most of the population, except the aristocracy, had been advancing in knowledge and in morals, Smiles selected "the middle classes especially" for making "the most rapid progress in the arts and sciences, making all nature tributary to them, extending . . . knowledge, and surrounding themselves with the results of art, and science, and refinement . . ."[218] Although this passage foreshadows Smiles' future allegiance to most of the middle class ideals, in the period 1839-1842 he shared with the Philosophical Radicals the hope of a middle-working class alliance, and like the Radicals visualised an underlying social structure of People versus Aristocracy.

At this time Smiles' political attitude was wholly in accord with that of the Philosophical Radicals, whose basic views consisted in a belief that a People versus Aristocracy conflict existed, and that radical extension of the suffrage was necessary.[219] Smiles also corresponded with at least two of the Philosophical Radicals, Place and Roebuck, and his position on several issues appeared identical with the Radicals. Thus Smiles also criticised the middle class (as well as the aristocracy) for their avaricious ways, and for refusing to support radical reform and the middle-working class alliance. Like the Radicals, too, Smiles came slowly to the reluctant conclusion that the existence of class consciousness and conflicting interests discredited the idea of "the People" as a unitary body. And in company with the Radicals he became suspicious of the physical force Chartists for their bias against the middle class, and for their refusal to follow the lead of the "rational" radicals. Finally, Smiles was in the Philosophical Radical tradition in advocating the political education of the working classes so that they could recognise their true interests and leaders.[220]

In short the 1830s and '40s were for Smiles a time of intellectual questioning, and also of reorientation, from the simple concept of a society based on two conflicting interests, the People and the Aristocracy, to an understanding of a much more complex three-class society, each with its own interests and aims. Did Smiles choose the middle class as potential leaders of society? The choice would seem to be a foregone conclusion, since the aristocracy had been rejected toally, and by the 1850s the working class had failed to respond to Smiles' hopes. Actually Smiles' choice settled on those members of society who combined character, culture, industry, and socially beneficial enterprise. This group often were members of the middle class, but it is clear that the middle class did not necessarily coincide with this group. Indeed Smiles is particularly careful to point out in Self-Help that his models came from every condition and class, and that class, wealth or rank had no connection with true merit. The "true gentleman" was in fact classless, and any attempt to see Smiles as a strong supporter or exponent of middle class morality (as is often done) must take this into account, together with his condemnation of money worship and his deep suspicion of the middle class man in the arly 1840s. Indeed Smiles seems in Self-Help to be trying to find a moral *elite* composed of men of all classes, those men of character who had improved the quality of life in the country, besides improving themselves. This position is curiously similar to Matthew Arnold's attempt to find a special "remnant" from among the three classes, who would not be subservient to habits of their class, but by perfecting their best selves would help to influence the mind of the nation.[221] Arnold's further comments on the State as an instrument of power would not have interested Smiles, but Self-Help can be seen as Smiles' reflections on the inadequacy of radical reform, of government, of the leadership potential of any of the three classes, and of the atheism and money-worship of the age. There were not many solutions left, apart from the examples of those who aspired to a higher ideal than class, rank or wealth.

However, to balance this statement, and to anticipate a little, it must be said that under the spur of the growing movement for democracy, Smiles did invoke the middle class as a counter balance to the other two orders, and did attempt to use middle class independence (social and financial) as an example for the working class to follow.

From the point of view of class roles, the 1830s and '40s also reflected Smiles' effort to evaluate the ideal of self-help, and to find its application among the groups of the new industrial society. In this quest he sometimes despaired, noting in August 1840 that "the people have not yet attained either the will or the power to 'help themselves.'" But it was in this connection that Smiles considered the middle class to have a vital role to play, because the only way for the people themselves to break the grip of the aristocracy was for the middle class to form an alliance with the working class, in accordance with Philosophical Radical doctrine. This alliance should therefore "be the object of all true Liberals . . . to cement."[222]

The first reqirement of the middle-working class alliance was that the middle class desire the alliance. This was by no means clear, and Smiles criticised "the new Aristocracy of the middle classes" for their aloof and exclusive spirit. Moreover, the middle class had failed to support the campaign either for Universal, or, what was more surprising, Household Suffrage, and so Smiles was forced to conclude that the middle classes were, as he told Cobden, still "in the dark" about reform.[223] This lack of interest in reform was all the more remarkable, Smiles felt, because the middle classes "are squeezed to death between the oppressors and the oppressed - between the privileged and the poor; for the aristocracy have . . . thrown on them the chief burden [taxation] of supporting the victims of their shameful legislative oppression . . ."[224]

Smiles was quickly able to make a distinction, therefore, between the three classes of society - at least in terms of economic exploitation and taxation. But his hopes for the union of the lower and middle classes in the 1840s were shattered by the refusal of the middle class, not only to support the alliance, but to free themselves from habits of dependence on the aristocracy. Here is the genesis of one of the drives behind the self-help ideal - that each individual and class should be independent of outside help, and thus remain free of class spirit and servile attitudes. So at the beginning of 1842 Smiles was distressed to find that the middle class man was still in the grip of old ideas: "His desire for independence struggling with his original obsequiency to rank and birth, and his consciousness of newly acquired strength contending fiercely with his old habits of political servitude and submission."[225] This middle class struggle for an independent attitude of self-help was evidently still unresolved, as events were to prove.

As the year 1842 progressed Smiles became more and more disenchanted with middle class failure to help with repeal of the Corn Laws, and accused the middle class of worshipping exactly what the aristocracy stood for - Rank and Wealth. "The middle classes of this country," charged Smiles in March 1842, "worship aristocracy: they exhibit a slavish subserviency to it: they ape aristocratic manners and customs: they are thoroughly imbued with the spirit of class and caste . . ."[226] In this particular case Smiles was arguing for middle class support on a specific political issue, but the feeling behind his attack also represented the strong Calvinistic emphasis on individuality, coupled with his own school-acquired bias against unearned social and financial advantage (rank and wealth).

As the years passed, Smiles was able to forget the pusillanimity of the middle class in 1842, especially as the rise of social democracy in the form of Trades Unions and pressure for social legislation began to alienate him. In 1867, while reflecting on the events that caused the French Revolution of 1789, Smiles was finally able to idealise the role of the middle class. In France it was the Protestants who supplied

> that enterprising and industrious middle class which gives stability to every state. They provided remunerative employment for the population, while at the same time they enriched the kingdom by their enterprise and industry. Moreover, they furnished that virtuous and religious element in society without which a nation is but as so much chaff that is driven before the wind.

Smiles went on to surmise that with the flight of the Huguenots from France, the misgovernment of the ruling class went unchecked and the working orders were left to idleness and famine.[227]

By 1867, therefore, Smiles saw the function of the middle class as that of providing a solid bulwark between the upper and lower classes, of employing the otherwise idle working class, checking the abuses of the ruling class, and perhaps most important of all, providing the moral and social stability of the state. In Smiles' mind, the middle class ideal evidently represented the goal of self-help; morally, socially and economically.

If this was to be the eventual contribution of the middle class, what was the function of the working class? Smiles saw the role of the working class to be defined, though not necessarily limited, by the work needed to keep the country going. Work was in fact the condition of existence, and Smiles considered the position of the labourer as honourable, because labour was both essential and ultimately God-given. The labourer "is the true Producer [an echo from Carlyle]. By his handiwork society is kept alive - it is fed, clothed and lodged by him." Smiles was careful to define work as including either "hands or head," and thus once again set up the two-fold division of work (middle and lower classes) versus idleness (the aristocratic "titled idler").[228] Unfortunately, as in the middle class situation, the working class also proved recalcitrant in supporting the middle-working class union. Smiles was continually calling on the working class radicals to cease attacking the "money-mongers," "Jews" and "mercenary ruffians," namely the middle classes. The idea was reconciliation of "all the elements of society" and not division, although permission was granted to attack "aristocratic selfishness alone . . ." As with the Philosophical Radicals, the question in 1839 was between two camps only, "between democracy and aristocracy," and for the "people" to win.

The slogan was "Heaven only helps those who help themselves."[229] Self-help was an essential element of reform politics.

While Smiles was sincere in his hope for middle-working class union (lamenting in an 1842 letter to Cobden that the Chartists were doing their best to hinder such an alliance) he also wrote as though the functions of the two classes were irrevocably separate. He feared that the laws of the aristocracy were "crushing the middle classes down into the rank of operatives, and elevating the larger capitalists to the condition of lords and princes."[230] And again he seemed to suggest that the only function of the working class was to work on, with no particular purpose in life except simply staying alive and relieving the middle class of poor rates. "Neither do they [the people] wish to eat the bread of idleness; they are willing and anxious to labour; they have no avaricious desire for increased comforts and luxuries." Nor apparently did they "require that any other class of the community shall be taxed for their support . . ." All that the people wanted, according to Smiles, was that they be permitted to live on the fruits of their own labour.[231]

To be fair, the constant stress that Smiles laid on the desire of the workers to work, and the seeming limit of his vision, was motivated by the one overriding fear that haunted Leeds in the 1840s, the fear of unemployment. Unemployment meant two things - to the workers it meant hunger, poverty and even death, while to the middle and upper classes it meant destruction, riot and danger. Thus Smiles noted in very evident alarm in March 1842 that the people "have nothing to protect - have no other patrimony than their bare hands! Is not this a most dangerous state of society? A people without property will ever be a reckless and improvident people. They will neither be thoughtful, prudent, nor orderly . . ."[232] The fear of unemployment, and its visible consequences in Leeds,[233] was deeply impressed on Smiles' mind.

The admonitions to the working class on saving and thrift in Smiles' books were almost invariably accompanied by the spectre of unemployment in the shape of such euphemistic phrases as "in commercial crises," or in "time of pressure," and it was made clear that in such times, men without savings "must inevitably go to the wall." This was an age before the welfare state, when the only safety-net was unreliable private charity and poor laws, and when a growing population, coupled with frequent unemployment, was a threat so evident that Smiles later believed industry alone had averted revolution:

> Could agriculture have supported the continuous increase of population? Is it not more probable that this country would have become overrun by beggars, or that property would have been assailed and the constitution upset, as was the case in France, but for the extensive and remunerative employment afforded to the labouring-classes in the manufacturing districts? The steam-engine has indeed proved the safety-valve of England.[234]

Smiles' understanding of the function of the working class was therefore twofold. Because of the uncertainties of employment, the working man should aim at financial independence (saving and thrift), which in turn would help moral independence (refusal to accept charity, and freedom from servile attitudes). And moral independence would ultimately reflect back on the financial condition of the workman, so that Smiles frequently warned the working class against sectarian or hereditary bondage, and counselled self-reliance and self-dependence. (The subservient attitude of the working class must have seemed obvious to other observers in mid-century for another author in 1847 was able to condemn the working class for "the dependent and suppliant character of their proceedings in their efforts to amend their position.")[235] At the same time the primary function of the working class was to do the work of the nation, since this was the "ordinance of God." Yet Smiles also went to considerable lengths to try and include the working class _within_ the political system, for they were in a "dreadful extra-social position." He considered in 1841 that the basic reform needed was suffrage extension, and told Cobden that it was _the_ question for "all who look to responsible government as a means of securing the public well-being. Representative reform, conceal it as we will, is the _key_ to all great changes, whose object is to elevate the condition of the masses . . ."[236]

In effect Smiles wanted to forestall social unrest, and at the same time give the working class an outlet for their efforts at self-help by granting them the same starting privileges as any other class in the "race of life." To this end he concentrated on removing inequalities by pressing for organic reform (including repeal of the Corn Laws) and particularly the suffrage question. In February 1841 he wrote somewhat heatedly to Francis Place in London on the question of extending the suffrage: "Could you let us know when you have _done_ anything, and what progress you are making . . ." and at another time telling Cobden that he had formed a committee of operatives to investigate the real conditions of the workers in Leeds, and in return getting the sharp side of Cobden's temper for supporting other causes before the repeal of the Corn Laws: "It is no compliment to you," wrote Cobden, "to say that the [Leeds] Times is immeasurably superior to its Manchester namesake," for Cobden felt that commercial reform should come before "organic changes."[237] In 1844 Smiles spoke at a Leeds meeting suggesting that complete suffrage could be obtained through the radical step of bargaining with the war supplies for

Ireland (incidentally revealing that his support for middle class Household Suffrage was not an abandonment of Universal Suffrage), and in December of the same year pressed J.A. Roebuck (one of the original Philosophical Radicals) to stand for election to Parliament, so that someone could speak "to the people," since Smiles still apparently believed in a possible reconciliation of the middle and working classes - the Gentry (aristocracy) should still be led by "the people." As late as 1849 Cobden was once more urging Smiles to remember economic questions before "Organic Reforms."[238] In the 1840s, therefore, Smiles' commitment to radical reform favourable to the working class is clear.

What is not so clear is how "responsible government" or "representative reform" was supposed to help the working class (and the middle class) once the suffrage was extended, for Smiles' concept of the role of government in political and social reform was basically as negative as it was in the area of economics. Ultimately, Smiles' concept of the role of the government was to be stunted by his ideal of self-help, partly because he saw the government in exactly the same way as he saw the aristocracy, although not in quite the apocalyptic terms with which Cobden described it to Edward Baines (the Whig editor of the Leeds Mercury) as "the instrument of our destruction."[239]

In 1839 Smiles started from the basic position that the government, although "an association for mutual protection and benefit," could not achieve much since "the sources of national prosperity and happiness lie deep in the principles of human nature;" and that the chief object of government was to "regulate their operation, and to remove obstructions to their development." And so he borrowed a phrase from the radical Sheffield theoretician, Samuel Bailey, to describe the function of government as of a "negative rather than a positive nature . . ." Moreover, as presently constituted, the government was merely "legalised robbery," it oppressed, plundered, and caused "widespread misery and discontent."[240] This was the orthodox "Manchester school" position, but in Smiles' case it illustrates the sense in which self-help emerged as an antidote to government and aristocratic power; that is, since help was not forthcoming from above, it must come from below. So it was an attempt to outflank what was privileged (on behalf of the underprivileged Dissenters, shopkeepers, traders and the mass of workers) rather than a positive plan for the improvement of society. Starting from the belief that man contained within him all the necessary seeds[241] for potential growth and culture, self-help was a reaction against everything that prevented this flowering. It was, in short, a reaction rather than a positive move to promote social welfare - a reaction in favour of the self-helping work of the individual - a removal of evils.

The solutions that Smiles usually offered at Leeds political meetings therefore reflected the belief that the best and most likely reforms occurred naturally as outgrowths of self-helping attempts to achieve them. There was in fact no other source of reform, a lesson Smiles learned from his advocacy of suffrage extension and Corn Law repeal. Smiles thought (in an analogy of cause and effect, action and reaction) that only as much reform occurred as effort went into achieving it. To extend the analogy is really to explain 'political' self-help as another aspect of Smiles' faith in a just and Divinely ruled world - Heaven helps those who help themselves, in a merit and reward equation. So Smiles told a public meeting in 1843 on the subject of Church and State separation: "It was in themselves alone, in their own strength alone, that they should rely, for the attainment of their rights. Let them help themselves, and Heaven would help them (loud applause)."[242]

Of course another aspect of self-help was Smiles' belief that if reform did come from above, it was likely to result in mental slavery or subservience to those that had engineered the reform. In other words, Smiles opposed the paternalism of the ilk of "Young England." Furthermore Smiles supported the Benthamite 'naturalistic' concept of a society in which every man would naturally discover for himself the proper means of securing his own welfare - something that no civil government could do - and so the motto should be "Let Alone." The functions of a government were simply protection of Labour, Property, personal security, public opinion, and religious opinion. Together with some police and protection against foreign aggression this "nearly exhausted the functions required of the civil power . . ." But government should be cautious over the protection of personal security, for personal liberty was essential if man was to fulfill "those ends and purposes for which he was made a rational and intelligent being." These purposes were left vague (unlike John Stuart Mill's extended and brilliant definition of Liberty) for Smiles was more concerned at this point with the excesses of government power.[243] This position was reinforced by the conclusion that followed from the individualism of Utilitarianism, namely that the government, like the nation, was but the "reflex of the character and intelligence of the individuals composing the nation . . ." It was the people that made the government and not vice-versa, for if the people wanted honest and industrious legislators, they were bound to practice these virtues themselves and attempt to diffuse them throughout society.[244] Smiles made these comments late in 1842, and was evidently moving toward the more stringent attitude of Self-Help, namely that the people got the kind of government they deserved. But in 1842 Smiles was merely proposing the more limited argument that reform could only come from below.

However, Smiles' account of the negative role of government should not be seen just in terms of laissez-faire individualism. An historian of the mid-Victorian era has suggested that Victorians were perhaps more concerned with the struggle between localism and centralisation,[245] and Smiles was no exception. In 1839 Smiles launched into an attack on centralisation:

> Holding it to be the duty of enlightened and truly liberal statesmen to encourage the habit of self-dependence and self-government among the people . . . schemes of central organisation [in Jamaica, Canada, the Poor Law Amendment Act and the Rural Constabulary Force Bill] are . . . fraught with the utmost danger to national liberty and emancipation. The self-dependence of a people is ever the true source of their greatness. Society owes to this and not to political institutions, all its greatest steps in human improvement. Government, indeed, of whatever kind, is but a necessary evil at the best . . .

Here Smiles is worried about the mental slavery that could occur when a centralised government took over whatever functions had been organised locally, and thus insidiously undermined a people's habit of self-dependence. Hence government was dangerous because "subserviency and implicit subjection to it have in all ages been the chief agencies . . . by which . . . the many have been reduced to the condition of mere machines in the hands of a few." This is also an example of the many nuances of "independence" that Smiles packs in to his ideal of self-help. Independence could mean either freedom from the spirit of class, independence from the aristocracy, financial independence, or, as in this case, independence of a moral kind - simply the spirit of habitually thinking in a self-dependent way. Interestingly enough, Smiles concluded his article on centralisation with a quote from the apostle of spiritual freedom, Channing: "Society has made its chief progress by the minds of private individuals . . ."[246]

With Smiles' 'self-helping' attitude toward social reform and government interference, it is at first sight surprising to read two or three articles that he wrote during 1851, which seemed to reflect a volte-face on the question of government intervention. This is all the more unusual in view of a strong 'self-help' statement by Smiles in 1849 on the "true patriot spirit of self-help," which meant that men "must raise themselves - must work out their own salvation." However, the 1849 article was probably prompted by the Chartist visit to London in 1848 (although he appeared to approve generally of the 1849 continental revolutions), and on the other hand the 1851 articles benefitted from a more favourable atmosphere for reform generated by the years 1848-1851, which were particularly prolific in regulatory legislation.[247] But in fact the strongest reason for Smiles' new insistence on some form of intervention was his involvement with a movement to secure national (locally controlled), secular education. This movement started in April 1850, and Smiles backed it for some two or three years, although the country had to wait until 1870 for the Education Act to be passed. Smiles' renewed involvement with social reform was reflected in his more outspoken articles.

In July 1851 Smiles advocated secular education via local taxes (again the bias against centralisation), which he felt would be supported "by a vast majority of the moral force of the country . . ."[248] By August 1851 Smiles was on the offensive with a striking article entitled "Nobody Did It!". The article contains some interesting parallels to Carlyle's attack on "insolent Donothingism in Practice and Saynothingism in Speech," and indeed the article quotes Carlyle at length in a passage calling for the end of *laissez-faire* and the beginning of government intervention. If anything Smiles seems to be attacking his own 'self-help' position: "Nobody still says - let the poor educate themselves - let them rise out of poverty and helplessness of their own accord - let them rely on the voluntary principle, - in other words let them perish in their ignorance, *laissez-faire*; but let us hope Somebody will yet be found ready to help the feeble, to elevate the depressed, and to cultivate the ignorant . . ." "Nobody" had a theory, wrote Smiles; it was called *laissez-faire* and it caused social suffering, crime, poisoned water and food, cholera, typhus, illiteracy, prostitution and children in factories. But (and here Smiles reverts to his simplistic cause and effect terminology) "we may depend upon it that somebody is to blame. The responsibility rests somewhere . . ."

In the past "Somebody" had taken women and children out of the coal pits, the poor from their sickly cellars, and had relieved the starving Irish. If Poor Laws, Factory Laws and Sanitary Laws had been passed, why not a law for Education? How was this to be done? And here Smiles defines the situations in which men may be helped by law, rather than help themselves, and at the same time lays down a revealing precondition for the making of a law:

> We may not be able to cope with the evil as individuals, singlehanded; but then it becomes us to unite, and bring to bear upon the evil the joint moral power of society in the form of a law. A law is but the expression of a combined will; and it does that for society, which society, in its individual and separate action, cannot so well or efficiently do for itself. Laws may do too much; they may meddle with things which ought to be "let alone;" but the abuse of a thing is no proper argument against its use in cases where its employment is urgently called for.

As in Benthamite thought, the idea was the removal of evils (in this case the removal of ignorance through education) rather than any kind of welfare economics, and the law was to be used only in cases where "urgently" required.[249] Moreover, as in the previous article on public education, Smiles relied on the moral force or moral power of society to create law. Like Carlyle and Thomas Arnold, Smiles was thinking in terms of the moral reform of society (although Carlyle aimed his reformation more exclusively at the aristocracy and Arnold was more concerned with a religious revival), and like Rousseau, Smiles was saying that it was the moral power or agreement of society (the general will) that created law, law from below, not law from above in the shape of government decree.

So far, then, it seems that Smiles' form of intervention was more or less consistent with the self-help ideal. And if the criticism is levelled that this form of law creation might be unlikely to produce results, it must be said that Smiles was right in the mainstream of Philosphical Radical thinking, which laid an immense emphasis on the power of public opinion to change society.[250] This view referred to an atomistic concept of society, congenial to a philosophy of self-help, because every individual, however humble, could have some effect on his surrounding fellows. For Smiles, public opinion was strictly a question of organic growth and aggregation. "Public opinion is made up of the tiniest little bits of opinion, which, first sown in private, afterwards issue forth, and increase in public life."[251] Sooner or later, he believed, this sum of addition would result in legislation or social change. Similarly Smiles conceived of the individual as the centre of a potential circle of influence, so that the influence of opinion, action, example, or work, spread outwards like the ripples from a stone thrown into a pond. Thus "the energies of the strong form so many living centres of action, round which other individual energies group and cluster themselves; thus the life of all is quickened, and on great occasions, a powerful energetic action of the nation is secured." The starting point, as with so many Victorians, was the home, and "from this little central spot, the human sympathies [or opinions] may extend in an ever widening circle, until the world is embraced . . ." More specifically, the second "concentrating circle" after the home were one's relations, then fellow-citizens, and lastly the whole human race.[252]

This atomistic idea of society sets the background to Smiles' next series of articles (from 1852 onward), for he believed that the circle of each individual's actions or refusal to act, cut across the circles of other individuals and groups. It was not sufficient to "let alone" because "the man who doesn't care for others . . . and help them, is very often pursued even in this life with retribution" (in the shape of crime, fever, poor rates, taxes, etc.). And "it is not all the same whether a young man is idle or not, if the world needs his help. His idleness makes others idle, and propagates bad example. For there is no man, however mean, but helps to mould others."[253] But Smiles runs into trouble at this point, because the self-helping action of the people - the moral force and power of public opinion - was evidently not forthcoming. And here Smiles' solution of allowing the creation of law from below, of letting the people help themselves, simply breaks down. Plaintively he rebukes the people: "The governing class has recently proved itself to be decidedly ahead of the people at large . . . There is positively an active agitation <u>against</u> the Government, because it gives its aid to Education." And on Public Health: "The Bill was not sufficiently stringent; and its subsequent amendments invited the action of localities by voluntary association. But the voluntary action has not been called forth . . ." The conclusion was unmistakable: "The people really refuse to respond to the efforts of the Legislature to better their social elevation." Smiles had no answer at all, he threw up his hands in disgust and ended by calling on the people to "cease railing at the Government, which is . . . considerably in advance of the people themselves."[254]

Smiles had reached the point beyond which his self-help ideal could not go, and when he returned to the attack six or seven weeks later, he stopped at the same point. For Sanitation to be successful, he thought, local cooperation was necessary, and the "individual efforts of the community are therefore needed; and any legislative enactments which dispensed with these would be an evil." Although Smiles admitted that the poor "cannot do all," yet they could "do much to better their own condition," and so he concluded by asking the employers and capitalists to build clean homes for their employees, but specifically forbade the government from doing so.[255] Smiles apparently found it possible to draw an imaginary line between the role of the government and the free activity of the individual. Essentially it was a line drawn by common sense. Where the evils were obvious and urgent, they should be removed, the desirable methods being firstly by the people themselves, but if the people could not do so, or do it as well, or as efficiently, as the government, then the government was permitted to step in and remedy the situation. But this last action could only be taken if, on the local level, the people _voluntarily_ cooperated with the government in efforts at reform. Where the people refused to respond to the attempt by the government to help them help themselves, then _nothing_ could be achieved, the evils would remain.

Ultimately, therefore, reform depended on the self-help of the people themselves, because Smiles could not imagine a situation, or conceive of a workable mechanism, that would place the government in the position of introducing complete and all-embracing reforms from above. This was because such reforms affected all the individuals concerned, and it was axiomatic that these reforms would not be able to successfully penetrate the "concentring circle" of the individual and his Home.

Smiles' thinking on the limits of government at this time revealed at least four areas in which ideally the individual should be left to pure self-help. These were social relations, the work of the individual, the home, and personal morality. Of course if an evil that was both obvious and urgent occurred, then something might be done, but in general Smiles' frame of references toward the individual contained only organic metaphors, images of seeds and growth, of plants, and pebbles dropped in ponds, in which growth or influence radiated outwards - the reverse process of government influence penetrating and altering natural organic growth was opposed to the observed laws of nature, and was simply not present as a model in Smiles' categories of thought.

If parochial voluntaryism had failed in education reform, as Smiles intimated to Cobden in 1853, at least one reform bolstered Smiles' confidence: the aristocracy had been cut down to size. Early in 1854 Smiles declared optimistically:

> Time was when lords and gentlemen constituted 'the world;' when all beneath them were hewers of wood and drawers of water. That time has passed.

The day when honest work and industry of both head and hand replaced aristocratic idleness had apparently arrived, for in "recognising the great parvenue spirit of this age we merely recognise what, in other words, is designated as the dignity of labour, the rights of industry, the power of intellect." Now, claimed Smiles triumphantly, "the times have changed; 'blood' without talent or merit to redeem it is held of little account . . ."[256]

In summary it seems evident that Smiles' ideal of self-help owed a great deal to the opposition in his mind between the (good) industrious People and the (evil) idle Aristocracy. Since the aristocracy were obviously and unjustifiably the leaders of society and the possessors of most of the available wealth and privileges, then the only way to attack the system was work and self-help - to create a new aristocracy of charcter and industry to replace the old. This new "class" would theoretically provide the right leadership and models of behaviour (the necessary "moral force") to reform the evils of society, and to level up the masses through the provision of powerful examples of fine character and socially useful work. Smiles' disillusionment with other means of reform, his approach to the question of the "new" aristocracy, and what the complementary role of education was to be, together with a summation of the ideal of self-help, is the subject matter of the next section.

## Disillusionment, the role of the hero, and the importance of education, in the writing of SELF-HELP.

It was in November 1842 that Smiles began to realise the complexity of the task of improving social conditions. There was no single political answer: "mere political reform will not cure the manifold evils which now afflict society. There requires a social reform, a domestic reform, an individual reform."[257] And when living on Woodhouse Moor near Leeds (from approximately 1847), Smiles found the proportion of drinking places to churches so high (17 to 1) that he concluded political reforms, 'though useful, were obviously not enough. "They did not touch the lower classes of the population. They did not educate or elevate the people. They did not grapple with the worst vices of the age." Smiles therefore supported the new combined Woodhouse Mechanics Institute and Temperance Society, and delivered lectures conducive to improving the character of the people. These included (from January 1851 onward) "Self-Education," "Self-Help in Men" and "Character and Habits" and were aimed, not only to check vice, but (again in Smiles' organic metaphor) to "plant virtue," so that the disreputable might become "industrious, sober and intelligent . . ." and therefore "well fitted to their work in life."[258] To Smiles this was just one example of a wide and complex area of reform - the elevation of character - that mere political reforms could not approach.

By the beginning of 1852 Smiles was signalling his disillusionment and loss of faith in specific reforms. He recognised that his past efforts at promoting first one reform, and then another, were useful, but had not achieved what the first flush of enthusiasm had hoped for. Universal Suffrage had failed, Free Trade had succeeded, but with no astonishing results, Cooperation had fallen far short of his hopes in 1847 and 1848, and National Education looked to have but a slim chance of acceptance. He concluded therefore that no particular reform was going to save society - a position that could rationalise his retreat from support of specific reforms to advocacy of general reform; from the radicalism of the Leeds Times to the self-help of the 1850s. "As men grow older and wiser," he wrote in 1852, "they cease to have faith in any panacea. They find a little of good in everything . . . for they begin to find out that truth and patriotism are not confined to any particular cliques, or parties, or factions." Smiles had been involved with the whole spectrum of reform and had found various groups calling for more Church attendance, the Charter, National Schools, Total Abstinence, the end of war, the rejection of state schools and churches, cooperation and Communism, and so on, and although "sympathetic with many of them," he disliked the sectarian spirit behind the proposed reforms, "each of which, according to its special advocates, is the only thing to save society."[259]

Smiles felt that he had grown older and wiser, and obviously less radical. The autobiographical phrase "older and wiser" seemed to stick in his mind, and in the Lives of the Engineers (1861-62), he remarked that although the engineer Telford had read Tom Paine and become a radical, yet as he "grew older and wiser, he became more careful in jumping at conclusions on political topics."[260] This was evidently Smiles' own position, for he considered that the process of getting older engendered changes of mind, provided the individual allowed himself to "be freely acted upon by facts and events." This was Smiles' environmentalism again, but it was a beneficial environmentalism, usually enlarging the vision of the individual. Hence Smiles confidently remarked of the radical, Robert Nicoll (whom he had replaced as editor of the Leeds Times, and who was now dead), that if he had lived "we should have found his sympathies becoming more enlarged, and embracing other classes besides those of only one form of political creed."[261]

In fact Smiles' retreat to the classless and non-political advice of self-help was part of the mid-Victorian retreat from what was felt to be the rigid and extreme positions taken during the controversies of the preceding years.[262] As J.S. Mill put it in 1854:

> In the last age the writers of reputation and influence were those who took a side, in a very decided manner, on the great questions, religious, moral, metaphysical, and political; who were downright

> infidels or downright Christians, thorough Tories or thorough democrats, and in that were considered, and were, extreme in their opinions. In the present age the writers of reputation and influence are those who take something from both sides of the great controversies . . .

Possibly Mill's statement had something to do with his own discouragement at the ineffectiveness of his efforts at political reform in the years immediately after 1840,[263] but in any case this seems to have been a motive in Smiles' mind, for in November of 1852 Smiles' disillusionment with specific reforms was reinforced by disillusionment over the progress of reform as a whole:

> We form associations, organise societies, spend money and labour in committees. But the power of ignorance is too great for us. We almost despair while we work. We feel that much of our effort is wasted. And we are often ready to give up in dismay.[264]

If disillusionment with the progress of reform gave Smiles a solid reason to abandon attempts at finding specific solutions in favour of a general statement of self-help (not forgetting the emotional response of his early Calvinism and parental training as reflected in the phrase "Heaven helps those who help themselves"), there was another possible solution - the defeat of evils and difficulties through the work of the heroic individual. In this context, there are many parallels between Carlyle and Smiles in their approach to life. Both had rejected an early Calvinism, both attacked the prevalent worship of money, both felt the mechanical tendencies of the age, both took a deep interest in history (in 1844 Smiles wrote a History of Ireland and in 1845 delivered a series of lectures on 17th Century English history, and considered becoming a serious historian),[265] both thought of biography as history, both felt there was a value to work beyond rational reward, and perhaps most important both held that there was a serious and moral purpose to life.

How much of Carlyle Smiles had read is not certain[266] but some of Carlyle's early works read much like the later Self-Help. In 1829 Carlyle called for "faith in individual endeavour" and proposed individual reform instead of State reform: "the only solid, though a far slower reformation, is what each begins and perfects on himself." Not unlike Smiles' call for self-reform before government reform, Carlyle's essay on Novalis (also in 1829) remarks that "causes and effects connecting every man and thing with every other extend through all Time and Space . . ." This was certainly comparable to Smiles' favourite chain of events terminology, and Carlyle continues the same line of though in "Corn-Law Rhymes": the influence of a good man is everlasting, "his works do not die, but being of Eternity are eternal; and in new transformation and every-wider diffusion, endure, living and life-giving." And Carlyle uses the phrase 'self-help' liberally, applying it equally to J.P. Richter, Sir Walter Scott, and Samuel Johnson.[267]

It would be tedious to recite the very many references that Smiles gives from Carlyle, but at least two areas of agreement emerge. One was the idea of persevering work, and the other the serious moral purpose of life. If progress in life is slow, counsels Smiles, "some are scared from the diligent practice of self-culture and self-help . . ." But he remarks: "They must be satisfied to do their true work, and wait the issues thereof. How much, says Carlyle, 'grows everywhere if we do but wait!'" Smiles goes on to make the same argument as Carlyle on the intuitively known duty of the individual: "Let us have the honesty and wisdom to do the duty that lies nearest us," which in this case was "the culture of ourselves . . . We can cultivate such powers as have been given to us . . ."[268] At another time Smiles encouraged the humble to engage in active work by quoting

Carlyle: "The weakest living creature . . . by concentrating his powers on a single object, can accomplish something. . . ." This was the secret of perseverence, but Smiles applied it less to work "as a means of 'getting on in the world' . . ." than to self-culture "as a power for purposes of spiritual self-elevation, or of social usefulness."[269]

A sense of earnest moral purpose was as strong in Smiles as it was in Carlyle. Men were not sent into the world for their own selfish pleasures, nor for idleness, but for serious work and purpose. Every man was a priest sent to minister in the Temple of Immensity was Carlyle's message in one of Smiles' 1853 articles, and (in a somewhat familiar warning) Smiles berated the croaking of youths who refused to set to work, claiming that youth wanted "faith in their own improvement and in human improvement generally," and most of all, youth were without "moral purpose or mental energy."[270] In even more serious vein Smiles wanted men to know, in Carlyle's words, that they who were created by God, "work in any meanest moment of time what will last through eternity . . ." Perhaps Smiles was more worried here about the potential decline of the nation through idleness and luxuriousness,[271] but such a threat fitted in with the retribution that would surely follow if man forgot his true purpose and work in life, and allowed pleasure to usurp earnest duty. As he told his grandchildren: "Life is but short, and it is right that it should be used with justice and usefulness to yourselves, and with Glory to the Giver."[272]

Apart from these two areas of general agreement (persevering work and earnest purpose) there is specific evidence that Carlyle made some impact on Smiles with his ideas on the new dignity and importance of the individual (man was above money, but not above the dignity of labour); and with the anti-establishment attitude that "man perfects himself by work much more than by reading . . ."[273] However, too much should not be read into the similarities of Carlyle and Smiles, since all these comparisons and agreements can also be explained by the similar Calvinism of their youth, and the subsequent retreat from Calvinism that both adopted. Moreover, from the point of view of work and self-help their attitudes are different. To put it at its most simple, Carlyle externalised work, believing that inside man there was "a force for work . . . giving thee no rest till thou unfold it . . . ",[274] whereas Smiles internalised work, as well as rationalised it. For Smiles, work cultivated, disciplined and developed man internally, since without the stimulus of work the internal faculties and powers of man could not be animated into growth and fulfillment, while the passions and instincts of men also required work and self-denial as a discipline. Pragmatically Smiles also saw work as necessary for the survival and advance of the nation and, on behalf of the "industrious orders," a means of undercutting and even triumphing over the aristocratic-government complex.

The two concepts of work of Carlyle and Smiles are not necessarily exclusive in all their ramifications. For example, Smiles too can believe that work is the creation of order: "This succession of noble workers, - the artisans of civilisation, - has created order out of chaos, in industry, science and art . . ." just as Carlyle sees man as "the missionary of Order. Is not all work of man in this world a making of Order?"[275] Again, to assign to Carlyle a considerable influence over Smiles[276] seems to be an overstatement of the case. If anything, Smiles appears to have learnt the phrase of 'self-help' from Emerson,[277] and quite possibly many of his other ideas. Like Smiles, Emerson stressed Self-Reliance (the title of one of his early essays); believed in causation rather than luck; advocated adaptation to the "laws" of nature and the world; attacked exclusiveness and money-making as lower ideals; criticised Napoleon for the same fault noticed by Smiles, selfishness; hoped for a natural aristocracy of progressive men; and thought that the character of individuals shaped the country and the government, and not *vice versa*. And it is significant that Smiles used Emerson's title to head one of his essays in 1842, "Self-Reliance," in which he first spelled out the role of the hero in removing difficulties. All that was necessary, wrote Smiles, was "a great will - a hero purpose, and quick battle action . . ."[278]

What can be said in regard to Smiles' journey toward the ideal of self-help is that while in 1839 he blamed the condition of the working class on aristocratic institutions (denying even in 1839 that the workman could save money for the sake of independence because it was doubtful that the workman *had* anything to save),[279] beginning in the early 1840s Smiles started to affirm the ability and the power of the individual to work and help himself regardless of the circumstances (a different claim from the milder statement "Heaven helps those who help themselves," although a logical outcome from it). In this process Smiles evidently found encouragement, if not an intellectual basis, in the writings of Channing, Emerson and Carlyle, as he himself testifies in his important review of Emerson's *Man, the Reformer*.[280] Therefore too much emphasis should not be placed on Carlyle alone, nor should explanations of Smiles' arrival at the ideal of self-help, heroic or otherwise, disregard this intellectual changeover in the early 1840s, and particularly the change that occurs in 1842.[281]

It will be recalled that some of Smiles' early writings, *Physical Education* in particular, had used a sensationalist and somewhat deterministic psychology. Smiles' appreciation of these three authors in the early 1840s (Emerson, Channing and Carlyle), together with the failure of extra-personal reform to achieve any significant improvement in working class conditions, enabled Smiles to supplement his use of determinism and sensationalist psychology with the idea of an internal will power and energy that could overcome the forces of the environment. While Smiles had always believed in individualism, it was in 1842 that he began to emphasise man's own "force and capability" and "faculties of being and doing" as means of preserving "individuality." Smiles' whole emphasis appears to change in 1842, as he begins to adopt a much more stringent attitude toward the working classes, writing on temperance and the need for self-conquest, and in classically apologist fashion stating that "poverty sharpens the intellect, and disciplines the character of man, far better than wealth can do."[282] This new hard-line self-help was held in balance through Smiles' efforts during the 1840s at Free Trade, middle-working class union, universal suffrage and cooperation (in 1846 for example Smiles thought the principle of cooperation alone was likely to realise the social emancipation of the working classes),[283] but the failure of the majority of these hopes helped in the 1850s to refuel Smiles' faith in the principles of self-culture, self-help, individualism and heroic defeat of difficulties that he had found in Carlyle, Emerson and Channing, and which he had himself been brought up to believe in.

There were also other stimulants for Smiles' ideas on self-help and heroic work. In an interview Smiles is recorded as saying: "My friendship with Geo. Step. [*sic* - George Stephenson] had a lot to do with my ultimate determination to write *Self-Help*. Geo. Step. himself often proceeded on the same theme, and Dr. Smiles recalled with a laugh how he once heard the great engineer in the course of a lecture at Leeds roar out . . . 'Young men, persevere, persevere, persevere; its been the making o' me.'" Smiles was much taken with Stephenson's idea of persevering work, and later instructed his son to pass the advice on to his grandson: "Instill the great word of George Stephenson in Jack's mind - Perseverence. It is a grand word for a boy to remember."[284] Smiles' 1849 article on George Stephenson showed, however, that heroic work owed something to yet another source:

> The life of George Stephenson will form a highly interesting chapter in some future edition of "The Pursuit of Knowledge under Difficulties." No one of the numerous self-educated men whose histories are given in the pages of that fascinating book, had greater difficulties to encounter, or overcame those difficulties more triumphantly than he.[285]

Although in his Autobiography Smiles reiterated his debt to Stephenson stating that he had published Self-Help specifically to enforce and illustrate that "great word - PERSEVERENCE," at the same time Smiles acknowledged that his original idea for Self-Help came from G.L. Craik's The Pursuit of Knowledge under Difficulties, an extraordinarily influential book in its romanticism of the heroic efforts of the lower classes at self-education. Significantly Smiles wanted to teach Craik's lesson that "the most important results in daily life" came through the energetic use of ordinary qualities.[286] The point is that Smiles wanted to enforce the lesson of virtuous conduct and character in day to day living, of work and self-help in daily life, not any long drawn-out plan for success and social mobility.

In view of the impact of Craik's book on Smiles ("I had read it often, and knew its many striking passages almost by heart"), it is interesting to note that Craik specifically wrote his book for the S.D.U.K. and also made clear that he was not writing a 'success' book. Lord Brougham, on behalf of the S.D.U.K., thereupon tried either to change Craik's book into one more concerned with "self-exaltation," or perhaps find another author, but Craik stood firm, refusing to encourage the idea of rising in "rank" through self-education.[287] In any case, Smiles' own negative attitude toward success in Self-Help has already been clearly outlined, and it remains to suggest that Smiles very often visualised the role of heroic work in overcoming difficulties more in terms of the character training that it would entail, than in any results to be expected from the final defeat of the difficulties concerned. Thus without "the necessity of encountering difficulty, life might be easier, but men would be worth less. For trials, wisely improved, train the character and teach self-help." And Smiles goes on to intimate that without the presence of difficulty it would be hard to tell the idle and worthless apart from the virtuous and industrious. Besides, only the struggle involved in overcoming difficulty could produce a mind and character trained to "an almost perfect discipline . . ."[288] What Smiles wanted to illustrate was the "fact" that the pursuit of self-help created desirable moral habits.

The role of the heroic individual thus had a number of antecedents, from Carlyle, Channing and Emerson, through G.L. Craik, George Stephenson and Smiles' own training in Calvinist individualism. What was the actual role of the hero to be? Smiles appeared to visualise three kinds of model or hero.

The first hero represented the enlightened and self-helping common man, the working class man, labouring energetically and uncomplainingly in his fight against poverty. In this effort to improve his common moral and social condition Smiles recognised "a heroism of living men - aye, of poor working men, in this 19th Century." Smiles was sure that "the multitude of men who have successfully battled with and overcome the adverse circumstances of life . . . [rising] from out of the lowest depth of poverty . . ." had done so through their own efforts. The goal was moral, financial and political independence, and the agency was self-help - the reform of the individual from within.[289] Thus Smiles' first kind of hero was able to overcome external conditions through the use of moral habits created by the internal conquest of self. Smiles therefore implies that social and economic conditions were either unalterable or basically favourable, and that the real evil existed inside man. This indeed is a basic assumption of Self-Help and lies behind all Smiles' strictures on character formation and self-conquest.

The second class of hero comprised the man who performed socially beneficial work, almost always under extreme difficulties, and with considerable opposition to contend with. This class embraced all ranks of society, great or unknown, who had advanced the civilisation of the nation, and the examples ranged from Newton and industrialists to the heroism of the common soldier. (The recent Indian Mutiny and the Crimean war did much to strengthen the cult of the "average" hero in Self-Help.) Since life was a battle, victory was won not only by the generals, but by the "heroism of the privates," "men in the ranks" having "in all times" been amongst the "greatest of workers." The two traits common to these heroes were that they came from no particular class (thus forming a natural rather than an inherited aristocracy) and they all displayed a fine disregard for self (their work and deeds being therefore socially beneficial). It was for this reason that Smiles rejected Napoleon, despite his industry, will-power and energy - and produced a counter hero, Wellington. Napoleon displayed "intense selfishness," while Wellington eschewed self in favour of "Duty." The difference was in Napoleon's lack of "beneficence" and Wellington's "patriotic" valour. Similarly, one John Foster showed immense industry and valour in overcoming his difficulties, and consequently died wealthy. But Smiles remarked morosely "mere earth went to earth," for Foster had become a miser, and worse still, had not been a social "benefactor" and thus his life and end "were alike sordid."[290]

Finally, the third class of hero in Smiles' pantheon could come from either of the first two kinds of hero, but performed a slightly different function. This was to provide an example or model to those around them, and thus to become the centre of a circle or sphere of useful influence. Smiles was certain that moral example was contagious, believing that examples of industry, sobriety and honest purpose "pass unconsciously into the lives of others . . ." Thus there "is no individual so humble as not to be able to aid in the propagation of principles. For . . . the words and deeds of men affect not only the present time, but all time coming . . ."[291] Chapter XII of Self-Help is a resumé of the impact of good models and examples on the character of the nation. Smiles believed that the examples of great men, or of ordinary men of heroic and exemplary character, radiated outwards, forming "so many living centres of action . . ." Hence the value even of books, and particularly of biography, the chief use of which "consists in the noble models of character in which it abounds . . ." The enshrined biographic model worked subconsciously "breaking fresh life into us, helping us . . . to illustrate his character in other forms. Hence a book containing the life of a true man is full of precious seed . . ."[292]

The chief function of this third class of hero was therefore to provide a germinating example, allowing his moral influence to propagate and grow from one central spot through the subconscious imitation by others of his example. Presumably such an example could only infect those who came into personal contact with the examplar or his biography. But even when dead, Smiles resurrects the hero's example with an organic life of its own, still living and capable of helping fresh generations to industry and noble character. Once again Smiles uses his metaphors of organic growth ("full of precious seed") and expanding circles of influence, to explain the interaction between the work of the individual and society. And by the same token Smiles has the same growth process in mind in describing the influence of parents and the Home as "the very nucleus of national character . . ."[293]

If the work of the hero in society compensated in Smiles' thinking for his disillusionment with political and other methods of reform, and in some sense filled the vacuum left by the removal of unilateral government intervention as an agent of reform, then it was imperative that all the individuals in the state either recognise and support heroic individual efforts to reform society or themselves undertake their own self-reform and come to understand what each individual could himself do.[294] Furthermore, it was essential in the Utilitarian and individualistic concept of society that each individual should understand as much as possible about the means of social and economic progress (over and above the natural congruence of interests) in order to perform his part in life correctly. This was made potentially easier by a sensationalist psychology which might logically enable society to train the individual into the perfect unit. Accordingly it was no accident that the early 19th Century abounded in works on education, and that even the medical doctors followed the same line of thought. Hence the emphasis on early instruction in Dr. Andrew Combe's work, and similarly in Dr. Southwood Smith's book, The Philosophy of Health, which appeared at the same time as Smiles' Physical Education, and said much the same thing in much the same words, namely that early training of the child, the "plastic creature," would exert on it "a prodigious influence for good or evil."[295]

Consequently a doctor like Smiles (and from Scotland, the land of John Knox and education) who had written his first book on sensationalist principles of psychology, and whose early political leanings were evidently in the direction of Benthamism and the Philosophical Radicals, could not fail to accord an important place to education. More than this, if there was one permeating theme to the concept of self-help, and from which the idea of self-help actually evolved,[296] it was the ideal of education and self-culture, and especially self-education. Very evidently education had to be complementary to the work of the hero, for without a proper recognition of the evils and difficulties in society, and without and understanding of the social system and the means of progress, the great mass of society would not respond to the example of models and elevate themselves to respectability and independence.

In 1839 the question was still whether the working classes needed to learn anything or not, and Smiles certainly supported their right to learn. Yet he took a patronising attitude at first, wishing to "slot" the working man into his place. The poor man "MUST BE EDUCATED - morally, and intellectually; and instructed in the social and religious duties of life, in order that he may be enabled to perform them." Smiles even thought of knowledge as "the first great object of an efficient system of moral police," although he went on to admit that education should be used chiefly "to aid in the creation of MIND." Smiles also believed that ignorance and poverty were related, for if the poor man was elevated "in the scale of rational living" then he could reflect on causes and consequences and take advantage of circumstances to improve his lot. The pragmatic and self-helping aspects of education were therefore uppermost in Smiles' mind from the beginning, and in rebuking the Bishop of Exeter for opposing all working class eduation, Smiles saw education as both defensive and offensive: "Our ideas are that poor men, as well as Bishops, should cultivate their thinking faculties . . . as the best protection from knaves [read government, bishops and aristocracy] . . . and as the best means of their progression as rational and intelligent beings."[297]

This two-fold objective of education in 1839 both as a defense and a means of self-help, required as a pre-condition the stimulation of the nascent faculties into a literal "creation of mind." The mind would simply not exist in its proper form without stimulation from without. The "education and development of the human faculties" was actually "a creation of the moral and intellectual being of man . . ." But Smiles' bias against schools, both from his own experience and from his desire to undercut the educational advantages of the privileged, together with his sensationalist psychology, directed him to visualise the formation of the mind of the working class man in terms of a generalised self-education through the instructive external experiences or circumstances of life.

However, self-education was actually only one of three ways in which he approached the idea of education. The first, already referred to, was the influence of external experiences or circumstances over the individual, by which Smiles meant a broad kind of "practical" education or self-education. The second definition of education was the conventional meaning of regular schools and schooling. Smiles' third concept of education was that of self-culture - the self-improvement of the understanding and the cultivation of the intellect. These three definitions will be analysed in turn, and their relationship to work and self-help explicated.

The educational value of external experiences or circumstances meant that a man could receive education from all quarters - from the press, from public debate, from mutual improvement societies, and even the instructive events of every-day life. In 1846 Smiles noted that

> a man is educated by circumstances - by his daily avocations and pursuits - by his associates - by examples - by his struggles for subsistence - by his successes, his failures, his achievements. The education which a people receive in their homes goes for more than that which they receive in their schools.[298]

Ultimately it all meant self-education, which had one great advantage over regularised schooling: it usually evoked the virtues of self-help and self-dependent work. Borrowing evidently from his own experience, Smiles remarked "how many of the working as well as of the middle class can date the budding of their intellect, and the growth of the feeling of self-dependence, from the political agitation of the Reform Bill!" Smiles had himself been strongly affected by the 1832 event (he was then 20) and considered that the Reform movement had aroused "millions of minds to action." Likewise, when studying the formation of Mutal Improvement Societies and People's Colleges, Smiles predicted that such attempts as self-education would result in "manly independence, genuine self-respect, noble aims and achievements."[299]

Smiles' definition of "education" therefore covered an extremely wide spectrum, and he felt that the general diffusion of knowledge would confer equally wide-ranging benefits. Thus the 1848 Revolution in France was welcomed by Smiles because several of its leaders were men of intellect and education and were therefore constructive (unlike 1789 which was principally a time of destruction),[300] and similarly in 1842 Smiles favoured the Chartist movement (though not the physical force element) as "one of the most notable steps in the march of modern civilisation," for it was partly "the result of knowledge . . ." (knowledge in the broadest possible sense).[301] So in addressing the Leeds Mutal Improvement Society in 1846 Smiles claimed that "the general diffusion of intelligence and education amongst the working men, must be productive of the most beneficial results." And speaking to the Odd Fellows Society in the same year Smiles found their organisation to be

> the germ [note the metaphor] of a great educational movement - not perhaps to teach reading and writing . . . but to teach such things as - how to preserve their personal health; how to make the most of the means of social and domestic happiness which lay within their reach; how, in a word, to make them, in all respects, healthier, wiser and happier beings (cheers).[302]

In the 1840s therefore Smiles thought of education in a very broad sense. But by the 1850s he was beginning to fear that the results of self-education were somewhat meagre, and that national education might be preferable. In 1851 Smiles wondered whether the working man might "become a kind of machine . . . [by] being confined to one small mechanical process." But he reassured himself with the thought that men could be made "as far as possible self-dependent by means of a course of sound mental discipline and culture."[303] Significantly Smiles was now (1851) asking for a <u>course</u> of education, and the reason for this change from the self-education of 1846 was that, although Smiles recognised the dangers of mechanism and mass production, it was from another direction that the real dangers seemed to lie, and for the cure of which an organised system of national education seemed an urgent necessity.

Writing to the Leeds Mercury in December 1851, Smiles raised the alarm, pointing to

> the wide and growing gulph [*sic*] of separation which divides the educated upper and the uneducated lower classes of society, - the rapidly increasing numbers of the "dangerous classes" . . . - and the social insecurity . . . where a large portion of the people, with their desires whetted for the enjoyment of political privileges . . . [are] like some blind Samson, it may be, ready to pull down the pillars of the social fabric and lay it in ruins.

Smiles felt that ignorance was a serious and even revolutionary danger, responsible for nearly all the evils, for which "the costly repressive institutions of modern governments exist." The answer was (like preventive medicine) preventive education, which would remove "all the powers of [i.e. inclination to] evil."[304] The way in which Smiles thought this preventive education might be applied is interesting, for he evidently separated those for whom self-education and self-help could operate successfully from those for whom self-education and self-help just did not work. The generalised education of external circumstances only helped those who could take advantage of their experiences and help themselves, while the "destitute" could not help themselves, and therefore required education (schooling) to *prevent* them remaining a liability on the community, or worse. Smiles would have the destitute taught the value of property:

> I value life: well, I would have these destitute children taught the sacredness of life, its duties, its responsibilities, its destinies. I value property: I would have them taught a proper regard for it, its uses, its rights, and the obligations devolving on its possession. Without this sense of

> the sacredness of person and property pervading the community, neither my person nor possessions can for a moment be regarded as secure.[305]

In other words, education (schooling) would supply that understanding of the value of duty, work, property and earnest purpose which children would normally learn in the Home, but which destitute children lacked since they obviously had no homes.

Smiles' hopes were not realised and national education had to wait, and so Smiles fell back once again onto the broad concept of self-education via the stimulating experiences or circumstances of life. When Smiles became more specific about the utilitarian functions of this kind of education - generalised self-education - he referred to it as "practical" education. That is, like the proposed regular schooling of destitute children, "practical" education aimed at two precise objectives. The first objective would be to discipline the individual into an acceptance of his work and station in life. Such an "education" applied to the working classes particularly, tending "to discipline a man truly, and fit him for the proper performance of the duties and business of life . . ." This industrial discipline was necessary because the well-being of the country depended on how many "productive and well-trained labourers" there were available, and because the "dangerous" or "helpless" classes required particular discipline: "It is easy to see, also, how, by drilling the helpless classes to industrial habits, you increase their powers of self-dependence, and enable them . . . to provide for themselves without being a burden upon others at home . . ." Smiles was therefore pleased to observe the foundation of industrial schools for the "drilling of poor children [i.e. destitute or helpless] to industrial labour . . ."[306]

The second objective of the "practical" education of life was paradoxically the very opposite to the first, although still concerned with discipline, for Smiles believed that men could be trained to an individualism of "self-dependence." This "life-education," while "fitting Englishmen for doing the work" of society also fitted them for "acting the part of free men." Smiles considered that the "most self-dependent man is under discipline, - and the more perfect the discipline, the more complete his condition," and so, for example, the "happiest home is that where the discipline is the most perfect, and yet where it is least felt . . ."[307] Smiles meant that where a man had disciplined himself internally (or had been disciplined by "life-education," or, if helpless, by industrial schools), then he could act externally as a self-helping independent individual.

That is, through the education of the circumstances and experiences of the environment the individual could learn (or if "helpless" be taught) two things: firstly, internal self-control or the conquest of vice through moral habits, and secondly, as a result, acceptance of his work and place in society. Through these two moral victories, over the internal self and the external world, and involving the calm acceptance of his fate, the individual could reach his own sphere of free self-dependence. At the same time, Smiles felt that the habit of internal self-control, together with the acceptance of external work and social duty, would spill over into an habitual self-dependence and a free individualism of thought, action and character.

Smiles' view of education also included a third idea, that the diffusion of knowledge would automatically arouse the interest and desire for improvement of the working classes, and equally important, would enable every individual to aim at self-culture. Indeed Chapters X and XI of Self-Help are largely concerned with the idea that all men had a right to intellectual culture, and not merely the privileged classes, for all men were born with the potential for developing their God-given intellectual faculties, regardless of class or rank. Smiles laid great emphasis on this point, and it is significant that he supported Short Time in factories for the same reason as George Combe welcomed the invention of machinery - it would give the working class person time to develop his moral and intellectual faculties. Smiles did not want an "untaught, rude and savage generation, whom the workshop may drill into wealth-producing machines, but whose existence, as regards its higher ends, can only prove a miserable failure." And Smiles included in the self-culture aspect of education a cultiviation of the taste for the beautiful in art and nature, a cultivation of the "higher pleasures" rather than "a deceitful solace in sensual excess."[308]

Whether Smiles was sometimes motivated more by fear of a "savage" and "sensual" generation than by a real feeling for self-culture is occasionally open to question, but in any case he was committed to the intellectual self-help of self-culture, and his debt to Channing in this respect has already been noted, as well as his opposition to self-culture as a means of "getting on" in life. In this respect, Smiles' design for self-culture may be compared to that of J.H. Newman, who felt that the culture of the intellect was "noble in itself" and useful "not in any low, mechanical, mercantile sense, but as diffusing good . . . first to the owner, and then through him to the world." The intention was the same, but the means were slightly different, for Newman's Idea of a University by definition approached self-culture through disciplined schooling rather than individual self-culture. A more accurate comparison is that of Smiles and Matthew Arnold, since Arnold saw self-culture both as internal perfection and as a means of carrying the whole society forward through enlightenment. And like Smiles, Arnold also feared the uneducated savage generation, the "raw and rough" populace, which he hoped would learn both discipline and a happier attitude toward society through the attainment of right reason. But in the end, and unlike the Dissenting individualism of Smiles, Arnold opted for the State as the ultimate principle of authority.[309]

To summarise, what did education mean to Smiles? It will be recalled that Smiles' lectures to the working men of Leeds were very often concerned with education. Two of these lectures have been preserved through publication, The Diffusion of Political Knowledge Among the Working Classes (1842) and The Education of the Working Classes (1844), while Smiles' lead-off lecture to the Leeds Mechanics and Temperance Institute in 1851 was entitled "Self-Education." It was from these lectures, as Smiles notes in his Introduction to Self-Help, that that book gradually expanded, and the varied mixture of educational ideas that characterise the two published lectures on education show how politics, education, self-culture, self-help, and physiology were inextricably linked in Smiles' mind. So, for example, in one of his rare definitions, Smiles puts together the collection of ideas that for him describes education:

> The freedom of the mind - mental self-dependence - the free and unshackled use of the human faculties - earnest self-culture and development, so that the whole nature of man may become stronger, better, freer, happier . . . If Education has not given men greater power to overcome wrong, to resist evil, to work out good, to unfold the highest elements of character, and to liberate the intellect and the conscience . . . Education has failed of its great purpose.[310]

In Philosophical Radical tradition, Smiles thought that education could do almost everything to reform the individual, and as Cobden once told Smiles, the question of education was the one "which lies at the bottom of all others." The basic reason for this, as far as Smiles was concerned, was that he still believed in a tabula rasa psychology, which meant that all the virtues had to be learnt.[311] This was true, for example, of thrift and saving ("thrift is not a natural instinct") and indeed of social development as a whole, which "invariably resolves itself into a question of individual training." Man was "made the being that he is, chiefly by means of education," wrote Smiles referring to education via experience; this was a fact which "no rational person will now-a-days attempt to deny . . ."[312] If social reform required individual reform, then education in its three meanings had the potential to improve and reform the individual, and could lead to the adoption of the spirit of self-help in regard to life and work.

This section has been concerned with the more immediate way in which Smiles came to write Self-Help. His disillusionment with the sectarian nature of reforming groups and the seeming inability of political reform to achieve results, together with a new emphasis on the internal capabilities of the individual and the recognition of a classless "natural" aristocracy of heroic workers as leaders[313] and examplars, steered him toward the possibilities of universal self-help. As a necessary adjunct "education" enabled the individual to evaluate the potential of the heroic examplars as models, and at the same time prepare the individual for his own role and work in society. Smiles actually wrote Self-Help in the early 1850s, prior to his book on George Stephenson, published in 1857, but the example of Stephenson's heroic and persevering work in overcoming difficulties places the two books in the same mould. Moreover, Stephenson's objective achievements touch on the last element that went into Self-Help: the reflection in Smiles' writing of the growing confidence of English society in the 1850s.

In Smiles' case this appears to date from the beinning of 1854 in the shape of one or two articles and in particular a February 1854 article entitled "Parvenues." Smiles makes the remarkable statement that "all our great men, without exception, are parvenues. Our poets, our sculptors, our painters, our authors, are all men who have risen from the ranks."[314] Such an assertion reflected complacency as much as confidence, and still did not mean that this was an example to be followed by the mass of the working class, for such achievements were exceptional. Significantly, Smiles' article did not refer to business achievement, but to the arts, and, as the rest of the article makes clear, Smiles' partiality for the parvenues was really an indirect attack on the aristocracy through his promotion of a 'natural aristocracy' of talent. Chronologically, 1854 was also the year in which Smiles attempted to publish the manuscript of Self-Help, and in which he obtained a higher position in railway work (secretary of the South Eastern). The years 1854 to 1859 do represent a phase of confidence and complacency for Smiles, following the political and radical conflicts of the 1830s and 1840s, and preceding his growing reaction to the expanding strength of democracy from the 1860s onward. This phase of a few years' duration signified Smiles' new optimism for reform - a reform of society based on self-help as an ideal, and on the necessary public recognition of the value of work.

Seen in perspective, and as a whole, what was the meaning of Smiles' ideal of self-help? An answer to that question, and the relationship of Smiles' thought to what may be termed the self-help tradition, may be found in the following chapter.

## Chapter II - Footnotes

[1]Although the majority of the material in this Chapter comes from pre-1859 sources, the 'self-help' series of books by Smiles are also included: Self-Help (1859), Character (1871), Thrift (1875), Duty (1880), Life and Labour (1887) since they form a single unit which frequently complements and relates to the earlier material.

[2]Harrison, Learning and Living, pp. 204-205. Perkin, Origins of Modern English Society, p. 225. See also the Critical Bibliography for the overwhelming modern interpretation of Smiles as a "success" author.

[3]G.R. Cragg, The Church and the Age of Reason, 1648-1789 (New York, 1961), p. 171.

[4]Smiles at first followed the Philosophical Radicals in politics (and particularly J.A. Roebuck and J.S. Mill) before turning to Cobden and the Anti Corn Law League. He preferred to call himself an "independent radical" or a "rational radical," Leeds Times, Jan. 5, 1839, p. 4; Cobden to Smiles, Jan. 9, 1841 (Eva Hartree Collection, Fitzwilliam Museum, Cambridge) (hereinafter Hartree Collection), MS 76.

[5]Smiles' parents to Smiles, Oct. 17, 1829, Smiles Correspondence, SS/AII/1; Robert Smiles, "Obituary," The Railway News (London), April 23, 1904, vol. LXXXI, p. 661. Smiles, Autobiography, p. 15.

[6]Smiles to William, June 25, 1868, Smiles Correspondence, SS/AII/5a and b.

[7]Smiles, Autobiography, pp. 8, 13, 24. The Cameronians were named after Richard Cameron, a particularly fiery Covenanter, who renounced allegiance to Charles II. Richard Cameron's sermons dwelt much on sin and

conversion, and in view of Smiles' rejection of the pursuit of wealth for its own sake, may have some relevance: "What signifies so much gold and money . . . ye that can eat and drink, and never mind God, your souls are in a most dreadful case and situation," John Howie (ed.), Sermons delivered in Times of Persecution in Scotland (Edinburgh, 1880), p. 439. Rev. John M'Kerrow, History of the Secession Church (Revised edition; Edinburgh and London, 1848), pp. 465, 656.

[8]Smiles, Autobiography, p. 27. For example, in 1873 Smiles severely reprimanded his son, Samuel, for expressing atheistic views in public, and noted: "Remember that the greatest men who have ever lived have been believers in that which you may consider humbug . . ." Smiles to Duff, July 3, 1873, Smiles Correspondence, SS/AIII/9. By the 1880s Smiles was expressing the view that man worked in conformity to the purposes of the Divine Will, that man was guarded by the Higher Will, and that man could not choose to be rich or poor, but only worthy or worthless, Smiles, Duty, with Illustrations of Courage, Patience and Endurance (New York, 1881), pp. 17, 12, 14.

[9]See, for example, the Covenant declaration of the Secession Church, entitled a "Profession of Faith, and Engagement to Duties" in M'Kerrow, History of the Secession Church, pp. 423-25. The individualism and subjectivism of Calvinism in England and Scotland is well-documented, but it should be pointed out that this individualism operated in the religious area, and that the relation of the individual to the community in Calvinistic theory, despite the right to resist where the honour of God is at stake, was essentially conservative, Ernst Troeltsch, Protestantism and Progress (1912) (Beacon Paperback edition; Boston, 1958), pp. 150-54.

[10]Murray was editor of the Edinburgh Weekly Chronicle to which Smiles contributed regular articles during the mid-1830s, John A. Fairley (ed.), Autobiographical Notes: Also Reminiscences of a Journey to London in 1840 by Thomas Murray (Dumfries, 1911), p. 4. Smiles, Autobiography, p. 64.

[11]Georgia Harkness, John Calvin, the Man and his Ethics (New York, 1931), pp. 210-13. Ronald S. Wallace, Calvin's Doctrine of the Christian Life (Grand Rapids, Michigan, 1959), pp. 148-69. For this reason, both Smiles and Thomas Carlyle rejected a cash-nexus society in favour of a more mutually responsive society. A. Dakin, Calvinism (London, 1940), pp. 23-26, 224. Wallace, Calvin's Doctrine, p. 319. Harkness, John Calvin, p. 220. John T. McNeill, The History and Character of Calvinism (New York, 1954), p. 223, note.

[12]See Max Weber's interpretation of the phrase "God helps those who help themselves" in The Protestant Ethic, p. 115. Smiles' phrase occurs for example in the Leeds Times, April 13, 1839, p. 4; Feb. 8, 1840, p. 4; July 17, 1841, p. 4; Smiles, Self-Help; with Illustrations of character and conduct (Author's edition; Boston, 1860), p. 15. Weber, Protestant Ethic, pp. 115, 119; Wallace, Calvin's Doctrine, pp. 59 ff. and 229 ff.

[13]Samuel Brown to Smiles, n.d. (but soon after Smiles left the Medical School at Edinburgh, which would date it 1833 or 1834), Smiles Correspondence, SS/AIX/30a, b, c. This letter is of great interest, for it is one of the very few items relating to Smiles' early state of mind. Samuel Brown is replying to, and answering, some of Smiles' metaphysical queries. Smiles had evidently asked firstly whether matter and mind were not identical, to which Brown replied: "That matter and mind are distinct and different existences is demonstrable; it is a doctrine." Secondly, Brown posed Smiles' own question and answered it: "You ask 'is life not

the result of certain operations of organisations?' Undoubtedly not. It is the _cause_ of organisation."

Smiles' approach to materialism may well have been caused by attending lectures at Edinburgh, and in particular the lectures of Dr. Fletcher (Smiles, _Autobiography_, pp. 34, 52), who asked the same question: "Nothing, for example, is more common that the proposition, 'Life results from organisation,' but . . . the principal _words_ are entirely misapplied - the sentence should have stood, 'Vitality results from Organism'." Dr. John Fletcher, _Rudiments of Physiology_, ed. Robert Lewins (3 parts; Edinburgh and London, 1835), Part I, pp. 1-2, footnote (Microfilm, Yale Medical Library).

[14]A.H. Lincoln actually considered Priestley's determinism to be "in the strictest sense, a doctrine of philosophical self-help," in Lincoln, _Some Political and Social Ideas of English Dissent, 1763-1800_ (Cambridge, 1938), pp. 156-57.

[15]For the early 19th Century Unitarians as rational, emotionless and conservative, see Olive Griffiths, _Religion and Learning_ (Cambridge, 1935), pp. 156, 163; and John Colmer, _Coleridge, Critic of Society_ (Oxford, 1959), p. 40. For Unitarian-Utilitarian links, see Perkin, _Origins of Modern English Society_, pp. 204-205; R.K. Webb, _Modern England from the 18th Century to the Present_ (New York and Toronto, 1968), pp. 241-42; and R.K. Webb, _Harriet Martineau, A Radical Victorian_ (New York and London, 1960), p. 88. George Combe, the Edinburgh phrenologist, remarked in 1834 that it was "certain that the great body of educated men are either Deists or Unitarians, but publicly profess some one or other of the popular forms of moral belief . . .", Charles Gibbon, _The Life of George Combe_ (2 vols.; London, 1878), vol. I, p. 303. Smiles, _Autobiography_, p. 52.

[16]For the Monthly Repository, see F.E. Mineka, The Dissidence of Dissent, The Monthly Repository, 1806-1839 (Chapel Hill, 1944), passim. For Mary Leman Gillies (later Mrs. Grimstone), Bowring and Southwood Smith, see Smiles, Autobiography, pp. 52, 74-78. For the Unitarian affiliation of Bowring, Mineka, Dissidence of Dissent, p. 117; and for Southwood Smith, Grobel, "The S.D.U.K.", vol. II, p. 176.

[17]Smiles, Autobiography, pp. 91-96. For Hamer Stansfeld as Unitarian, see R.V. Holt, The Unitarian Contribution to Social Progress in England (London, 1938), p. 240. For J.G. Marshall as Unitarian, Grobel, "The S.D.U.K.", vol. II, p. 736. See also W.E. Channing to Hamer Stansfeld, March 31, 1841 in W.H. Channing, Memoir of W.E. Channing (3 vols.; Boston, 1848), vol. III, pp. 59-60.

[18]Kilburne, Annals, pp. 30, 213-14.

[19]Rev. C. Wicksteed, A Broad Foundation the Only Sure One (Leeds, 1841). Smiles to Cobden, Aug. 16, 1841, in Cobden Papers (West Sussex County Record Office, Chichester), postscript, no folio number. Smiles, "A work that prospered," Good Words, 1877, vol. XVIII, p. 387. Smiles to Janet, Nov. 9, 1883, Smiles Correspondence, SS/AI/173.

[20]Smiles, Autobiography, note p. 128. Holt, Unitarian Contribution, p. 345. Leeds Times, March 23, 1839, p. 6; May 16, 1840, p. 6; April 24, 1841, p. 4; Aug. 7, 1841, p. 6; Feb. 5, 1842, p. 6; Nov. 5, 1842, p. 4; Smiles, The Diffusion of Political Knowledge Among the Working Classes (Leeds, 1842), p. 19; Smiles, Self-Help, p. 342. Similarities between Smiles and Channing will be discussed later in the section.

[21]Smiles actually inclined to a Broad Church view of religion by the 1870s, attending the services of Teignmouth Shore, one of F.D. Maurice's curates, and finding support for his rational belief in William Paley's

Natural Theology (American Tract Society edition; New York, n.d. [catalogued as 1821 in Yale University Library]). Smiles to [?], March 15, 1873, Smiles Correspondence, SS/AI/49; and for Paley, Smiles to William, Oct. 23, 1868, ibid, SS/AII/14.

[22]Mineka, Dissidence of Dissent, pp. 176-77, 215, 257-59. Smiles, Autobiography, p. 52. W.J. Fox, "Poor Laws and Paupers," The Monthly Repository of Theology and General Literature (New Series; London), 1833, vol. VII, p. 372. Fox also recommended national education, repeal of taxes on knowledge, popular suffrage, and a plan for emigration - a programme which Smiles espoused in the 1840s. For one example, among many, of Smiles' rejection of the value and effectiveness of Trades Unions and strike action, see Smiles, "What is doing for the People in Leeds?" People's Journal (5 vols.; London, 1846-48), March 7, 1846, vol. I, p. 136, where he opposes strike action, referring to past strikes; "in nine out of ten cases, the strikes completely failed in their object."

[23]Smiles, Autobiography, p. 76. Smiles also appreciated her book, Character, or Jew and Gentile (2 vols.; London, 1833), and her emphasis on the role of woman in society, Smiles, Physical Education, p. 6. G.J. Holyoake, the apostle of Rationalism and Individualism, also found Mrs. Grimstone's articles stimulating, G.J. Holyoake, Rationalism (London, 1845), p. 38. Mary Leman Gillies, "Rich and Poor," Monthly Repository, 1835, vol. VIII, p. 342. Smiles, Thrift, p. 18.

[24]Mary Leman Gillies, "Self-Dependence," Monthly Repository, 1835, vol. VIII, p. 597. [Smiles], "Competition," Eliza Cook's Journal (hereinafter ECJ) (12 vols.; London, 1849-1854), April 24, 1852, vol. VI, p. 408. For attribution of Smiles' ECJ articles, see Appendix D.

Smiles, "Conditions of the Masses," Leeds Times, Sept. 26, 1840, p. 4. See also Smiles, Diffusion of Political Knowledge, p. 15.

[25]Mary Leman Gillies, "Universal Cooperation," Monthly Repository, 1835, vol. VIII, p. 781. Smiles, "How is the Community best to be educated?" Leeds Times, Oct. 5, 1839, p. 4.

[26]Mary Leman Gillies, "Antagonism of the Classes," People's Journal, Jan. 24, 1846, vol. I, p. 5. By this time (1846) Mary Leman Gillies' views and Smiles' were identical; she believed that what people achieved by themselves was more valuable than "monster meetings," and that conduct, moral dignity, honest independence and knowledge were the keys to improvement, not political dogmatism, Mary Leman Gillies, "A Happy New Year to the People," ibid, Jan. 17, 1846, vol. I, pp. 38-39. Mary Leman Gillies, "Power and the People," Monthly Repository, 1835, vol. VIII, p. 490.

[27]Mary Leman Gillies, "Self-Dependence," ibid, p. 597. This same confusion led another Unitarian, Harriet Martineau, to break away from necessitarianism. Smiles, "English Society," Leeds Times, April 16, 1842, p. 4.

[28]Smiles, Character (Harper and Brothers; New York, n.d.), pp. 373, 14. Although Character was published in 1871 and may represent a more conservative emphasis on duty, similar statements can be found in Self-Help, pp. 206, 274, 289, 360.

[29]Mary Leman Gillies, "Universal Cooperation," Monthly Repository, 1835, vol. VIII, p. 777.

[30]Smiles, The Education of the Working Classes (Leeds, 1844), p. 8.

[31]Milner, Elevation of the People, p. 212.

[32]"Anniversary of the Leeds Mutual Instruction Society," Leeds Times, Feb. 28, 1846, p. 3, speech by Smiles.

[33]Smiles, Self-Help, pp. 268, 315.

[34]Smiles, Autobiography, pp. 34, 52. From the point of view of Fletcher's influence on Smiles, it is worth noting that the man who was Fletcher's intimate friend, and who edited and published Fletcher's lectures was none other than the doctor to whom Smiles was apprenticed for three years in Haddington before going to Medical School in Edinburgh - Dr. Robert Lewins. Smiles considered Fletcher "a most profound lecturer," and thought that the posthumously published lectures showed "the calibre and genius of the man," ibid, p. 35.

[35]Fletcher, Rudiments of Physiology, Part I: "On Organism," passim, and Part III, p. 89.

[36]Smiles, Physical Education, p. 200 (emphasis mine). (The message of the book was that health depended on the adaptation of the individual to the laws of Nature. In the section on Ethics, Smiles' emphasis on Natural law will be discussed.) Smiles, Self-Help, pp. 312, 206, 274.

[37]Smiles, "Our present position and politics," Leeds Times, Nov. 16, 1839, p. 4. Smiles, "Government and the Chartists," ibid, July 13, 1839, p. 4. Smiles, "William Lovett," Howitt's Journal of Literature and Popular Progress (3 vols.; London, 1847-48), 1847, vol. I, p. 257. Smiles, A History of Ireland and the Irish People, under the Government of England (London, 1844), p. (i).

[38]Smiles, Duty, p. 11. [Smiles], "It's all the same!" ECJ, March 12, 1853, vol. VIII, p. 313. Smiles, Self-Help, p. 355.

[39]Ibid, p. 317.

[40]Hence, when Smiles was actually faced with a group of men who were evidently trying to reach middle class status (members of the Leeds Mutual Instruction Society), he reacted in a curiously neutral manner, acknowledging their purpose in his speech to them, but adding: "it was, however, the elevation and the enlightenment of the great mass of the people that was the most desirable object . . ." Smiles, speech at the "Anniversary of the Leeds Mutual Instruction Society," Leeds Times, Feb. 28, 1846, p. 3.

[41]Smiles, Education of the Working Classes, p. 9.

[42]Channing, "Self-Culture," cited in Leeds Times, March 23, 1839, p. 6. Channing's lecture on Self-Culture was printed in 1838 and was widely circulated in England, Channing, Memoir, vol. III, p. 56. D.P. Edgell, W.E. Channing (Boston, 1955), pp. 57, 99, 105 and passim.

[43]Ibid, pp. 130-139. Channing, "Self-Culture," cited in Leeds Times, March 23, 1839, p. 6.

[44]Smiles, "Select Thoughts," ibid, May 16, 1840, p. 6 (emphasis mine). The original is W.E. Channing, Lectures on the Elevation of the Labouring Portion of the Community (Boston, 1840), p. 6.

[45]Smiles, Self-Help, p. 190 (emphasis mine).

[46]Ibid, p. 32 (emphasis mine).

[47]Ibid, p. 17, and Channing, "Spiritual Freedom" (1830), The Works of W.E. Channing (New and Complete edition; Boston, 1900), p. 176. Smiles, Self-Help, pp. 294-295; Channing, Lectures, pp. 8-9.

[48]Channing, "On the elevation of the Labouring Classes," Works, p. 61 (Channing's lecture was delivered to a group of mechanic apprentices). Smiles, Education of the Working Classes.

[49]Ibid, pp. 14, 7, 8: "Miserable, unhappy, useless, is the man or woman who has not learnt to work!" p. 9. Channing, Lectures, p. 10: "alas, for the man who has not learned to work!" p. 7.

[50]"Gleanings," Leeds Times, July 17, 1841, p. 6. The original is from Channing, Lectures, p. 6.

[51]Smiles, Duty, p. 121. On the uses of pain in stimulating the intellectual faculties, see Smiles, Physical Education, note on p. 106. For Channing on the uses of suffering, see Edgell, Channing, p. 131.

[52]Smiles, "The greatest thing in a city," Leeds Times, Feb. 5, 1842, p. 6; Smiles, "The Present Age," ibid, Aug. 7, 1841, p. 6. Both articles refer to Channing.

[53]Smiles, "The Education of the People," ibid, Feb. 23, 1839, p. 4; Smiles, "The prevention of Crime," ibid, March 30, 1839, p. 4.

[54]Smiles, Self-Help, p. 194.

[55]This can be seen in the Leeds Times, March 30, 1839, p. 4; and in Smiles, Education of the Working Classes, pp. 7-8. As noted above, Smiles showed himself sympathetic to the idea of the elevation of the condition of the entire working class, which was after all only common sense. But Smiles, like the Philosophical Radicals, often thought of society as having one major social category - the "People" - which comprised all of society, apart from the relatively small aristocracy. Thus if the rest of society had advanced, but not the working classes, then by a process of "levelling-up," the condition of the working classes should be brought in line with the rest of the "People." The question of individual advance was academic in comparison to the real need of "levelling-up." Thus, "it is not governments, them, but THE PEOPLE who must educate the people . . ." Smiles, ibid, p. 5. For the concept of "the People" among Radicals, see

Joseph Hamburger, Intellectuals in Politics: John Stuart Mill and the Philosophical Radicals (New Haven and London, 1965), p. 33. Another example of Smiles' use of "People" comes in Dr. Smiles, "Government and the People - the Public Health," ECJ, March 6, 1852, vol. VI, p. 289.

[56]Smiles, "Dr. Channing," Leeds Times, Nov. 5, 1842, p. 4. The three lectures were On the elevation of the Labouring Classes, Spiritual Freedom, and Ministry to the Poor.

[57]Smiles, "Money versus worth," ibid, Oct. 15, 1842, p. 6. The three other reformers were Carlyle, Orville Dewey, and Emerson.

[58]Anniversary Celebrations and Pieces delivered at the Zion Sunday School, New Wortley (leeds University Library), MS 116, n.d., pp. 21-23.

[59]A letter from Channing to George Combe (with whom Smiles corresponded) reveals something of Channing's Calvinistic emotional commitment: "I do not expect that any improvements of the race will exempt the individual from the necessity of struggle and self-denial in the formation of his own character, or will in any way do for him what every free being must do for himself." Channing to George Combe, Nov. 29, 1828, Channing, Memoir, vol. II, p. 408. Smiles would have agreed.

[60]Smiles, "Court and People," Leeds Times, March 16, 1839, p. 4; Smiles, "A Word on an almost prescribed Topic" (i.e. a Republic), ibid, May 25, 1839, p. 4; Smiles, "Prospects of the People," ibid, Jan. 5, 1839, p. 4; Smiles, "The 'Greatest Happiness' Principle," ibid, July 24, 1841, p. 4 and following weeks.

[61]Smiles, "Literature," ibid, April 30, 1842, p. 6.

[62]Smiles, Physical Education, pp. 166-67; Smiles, "Woman, the great Social Reformer," The Union (London), April 1, 1842, vol. I, p. 13.

[63]Bentham, Economic Writings, vol. III, p. 427.

[64]Smiles, "Money versus Worth," Leeds Times, October 15, 1842, p. 6. Smiles, "Attempt on the Queen's Life," ibid, June 4, 1840, p. 4.

[65]Smiles, "The Tory Government on Popular Education," ibid, July 23, 1842, p. 4; Smiles, "The Oppressed Poor," ibid, March 12, 1842, p. 4; Smiles, "Our Social Distractions," ibid, Nov. 2, 1839, p. 4. "Riches are no proof whatever of moral worth . . ." Smiles wrote in Self-Help, p. 287.

[66]Smiles, "America and its Democratic Institutions," Leeds Times, October 29, 1842, p. 4. A similar statement occurs in Smiles, "The Duty of the State to the People," ibid, Aug. 29, 1840, p. 4. For Smiles' approval of Adam Smith, see Self-Help, p. 75.

[67]Smiles, Character, pp. 14, 346. Smiles also thought early education most important, see Chapter II, section (iii). The Victorian sense of intuitively recognised duty is neatly caught in a verse by Charles Swain:

> "Life is duty! - noblest therefore
> He who best that course selects;
> Never waiting, asking 'wherefore?' -
> Acting as his heart directs!"

Charles Swain, "Lines on the death of Sir John Potter, M.P." [Founder of a Free Library], in Charles Swain, Art and Fashion (London, 1863), p. 177.

[68][Smiles], "Earnest Purpose," ECJ, Aug. 30, 1851, vol. V, p. 286; S. Smiles, "It will do!" ibid, Jan. 17, 1852, vol. VI, p. 191.

[69]Smiles, Duty, p. 390.

[70]See, for example, T.T. Segerstedt, The Problem of Knowledge in Scottish Philosophy (Lund, 1935), p. 6. Smiles wrote a section on the Scottish common sense philosopher, Dugald Stewart, in the Leeds Times, Dec. 14, 1839, p. 6. Also, S.A. Grave, The Scottish Philosophy of Common Sense (Oxford, 1960).

[71]Smiles, Autobiography, p. 62, where Smiles refers to Andrew Combe's book, The Principles of Physiology (2nd edition; Edinburgh, 1834) as "of

great use . . ." and to Andrew Combe himself as "that excellent man . . ." Andrew Combe had also been brought up in Calvinism, and had likewise rejected its severities. Smiles also acknowledged his debt to the Combe brothers in the preface to his Physical Education, and in footnotes in the book. See also the D.N.B. (Dictionary of National Biography) article on George Combe by Leslie Stephen. On Unitarianism, see footnote 15 above, and Perkin, Origins of Modern English Society, pp. 204-205, where it is implied that George Combe is a Unitarian; Harrison, Learning and Living, pp. 114-17, for an explanation of phrenology. Smiles cautiously accepted phrenology, but relegated it to "a subordinate branch of natural history," Leeds Times, April 20, 1839, p. 6; Channing reviewed many of George Combe's books, George Combe, The Life and Correspondence of Andrew Combe (Edinburgh, 1850), endpapers, p. 1.

[72]Gibbon, Life of George Combe, vol. I, p. 255. Significantly, Gibbon mentions Smiles as having similar ideas to George Combe, ibid, vol. II, p. 8. Smiles Autobiography, pp. 42, 44.

[73]Smiles to George Combe, 20 Dec. 1837 (MS 7244, National Library of Scotland), ff. 10R-11V.

[74]George Combe to Smiles, 22 Dec. 1837 (MS 7387, ibid), f. 504R.

[75]George Combe, Moral Philosophy; or the Duties of Man (Edinburgh, 1840), p. (iv). Smiles, Autobiography, p. 64. Smiles cites G. Combe's Constitution of Man, for example, in a note on pp. 46-47 of Physical Education. Unfortunately copies of the Edinburgh Weekly Chronicle have apparently passed from the face of the earth.

[76]George Combe, The Constitution of Man considered in Relation to External Objects (2nd edition; Edinburgh, 1835), pp. 59-62, Chapters IV and V, passim; G. Combe, Moral Philosophy, pp. 22, 57-58, 62. Smiles' medical

instructor, Dr. Fletcher, used much the same schema of man's impulses to action, dividing them into Instinct and Passion, Fletcher, Rudiments of Physiology, Part III, pp. 89, 92.

[77]G. Combe, Moral Philosophy, p. 65. Note the resemblance between Combe and Smiles in the use of the "scale" analogy. Smiles also quotes from this section of George Combe's book in advancing the idea that machinery would eventually give sufficient leisure for the masses "to enjoy their moral, intellectual, and religious endowments," Smiles, "The Revolution Working Out by the Discovery of James Watt," Leeds Times, Jan. 4, 1840, p. 4.

[78]The best summary of this tradition occurs in Peter J. Stanlis, Edmund Burke and the Natural Law (Ann Arbor Paperback edition; Ann Arbor, Michigan, 1965), pp. 3-28. Stanlis notes the distinction between physical science and the Natural Law of ethics, politics, human behaviour, etc., and also points out the break made by the subjective "natural rights" ethics of Hobbes and Locke with the objective theistic Thomist Natural Law tradition.

[79]Article on Andrew Combe, M.D. in The Dictionary of National Biography: From the earliest times to 1900, ed. Sir Leslie Stephen and Sir Sidney Lee (London), vol. IV, pp. 881-82.

[80]Smiles, Physical Education, p. 1; Smiles, "Distress of the Working Classes - Emigration," Leeds Times, May 30, 1840, p. 4.

[81]Smiles, Physical Education, p. 9.

[82]Smiles, Thrift, p. 18.

[83][Smiles], "Helps to Self-Culture," ECJ, Oct. 4, 1851, vol. V, p. 365. Smiles, Thrift, p. 37.

[84][Smiles], "Competition," ECJ, April 24, 1852, vol. VI, p. 407. [Smiles], "Helps to Self-Culture," ibid, Oct. 4, 1851, vol. V, pp. 365-66.

[85] Every man, for example, could attain physical comfort "in this abundant and plenteous country, rich in all the wealth which nature yields." The stumbling block for Smiles were the Corn Laws, but these were repealed in 1846, Smiles, "How abolition of the Corn Laws would benefit the Working Classes," Leeds Times, Jan. 12, 1839, p. 4. For bounty of Nature, see also Smiles, "Late Sayings and Doings in and out of Parliament," ibid, Feb. 20, 1841, p. 4.

[86] [Smiles], "The Lot of Labour," ECJ, Nov. 13, 1852, vol. VIII, p. 47; [Smiles], "Attend to Little Things," ibid, Sept. 24, 1853, vol. IX, p. 344; [Smiles], "Gibson and Thorburn the Artists," ibid, Sept. 22, 1849, vol. I, p. 333.

[87] Smiles, Duty, p. 204.

[88] [Smiles], "It's all the Same!" ECJ, March 12, 1853, vol. VIII, p. 314. Smiles, Self-Help, p. 354.

[89] Ibid, p. 355. Smiles also quotes a long passage from Charles Babbage to the same effect (Charles Babbage, The Ninth Bridgewater Treatise (2nd edition; London, 1838), pp. 111-116). Babbage concentrated on Laplace's Law of Action and Reaction and thereby showed that man's every action has considerable significance, a theory which Smiles took over.

[90] [Smiles], "Young Men's Mutual Improvement Societies," ECJ, May 19, 1849, vol. I, p. 34.

[91] [Smiles], "Industrial Schools for Young Women," ibid, June 9, 1849, vol. I, p. 81.

[92] [Smiles], "Drill!" ibid, Nov. 8, 1851, vol. VI, p. 17.

[93] [Smiles], "Young Men's Mutual Improvement Societies," ibid, May 19, 1849, vol. I, p. 34. Robinson, Self-Education, p. 118.

[94]Dr. Smiles, "Abbey Life in Old England," ECJ, Jan. 18, 1851, vol. IV, p. 180.

[95]Dr. Smiles, "Samuel Bamford," Howitt's Journal, May 20, 1848, vol. III, p. 328.

[96][Smiles], "Dutch Pictures," ECJ, Sept. 25, 1852, vol. VII, p. 343. Smiles, The Huguenots: Their settlements, churches and industries in England and Ireland (London, 1867), p. (v). Dr. Smiles, "Abbey Life in Old England," ECJ, Jan. 18, 1851, vol. IV, p. 177.

[97]Smiles, Thrift, p. 114.

[98]Smiles, "Unsatisfied Appetites," Leeds Times, Dec. 7, 1839, p. 6. For J.S. Mill, see Karl Britton, John Stuart Mill (2nd edition; Dover, N.Y., 1969), pp. 85, 93.

[99]Smiles, Lives of the Engineers (5 vols.; Popular edition; London, 1904), vol. V, p. 328; most of this volume was originally published as The Life of George Stephenson, railway engineer (London, 1857). The same idea of railways as levelling and democratic occurs in [Smiles], "Railway Travelling," ECJ, June 16, 1849, vol. I, pp. 97-99; and in [Smiles], "The Scottish Borders," ibid, March 4, 1854, vol. X, p. 295, where Smiles comments that the age of monasticism has been overtaken by "the all-levelling railroads of the 19th Century." [Smiles], "George Stephenson," ibid, June 2, 1849, vol. I, pp. 66-67.

[100]Smiles, Lives of the Engineers, vol. III, p. 122. S.S. (Samuel Smiles), "Love of Country in Town," ECJ, May 5, 1849, vol. I, p. 14. Smiles, Lives of the Engineers, vol. III, p. 153.

[101][Smiles], "George Stephenson," ECJ, June 2, 1849, vol. I, p. 67.

[102][Smiles], "Heads!" ibid, Dec. 4, 1852, vol. VIII, p. 91. Referring to African slaves, Smiles commented: "Men, with any large force of

character, or power of brain, could not thus have been treated for centuries," p. 91.

[103] Smiles used both phrases frequently. Two examples are: Smiles, "The Education of the People," Leeds Times, Feb. 23, 1839, p. 4; Smiles, "How is the Community best to be Educated?" ibid, Oct. 5, 1839, p. 4.

[104] Smiles, Physical Education, pp. 24, 25, and for references to Rousseau's Emilius on sense-experience and the late development of the brain, pp. 156, 194. Smiles' teacher at Edinburgh, Dr. Fletcher, may also have influenced him in this direction, for Fletcher admitted that the chief effort of his lectures had been to establish Lockean tabula rasa and sensationalist theory. Fletcher, Rudiments of Physiology, Part III, p. 113.

[105] Smiles, Physical Education, pp. 165, 26.

[106] Smiles, Self-Help, p. 350.

[107] J.J. Rousseau, Emilius; or a Treatise of Education (3 vols.; Edinburgh, 1768), vol. II, p. 73. Smiles, Self-Help, p. 21.

[108] Smiles, "Woman, the great Social Reformer," The Union, April 1, 1842, vol. I, p. 10.

[109] Smiles, Self-Help, p. 16; Smiles, "Woman the Great Social Reformer," The Union, April 1, 1842, vol. I, p. 9. This was, of course, a common Utilitarian position, and will be considered in the next section.

[110] Smiles, Diffusion of Political Knowledge, p. 9.

[111] Smiles, "The Most Unreformed of all Rotten Corporations," (i.e. the Government), Leeds Times, June 22, 1839, p. 4.

[112] Smiles, Physical Education, p. 26.

[113] [Smiles], "Home Power," ECJ, Dec. 29, 1849, vol. II, p. 129; Smiles, "Woman, the great Social Reformer," The Union, April 1, 1842, vol.

I, pp. 11, 10. [Smiles], "Home Power," ECJ, Dec. 29, 1849, vol. II, p. 129.

[114] Smiles' ideas on the importance of women owed much to the French author, Aimé-Martin, Smiles, Autobiography, p. 52. On the other hand, Smiles also claimed that his ideas on women came from Mary Leman Gillies, Smiles, Physical Education, p. 6. And see Rousseau, Emilius, vol. I, p. 8, note, for the influence of mothers. Smiles, "Woman, the great Social Reformer," The Union, April 1, 1842, vol. I, pp. 12, 13.

[115] Smiles, Self-Help, pp. 352, 353. The emphasis on the eye rather than the ear seems to stem partly from common-sense - it was much easier to conceive an image or action being permanently imprinted on the wax-like mind through the eye than the same process through the ear - and perhaps partly through the emphasis placed on the method of observation by the Scottish common sense school of philosophy, Elie Halevy, The Growth of Philosophical Radicalism, tr. Mary Morris (Boston, 1955), p. 439. And see Smiles' stress on the visual element in theorising, Smiles, Autobiography, Chapter IV.

[116] Smiles here refers to his separation of the moral and intellectual faculties of man.

[117] Smiles, Self-Help, p. 384. It is interesting to note that Smiles eliminated these passages from the 1866 edition of Self-Help. Smiles also likened habits to "letters cut on the bark of a tree" which grow and widen with age, ibid, p. 385.

[118] Smiles, Physical Education, p. 13.

[119] To take just one example, Chapters III (Improvidence) and XIII (Great Debtors) in Thrift (1875).

[120] On the determinism and the rationalism of the 18th Century, see Houghton, Victorian Frame of Mind, pp. 336 ff.

[121] For Carlyle and Emerson, see Chapter III. It is significant that Smiles, as he says, "rose" from the poetry of Shelley and Keats to Coleridge and Wordsworth, Smiles, Autobiography, p. 52. It was no accident that Carlyle, the great foe of the Lockean tradition, rejected Lockean psychology because of its "genetic history of the mind," cited in R. Wellek, Kant in England (Princeton, 1931), p. 183. See also G. Bryson, Man and Society: The Scottish Inquiry of the 18th Century (Princeton, 1945), pp. 26-28 for the general reaction against sensationalism.

[122] J.S. Mill, Autobiography, ed. C.V. Shields (Library of Liberal Arts edition; 1957), p. 109.

[123] [Smiles], "Young Men's Mutual Improvement Societies," ECJ, May 19, 1849, vol. I, p. 34.

[124] Smiles, Physical Education, p. 26.

[125] Ibid.

[126] Ibid, p. 25.

[127] Samuel Bailey, Essays on the Formation and Publication of Opinions (3rd edition; London, 1837), p. 175. For Smiles on Bailey's Essays, see Smiles, "The 'Greatest Happiness' Principle," Leeds Times, July 31, 1841, p. 4.

[128] Smiles, "Woman, the great Social Reformer," The Union, April 1, 1842, vol. I, p. 10.

[129] Smiles, "Self-Respect and Self-Dependence in Youth," Leeds Times, Dec. 7, 1839, p. 6.

[130] Smiles, Physical Education, pp. 26, 25.

[131]Smiles, "Self-Respect and Self-Dependence in Youth," Leeds Times, Dec. 7, 1839, p. 6.

[132]For example, Smiles opposed civil service examinations because well-crammed minds would be secured at the expense of energy, vigour, robust manhood, ordinary industry and independence, Smiles, Self-Help, p. 318.

[133]Ibid, p. 291.

[134]Ibid, p. 277. The existence of the principles within explains why Smiles desired consistent conduct, because inconsistent conduct revealed, besides lack of decision, also lack of principles.

[135]Smiles, Physical Education, p. 25.

[136][Smiles], "Young Men's Mutual Improvement Societies," ECJ, May 19, 1849, vol. I, pp. 33, 34.

[137]Smiles to "Gingers," March 21, 1860, Smiles Correspondence, SS/AI/2.

[138]Smiles, Character, p. 165. Weber, The Protestant Ethic, p. 119.

[139]Tweedie, Man and his Money, p. 148; J.W. Alexander, The Young Man in Business Cheered and Counselled (London, 1861), p. 70; Gilbart, Moral and Religious Duties, p. 18.

[140]Smiles, "The Voluntary Principle," Leeds Times, May 1, 1841, p. 7. For similar statements by Smiles, ibid, July 10, 1841, p. 4.

[141]Robert Vaughan, D.D., The Age of Great Cities: or, Modern Society viewed in its relation to intelligence, morals and religion (London, 1843), p. 282.

[142]Weber, The Protestant Ethic, pp. 115, 119. Smiles much admired Paley's Natural Theology (see note 2, p. 192 above) which aptly illustrates this concept. "Virtue is infinitely various. There is no situation in

which a rational being is placed . . . which affords not room for moral agency, for the acquisition, exercise, and display of voluntary qualities, good and bad. Health and sickness, enjoyment and suffering, riches and poverty . . . have all their offices and duties, all serve for the formation of character; for when we speak of a state of trial, it must be remembered that characters are not only tried or proved or detected, but that they are generated also and formed by circumstances." Paley, Natural Theology, p. 339 (emphasis mine).

[143]Smiles, Self-Help, pp. 32, 330, 333. This is one reason why Smiles had been greatly attracted to G.L. Craik's Pursuit of Knowledge under Difficulties, which he had read often and knew many passages almost by heart, Smiles, Autobiography, p. 222. It was no coincidence that Channing saw temptation and suffering as enabling men "to perfect himself by conflict with the very forces which threaten to overwhelm him," Channing, Lectures, p. 32.

[144]Smiles, Character, p. 352.

[145]Smiles, Self-Help, pp. 332, 333-334. S. Smiles, "Music in the House," ECJ, Jan. 31, 1852, vol. VI, p. 209.

[146]Smiles, "Moral and Physical Condition of the Working Classes," Leeds Times, May 18, 1839, p. 6.

[147][Smiles], "Drill!" ECJ, Nov. 8, 1851, vol. VI, pp. 18, 19.

[148]Smiles, Character, p. 97. [Smiles], "Quite the Gentleman!" ECJ, May 22, 1852, vol. VII, p. 62.

[149][Smiles], "Success in Life," ibid, May 7, 1853, vol. IX, p. 30.

[150]Smiles, Self-Help, p. 289; the discussion on the uses of work and difficulty occurs in Chapter XI, "Facilities and Difficulties."

[151]Smiles to William Buckles, Dec. 28, 1857 (British Transport Historical Records, London), MS f. W2/109.

[152]Smiles, Self-Help, pp. 376, 377.

[153]Smiles, "Self-Respect and Self-Dependence in Youth," Leeds Times, Dec. 7, 1839, p. 6.

[154]Smiles, Self-Help (Sphere edition; 1968 [reprint of 1866 edition]), p. 204; ibid (Boston, 1860), p. 305.

[155]Smiles, Thrift, pp. 13-22.

[156]Smiles, Lives of the Engineers, vol. I, p. 329.

[157]Smiles, Self-Help, p. 75. For a summary of Adam Smith's economic ideas, see William J. Barber, A History of Economic Thought (Penguin Books edition; Middlesex, 1967), pp. 23-54.

[158]Smiles, "Late Sayings and Doings in and out of Parliament," Leeds Times, Feb. 20, 1841, p. 4.

[159]Thomas Murray, LL.D., Summary of Lectures on Political Economy (Privately printed; "as published in the Edinburgh Weekly Chronicle;" Edinburgh, Winter 1836-37), pp. 4-12, 75, 10, 34 (original in Edinburgh University Library).

[160]Perkin, Origins of Modern English Society, pp. 222-226.

[161]Smiles, A publisher and his friends. Memoir and correspondence of the late John Murray (2 vols.; London, 1891), vol. II, p. 517. [Smiles], "The Lot of Labour," ECJ, Nov. 13, 1852, vol. VIII, p. 46. [Smiles], "Patience is Genius!" ibid, March 26, 1853, vol. VIII, p. 350.

[162]Smiles, History of Ireland, p. 371.

[163]For example, Smiles, Lives of the Engineers, vol. I, pp. xxiii, xx; and Smiles, Thrift, p. 16.

[164]Ibid, pp. 15-16, 14. Smiles, "Relief of the Destitute - Signs of the Times," Leeds Times, July 11, 1840, p. 4. Smiles, Self-Help, p. 268.

[165]Smiles, "The condition of factory women - what is doing for them?", People's Journal, Nov. 7, 1846, vol. II, p. 258. The question of middle class entrepreneurs will be taken up again in Chapter IV.

[166]Smiles, "Working Class respect for Property," Leeds Times, Sept. 10, 1842, p. 4. (And see also Smiles, "What is the Aim of the Torchists?" ibid, Jan. 12, 1839, p. 4.) Smiles, "Strikes," Quarterly Review (London), July-Oct. 1859, vol. CVI, pp. 508, 509.

[167]Smiles, "Masters and Men," Leeds Times, Sept. 17, 1842, p. 4. Smiles, "Distress of the Working Classes," ibid, May 30, 1840, p. 4. In view of Smiles' Unitarian associations it is interesting to record Joseph Barker's comment: "The Unitarians themselves, both ministers and people, advocated Free Trade. Many of them were most zealous in its advocacy." Barker, "The Unitarians and Chartism," The People (Wortley, Leeds), 1849, vol. I, p. 4.

[168]Smiles, "Factory Legislation," Leeds Times, July 6, 1839, p. 4; and Smiles, "Relative Position of the Employers and Employed," ibid, Aug. 8, 1840, p. 4.

[169]Smiles, "Pinching and Pining," ibid, Feb. 13, 1841, p. 4; and similarly Smiles claimed that as long as the Corn Laws existed, men would need to work long hours to survive, Smiles, "An Agitation gone Astray," ibid, Aug. 14, 1841, p. 4.

[170]Smiles, "Beware the 'Fraud'!" ibid, Jan. 29, 1842, p. 4; Smiles, "Peel and Short-Time," ibid, Feb. 5, 1842, p. 4.

[171]Smiles, "How Abolition of the Corn Laws would Benefit the Working Classes," ibid, Jan. 12, 1839, p. 4.

[172] Smiles, "The Condition of Factory Women - What is Doing for them?", People's Journal, Nov. 7, 1846, vol. II, p. 258.

[173] Smiles, "Men of the People. Richard Cobden," ibid, July 25, 1846, vol. II, p. 46.

[174] Smiles, "The Phalanstery," Leeds Times, Sept. 17, 1842, p. 6. Smiles, "How we can permanently elevate the condition of the labourer," ibid, March 7, 1840, p. 4.

[175] Smiles, "What is doing for the People in Leeds?" People's Journal, March 7, 1846, vol. I, p. 137.

[176] "First Soirée of the Leeds Redemption Society," The Herald of Redemption (Leeds), Jan. 1847, no. I, p. 11.

[177] "God help those who help themselves," ibid, March 1847, no. III, pp. 18, 17.

[178] Smiles, "Men of the People. Richard Cobden," People's Journal, July 25, 1846, vol. II, p. 46.

[179] S. Smiles, "Nothing like Leather!" ECJ, Feb. 7, 1852, vol. VI, p. 239.

[180] Smiles, Life of George Stephenson, p. 459. The reference is to the way railway lines were being duplicated.

[181] [Smiles], "Competition," ECJ, April 24, 1852, vol. VI, pp. 407-408.

[182] See Perkin, Origins of Modern English Society, Chapter IX, "The Rise of a Viable Class Society."

[183] Smiles, "The Prevention of Crime," Leeds Times, March 30, 1839, p. 4. Smiles, "How is the Community Best to be Educated?" ibid, Oct. 5, 1839, p. 4. For an early 'self-help' article, see Smiles, "The Late Division - Relative Merits of Whigs and Tories," ibid, Feb. 8, 1840, p. 4.

[184]Smiles, "Why Should the People be Transported?" ibid, Oct. 8, 1842, p. 4. Smiles, "Distress of the Working Classes - Emigration," ibid, May 30, 1840, p. 4. Smiles, "How Abolition of the Corn Laws would Benefit the Working Classes," ibid, Jan. 12, 1839, p. 4. Adam Smith also visualised a generous Nature, Barber, History of Economic Thought, p. 43.

[185]Smiles, "Relative Position of the Employers and Employed," Leeds Times, Aug. 8, 1840, p. 4.

[186]Smiles, (review of) "W. Cooke Taylor, Notes on a Tour in the Manufacturing Districts of Lancashire, 1842," ibid, Aug. 13, 1842, p. 6. Cooke Taylor presented a generally favourable view of manufacturing.

[187]Smiles, "Remember the Poor," ibid, Dec. 26, 1840, p. 4. Smiles, "Peel and Short-Time," ibid, Feb. 5, 1842, p. 4.

[188]Smiles, Physical Education, pp. 10, 21, 5.

[189]Ibid, pp. 10, 8, 43, note p. 106.

[190]Smiles, Self-Help, p. 355. Smiles, Industrial Biography; ironworkers and tool-makers (London, 1863), pp. 167-68 (emphasis mine). [Smiles], "Young Men's Mutual Improvement Societies," ECJ, May 19, 1849, vol. I, p. 34.

[191]Sir Arthur Helps, The Claims of Labour. An Essay on the Duties of the Employers to the Employed (2nd edition; London, 1845), p. 12. Echoes of Helps' book appear in Smiles' writings, and it is interesting that in the Goldsmith's Library of London University there is a copy of The Claims of Labour with Smiles' signature on the fly leaf, addressing the book as a gift to the Leeds transcendentalist, G.S. Phillips.

[192]Fletcher, Rudiments of Physiology, Part III, p. 89.

[193]Smiles, Self-Help, pp. 355, 16. Smiles even carried the idea of aggregation into morality, for he once wrote that kindness was a sort of

"moral savings bank, . . ." Smiles, George Moore, Merchant and Philanthropist (2nd edition; London and New York, 1878), p. 515.

[194]Smiles, Self-Help, p. 18.

[195]Smiles, Character, p. 40. Smiles, Self-Help, p. 395.

[196]For a discussion of the conservation and proportionality of energy, see Cecil J. Schneer, The Search for Order (New York, 1960), pp. 186 ff. Smiles, Self-Help, pp. 17, 377.

[197]Smiles, Autobiography, pp. 44, 52, and for references to parental example and past generations, pp. 13, 15. The considerable emphasis Smiles placed on the role of women is reflected in Physical Education, several articles for The Union periodical, and in most of the 'self-help' series of books.

[198]Smiles, Character, p. 194; Smiles, Duty, p. 393.

[199]Smiles, Thrift, p. 16. The idea of time as a 'financial' loan to be repaid to God is strikingly put by Samuel Bridgett, a Methodist, who had "a deep conviction" that Time "is not our own, but an important talent put into our hands, for which we must give a strict account at the grave, the general audit of all our accounts with our Maker, . . ." cited in W. Arthur, The Successful Merchant (London, 1852), p. 60.

[200][Smiles], "Patience is Genius!" ECJ, March 26, 1853, vol. VIII, p. 350. Other random examples of Smiles' sense of debt to past generations occur in Self-Help, pp. 18-19, 357, 395; Duty, p. 53; Character, pp. 38, 39, 273. Carlyle, "Signs of the Times," Works, vol. XV, pp. 462-487. For E.L. Bulwer, see Appendix C.

[201]For James Hole, see Harrison, Learning and Living, pp. 126-27.

[202]Smiles, History of Ireland, pp. 310-11. Smiles' favourable attitude to the Irish reform movement at this time (1840s) was to undergo a

violent change by the 1880s. A more recent analysis makes sense of Smiles' alternative solutions of self-help and government legislation, T.H.E. Travers, "Samuel Smiles," Biographical Dictionary of Modern British Radicals, (1830-1870),, vol. 2, Sussex, 1984, pp. 455-460.

[203]Smiles, Autobiography, p. 8. Smiles to Janet Hartree, April 7, 1882, Smiles Correspondence, SS/AI/137a. Smiles, Self-Help, p. 346.

[204]Smiles to Thomas Hutchinson, Oct. 10, 1891, Literature, Science, Art and Music. Autographs (MS, Brotherton Liberary, University of Leeds).

[205]Smiles, "Prospects of the People," Leeds Times, Jan. 5, 1839, p. 4.

[206]Smiles, "Tendencies of Society," ibid, Sept. 17, 1842, p. 4; Smiles, "Court and People," ibid, March 16, 1839, p. 4.

[207]Smiles, "Liberation of William Lovett," ibid, July 11, 1840, p. 4; Smiles, "The Women of the Working Classes," The Union, Jan. 1, 1843, vol. I, p. 430.

[208]Smiles, "Corn Laws and Poor Laws," Leeds Times, Jan. 26, 1839, p. 4; Smiles, "Autocracy and Plutocracy - Wealth and Corruption," ibid, Aug. 6, 1842, p. 4.

[209]Smiles, "The Exclusive Spirit - Haut Ton," ibid, Dec. 3, 1842, p. 4.

[210]Smiles, "The Ultimate Question," ibid, April 11, 1840, p. 4; Smiles, "The 'Greatest Happiness' Principle," ibid, July 31, 1841, p. 4; Smiles, "The 'Greatest Happiness' Principle," ibid, July 24, 1841, p. 4.

[211]Smiles, "The 'Greatest Happiness' Principle," ibid, July 31, 1841, p. 4; Smiles, "What will the Lords do?" ibid, Aug. 21, 1841, p. 4; Smiles, "The Urgent Necessity for a Second Reform Bill," ibid, Nov. 23, 1839, p. 4.

[212]Smiles, Self-Help, pp. 268-69.

[213]Dakin, Calvinism, p. 228; Smiles, "Warning Hints to Landlords," Leeds Times, Aug. 7, 1841, p. 4.

[214]Smiles, "The Truth Oozing Out," ibid, Feb. 19, 1842, p. 4.

[215]Smiles, "Aristocratic Morality," ibid, Nov. 5, 1842, p. 4.

[216]For comparison, J.M. Robson remarks that J.S. Mill also regarded the landowning class as (a) unjust and (b) useless, deriving this attitude from Ricardian economics and Benthamite politics, J.M. Robson, The Improvement of Mankind: The Social and Political Thought of John Stuart Mill (Toronto, 1968), p. 252.

[217]Smiles, "The Approaching Festival," Leeds Times, Jan. 16, 1841, p. 4.

[218]Smiles, "Aristocratic Morality," ibid, Nov. 5, 1842, p. 4.

[219]For discussion of the Philosopical Radicals' position, see Hamburger, Intellectuals in Politics pp. 33, 64, and passim. For Smiles' position and contact with Radicals, see the rest of this section.

[220]Smiles, Diffusion of Political Knowledge, passim.

[221]For comments on Matthew Arnold's "remnant" see Raymond Williams, Culture and Society, 1780-1985 (Harper Torchbook edition; New York, 1966), pp. 121 ff. To a lesser extent Coleridge's "clerisy" were to play the same kind of role.

[222]Smiles, "Summing up of the Session," Leeds Times, Aug. 15, 1840, p. 4; Smiles, "Progress of opinion on the Starvation Laws," ibid, Feb. 2, 1839, p. 4. "Liberal" was often used as a name for the Philosophical Radical viewpoint.

[223]Smiles, "Progress of Political Dissatisfaction between the Middle and Working Classes," ibid, Aug. 10, 1839, p. 4. For lack of middle class support on Universal Suffrage, Smiles, "The New Political Movement," ibid,

July 11, 1840, p. 4; and for Household Suffrage, Smiles, "A promising move - the Suffrage," ibid, Nov. 27, 1841, p. 4; Smiles to Cobden, Aug. 16, 1841, in Cobden Papers (West Sussex County Record office, Chichester).

[224] Smiles, "Necessity for a Socio-Political Reform," Leeds Times, Sept. 21, 1839, p. 4.

[225] Smiles, "Union of the Middle and Working Class," ibid, Jan. 15, 1842, p. 4.

[226] Smiles, "The Middle Classes and the Aristocracy," ibid, March 26, 1842, p. 4. See also Smiles, "Respectable Fashion," ibid, Nov. 19, 1842, p. 6, for attacks on middle class worship of rank and wealth.

[227] Smiles, The Huguenots . . . in England and Ireland, pp. 446-47. Smiles' explanation had a lot to do with his Protestant aversion to Catholics.

[228] Smiles, Education of the Working Classes, pp. 8, 9.

[229] Smiles, "Factory Children," Leeds Times, March 9, 1839, p. 4; Smiles, "The Progress of the People," ibid, April 6, 1839, p. 4; Smiles, "Forwards or Backwards - Democracy or Aristocracy? ibid, April 13, 1839, p. 4.

[230] Smiles to Cobden, May 17, 1842, in Cobden Papers (West Sussex County Record office, Chichester); Smiles, "Accumulations of Wealth," Leeds Times, March 12, 1842, p. 6.

[231] Smiles, "Hope Deferred," ibid, June 18, 1842, p. 4; Smiles, "What Do the People Want?" ibid, Dec. 4. 1841, p. 4.

[232] Smiles, "Accumulations of Wealth," ibid, March 12, 1842, p. 6.

[233] In Leeds during 1841-42, 15-20% of the population had an income of less than a shilling per week, while it was estimated in 1842 that meat consumption among the working classes in Leeds had declined by 50% since

1835-36, Hobsbawm, Labouring Men, pp. 88, 120. In 1841 it was estimated that more than one-third of the adult Leeds population had no regular employment, John Burnett, Plenty and Want (Pelican edition; 1968), p. 177. Also Smiles, Autobiography, pp. 114-15.

[234] On euphemistic phrases, Smiles, Self-Help, pp. 264, 265; for quotation, Smiles, Thrift, p. 207.

[235] For example, Smiles, Education of the Working Classes, p. 5. "God helps those who help themselves," Herald of Redemption, March, 1847, no. III, p. 17. Naturally the opposite course of the Chartists should also be avoided.

[236] Smiles, "Accumulations of Wealth," Leeds Times, March 12, 1842, p. 6; Smiles to Cobden, Aug. 16, 1841, in Cobden Papers (West Sussex County Record office, Chichester).

[237] Smiles to Place, Feb. 9, 1841, in Place Papers (British Museum), f. 310; Smiles to Cobden, Sept. 20, 1841, in Cobden Papers (British Museum), f. 57; Cobden to Smiles, Oct. 21, 1841, Hartree Collection, MS 80.

[238] Speech by Smiles, reported in "Stopping the Supplies," Leeds Times, Jan. 6, 1844, p. 7. (Smiles also spoke on behalf of Complete Suffrage during 1843, "Complete Suffrage Association," ibid, Nov. 25, 1843, p. 4) Smiles to J.A. Roebuck, Dec. 23, 1844, Smiles Correspondence, SS/AIV/8b; Cobden to Smiles, Jan. 2, 1849, Hartree Collection, MS 86.

[239] Cobden to Edward Baines, Oct. 12, 1841 in Baines Collection (Archives, Leeds Public Library), no folio number.

[240] Smiles, "The Most Unreformed of all Rotten Corporations," Leeds Times, June 22, 1839, p. 4.

[241] The organic imagery of seeds, planting, growth, etc. is very prevalent in Smiles' thought, as is the counterpart, the springing up of

the "fresh luxuriance" of evils, cured only by radical (root) improvement. Smiles did think of men and classes as comparable to plants - to be left free to grow and cultivate themselves - and not to be stunted or forced. For examples, see Smiles, Self-Help, pp. 16, 23, 29, 316, 350.

[242] Report of speech by Smiles at a "Great Public Meeting," Leeds Times, May 20, 1843, pp. 7-8. Similarly Smiles stressed the statement: "you must become your own social and political regenerators, or you will never enjoy freedom," "Moral and Intellectual Aspects of Chartism," ibid, April 17, 1841, p. 7.

[243] Smiles, Education of the Working Classes, p. 5; Smiles, "The Duty of the State to the People," Leeds Times, Aug. 29, 1840, p. 4.

[244] Smiles, "America and its Democratic Institutions," ibid, Oct. 29, 1842, p. 4.

[245] W.L. Burn, The Age of Equipoise. A Study of the Mid-Victorian Generation (Norton Library edition; New York, 1965), p. 167.

[246] Smiles, "Whig Projects of Centralisation," Leeds Times, Aug. 3, 1839, p. 4. Smiles' quotation of Channing was from his Character of Napoleon.

[247] [Smiles], "Providing against the Evil Day," ECJ, Oct. 6, 1849, vol. I, p. 355. For 1848-1851, Burn, Age of Equipoise, p. 153.

[248] On the education movement, Smiles, Autobiography, pp. 167 ff; Dr. Smiles, "State of Popular Education," ECJ, July 5, 1851, vol. V, p. 147.

[249] Carlyle's reference came from Past and Present, Book III, Chapter III. [Smiles], "Nobody Did It!" ECJ, Aug. 2, 1851, vol. V, pp. 223-24. A useful discussion of the evolution of the two strands of Benthamite thinking into 'natural' Benthamism (pure self-help) and 'artificial' Benthamism (the removal of barriers to self-help), is in Eric Midwinter,

Victorian Social Reform, London 1968, 1973, pp. 20 ff. It can be seen that Smiles moved uneasily between these two strands of Benthamite thought.

[250]Hamburger, Intellectuals in Politics, pp. 126 ff.

[251]Smiles, "Woman, the Great Social Reformer," The Union, April 1, 1842, vol. I, p. 10.

[252]Smiles, Self-Help, pp. 20, 353. Smiles, Duty, p. 11. The individualistic concept of the power of each member of society to react on, and influence his neighbours in an ever extending circle, is also remarked by Davenport Adams in his The Secret of Success, p. 125: Each person "is the centre of a circle . . . and that circle must accordingly react on another and wider circle, and that again on yet another . . . just as we see that the dropping of a stone in the water creates a series of waves . . . far away into the distance."

[253][Smiles], "Don't Care!" ECJ, Dec. 20, 1851, vol. VI, p. 128; [Smiles], "It's all the same!" ibid, March 12, 1853, vol. VIII, p. 313.

[254]Dr. Smiles, "Government and the People - The Public Health," ibid, March 6, 1852, vol. VI, pp. 289-292.

[255]Dr. Smiles, "Improvement of Homes," ibid, May 1, 1852, vol. VII, pp. 1-3.

[256]Smiles had written to Cobden on the theme of local failure of voluntaryism, and Cobden repeats Smiles' statements rhetorically. Cobden to Smiles, Dec. 23, 1853, Hartree Collection, MS 90. [Smiles], "Parvenues," ECJ, Feb. 11, 1854, vol. X, pp. 254-55.

[257]Smiles, "Literature," Leeds Times, Nov. 19, 1842, p. 6.

[258]Smiles, "A Work that Prospered," Good Words, 1877, vol. XVIII, pp. 386, 389-92.

[259]S. Smiles, "Nothing like Leather!" ECJ, Feb. 7, 1852, vol. VI, pp. 239-240.

[260]Smiles, Lives of the Engineers, vol. III, p. 177. Smiles incidentally attacks Paine for his "shallow infidelity," conceiving him as a "restless, speculative, unhappy being . . ." ibid, pp. 212, 213.

[261]Dr. Smiles, "Victor Hugo," Howitts Journal, June 10, 1848, vol. III, p. 369; in this article Smiles also makes an evidently autobiographical comment on the way in which he himself had undergone a radical change over the last ten years, i.e. 1838-1848. Dr. Smiles, "Robert Nicoll," ibid, Feb. 26, 1848, vol. III, p. 135.

[262]The change from the extremism of the 1830s and 1840s to the compromise and settlement of the 1850s and 1860s is neatly reviewed in Chapter II of Burn, Age of Equipoise, pp. 55-91. See also Midwinter, Victorian Social Reform, p. 47.

[263]J.S. Mill, Letters, ed. H.S.R. Elliot (2 vols.; London and New York, 1910), vol. II, pp. 360-61. On Mill's discouragement after 1840, see Hamburger, Intellectuals in Politics p. 111.

[264][Smiles], "Ignorance is Power," ECJ, Nov. 6, 1852, vol. VIII, p. 30.

[265]Smiles, Autobiography, p. 129. However, when his son suggested he write a Social History of England, Smiles rejected the idea as it would take too long and be very difficult, Smiles to Billio, Oct. 30, 1868, Smiles Correspondence, SS/AII/15.

[266]Smiles had at least read Carlyle's Life of Sterling, Chartism, and judging from his references, the Miscellanies. Smiles to Billio, 23/10/68, Smiles Correspondence, SS/AII/14. Leeds Times, May 30, 1840, p. 6. Smiles, Character, pp. 33, 34, 275, 352. It is most probably that Smiles,

being a voracious reader and well-informed on political and social matters, would have read the greater part of Carlyle's work.

267 Carlyle, "Signs of the Times" (1829), Works, vol. XV, pp. 468, 487. Carlyle, "Novalis" (1829), ibid, vol. XVI, p. 17. Carlyle, "Corn Law Rhymes" (1832), ibid, vol. XVIII, p. 143. References to 'self-help' in Carlyle, "Jean Paul Frederick Richter" (1830), ibid, vol. XVI, p. 94. Carlyle, "Sir Walter Scott" (1838), ibid, vol. XVII, p. 417. Carlyle, On Heroes, pp. 281-82.

268 [Smiles], "Helps to Self-Culture," ECJ, Oct. 4, 1851, vol. V, p. 366. Carlyle, of course, also believed in self-culture: "For the great law of culture is: Let each become all that he was created capable of being; expand, if possible, to his full growth; . . ." Carlyle, "Jean Paul Frederick Richter" (1827), Works, vol. XV, p. 20.

269 [Smiles], "Earnest Purpose," ECJ, Aug. 30, 1851, vol. V, p. 286.

270 [Smiles], "It's all the same!" ibid, March 12, 1853, vol. VIII, pp. 314, 313.

271 Smiles, Character, p. 34, note and pp. 38-40. The reference is from Carlyle's essay on "Sir Walter Scott," see note 267 above.

272 Smiles to grandchildren, 23 Dec. 1887, Smiles Correspondence, SS/AII/129.

273 Smiles, "Money versus Worth," Leeds Times, Oct. 15, 1842, p. 6. Smiles, Character, pp. 33 ff. Smiles, Self-Help, pp. 21, 311.

274 Carlyle, "Past and Present," Works, vol. XIX, p. 194.

275 Smiles, Self-Help, p. 18. Carlyle, On Heroes, p. 319.

276 Comparisons between Smiles and Carlyle are made by Royden Harrison, "Afterword," in Smiles, Self-Help (Sphere Books edition; 1968), p. 265; and Houghton, Victorian Frame of Mind, p. xvi.

[277]The first time'self-help' appears in the Leeds Times is in an excerpt from Emerson, Man, the Reformer, Smiles, "Money versus Worth," Leeds Times, Oct. 15, 1842, p. 6.

[278]Emerson's ideals are analysed in John G. Cawelti, Apostles of the Self-Made Man (Chicago, 1965), pp. 86-98. For Smiles on Napoleon, Smiles, Self-Help, p. 195. Smiles, "Self-Reliance," Leeds Times, July 23, 1842, p. 6.

[279]Smiles, "How is the Community best to be Educated?" ibid, Oct. 5, 1839, p. 4.

[280]Smiles, "Money versus Worth," ibid, Oct. 15, 1842, p. 6. Smiles also mentions Orville Dewey.

[281]Most commentators see Smiles' change from the Leeds Times and politics to business as significant, e.g. Briggs, Victorian People, p. 121; Royden Harrison, "Afterword," p. 266.

[282]Smiles, "Self-Reliance," Leeds Times, July 23, 1842, p. 6. Smiles, "Temperance - Social Progress," ibid, May 28, 1842, p. 7. Smiles, "Legislation for all," ibid, Oct. 8, 1842, p. 4. And other examples occur, e.g. Smiles, "Literature," ibid, Nov. 19, 1842, p. 6.

[283]Smiles, "What is doing for the people in Leeds?" People's Journal, March 7, 1846, vol. I, p. 136.

[284]Alf Mattison papers (Leeds Public Library), Folder 34, p. 3. Smiles to Willie, 2 July 1889, Smiles Correspondence, SS/AII/141.

[285][Smiles], "George Stephenson," ECJ, June 2, 1849, vol. I, p. 65.

[286]Smiles, Autobiography, p. 222 (emphasis mine). Craik's Pursuit of Knowledge was so popular that it was soon out of print, Monica Grobel, "The S.D.U.K.," vol. II, p. 398.

[287]See Appendix E.

[288]Smiles, Self-Help, pp. 333, 335.

[289]Smiles, "What is doing for the people in Leeds?" People's Journal, March 7, 1846, vol. I, p. 137. Smiles, Self-Help, p. 16.

[290]Ibid, pp. 19, 195, 285.

[291]Smiles, "Female Education, I, Social," The Union, Nov. 1, 1842, vol. I, p. 325. Smiles, Self-Help, p. 19. Smiles, Diffusion of Political Knowledge, p. 16.

[292]Smiles, Self-Help, pp. 20, 364.

[293]Ibid, p. 353.

[294]Smiles' position may again be compared with J.S. Mill's, for although Mill was undoubtedly his intellectual superior, their attitudes and changes of mind were very often similar. Thus Mill also came to see that institutional changes really achieved little, and that the influence of the individual was pre-eminent, Robson, Improvement of Mankind, pp. 125 and 127 ff.

[295]Southwood Smith, The Philosophy of Health (2 vols.; London, 1838), vol. I, p. 6.

[296]Smiles, Autobiography, p. 222. The debt was, of course, to G.L. Craik's book on self-education.

[297]Smiles, "The Prevention of Crime," Leeds Times, March 30, 1839, p. 4. Smiles, "Moral Police," ibid, April 27, 1839, p. 4. Smiles, "Bishops versus Education," ibid, July 13, 1839, p. 6.

[298]Smiles, "The Tory Government on Popular Education," ibid, July 23, 1842, p. 4. Smiles, "What are the people doing to educate themselves?" People's Journal, April 18, 1846, vol. I, p. 222.

[299]Smiles, "The Advantages of Political Knowledge to the Working Classes," Leeds Times, Oct. 16, 1841, p. 7. Dr. Smiles, "Robert Nicoll,"

Howitts Journal, Feb. 26, 1848, vol. III, p. 133. (The formation of Smiles as a Radical owed much to the impact of the Reform movement, as the article on Robert Nicoll makes clear, as well as pp. 36-42 in Smiles, Autobiography.) Smiles, "What are the people doing to educate themselves?" People's Journal, April 18, 1846, vol. I, p. 230.

[300]Dr. Smiles, "Victor Hugo," Howitts Journal, June 10, 1848, vol. III, p. 370.

[301]Smiles, Diffusion of Political Knowledge, p. 14. However, Smiles also thought that Chartism had other causes besides the desire for knowledge, including the cheap press, the 1832 agitation, and the desire for individual happiness, ibid, p. 15. J.F.C. Harrison perhaps unduly narrows Smiles' view of Chartism as only a "knowledge agitation," and Harrison's claims that Smiles abandoned Chartism in 1840 and universal suffrage in 1842 should be modified. J.F.C. Harrison, "Chartism in Leeds," in Asa Briggs (ed.), Chartist Studies (Papermac edition; London, 1962), pp. 83, 85.

[302]Report of speech by Smiles, "Anniversary of the Leeds Mutual Instruction Society," Leeds Times, Feb. 28, 1846, p. 3. Report of speech by Smiles, "Grand Soirée of the Odd Fellows," ibid, Dec. 26, 1846, p. 3.

[303][Smiles], "Drill!", ECJ, Nov. 8, 1851, vol. VI, p. 18.

[304]Smiles, National Education. Is the Voluntary Principle adquate to our National Exigencies? A letter from Dr. Smiles, of Leeds, to Edward Baines, Esq., 29 Dec. 1851. Privately printed by the National Public School Association (Manchester, n.d.). [Smiles], "Ignorance is Power," ECJ, Nov. 6, 1852, vol. VIII, p. 30. There is no doubt that Smiles was using fear of revolution as a lever to achieve educational reform, but at the same time (like Disraeli) he evidently felt some considerable sense of

alarm at the separation of the two nations of rich and poor. An amusing example of the way in which mid-Victorian reformers thought of reform as the removal of evils comes from Mary Leman Gillies who stated (prematurely) that "the absence of a system of national education is about to be removed," M.L. Gillies, "National Education," People's Journal, Oct. 24, 1846, vol. II, p. 227.

[305] S. Smiles, "Education of destitute children," ECJ, May 23, 1853, vol. IX, pp. 72, 71.

[306] Smiles, Self-Help, p. 20. [Smiles], "Drill!" ECJ, Nov. 8, 1851, vol. VI, p. 18.

[307] Smiles, Self-Help, p. 20. [Smiles], "Drill!" ECJ, Nov. 8, 1851, vol. VI, p. 18.

[308] Ibid, p. 19. Smiles, "What is doing for the People in Public Amusement and Recreation," People's Journal, July 4, 1846, vol. II, p. 14.

[309] J.H. Newman, The Idea of a University ([1st edition, 1852]; London, 1919), p. 164. Matthew Arnold, Culture and Society (1869), ed. Dover Wilson (Cambridge, 1969), pp. 81, 204.

[310] Smiles, Education of the Working Classes, pp. 4-5. Information on Smiles' lecture, "Self-Education" is from Smiles, "A work that prospered," Good Words, 1877, vol. XVIII, pp. 387, 388-389. Smiles' reference to his Leeds lectures is in Smiles, Self-Help, p. vi.

[311] Cobden to Smiles, Nov. 17, 1853, Hartree Collection, MS 88, and Smiles, Autobiography, p. 174. Confirmation of Smiles' continued belief in tabula rasa psychology comes in an article from Eliza Cook's Journal of 1852 that he rewrote for the American journal, Youth's Companion in 1884. While in 1852 Smiles wrote that the human mind could create nothing apart from what experience and meditation on that experience brought to light, in

1884 Smiles had only shifted very slightly, and wrote that the human mind could "create little," [Smiles], "Gifts of Memory," ECJ, Dec. 4, 1852, vol. VIII, p. 95. Dr. Smiles, "The Gift of Memory," Youth's Companion (Boston), March 20, 1884, vol. V, pp. 113-114. For Smiles' articles in Youth's Companion, see Smiles to Janet Hartree, 14 Feb. 1883, Smiles Correspondence, SS/AI/154.

[312]Smiles, Thrift, pp. 14, 20. Smiles, "Woman, the great social Reformer," The Union April 1, 1842, vol. I, pp. 9, 10.

[313]For example, Smiles characterised the "natural" leaders, the "men of mark" in society, as those men who were not necessarily rich, but who were "of sterling character, of disciplined experience, and of moral excellence," Smiles, Self-Help, p. 290.

[314][Smiles], "Parvenus," ECJ, Feb. 11, 1854, vol. X, pp. 254-55.

## CHAPTER III

## SELF-HELP AND THE SELF-HELP TRADITION

What was Smiles' ideal of self-help? The question has usually been answered in terms of success and social mobility. Portions of Chapter II have been devoted to refuting this idea, which seems to have grown up through a cursory reading by modern critics, rather than through an attentive appreciation of Smiles' work. Hence, even George Orwell (normally a perceptive critic, and one whose books are often concerned with social attitudes toward work) characterises Smiles as proposing the "cult of success," or even "the money-grubbing Smilesian line." On the other hand the Leeds Mercury in an obituary dated 1904 confidently asserted that many supposed Self-Help was

> a glorification of mere success; but nothing was further from the intention of the author than to inculcate by his writings an enlightened form of self-interest not easily distinguishable from sheer selfishness. 'I have tried to rectify the strong tendency toward selfishness,' Dr. Smiles once remarked to an interviewer . . . 'The selfish man becomes a curse to himself and to others. I have never advocated mere money-getting, or working solely for personal advantage.'[1]

If Smiles is accused here of trying to sit on the fence, it is answered that he clearly disliked selfishness and admired unselfishness. Smiles had criticised the way in which from boyhood man was taught to trust to himself as "the only means of pushing his way through the world. The selfish part of his nature is over-developed; the sympathetic scarcely at all." And in a letter concerning the subject of one of his later books, Jasmin, the French barber-poet, Smiles expressed admiration for the barber as "one of the most unselfish beings that ever lived . . ."[2]

Smiles' Self-Help has also been compared to Darwin's The Origin of Species in that both were supposed to have taught the same lesson of struggle for existence and survival of the fit.[3] There is some truth in this comparison, since Smiles certainly considered that life was a struggle, that nature/society "rewarded" the virtuous in relation to their strivings to improve themselves, and that it was necessary for man to adapt to the 'laws' of nature. Smiles was also a strong individualist, and considered that if men did not provide for the future they might "go to the wall." But all these were fairly common attitudes in the mid-Victorian era, and in one important respect Smiles differed from both Darwin and Malthus. Because nature was bountiful he did not think that there were more of the human species born than could survive, and thus the individual did not have to fight with others of the same nation for survival, but only with his own internal vices. The struggle for survival took place within each individual, not between individuals, and adaptation to the laws of nature and economics meant the survival of all, not just the fittest. In only one case before 1859 did Smiles see some kind of survival of the fittest, and that was the conflict of races that occurred during the process of colonisation, where the "weaker races" would "disappear" under the impact of the white colonisers. This was certainly Darwinian, but it did not apply within the species, within Britain, but specifically where races collided, and hence did not apply to the message of Self-Help. Moreover, as previously noted, Smiles was careful to mention the sympathetic side of man, and he recalled that the artisans of the Leeds Mechanics and Temperance Institute learnt equally "sympathy, and the benefits of self-help and mutual help."[4] Lastly it can be argued that Smiles did not conceive of the competitive system of economics as unrestricted, for he was quite prepared to see the Free Trade idea restrained and the removal of urgent evils undertaken.

A comparison of Darwin and Smiles would have more validity, however, if made after 1859, or in the 1830s. By 1832 both had studied medicine at Edinburgh University (Darwin left in 1827 before graduating, and Smiles in 1832), and at that time Smiles was still a sensationalist without qualification, and almost a materialist. But here again the comparison is not a good one, since, from the point of view of the individual, Smiles conceived of the class structure of society as more static than evolutionary, and from the 1840s onward moved toward some form of innate morality of conscience - whereas the struggle for survival favoured social mobility and a neutral morality. Smiles continued to be a sensationalist, but endowed every man with the internal equipment necessary to overcome the environment, and in terms of class-struggle advocated levelling up, rather than dragging down or eliminating. But after 1859 Smiles did seem to catch something of the Darwinian struggle in his descriptions of the invention of machinery and the material progress of the nation. New methods of production were desirable, he thought, "though the weak and unskilled may occasionally be pushed aside, or even trodden underfoot. The consolation which remains is, that while the few suffer, society as a whole is vastly benefitted . . ."[5] Smiles obviously regarded this process as both inevitable and ultimately beneficial, but he did not so much approve the suffering of the few, as record what he thought was actually happening. In any case Smiles did not hold this up as an ideal, nor advocate the survival of the fittest as the rule of life.

Yet, if Smiles' ideal of work and self-help was neither financial success, nor social mobility, nor the grim and selfish survival of the fittest, what then was he trying to say? The answer comes on two levels. The first level constitutes a varied explanation. Smiles conceived of work and self-help as a law of God, and as a necessary adaptation to a pre-established order in nature and society. Work and self-help also logically resulted from the duty of each individual to develop his God-given internal faculties and powers through conflict and cooperation with the environment. Work performed the further function of disciplining the moral faculties and character of the individual. Moreover work and self-help were the obvious means to undercut and discredit the power of the aristocracy and their value system of elegant idleness and conspicuous consumption rather than production and self-denial. Finally, the work of the individual was essential for the progress of the nation toward an ultimate civilisation, and was in some way a repayment for, and continuation of, the work of past generations. This first level of explanation, therefore, as intimated at the beginning of Chapter II, makes use of the five starting points of Religion, Ethics, Psychology, Economics and Politics, to show the varied origins of the ideal of self-help.

The second level of explanation subsumes the first, and is the underlying explanation of all Smiles' strictures on work, character, self-help, and the aristocracy. In a brief phrase, Smiles wanted to reform and improve society by moralising it - he wanted to reform the behaviour of the individuals who were the units that composed society, and particularly to improve the condition of the working classes by improving their behaviour. Smiles' message was obviously aimed at the moral improvement of the character of the individual rather than external success, for as he once remarked, the motive power of society were the men of character and conscience, "it is moral qualities . . . which rule the world . . ." Moral reform also appealed to Smiles because early in life he had seen attempts to reform, educate and punish individuals with physical force, and the sight had not only struck him "with horror," but in his own case he had been able to compare the physical cruelty of one schoolmaster with the "moral suasion" of another who had nevertheless maintained "perfect order," so that he soon learned to appreciate moral persuasion rather than physical coercion. In the same way Smiles disapproved of the physical force Chartists and their method of reform, and the physical violence of the mob - "always the biggest of despots."[6] It was natural, therefore, that Smiles should seek a moral solution to the condition of the working classes (and others), and if, as Smiles believed, the nation was only the sum of its individuals, and if reform from above had failed, or was simply not feasible, then the way to reform society was to reform the individual.

Smiles came to think that the unhappy condition of the working class was "the result of moral causes" and that therefore "the end of all reform is the improvement of the individual. Everything that is wrong in society results from that which is wrong in the individual. When men are bad, society is bad."[7] With this problem in mind, Smiles had recourse to the only solution which was available to him from his inherited value system, and that was the improvement of society through the old moral virtues as expressed in the phrase 'Heaven helps those who help themselves.' As he noted, this advice was as old-fashioned "as the Proverbs of Solomon," but, in a Divinely-ruled rational world of cause and effect, if men could be brought to an habitual reliance on a spirit of self-help, everything else would follow. The assumption of the spirit of self-help was important because it represented an internal conversion - a moral reform - and thus was "the root of all virtues, knowledge, freedom and prosperity."[8] It was the organic seed from which all the branches of virtue sprang.

Moral reform was generated in two ways. The first means was the way in which people often seemed to unconsciously imitate their betters. The need was for outstanding models and examples, because if in 1838 Smiles had relied on a sensationalist psychology and early domestic training, by 1859 he acknowledged that the training would have to be done by arousing the spririt of self-help through the stimulating example of heroic models and their true biographies. So, for example, in 1846 Smiles wrote an article pointing out "for admiration and encouragement" certain workers for the people, and in particular Richard Cobden, one of the best specimens of English character: "Would that all Englishmen strove to imitate him!"[9] Obviously biography had its drawbacks from the point of view of effectiveness, and Smiles preferred the early training that parents, and especially mothers, could give, although models did have the advantage of extending beyond childhood, and of unfolding a wide range of virtues to be imitated. And, to reiterate, Smiles used his models to demonstrate not the results to be achieved, but the virtues revealed in the struggle.

The second means of producing moral reform was through the actual formation of character by the individual. This could be achieved partly through Smiles' broad concept of "education," stimulating men to discipline themselves to moral habits and character through contact with the "school of life" (or if "helpless" be disciplined in an actual school); and partly through the struggle to conquer internal vices. In the latter case, the struggle to overcome internal deviations would be supplemented by the heroic battle against external difficulties, and both struggles would be initially stimulated by the adoption of the spirit of self-help. Thus both "education" and the initial struggle for internal control and external independence were the starting points, and the final product was the disciplined character. Once again the most striking omission in Self-Help was that of any particular goal or aim to be achieved (apart from 'independence') and the logical deduction is that Smiles wanted to emphasise the struggle (and hence the formation of character) rather than the end result.

Self-Help was in fact supposed to be a moral guide to the conduct of everyday life - a guide principally for the new reading public of the artisans and mechanics, who had no continuity of class experience to fall back upon, and whose expectancy of the future lacked suitable models. In this sense Self-Help falls into the category of those Victorian etiquette books which were beginning to appear in mid-century, such as How to Behave: A Pocket Manual of Etiquette, and guide to Correct Personal Habits (Glasgow, 1865). Just as these etiquette books explained the means by which the untutored could identify socially acceptable forms of behaviour, so Self-Help explained the way in which work, perseverence and other virtues were the correct forms of behaviour to follow in the new industrial society. Moreover, these virtues were evidence of true moral worth to Smiles' classless elite (the 'true' gentlemen) and as such, socially acceptable in that elevated sphere of society which depended for its identification on internal merit rather than outward rank or show. And, of course, members of this elite could be identified through their characters; character being the "crown and glory of life . . . the noblest possession of man, constituting a rank in itself . . ."[10] Hence Self-Help was quite consciously something of an etiquette book (especially the last chapter, "Character: The True Gentleman"), but it obviously contained a more earnest appeal than outward refinement of manners - it encouraged some kind of "religious" conversion experience - the internal moral reform of the character of the individual.

More surprising, perhaps, is that this encouragement registered some success, as the surviving evidence indicates. One letter to Smiles claims that Self-Help "came in the nick of time. I read it, and pondered over it until it seized entire hold of me; . . ." another wrote that the book "helped me to a new life and I now look upon it as my prayer book. Because every time I read it I feel as if I have been born anew." Another letter from a grateful father reports that his son's reading of Self-Help "has been the cause of an entire alteration in his mode of life . . ." In the same vein a reader mentions that Character did him more good that "all the Sermons I have heard, for years" and promises to follow Smiles' examples and "obey the precepts there laid down . . ."[11] The parallel to the way in which religious conversion alters a person's entire life (as with the Methodists) is clear, and the end result was much the same, industry and temperance instead of idleness and drunkeness.

This emphasis on character and moral improvement suggests that the message of Self-Help (like Smiles' own life) was aimed toward an inner-directed regulation of life. Smiles' own attitudes toward work and society had been 'set going' by his early parental and religious instruction; had been stimulated by various sanctions along the way, including guilt and anxiety (for example, Smiles' guilt complex about the past, and his frequent repetition of the phrase "I could not be idle"); and had been further regulated by a number of internalised 'principles'. Self-Help was the medium through which Smiles expressed and passed on his own inner-directed discipline to the new (and some of the old) reading public and to those who apparently required a written guide to the conduct of life. If education (however little), the press, and changing work roles had given the new working classes a measure of individuality and independence, so Self-Help was a means (conscious or unconscious) of guiding and disciplining those newly found possibilities.[12]

Such guidance and discipline were necessary because ultimately Smiles was thinking of national progress toward an eventual higher civilisation through the moral reform of the individuals constituting the nation. To this end Smiles developed the insight that if progress required some form of freely competitive society (however modified), then that same society required a corresponding moral discipline. Just in proportion as society rejected government intervention and state power as the means of progress, and permitted an individualism of self-help and free opportunity for all men, so would this individualism have to be balanced by moral discipline. It need not arouse surprise, then, that Smiles "could not resist the magic of organised discipline"[13] for such discipline was the essential *alter ego* of the self-help ideal. It was for this reason that Smiles took the paradoxical position (like Matthew Arnold's balance of Hebraism and Hellenism) that education in the broad sense should provide an independence of spirit linked with a moral discipline of character. Moreover, Smiles' Calvinist youth had prepared him for this conclusion, since as R.H. Tawney once observed, Calvinism contained two disparate elements, "it had at once given a whole-hearted *imprimatur* to the life of business enterprise . . . and had laid upon it the restraining hand of an inquisitorial discipline." Hence the Calvinistic emphasis on character and self-control as the necessary groundwork for this disciplined attitude toward work.[14] Furthermore Smiles believed that work and thrift were the necessary foundations of civilisation (unlike the mid 20th Century tendency toward a rejection of the values of work and self-denial) and like Freud, he understood that civilisation had been built up through a considerable measure of self-repression and guilt. And so Smiles produced an appropriate message for his time, the ideal of self-help and the gospel of work.

These two levels of explanation (work internalised and rationalised, and the underlying moral reform) may help to explain the message and the medium, but not the author. For here a curious dichotomy of personality appears. The study of Smiles the man reveals a constant tension between ideals, a tension that came from the conflict between the 18th Century and the 19th Century view of man and society, as might be expected from a well-educated and politically involved individual whose life (1812-1904) began close to the 18th Century and spanned the entire Victorian age. This tension is particularly evident in Smiles' original occupation as a doctor, surely a profession involving more mutual help than self-help. Again Smiles' problem with determinism and free will in relation to the early authoritarian training of the child and its lasting effects, was an outcome of 18th Century sensationalist psychology in conflict with the reformer's 19th Century stress on the liberty, will power, capabilities and dignity of every individual. Other tensions are illustrated in Smiles' uneasy balance between potentially opposite positions: self-help and cooperation, work internalised and work rationalised, self-education and national education, individual reform and organic political reform, private economy and political economy, and, quite strikingly, the claims of individual self-development versus the requirements of national development. Perhaps the real problem was that Smiles was trying to use two different concepts of the individual: man as swayed by passions and prejudice versus man as rational; and again, man as full of potential (capable of developing all his powers and faculties) versus man as trapped within the inexorable laws of society, economics and historical development. In short, Smiles' view of the nature and function of man was split between the conflicting principles of self-development and the authority of natural law and past experience.

With this analysis in mind, the question of Smiles' relationship to the Victorian work ethic may be raised. It will be recalled that Chapter I presented an outline of several attitudes that seemed to be evident at mid-century, including Rational, Promethean, and Protean concepts of work. Smiles related to the polar positions of Carlyle (Promethean) and the Utilitarians (Rational) without ever becoming totally committed to either, for while on the one hand Smiles paralleled the religious (Calvinist) and inherited values of work, moral purpose, intuitive conscience, and internal will power of Carlyle, yet he never reached Carlyle's almost frantic externalisation and dedication to work.[15] On the other hand Smiles followed the rationalism, sensationalism, political economy, belief in education, and politics of the Radicals and Utilitarians without ever admiring the pursuit of pleasure and wealth through the hedonistic calculus of the work and reward equation. At the same time Smiles added a third dimension to his ideal of self-help by expressing ideas that were particularly close to the Protean attitude toward work - individual self-culture, self-improvement and self-reform (with assists from Channing, the Combe brothers, and Scottish faculty psychology). The ideal of self-help therefore formed a tenuous triangular relationship of religious/inherited values, rationalism, and self-improvement.

It can be argued that this relationship of ideas (together with a fourth impulse, Smiles' opposition to the aristocratic-government complex) formed a distinctive self-help ideal. Distinctive because although drawing on some of the work attitudes mentioned above and in Chapter I, Smiles' ideal was not identical with any of them, and was particularly set apart by the incorporation of the possibilities of self-culture and self-development into his concept of self-help. The addition of self-culture, and the opposition to government and aristocracy, gave a progressive slant to what would otherwise have been a somewhat authoritarian and traditional set of values, even if the ultimate goal was to be a splendid future state of civilisation. However, it can also be argued that Smiles' position was not unique at mid-century. There was, for example, a 'Self-Help Association' operating from 1847 in Edwinstone (near Nottingham), composed largely of Odd Fellows (the particular Friendly Society that Smiles had been closely connected with in Leeds in the 1840s). This Society stressed some of the ideas that Smiles had advocated in Leeds - cooperation, association and thrift. "By self-help you will raise your class," predicted the founder of the Association, to moral worth, and "to be industrious and honest, and to enjoy the reward of labour, [which] is God's true patent of nobility . . ."[16]

Furthermore, the means (and often the message) which Smiles used to put forward his ideal - biography - was something of a commonplace in Victorian literature by mid-century. E.P. Hood, writing in 1852, thought one value of biography was that "it possesses the power of transfusing character into the reader." This was important because "the great cause of failures in life, of all weakness, of much sin and suffering is the want of character; few men are trained to a proper sense of their individual value, of their own proper power." And Hood went on to declare that didactic biography taught the "elegance and dignity of self-help . . ." G.J. Holyoake also saw that biography helped to form character and decision, and William Robinson believed that "no species of composition operates at once so powerfully and so beneficialy on the morals of readers as biography," for biography "touches the mainspring of virtuous action."[17] Because biography was the <u>true</u> story of the lives of noble men and women, it was thought to be capable of favourably influencing and improving the internal character of the reader.

However, biography could teach many lessons, and <u>Self-Help</u> certainly offered a wide variety of suggestions, including the need to struggle toward moral and financial independence. Inevitably the temptation arose to go beyond Smiles' limited goal of independence toward social or financial success, and this was the case with the Rev. Anderson (Congregational) who published a book in 1861 entitled <u>Self Made Men</u>. Thus Anderson condemned those who remained in their "present position" after seeing so many examples of social mobility - yet also contrived to sound much like Smiles' ideal of imitative self-help:

> Intercourse with superior minds is an important means of self-culture; but it is sometimes difficult to find suitable acquaintances. Biographies of men, who have honoured their country by their virtues and talents, are within the reach of all. In these books we see noble and encouraging specimens of men, self-raised and self-advanced . . . who have triumphed [not by fortune or genius] . . . but by industry, perseverence, fidelity to duty, and the wise use of . . . opportunities. Coming in contact with such examples, you are . . . constrained to tread in their footsteps . . .[18]

Anderson, who had read Smiles' <u>Life of George Stephenson</u>, was at one with Smiles in thinking that "example is the plastic power that draws. Imitation is one of the great characteristics of the human species . . ."

Anderson was also an exponent of the self-help ideal in pressing for the moral reform of the individual, and particularly the importance of habits in forming character: "Separate acts, frequently repeated, form character; character yields consequences; consequences are often irreparable. Habit is a second nature . . ." The emphasis on internal perfection was the striking element of Anderson's book, and, as with Smiles' advice on self-conquest, the advice of Self Made Men was based on the belief that the enemy lay within - self-control, perseverence, hard work and will power were necessary because of "evil habits, appetites and passions."[19]

Anderson also shared with Smiles an opposition to the aristocracy, and a corresponding interest in the cultivation of the faculties and powers of *every* individual. Self-culture, the development of the faculties and powers of the individual, was a very strong theme in Victorian thought, especially when linked with the idea that God had placed the underdeveloped faculties in man for the explicit purpose of their development by the individual. This theme was of course a component of Smiles' thought, and one author who had read Smiles and who favoured this aspect of the self-help ideal was the Methodist, William Unsworth. Writing in 1861, Unsworth quoted Smiles several times, and stated his intention of encouraging the moral and social elevation of the working classes: "God helps those who help themselves," noted Unsworth, and "were it but universally acted upon, society would be speedily revolutionised . . . [It] would entirely annihilate nine-tenths of the evils which now curse and afflict the commonwealth." Self-help menat the "cultivation of the powers and faculties nature has given you . . . to the greatest degree . . . to improve your own condition here . . ." For Unsworth, self-help and self-culture were the obvious answers to the problems of the working classes, as they were for E.P. Hood, who wrote in 1852: "It is beginning to be seen that the chief end of man . . . is the development of all his faculties, capacities, and affections . . ."[20]

It has been pointed out in Chapter II that Smiles' ideal of self-help also originated in some degree from G.L. Craik's study of self-education under difficulties. A parallel line of development in the self-help tradition can be seen in those volumes inspired by Craik's work, such as Capel Lofft's Self-Formation; or, the History of an Individual Mind: Intended as a guide for the intellect through difficulties to success (1837), which advised self-sufficiency, energy, determination, and perseverence as the means of overcoming difficulty; or in the case of T. Claxton's Hints to Mechanics, On Self-Education and Mutual Instruction (1839) which also drew on Craik's book (and George Combe) and which anticipated Smiles in many respects. Claxton praised the value of internalised principles and character, and felt that

> there are no circumstances so bad but that they may be bettered by one's own efforts, nor any obstacles to self-improvement so serious that energy and industry, and courage and perseverence, will not triumphantly surmount them all. This book is full of instances wherein men have done this . . .[21]

However, Claxton's ideal of self-help led not toward Smiles' concept, but in the direction of the Rev. Anderson's Self Made Men and Henry Birkett, the story of a man who helped himself (1860). That is, toward the promise of financial gain and social mobility as well as character formation and principled behaviour.[22] On the other hand, Smiles' concept of self-help (and William Unsworth's), tended to concentrate on character formation and moral reform without dwelling on their results.

Indeed a remarkable number of books were published from the 1850s onward emphasising the formation of character, self-help in the face of difficulty, and the struggle for moral improvement. "Help yourselves! God helps those who help themselves!" declaimed one anonymous author of religious persuasion in 1852: "in the race of life character is everything" for a noble character "is always more than gold!" In 1860, another nameless author described industrious habits and purposeful determination as invincible qualities likely to "do anything" in the world, but still directed the readers' attention not to the acquirement of "worldly fame, but to the formation of a heavenly mind and character." And an S.P.C.K. writer recommended a hero who possessed the "self-reliance of a strong character" and the determination toward self-improvement, which was "the true secret of success" - yet the ultimate message was not wealth and comfort, but only duty in "that state of life" assigned by God.[23] These attitudes did not properly correspond to Smiles' ideal of self-help, for in the main they were attempts by the Church and its affiliates to turn men's minds away from the snares of the world, and back to introspection, self-examination and religion. Nevertheless, Smiles' own stress on character originated largely from his religious values, and although he was more progressive in relation to the potential of the individual, his negative attitude toward the government drove him close to the same introspective position.

Smiles' ideal of self-help received recognition in 1861 from a lecture delivered to the Y.M.C.A. by the Rev. T. Pearson. It will be recalled that Smiles had feared the growing mechanism of the day, and the way in which education was made too easy - that is, education was divested, in Smiles' eyes, of its need for persevering labour. The Rev. Pearson equally condemned the age of "calculating machines and ready-reckoners . . ." and declared that the "heroism our age most needs is resolute loyalty to deliberately-formed convictions." The Rev. Pearson's convictions pointed toward "the utmost possible self-culture, self-help, self-action, compatible with the welfare of the whole," for "Saviour-help accrues only where there is individual determined self-help." Predictably the lecturer asked for individual reform, and the determination "to improve your moral, social, and intellectual status." This question of individual moral reform (the underlying message of Self-Help) was, not surprisingly, common to many church groups, and in the same series of Y.M.C.A. lectures, the Rev. James Bardsley delivered an address entitled "The Formation of English Character," in which he declared that "God's method of reforming society is to reform individuals . . ." But as a secularised message it was also in vogue before 1859: "personal reform is at the root of all national improvement," wrote Joseph Bentley in 1852, and in 1850 the ubiquitous E.P. Hood defined moral reformers as "those who believe that all healthy change is organic, and must commence within; this is the first principle of all action . . ."[24]

The mention of E.P. Hood brings to a useful close these observations on the self-help tradition, for if anyone could be said to represent such a tradition before (and after) the publication of Self-Help, it was E.P. Hood. The author of some eleven books in the 1850s, Hood frequently used the phrase 'self-help,' and in nearly every respect, paralleled Smiles' ideal of self-help. That is to say, he favoured self-education and self-culture, opposed government intervention and the power of the aristocracy, felt that character and moral reform was more important than the search for success, upheld the individuality of man against religious, economic and political intolerance, favoured the use of biography as an agent of self-help ("All real biography is constantly saying to us, 'Be thyself! Help thyself!'"), warned of the value of time and opportunity, and above all urged the duty of work:

> Better . . . to work hard, even to the shortening of existence, than to eat and sleep away the precious gift of life, giving no other cognizance of its possession. By work, or industry, of whatever kind it may be, we give a practical knowledge of the vale of life, of its high intentions, of its manifold duties. Earnest, active industry, is a living hymn of praise, a never-failing source of happiness; it is obediance, for it is God's great law of moral existence.

Like Smiles, Hood wanted to encourage those who would help themselves, without going too much the other way and fomenting the worship of Mammon and a restless discontent with social status. Hood's intention, as he noted in his book, Self-Education (1851), was simply "to hold out a hand to those who, by the circumstances around then, are compelled to be self-helpers . . ."[25]

To summarise the preceding description of the self-help ideal as outlined by Smiles and others is difficult, for Self-Help itself was in a sense a Gospel - many would come to drink at the fountain, and go away replenished in numerous different ways. As far as Smiles was concerned, four points can be made. Firstly, he finally came to the conclusion that the remedy for social ills lay with the individual, and so logically the first step was individual moral improvement. Secondly, Smiles did not wish to advocate success so much as character formation and consistent behaviour - in particular, hard work and a persevering application to duty and vocation. Moreover, his negative attitude toward success reflected a desire to raise the condition of the entire working class, and not merely the occasional individual. Thirdly, the ideal of self-help aimed at a manly individualism, embracing independence not only in opposition to the interests of the aristocracy and the government - a moral independence -

but also from surrounding circumstances, difficulties and poverty - an independence of thrift and will power. And fourthly, Smiles achieved a somewhat uneasy compromise between his reformer's instinct and his sense of religious and inherited values - hence Self-Help was an interesting via media between the needs of the individual, the needs of the nation, and the need to conform to a transcendent structure of moral values and natural law.

As far as other supporters of the self-help tradition were concerned, they too thought of it as primarily a solution (in an age that generally denied the value of government intervention) to the problems of society and the condition of the working classes. Starting originally in the drive for self-education among the Mutual Improvement Societies and the Mechanics Institutes, the self-help tradition concentrated on individual improvement, whether in the Protean sense of character formation, or more liberally as self-culture and the development of the powers or faculties of the individual. But by the 1860s the self-help tradition faced the dilemma of either having to emphasise its rewards in terms of concrete financial success and social mobility - the self made man[26] - or of continuing to concentrate on the moral virtues, self-improvement, and limited aims of Smiles' brand of self-help. Most authors chose the via media of Smiles' solution, and it was only toward the end of the century that financial or social success came to be separated from the accompanying virtues of character, hard work and perseverence. But that is a story for another chapter.[27]

Smiles' Self-Help also dwelt extensively on another point - the need for individual and national power and energy. This was natural in view of the quantified Victorian approach to understanding the universe, and their strong sense of the 'opposition' to man of difficulties, circumstances, matter and mechanical/natural laws. It is in this context that the cult of manliness can be explained, for man had to conquer not only his inner self, but had also to meet a considerable external challenge. Hence Smiles' books often dealt with the reassuring triumphs of the power of man, whether industrial, technical, or individual. An explication on this subject (and a description of the public reception of Self-Help) will be found in the following chapter.

## Chapter III - Footnotes

[1]George Orwell, "Charles Dickens" (1939) in George Orwell, A Collection of Essays (Doubleday Anchor Book edition; New York, 1954), pp. 109, 74. Clipping from Leeds Mercury, April 18, 1904, p. 5 in Alf Mattison Papers (Leeds Public Library), Folder 34.

[2]Smiles, "Female Education, I, Social," The Union, Nov. 1, 1842, vol. I, p. 322. Smiles to Jack Hartree, 13 March 1889, Smiles Correspondence, SS/AI/212.

[3]Sir James Baillie, Address delivered at Zion School, Wortley, Dec. 4, 1937 (typewritten; Leeds Public Library), p. 2. And see Jacques Barzun, Darwin, Marx, Wagner (Doubleday Anchor Book edition; New York, 1958), p. 37.

[4]Smiles, "A work that prospered," Good Words, 1877, vol. XVIII, p. 392.

[5]Smiles, Industrial Biography, p. 210.

[6][Smiles], "Quite the Gentleman," ECJ, May 22, 1852, vol. VII, p. 62. Smiles, Autobiography, pp. 17, 9-11, 123, 37. Obviously Smiles was not alone in favouring moral reform - witness Thomas Arnold, Matthew Arnold, Carlyle, Harriet Martineau and others.

[7]Smiles, Thrift, pp. 51, 52.

[8]Smiles, Self-Help, p. (v). [Smiles], "Providing against the evil day," ECJ, Oct. 6, 1849, vol. I, pp. 354-355.

[9]Smiles, "Men of the People. Richard Cobden," People's Journal, July 25, 1846, vol. II, pp. 44, 46.

[10]Smiles, Self-Help, p. 376.

[11]Smiles, Autobiography, p. 226; Anon to Smiles, n.d., Smiles Correspondence, typewritten copy between SS/AIX/182; Joseph Watson to Smiles, Jan. 26, 1872, ibid, SS/AIX/184.

[12]It will be recognised that some of this paragraph is based on David Reisman's The Lonely Crowd (Yale paperbound edition; New Haven and London, 1961), especially pp. 24-25, 88-89. It is significant that Smiles described one of the later 'self-help' books, Character (1871), in terms of guidance values, that is, as providing examples of "noble behaviour," Smiles, Autobiography, p. 293.

[13]Briggs, Victorian People, p. 127

[14]Tawney, Religion, p. 194, and pp. 101, 191 for the emphasis on character.

[15]Although Smiles later expressed a more explicitly Promethean attitude, for example, "by labour man has subjugated the world, reduced it to his dominion, and clothed the earth with a new garment, . . ." Smiles, Men of Invention and Inudstry (London, 1884), p. 107.

[16]Smiles' link with the Odd Fellows is detailed in Smiles, Autobiography, pp. 141-42. The 'Self-Help Association' was discussed in "Self-Help," The Herald of Cooperation, Jan. 1848, no. 13, p. 102, and the quote is from the founder, Christopher Thomson, Autobiography of an Artisan (London, 1847), p. 385 (also p. 378 for mention of Odd Fellows).

[17]E.P. Hood, The Uses of Biography, Romantic, Philosophic and Didactic (London, 1852), pp. 28, 29, 108. G.J. Holyoake, The Value of Biography in the Formation of Individual Character (London, 1845), p. 15. Robinson, Self-Education, pp. 52, 53. See also J.S. Blackie, On Self-Culture Intellectual, Physical and Moral, A Vade Mecum for Young Men and Students

(Edinburgh, 1874), p. 81, who declared "there is no kind of sermon so effective as the example of a great man."

[18]Anderson, Self Made Men, pp. 303, 286.

[19]Ibid, pp. 127, 289-290, 42. For other common examples of the importance placed at this time on self-control, cf. "the still greater conquest of himself," Edgeworth, Fireside Stories, p. 23, and Blackie, On Self Culture, p. 58.

[20]Unsworth, Self-Culture, pp. 4, 6, and for references to Self-Help, pp. 10, 24, 48. Hood, Common Sense, p. 132. Similar statements can be found in any number of books and lectures, including for example, Edward Baines' notes for a lecture to the Leeds Literary Society in the 1840s, in Baines Collection (Archives, Leeds Public Library), MS 52, p. 20: "every human being comes upon the stage of active life, charged with important duties, gifted with faculties for the fulfillment of those duties, and responsible therefore for the cultivation or neglect of those faculties . . ."

[21]Capel Lofft, Self-Formation; or, the History of an Individual Mind: Intended as a guide for the intellect through difficulties to success (2 vols., London, 1837), vol. II, pp. 109, 113. Timothy Claxton, Hints to Mechanics, On Self-Education and Mutual Instruction (London, 1839), p. 149, and for Craik, pp. 107, 182-83, and Combe pp. 63, 111.

[22]Henry Birkett, for example, noticed "the opportunities which were afforded to young men for self-improvement . . . He noticed one after another 'rising from the ranks,' obtaining promotion . . ." These self-improvers belonged to "a class of men which in England is not uncommon, but yet is hardly understood," Henry Birkett, pp. 278, 333. On

the other hand, Robinson's Self-Education was in the self-education to moral self-help line, rather than self-education to succes.

[23]Hammers and Ploughshares (London, 1852), pp. 74, 41 (written for the Nonconformist publishers, Partridge and Oakley). Men who were Earnest: The Springs of their Action and Influence (London, 1860), pp. 121, 203. The Village Beech-Tree (S.P.C.K.), pp. 102, 223, 256. G.J. Holyoake also published a book referring to cooperation as the "art of self-help," Self-Help by the People. History of Cooperation in Rochdale (London, 1858), p. 1. The Victorian interest in character has also been discussed in Chapter I through the Protean attitude toward work.

[24]Rev. T. Pearson, "Individuality," Lectures delivered before the Y.M.C.A., pp. 97, 117, 93, 113. Rev. James Bardsley, "The Formation of English Character," ibid, p. 374. Joseph Bentley, Health and Wealth (London, 1852), p. 293. E.P. Hood (ed.), The Moral Reformer's Almanack, a manual of advancement and civilisation (London, 1850), p. 3. Hood became a Congregationalist minister in 1852.

[25]Hood, Uses of Biography, pp. 110, 139; E.P. Hood, Self-Eduction: Twelve Chapters for Young Thinkers (London, 1851), p. 26.

[26]The rejection of the paternalism of the past, and the symbolic enshrinement of the self-made man is strikingly captured by the Rev. Thomas Binney: "Unquestionably, the greatest thing that can be said of a man is, that he had no father; that he sprang from nothing, and made himself; that he was born mud and died marble," cited in Anderson, Self Made Men, title page.

[27]See Chapter VI, opening pages.

## CHAPTER IV

## *Self-Help* AND AFTER - BIOGRAPHY, TECHNOLOGY AND THE NEW MERITOCRACY

*Self-Help* was published toward the close of 1859, and was received with cautious praise. Periodicals such as the 'improving' magazine of the Edinburgh Chambers brothers, *Chambers' Journal*, and the individualistic *Reasoner* predictably liked the work, while on the other hand the more conservative *Macmillan's Magazine* cautioned that self-help might arouse too much selfishness: "Help-scorning is no true manly habit," since it might impair the truest culture of self and also prevent a readiness to help others. The reviewer noted that *Self-Help* should and did prove "how real and how worthy is the help that the self-helper must and does receive from others," and pointed out that it was God who really provided help for the self-helper. Evidently this reviewer felt that *Self-Help* was, in some sense, a secularising book, emphasising independence of self rather than humility and spiritual dependence. A more accurate review, however, came from J.A. Froude's socially-conscious *Fraser's Magazine*, which estimated the message to be "above all, strict conscientiousness in the performance . . . of whatever duty may be nearest us in the common life of everyday." This meant a serious acceptance of one's work and social status, explained the reviewer, for all should "do their duty in that state of life to which it has pleased God to call them." Nor should one forget that there was no work or knowledge to be pursued in the grave "whither they are all hastening." This earnest review was written in June 1860, and it noted that a second edition of *Self-Help* was already off the press, and 20,000 copies sold of the first edition.[1]

During the 1860s the phrase 'self-help' and the book itself slipped into the popular mythology as a paradigm or touchstone of social attitudes. Even the Grand Old Man, Gladstone himself, proclaimed "it is SELF-HELP that makes the man . . ." and that thrift was the means "by which Self-Help for the masses . . . is principally made effective."[2] An opposing social philosophy was put forward by George Potter, the Trades Union leader, in 1861. Potter singled out Smiles for attack:

> We are perpetually told to follow George Stephenson, and Benjamin Franklin, and a few other exceptional, mighty geniuses of mind, and giants in body set forth in "Self-Help" as guides and examples for universal attainment. Verily working men would be fools to dream of a better future, or seek its realisation; but double-distilled we should be, to follow these Solomons; in hopes of either health, life, or comfort or remuneration . . . Were our would-be teachers a little more reasonable perhaps they would be more attended to. Away then with the falsehood of telling working men: ceaseless work is their only doom, and poverty their destiny, and that this is the decree of providence, the order of nature. No other meaning can be the end of such advice . . .[3]

That was not actually the meaning of *Self-Help*, but it did touch the ideal of self-help at its weakest point, namely the limited value of seeing individual reform as the most likely solution to the condition of the working classes. On the other hand an anonymous author (perhaps with deliberate sarcasm) used the pseudonym "Self-Help" in penning an Owenite pamphlet calling for cooperative production, strikes, and an exchange of goods based on labour-value, in order to "extinguish the middle class tyranny . . ."[4] The phrase "self-help" was also equated with *laissez-faire*, and criticised on those grounds - one article in 1866, for example, attacked those philosophers of recent years who had warned against government assistance as likely to "undermine the incentives to self-help."[5] In general Smiles' contemporaries in the 1860s did not read

Self-Help with much more care than his modern critics, or perhaps did not read his book at all, as seems likely in the case of Charles Knight, publisher for the Society for the Diffusion of Useful Knowledge, who stated erroneously that "the great distinction between the love of knowledge for its own sake, and the love of knowledge as the means of worldly advancement may be traced very distinctly in the two popular volumes of Mr. Craik, and the equally popular "Self-Help" of Mr. Smiles."[6]

Ironically, the publication of Self-Help occurred just as public opinion was beginning to turn away from individualistic opposition to government intervention. Self-Help was a book for the 1850s, not for the 1860s and beyond.[7] One example of the change in the 1860s was a book that the agnostic and independent minded Frances Power Cobbe wrote in 1867, entitled Hours of Work and Play:

> The simple fact forces itself upon us, that religious instruction and secular education, churches, schools, clubs, institutes . . . are all inadequate to cure the dreadful evil in question [poverty]. Other forces must be brought to bear . . . [i.e. government intervention].[8]

The debates over the Companies Acts (1856-1862), to take another example, signalled a similar change in public attitudes toward laissez-faire individualism. Limited Liability and Joint Stock Companies represented an effort to facilitate the use of capital, and at the same time protect the entrepreneurs and stockholders, by restricting the financial responsibilities of those who utilised capital in a joint venture. Thus the link that Smiles saw between individual effort and result (the necessary incentive for a competitive society) was at least weakened, if not broken. In this vein, one opponent of Limited Liability remarked indignantly: "That risk should in all cases accompany profit seems so perfectly reasonable, that I cannot understand how it can be impugned."

Another professed astonishment: "It was perfectly absurd to suppose that ordinary trades could be carried on by companies as well and as prosperously as by individuals." And a third did not believe that any Company

> could command that decision of purpose, that untiring exertion, and that concentrated power which an individual, whose sole interest was at stake, could always display. In fact, no Company could exist in competition against an energetic tradesman who understood his business, and who was industrious, honest, and persevering.[9]

On the other hand, as if to illustrate the complexities of a growing industrial society into which Smiles had in some sense stumbled with his easy solutions of character, work and thrift, one of the supporters of Limited Liability claimed that the measure was in fact a Free Trade Bill, which would permit the lower and middle classes to consolidate capital "enabling the poor and enterprising to better their condition . . ." It was, said Viscount Palmerston, "a question of free trade against monopoly" [monopoly of the large capitalists].[10] Curiously enough both sides invoked the authority of Free Trade, and one opponent even appealed to the causal link between labouring in a trade, and the necessary incentive of profit and loss in that trade, as a "natural law which it is beyond the province of legislation to interfere with . . ."[11] The whole argument really centred on the nature of a competitive society, and the kind of adjustment to a competitive system which would facilitate economic progress and allow safe entry into that system for some at least of the middle and lower classes. Smiles would have approached the argument in a characteristically ambivalent fashion, approving the opening up of the system, and disapproving of the human alteration of the natural proportionality of individual energy to its results. That the individual should be responsible for the profit of his work, but not for all the risks of that work, was not part of the cause and effect thinking of self-help.[12]

Furthermore, the formation of Limited Liability companies restricted the role of the individual in at least two areas - the need for team work rather than individual work, and the need for a different set of skills than those prized by Smiles. However, Smiles' set of values were almost completely formed by 1859, and so his books after that date continued to fix on the values of self-help, work and character. But there was a difference: Smiles' production after 1859 concentrated almost entirely on two areas - either biographical treatment of individuals involved with industrial and technological invention and discovery (whereas Self-Help had dealt to a considerable extent with the arts and cultural matters), or biographies of strongly individualistic men, overcoming great hardships in the cause of science and other pursuits.

Smiles' continued emphasis on biography was in accord with his belief that the story of virtuous and hard working lives were valuable as models of moral character for imitation by the still unformed characters of the new reading public. As William and Robert Chambers were to put it, biography provided "the great educational principle of imitation, which, though inferior to training and exercise, has a decided advantage over precept . . ."[13] And so although Smiles thought that Boswell's Johnson and Lockhart's Scott were the two best biographies he had read, his own efforts were aimed as much at encouragement as at literary merit. The "great lesson of biography," wrote Smiles, was "to teach what man can be and can do at his best. It may thus give each man renewed strength and confidence. The humblest, in sight of even the greatest, may admire, and hope and take courage." Hence Smiles' biographies followed Self-Help in emphasising models of character and behaviour, and he refused requests to write the official biographies of various individuals, including Macdonell, editor of the London Times, and J.B. Smith, one of the leaders of the Anti Corn Law League, evidently because they did not fit into his category of suitable examples.[14]

Indeed, the one biography that Smiles was pressured to write, that of George Moore, the merchant, he found boring and disliked, almost it seems because Moore "made a lot of money," while the life of Robert Dick, the penniless but self-helping Thurso baker and geologist, was much more to his liking.[15] Characteristically, however, Smiles found a suitable social message in Moore's hard work and eventual philanthropy: "Character is the true antiseptic of society. The good deed leaves an indelible stamp . . . [T]he great worker lives for ever in the memory of his race." Similarly Robert Dick's life was "an encouragement to others," for he had perfected "himself in knowledge" and advanced the cause of science, while honestly pursuing his calling as a baker. "It is by men such as he," Smiles noted approvingly, "that the character of a country is elevated to the highest standard, and raised in the scale of nation."[16] And like the life of Dick, the biography of Thomas Edward showed how a man in humble and difficult circumstances could persevere in the cause of science. It was families like the Edwards', argued Smiles, "that maintain the character and constitute the glory of their country."[17] Thus the character of the individual, formed by the arduous pursuit of science, or through the difficulties of daily work, or reflected in the example of a noble philanthropist, all helped to mould the character of the entire nation.

Smiles' biography of Jasmin, the French barber poet, therefore stressed the "character of the man as a philanthropist" and considered his role to be one of influencing "his country by spreading the seeds of domestic social virtues . . ." Smiles himself aspired to Jasmin's particular role of domestic and social reformer, and he admired the way in which France accepted the work of Jasmin, showing "almost the equality of all ranks of society, and the comparatively small importance attached to wealth or condition wherever there is intellect and power."[18] It was a long-standing complaint with Smiles, dating back to the early 1830s, that men of intellect had been ignored in Britain, and his appreciation of Jasmin's social acceptance was evidently reinforced at this time by the refusal of the law of England to let him (Smiles) sport his newly acquired Italian title (Chevalier of S.S. Maurice and Lazare), thus eliciting the comment to his son-in-law: "we honour men who kill not men who save." There is also no mistaking the feeling of social rejction (as opposed to literary acceptance) in Smiles' comment after his 1889 visit to Italy: "I came to the conclusion that I am much better known in Italy than at home; indeed, I have received more recognition there from the King and Queen down to the humblest of their subjects than in my own country."[19]

Smiles continued, therefore, to write biographies about the socially still unaccepted natural aristocracy of talent, character and work, and his animus against the class structure again shows up in his comment that Robert Dick achieved in science "much more than thousands of men furnished with the best available education, and with ample means at their command, had been able to achieve . . ." The belief that capable men were forced to fight against the political and social system to prove themselves is also reflected in Ruskin's letter to Smiles on receiving the latter's account of the poverty-stricken and work-filled life of Thomas Edward: "this history of all good and able men must always be tragic, in these days of ours."[20]

Much of the reason then for Smiles' turn to individual biographies of men of invention and science, and of men of humble condition but heroic results, stemmed from his feeling that British society venerated the wrong values and rewarded destructive military heroes rather than constructive workers. Thus if Harrison, inventor of the naval chronometer, had "been a destructive hero," Smiles declared, "and fought battles by land and sea, we should have had biographies of him without end. But he pursued a more peaceful and industrious course . . ." Smiles felt that those "public benefactors" who established new branches of industry, or pushed society forward with invention and production, were "shortly forgotten."[21] He therefore proposed to change the situation by writing the necessary biographies, as he told Cobden in 1863, to open "up a new field of biography - heretofore neglected."[22]

Smiles actually devoted the greater part of his literary output after 1859 to the history of scientific and mechanical discovery. He was determined to introduce to the public these practical inventors and engineers as the true meritocracy of Britain. More than that, this meritocracy did what Smiles believed was absolutely essential for progress and what had not been done before - they quantified power. If man was a part of Nature, required by reason to adapt to the laws of Nature, yet man was also challenged by the determinism of the Newtonian mechanical universe of quantitative laws, atomic or mechanical.[23] Despite Smiles' belief in the bounty of Nature, he recognised that the material resources of Nature were inanimate and thus required active exploitation. Yet he also seemed to think that Nature, through its very objective existence and enormity, presented a challenge to man that could only be met and defeated on its own terms, through the application and quantification of power. Like Carlyle, he felt something of the same Christian mission to subdue the earth, and like Carlyle he also became fascinated with the romantic concept of power. Specifically Smiles visualised the enslavement of the earth's resources through power, and this power was built up and controlled only by the use of ever-more improved tools and machines. Hence Smiles considered

> that handicraft labour was the first stage of the development of human power, and that machinery has been its last and highest. The uncivilised man began with a stone for a hammer . . . each stage of his progress being marked by an improvement in his tools. Every machine calculated to save labour or increase production was a substantial addition to his power over the material resources of nature, enabling him to subjugate them more effectually to his wants and uses . . .[24]

Smiles' fascination with power related to man as well as to machines, and harked back to his stress on perseverence. Ordinary patient work and perseverence produced results because it represented the addition or accumulation (quantification) of power until it equalled and topped the difficulty or obstacle to be overcome. Hence "success in removing obstacles depends upon this law of mechanics - the greatest amount of force at your disposal concentrated at a given point." Equally, the stored-up (accumulated) experience of the past represented not only wealth, but the "power of our race," and a quantity of saved money was really "husbanded power," although "the power of money" was not so noble as the "powers" of intelligence, public spirit and moral virtue.[25] When man came to attack the "rude uncultivated wilderness," both work and power were called for, "human energy, power and industry. These enable men to subdue the wilderness, and develop the potency of labour . . ." In this task the power of machinery was enlisted:

> Had Watt, at the outset of his career, announced to mankind that he would invent a power that should drain their mines, blow their furnaces, roll and hammer

> their metals, thrash and grind their corn, saw their timber, drive their looms and spindles, print their books, impel ships across the ocean . . . he would have been regarded as an enthusiast, if not as a madman. Yet all this the steam engine had done and is now doing. It has widely extended the dominion of man over inanimate nature.[26]

Similarly, the invention of Stephenson's Rocket showed that "a new power had been born into the world . . ." It was clear that steam and machinery had "placed an almost unlimited power at the command of the producing classes . . ." Fortunately this power of steam was considered by Smiles to be "docile" so that, for example, the hydraulic press exercised power in a concentrated yet tranquil form.[27]

Smiles emphasised power because only power could master the environmentalism and determinism of the Lockean and Newtonian quantified universe. Power represented not only machinery and human activity but also the construction of concrete things, and Smiles thus visualised the Tweed railway bridge as having "the impress of power grandly stamped upon it." Smiles thought of the production of tangible objects such as roads, bridges, canals, docks and harbours as an essential part of the history of England - what was England "without its tools, its machinery, its steam-engine, its steam-ships, and its locomotive. Are not the men who have made the motive power of the country, and immensely increased its productive strength, the men above all others who have . . . [made] the country what it is?"[28] But this creation of non-human objects did not lead to the kind of alienation that Marx envisaged between the labour of man and the objective results of that labour, for Smiles did not see the results of man's labour as alien, nor did he see any break between labour and the essential nature of man, and indeed was committed to the idea of industrial progress as a necessary element of civilisation. Furthermore, Smiles did not consider that man would become an appendage to machinery as Marx did (although he conceded the possibility), but rather he thought of machinery as becoming an appendage of man.

That is, Smiles actually humanised machinery. Like man, the steam engine or locomotive power was "born into the world, full of activity and strength, with boundless capability of work." And like man, machinery must work after birth, "the printing machine had been fairly born, and must eventually do its work for mankind." The steam engine grew old too, working "steadily and manfully in youth and old age," and Smiles once saw one of Boulton and Watt's machines - "Old Bess" - "working as steadily as ever, though eighty years had passed over her head." Like the faculties of man, Smiles also found that the powers of the locomotive engine "slumbered within it" until stimulated into action by external events.[29] Thus in describing the preparation for sea of the ship Warrior through the introduction of steam, Smiles humanised its work:

> The immense machine began as if to breathe and move like a living creature, stretching its huge arms like a new born giant, and then, after practicing its strength a little and proving its soundness in body and limb, it started off with the power of above a thousand horses . . .

All that the steam engine, "with its bowels of iron and heart of fire" needed to keep on working "without rest or sleep" was coal, water and some oil. Machinery in general worked "with millions of fingers," while one of Watt's copying machines seemed to work "as it were, with two hands . . ." And in even more convoluted fashion Smiles did not consider the steam engine satisfactory until, mammal-like, it could give birth: "The steam-engine itself was never complete until it could make itself - that is manufacture the self-acting tools which could never go wrong in the process of constructing it."[30]

Smiles' endowment of machinery with human characteristics may well have been a compensation for his apprehension over the mechanical tendencies of the century - "our life, like our literature," he once wrote, "is becoming more mechanical."[31] On the other hand, Smiles also visualised machines as simply superhuman workers, becoming man-like through the process of doing the same work as man and in fact taking man's place at the shuttle and the bench. Of course the work was done more efficiently and more regularly - the steam engine was "alike docile, regular, economical, and effective, at all times and seasons . . ." This "humanisation" of the machine through its work-role was particularly evident in the case of self-acting machines (almost mechanical humans) working with "unfailing precision and indefatigable patience and strength . . ." Indeed, Smiles evidently did think of these self-acting machines as reliable workmen, replacing the less reliable human workmen.[32] The humanisation of the machine in Victorian Britain was, it seems, quite a regular phenomenon, for it occurs in other authors besides Smiles. Perhaps the introduction of vast numbers of machines into a largely religious society actually demanded that such a vitalisation take place. In any case, one author pictured the changing aspect of the steam engine quite dramatically: "Of a sudden, a soul had been put into that wonderful creature of man's working, that inert mass of wood and metal, mysteriously combined. The monster was alive!" And another author wrote of a mechanic repairing his machine and thus suddenly finding an affinity with it: "All his labour was in a new spirit. The machine had become to him a living creature; he had obtained an insight into the power which moved it."[33]

Smiles' own particular instinct was to vitalise anything that he found merit in or wished to praise, whether it be machinery, or the still active effects of a dead examplar enshrined in biography or even an inert metal like iron, which he elevated to the status of "the soul of every manufacture, and the mainspring perhaps of civilised society . . ." Very often Smiles reverted to his organic metaphor of seeds and growth, as in his analogy of England at the time of Elizabeth I to human growth: "Modern England was then in the throes of her birth. She had not yet reached the vigour of her youth, though she was full of life and energy. She was about to become the England of free thought, commerce, and manufactures, to plough the ocean with her navies, and to plant her colonies over the earth."[34]

Underlying Smiles' humanisation of machinery and his use of the organic metaphor lay another concept, that of the 19th Century idea of historical process and change. For Smiles, change was at once deterministic, immanent and inevitable, and yet also caused by the work of individuals in bringing about industrialisation and technological change. New means of communication and new sources of power were for Smiles the obvious causal agents in English history, although Saxon and Norman racial contributions, the Protestant religion, the establishment of free institutions, and the stimulation of the Northern climate and soil, also played a part. If Smiles welcomed machinery and technological change (and humanised machinery to make it more acceptable to his readers) how did he explain the Industrial Revolution which brought about the application of machinery and technology?

To begin a little earlier, it is noteworthy that Smiles conceived of an original civilisation in Britain, occurring after the Romans had retired, and stimulated almost entirely by the early churchmen. This civilisation lasted approximately until the reign of Edward I (1272-1307) after which time agriculture, bridge building, and the arts fell into decay. The country was decisively rescued from this decline in the middle of the 18th Century. Smiles gives the cause of this rennaissance as the Industrial Revolution:

> England was nothing, compared with continental nations, until she had become commercial. She fought wonderfully . . . but she was gradually becoming less powerful as a state, until about the middle of last century, when a number of ingenious and inventive men, without apparent relation to each other, arose in various parts of the kingdom, and succeeded in giving an immense impulse to all the branches of the national industry; the result of which has been a harvest of wealth and prosperity . . .[35]

Such an explanation obviously emphasised the heroic work of the individual. But elsewhere Smiles notes that individual invention was not enough for at least three reasons.

The first reason was (in a Marxian sense) deterministic, that the individual was frequently born before his time, such as a certain Dr. Roebuck who was "working ahead of his age, and he suffered for it. He fell in the breach at the critical moment . . ." Smiles simply meant that inventions often occurred before they could be technically executed or practically applied, "before the world could make adequate use of them . . ."[36] The second reason was that invention and ingenuity required capital before development was possible. Smeaton, the engineer, had to wait until a "new race of capitalists, engineers and contractors had sprung into existence." And James Watt was initially thwarted because the manufacturing class in Glasgow "though growing in importance, had full employment for their little capital in their own concerns." In short, the great engineering works of Britain could simply not have existed without "the liberality, public spirit, and commercial enterprise of merchants, traders, and manufacturers."[37] Interestingly enough, Smiles makes a sharp distinction here between the role of the inventor, which he romanticised, and the role of the entrepreneur, which he thought necessary, but not worthy of commemoration in any of his individual biographies, unless George Moore and Josiah Wedgewood be labelled entrepreneurs. Plainly it was practical work and social advance he considered important, not fortune building.

The third reason was much more elusive and abstract. Even if the time was right, the capital existed, and the inventor was inventing, Smiles considered that the final push came from an entity variously labelled as spirit, enterprise, or energy. In the 1760s Smiles felt that the country was too poor "or too spiritless to undertake the improvement of the means of commercial intercourse . . ." This spirit either existed or it did not, the "stages of improvement which we have recorded indeed exhibit a measure of the vital energy which has from time to time existed in the nation," and so, for example, 17th Century England suffered from poverty and starvation partly because there was even less "spirit."[38]

Ultimately, however, Smiles exhibited the duality of his whole approach to society and history, and came down in favour of two pre-conditions as causal agents of the Industrial Revolution - one was historical determinism and the other was the free individual response to that determinism. The individual inventor and the three qualifying conditions already mentioned can be classified under these two pre-conditions. The greatest enterprises of the English sprang "like their constitution, their laws, their entire industrial arrangements, from the force of circumstances and the individual energies of the people." Thus on the one hand the early engineers "were the offspring of necessity" called into action by the needs of the time, and following rather than anticipating "public wants," while on the other hand the change around 1750 was the "outgrowth in a great measure of individual energy . . ."[39] On one remaining point, however, Smiles had difficulty, and it has turned out to be a crucial point.

For the Industrial Revolution to reach the take-off stage, according to modern historians, it was essential that the population should have been increasing at just the right rate, slow enough to maintain wages, but fast enough to expand aggregate demand.[40] Smiles seems to have had some vague idea of this when he wrote of "the growing wants of the population" demanding improved communications, but with the experience of large-scale unemployment in Leeds behind him, Smiles conceived of a large unemployed population already in existence, waiting passively for industry and invention to relieve them of hunger, want and idleness. Hence Smiles realised that population was a factor in industrialisation, but, not surprisingly, did not comprehend its role as a platform for industrial take-off. Consequently, he visualised Boulton and Watt's machines creating new industry "which gave regular employment to hundreds of families" and machinery in the Scotch iron districts producing employment for "vast numbers of our industrial population," and public-spirited men like Wedgewood, who "were actively engaged in devising new sources of employment for the population . . ."[41]

Smiles therefore visualised English society on the eve of the Industrial Revolution as divided into four sections. The aristocracy were largely inert and self-serving;[42] the merchants and traders (roughly the middle class) were poised with their capital; the true meritocracy of labour, the inventive and ingenious mechanics and engineers, were separately preparing to produce practical and applicable inventions; and the large mass of the population subsisted either lazily or in extremis, awaiting the discipline and employment of work. The first break-through came in the construction of roads, partly because they facilitated trade and traffic (especially the movement of food) but also because the task of road making had

> an important moral influence. The roads stimulated industry amongst a people who had hitherto been unused to it. In constructing them the people learnt to work, to use tools, and to apply themselves to continuous labour. Telford himself regarded the Highland roads in the light of a Working Academy, which annually turned out about 800 improved workmen."

Smiles laid great emphasis on the training of the population into workhabits, presupposing that prior to the construction of roads the population lived in a state of "inconceivable listlessness and idleness," or again of "sloth and idleness" which "gradually disappeared before the energy, activity, and industry . . . called into life by the improved communications."[43]

Communications also implied trade and the need for regularity (for example the time-tables of the railways, and even of the earlier stagecoaches) and regularity implied subordination to one accepted standard. This related to work-habits as much as to travel. The early manufacturing establishments such as Boulton and Watt required a force of foremen to oversee the work, and thus to overcome "the difficulties occasioned by the irregular habits of the work people . . ." Through various expedients the Duke of Bridgewater changed his work force of canal builders from "a half-savage class" into men of a high character of "sobriety, intelligence and good conduct . . ." Similarly with the draining of the Fens and the construction of roads, the inhabitants "subsided into the ranks of steady industry . . ."[44] Smiles is here referring to two related industrial needs - the detachment of work from other activities and hence its subordination into a "working day" of regularised and continuous work - and the formation of a work-force large enough to supply the needs of industry. Hence because the Scottish labour force was trained through "a century's discipline of work and technical training, the result is altogether different [from earlier idleness] . . . Mechanical power and technical ability are the result of training . . ."[45] Through this kind of work training (on the construction of early communication routes, and in the early manufactories) Britain was ready to embark on the next stage of the Industrial Revolution, the rapid expansion of industry.

It was clear to Smiles that if the construction of roads and canals had provided the initial stimulus to commerce and the nucleus of a stable work force, it was the parallel and complementary surge of invention in the mid 18th Century that provided the solid take-off point for industrial expansion. Glasgow, the "old city of tobacco . . . lords" was transformed into "a great centre of manufacturing industry; it was rich, busy, and prosperous; and the main source of its prosperity had been the steam engine." Hence if prosperity and employment came through the steam engine; and if the road to civilisation originally began with the use of tools as encapsulated sources of power; then machinery and its inventors were the key to the future. Indeed Smiles warned that if machines and tools were destroyed "the human race would [be] . . . reduced to their teeth and nails, and civilisation summarily abolished."[46] This did not necessarily mean that Smiles equated civilisation with machines and tools, but their presence was the essential base for civilisation (cf. Marx), and thus the inventors themselves, the "number of ingenious and inventive men" of the mid 18th Century, despite the qualifying conditions, were the really dynamic force for historical change.

How did these inventors produce such significant inventions, given the lack of previous examples of the method of invention? Smiles believed that no invention occurred suddenly, but rather (in a Baconian argument) that it was the outcome of a long process of advancement, often stimulated by the needs of the time, and leading to two results - the accumulation (quantification) of past efforts and the practical application of the accumulated knowledge:

> And rarely does it happen that any discovery or invention of importance is made by one man alone. The threads of inquiry are taken up and traced, one labourer succeeding another, each tracing it a little further, often without apparent result. This goes on sometimes for centuries, until at length some man, greater perhaps than his fellows, seeking to fulfill the needs of his time, gathers the various threads together, treasures up the gain of past successes and failures, and uses them as the means for some solid achievement.[47]

Smiles' further analysis of the method and style of invention helps to reveal why he idealised the inventor and engineer. These men belonged to a class of workers who were considered "unscientific and ungenteel" by the higher classes, but who (though denied education) achieved great results through a combination of natural ability and ordinary hard work. Great mechanics were the natural aristocracy of the country, for they did not "belong to the educated classes. They received no college education. . . . But where learning failed, natural genius triumphed. These men gathered their practical knowledge in the workshop, or acquired it in manual labour." In short they were a meritocracy of work, producing results through the intensive use of common qualities, "by their habits of observation, their powers of discrimination, their constant self-improvement, and their patient industry."[48] However, Smiles' explanation of invention was slightly contradictory, for as usual he became involved in a dual explanation, namely that invention was due both to extraordinary natural ability and also to very ordinary qualities.

Smiles considered that Brindley's "extraordinary ability . . . was in a great measure the result of close observation, painstaking study of details, and the most indefatigable industry." These were the moral values that Smiles prized, but was he referring to natural genius or to ordinary qualities made great? For Smiles often seemed unsure as to whether engineers were born or made: "Engineers were the product of circumstances, and of their instinct for construction; and this was often the instinct of genius . . ." Equally James Watt did not seem to build up his ability through persevering study since invention "was the natural and habitual operation of Watt's intellect, and he could not restrain it."[49] Perhaps the most accurate rendition of Smiles' position is to say that he did believe some engineers and inventors were born with "constructive instincts" and "inventive faculties," reverting here to his faculty psychology, and that others became inventors and engineers through the use of average faculties; thus the early mill wrights became engineers by working with tools and hence "cultivating the faculties of observation and comparison, acquiring practical knowledge of the strength and qualities of materials, and dexterity . . ." But both kinds of inventors and engineers had to work hard at their inventions and trades even in those very unusual cases where "the inventive faculty is so strong . . . that it may be said to amount to a passion, and cannot be restrained . . ."[50] This position generally allowed Smiles to romanticise the uniqueness of the inventor but at the same time insert the useful moral virtues of hard work and practical energy into the method of invention.

Three qualities which Smiles included in the vast majority of his explanations of invention were: observation; classification or study of details; and hard work. Observation particularly was an every-day quality to which Smiles attributed an inordinate value in all walks of life. James Watt possessed "an almost prophetic eye;" Maudsley had the necessary "quick eye;" Henry Cort was "clear sighted;" Wedgewood developed a talent for "keen observation;" the geologist Charles Peach "was as accurate and quick-sighted in business as in science;" and (perhaps essential in a naturalist) Thomas Edward possessed the "qualities of observing and seeing. Nothing that once came under his eyes was ever forgotten." Smiles felt that observation did two things: it revealed the wonders of Divine Creation, and at the same time it usefully classified and ordered the facts and laws of nature. The "seeing eye," wrote Smiles, "finds wonders in everything. Where the unseeing eye sees nothing, it detects differences, and varieties, and classifications."[51]

In a similar way, Henry Mayhew gives a particularly clear example of the uses of scientific classification: "By these means the mental and natural chaos of the world to ignorant eyes, is brought into something like the order the Almighty has impressed upon creation . . ." Mayhew believed that the study of science would reveal with certainty the harmony of the world (something of a parallel activity to Carlyle's use of work in producing order) and an updated argument for the existence of God from design. Mayhew was confident that "the endless chapter of accidents of which life and nature appear to the vulgar to be composed, have been shown to be part of one mighty system, where all is harmony and proportion, law and order . . ."[52]

Smiles' emphasis on observation and visual discovery was thus not unique, it was part of the Victorian search for knowledge coupled with the underlying belief that the elucidation of nature's secrets revealed the hand of the Divine Creator. It was no accident, therefore, that many Victorians combined a deep sense of religion with the (often amateur) study of Nature (Charles Kingsley and the father of Edmund Gosse come to mind), or that Smiles himself could state that "theories are human, but facts are divine," and hence write approvingly of Telford and Smeaton's rejection of theoretical deduction, and subsequent reliance on visual observation, experience and experiment.[53] Charles Kingsley provides an excellent example of the Victorian emphasis on visual discovery in an 1863 lecture to the boys of Wellington College:

> When we were little and good, a long time ago, we used to have a jolly old book called Evenings at Home, in which was a great story called 'Eyes and no Eyes,' and that story was of more use to me than any dozen other stories I have read.

The moral of the story concerned the visual accumulation of information:

> So it is. One man walks through the world with his eyes open, and another with them shut; and upon this difference depends all the superiority of knowledge which one acquires over the other . . . William, continue to make use of your eyes; and you, Robert, learn that eyes were given you to use.[54]

Smiles believed too that the "man who observed patiently and intelligently, and who tests his observation by careful inquiry, becomes the discoverer and inventor," and so with a little application, all men, regardless of rank, would be able to fasten onto the abundant (and democratic) facts of Nature: "the facts of nature are open to the peasant and mechanic;" wrote Smiles, "they are alike capable of making a moral use of those facts . . .

Even in the lowliest calling, the true worker may win the loftiest results."[55]

Smiles evidently conceived the world about him as rational, orderly and capable of being understood - a situation which enabled any individual, using his God-given capacities, to capture and order the facts of nature. This was essentially the task of the inventor: by careful observation and assiduous work and study the inventor could penetrate the facts and laws of nature, and by re-arranging these facts and using previously accumulated knowledge, could apply his 'insight' into practical inventions. However, one difficulty was that the artisans and mechanics who were likely to become inventors needed a certain amount of leisure to pursue their interests, and this was not always available. But here a number of comparable situations are related by Smiles, which frequently enabled the inventors to find time and make up for their deficient education, although he evidently did not notice the similarities. This is that at some stage many inventors suffered from illness, thus giving them an enforced leisure. James Watt was a sickly youth, spending long hours indoors, during which time, according to Smiles, he developed his mechanical dexterity; Josiah Wedgewood's self-education and experiments resulted from "the enforced leisure of his many illnesses . . ." and several amateur astronomers found an unexpected leisure in their various illnesses. Strangely it was ill-health which also gave Smiles himself an opportunity, for he recalled that as a boy "labouring under ill-health, he rummaged and read the books of nearly the whole library [Dr. Brown's itinerating library at Haddington] and thus laid the foundations of a considerable amount of useful knowledge."[56]

Smiles' inventors, and their every-day method of invention were designed to reveal two lessons. The first showed that invention and discovery might follow from a simple persevering spirit of self-help; and the second illustrated "how the moral and industrial foundations of a country may be built up and established;" that is, to emphasise the role that the new meritocracy of engineers, inventors and mechanics had played and were still playing in the progress of the nation. For Smiles was very conscious of historical change and thought that England was still at the exciting beginning of the journey toward civilisation - a journey made possible by the Industrial Revolution:

> Everything in England is young. We are an old people, but a young nation. Our trade is young; our engineering is young; and the civilisation of what we called "the masses" has scarcely begun.[57]

Smiles' ultimate ideal was that of national progress toward civilisation, and while self-help provided the moral reform of national character as the necessary human superstructure for the final end of civilisation, the Industrial Revolution provided the material substructure. Civilisation was therefore both moral and material.[58]

The moral superstructure and the material substructure were capable of interaction because it was the function of the new meritocracy of mechanics, engineers, inventors and true workers (including those who contributed to the character of the nation like Edward, Dick, and Moore) to combine moral and material advance in a socially beneficial way. A typical example would be Josiah Wedgewood, who not only experimented and invented to produce the material benefits of a large-scale industry, but also educated the working population morally in "habits of industry" and who, by his example of diligence and perseverence, influenced "public action in all directions," thus contributing "to form the national character." Another example was one of the original road builders, the blind Metcalf, "acting as an effective instrument of progress," for the building of roads always had the same result "everywhere," progress, material and moral, the "development of industry and increase of civilisation." And so Smiles' biographies after 1859 idealised a new kind of hero, not the aristocratic leader of the past, not the destructive military hero, not the Carlylean autocrat, but the democratic hero of technology, work and invention, exerting leadership by moral example, encouraging "men to follow with anxious and persevering industry. It is always the Man society wants."[59] It was the values of a new classless meritocracy that Smiles wanted to bring to the notice of the public, for these men provided both moral character and material advance - the two elements of civilisation. Moreover, the meritocracy of inventors, scientists and engineers were only able to stimulate moral and material advance because they belonged to that wider community of a natural aristocracy who combined the two qualities, that, according to Smiles, distinguished the true world-moving individuals from the false aristocracy of rank: namely, brains and work:

> Intellectual workers, who 'stand first in worth as in command,' form the true aristocracy of labour. They are the capitalists of society - the men of _caput_ or head; for it is not money nor station, but brains and work, that confer the highest rank, and constitute the motive power of mankind.[60]

Smiles' vision of the way in which mankind could advance was soon to receive a challenge, however, and this was the challenge of Socialism and a new attitude toward work and society.

Chapter IV - Footnotes

[1]"Self-Help," Chambers' Journal (3rd Series; London and Edinburgh), Dec. 24, 1859, vol. XII, pp. 413-15; "Self-Help." The Reasoner (London), March 25, 1860, vol. XXV, p. 101; R.C., "Self-Help," Macmillan's Magazine (London), March 1860, vol. I, pp. 402-406; "Self-Help," Fraser's Magazine for Town and Country (London), June 1860, vol. LXI, pp. 778-786.

[2]Cited in Bowden Green (ed.), Portraits, p. 48; and see W.E. Gladstone, Address and Speeches delivered at Manchester before the Mechanics Institute (London, 1862), p. 38. It would be tedious to spell out in the text the diffusion of Smiles' influence from the 1860s on, but his name, his works or adversions to 'self-help' appear e.g. in the following: Lectures delivered before the Y.M.C.A., pp. 93, 106; Unsworth, Self-Culture, pp. 10, 48; Page, Noble Workers, pp. 126, 359; J.M. Darton, Brave Boys, who have become Illustrious Men of our Time: forming bright examples for emulation by the youth of Great Britain (London, 1879), p. 247; Davenport Adams, Secret of Success, a palpable imitation of Smiles, and thus references occur throughout; The Way to Fortune (London, 1881), pp. 9, 56; and Henry Sidgwick, Principles of Political Economy (London, 1883), p. 538. Naturally this list is not exhaustive.

[3]George Potter, The Labour Question (London, 1861), p. 13.

[4]"Self-Help," Equity of Labour; or, the Working Man's Exodus from Poverty to Lasting Plenty (London, 1863), passim.

[5]The Working Man, July 21, 1866, No. 3 (New Series), p. 25.

[6]Charles Knight, Passages of a Working Life (3 vols.; London, 1864-65), vol. II, p. 133. Exactly the same mistaken critique of Smiles

appears in "Self-Culture: Uses of Books," Meliora (London), 1866, vol. IX, pp. 193-204; and in Davenport Adams, Secret of Success, p. 307.

[7]Symptomatic of changing attitudes are two paintings in the Tate Gallery, London, of similar subjects. One, entitled "Kit's Writing Lesson," was painted in 1852 by R.B. Martineau and shows a young boy painfully and perseveringly working at his school lesson. The second, entitled "The Writing Lesson," was painted in 1863 by Ford Madox Brown (who also painted the well-known study "Work"), and shows a young girl, happily oblivious of her work, chewing on an apple. The eleven years between the two paintings do represent some kind of change, and some historians accept the 1860s as a turning point, whether in agreement with A.V. Dicey or not, cf. Perkin, Origins of Modern English Society, pp. 439 ff.

[8]F.P. Cobbe, Hours of Work and Play (London, 1867), p. 43.

[9]A. Blair (Treasurer of the Bank of Scotland) in Parliamentary Papers, 1854-55, vol. XVIII (Reports from Commissioners, 4), "Appendix A to Second Report," Second Report of Mercantile Law Commission, p. 101. Mr. Strutt (Member for Nottingham), July 26, 1855, 3 Hansard's Parliamentary Debates, vol. CXXXIX, p. 1387. Mr. Muntz (Member for Birmingham), July 26, 1855, ibid, pp. 1380-81.

[10]Mr. Cordwell, June 29, 1855, ibid, p. 1349. Palmerston, July 26, 1855, ibid, p. 1390.

[11]J.G. Kinnear (merchant) in Parliamentary Papers, 1854, vol. XVII (Reports from Commissioners, 4), First Report of Mercantile Law Commission, Lords and Commons, p. 89. Justice Bramwell equally appealed to reason, authority, experience and Free Trade in favour of Limited Liability.

[12]An article in a journal founded by Smiles queried "whether a man will work for a company with the same inexhaustable zeal and untiring

diligence that he would for himself . . ." "Joint Stock Votes," Railway News, April 23, 1864, vol. I, p. 415. The claim that Smiles founded Railway News in 1864 occurs in "Dr. Samuel Smiles," The Railway Gazette, Oct. 1, 1937, vol. LXVII, pp. 544-45.

[13] [Chambers], Exemplary and Instructive Biography for the study of Youth (Edinburgh, 1836), preface note. On the other hand, the book also thought of biography in terms of success models, pp. 328-31. For the didactic use of biography, see Joseph Reed, English Biography in the early 19th Century (New Haven, 1966), p. 27 and passim.

[14] Smiles to Janet Hartree, December 21, 1881, Smiles Correspondence, SS/AI/129. Smiles, Character, p. 95. Smiles to Janet Hartree, September 21, 1879, Smiles Correspondence, SS/AI/106.

[15] Smiles to William, 14 June 1878, ibid, SS/AII/92.

[16] Smiles, George Moore, p. 517. Smiles to J.N. Dick, n.d., Smiles Correspondence, SS/AIV/1. Smiles, Robert Dick, Baker of Thurso, Geologist and Botanist (New York, 1879), pp. (vii) and 432.

[17] Smiles, Life of a Scottish Naturalist, Thomas Edward, Associate of the Linnaean Society (New York, 1877), pp. 13, 325. Smiles once conceded that he did idealise Edward a bit, Smiles to Janet Hartree, 4 January 1878, Smiles Correspondence, SS/AI/81.

[18] Smiles, Jasmin, Barber, Poet, Philanthropist (New York, 1892), pp. (vi), 188, 196. Typically, Smiles was happy to note that Jasmin only worked for the benefit of those "who could not help themselves" (p. 215) - the same category of "helpless" or "destitute" people that genuinely could not practice self-help.

[19] Smiles to Jack Hartree, 21 January 1890, Smiles Correspondence, SS/AI/111. (Jasmin was first published in 1891.) In the early 1830s

Smiles had already noted the differences in reward for warriors and for philosophers, Samuel Brown to Smiles, n.d., but c. 1833/1834, ibid, SS/AIX/30a-c. Smiles, Autobiography, pp. 409-410, and for title, pp. 344-345.

[20]Smiles, Robert Dick, p. 105. Ruskin to Smiles, n.d., but 1876 or soon after, Hartree Collection, MS 160.

[21]Smiles, Men of Invention, pp. 77-78. Smiles, Self-Help, p. 57.

[22]In 1881 Smiles considered that his best books had been Industrial Biography, and the lives of Boulton and Watt (vol. IV of the 1904 edition of Lives of the Engineers, originally published in 1862). This would put his most significant work, according to his own judgement, in the short period from 1862 to 1863, Smiles to Janet Hartree, 11 November 1881, Smiles Correspondence, SS/AI/128. Smiles to Cobden, 6 Nov. 1863 in Cobden Papers (West Sussex Record Office, Chichester).

[23]L.L. Whyte, "Man and Nature," in Ideas and Beliefs of the Victorians (Dutton Paperback edition; New York, 1966), p. 241.

[24]Smiles, Industrial Biography, p. 399. Smiles may well have obtained his idea of tools as a necessary basis of civilisation from Carlyle, whom he quotes extensively on the subject, ibid, p. 204. For Carlyle on machines and inventors, see Herbert L. Sussman, Victorians and the Machine (Cambridge, Mass., 1968), pp. 13-40. For the Victorian glorification of force, see Chapter IX in Houghton, Victorian Frame of Mind, especially pp. 196-201.

[25]Smiles, Life and Labour, p. 7. Smiles, Industrial Biography, p. 169. Smiles, Self-Help, pp. 265, 288, 289.

[26]Smiles, Men of Invention, p. 277. Smiles, Lives of the Engineers, vol. IV, p. 471.

[27]Ibid, vol. V, p. 263. Smiles, Industrial Biography, p. 400. Smiles, Self-Help, p. 46. Smiles, Industrial Biography, p. 235.

[28]Smiles, Lives of the Engineers, vol. V, p. 384 and vol. I, p. (xxiii).

[29]Ibid, vol. V, p. 263. Smiles, Men of Invention, p. 181. [Smiles], "George Stephenson," ECJ, June 2, 1849, vol. I, p. 65. Smiles, Lives of the Engineers, vol. IV, p. 212 (note) and vol. V, p. 74.

[30]Smiles, Industrial Biography, pp. 227, 400, 399. Smiles, Lives of the Engineers, vol. IV, p. 448; vol. I, p. (xix).

[31]Smiles, Self-Help, pp. 320 and 321. Carlyle faced a similar problem in reconciling transcendentalism and technological progress, Sussman, Victorians and the Machine, p. 24.

[32]Smiles, Lives of the Engineers, vol. IV, p. 327. Smiles, Industrial Biography, p. 327 and for other self-acting machines, pp. 326, 329, 331.

[33]Mrs. Craik, John Halifax, vol. II, p. 299. Jewsbury, Marian Withers, vol. I, p. 27.

[34]Smiles, Men of Invention, pp. 108, 13. The place of organic metaphor and life cycle analogy in Western culture has been studied by R.A. Nisbet, Social Change and History (Oxford, 1969).

[35]Smiles, Lives of the Engineers, vol. II, pp. 54, 66, 220; vol. I, p. (xvii); and see also vol. III, p. 71: "at some remote period [in Scotland] a degree of civilisation and prosperity prevailed, from which the country had gradually fallen."

[36]Smiles, Industrial Biography, pp. 179, 213, 214.

[37]Smiles, Lives of the Engineers, vol. II, pp. 160-61; vol. IV, p. 101; vol. I, p. (xx).

[38]Ibid, vol. II, p. 159; vol. III, p. 348; vol. I, pp. 150-51.

[39]*Ibid*, vol. V, p. 275; vol. I, pp. (xxii), 152. Smiles did occasionally distinguish between Scotland and England, and in the case of the former he felt that education played a significant part in the c. 1750 advance, because the people were stimulated to action through being educated "in advance of their material condition . . ." *ibid*, vol. II, p. 227.

[40]Perkin, *Origins of Modern English Society*, p. 105 and pp. 101-106 generally.

[41]Smiles, *Lives of the Engineers*, vol. I, p. 225; vol. IV, p. 168. Smiles, *Industrial Biography*, p. 203. Smiles, *Lives of the Engineers*, vol. I, p. 306.

[42]But not entirely so, for example, the Duke of Bridgewater, *ibid*, vol. I, p. 246.

[43]*Ibid*, vol. I, p. (xi); vol. III, pp. 60, 251.

[44]*Ibid*, vol. IV, p. 437; vol. I, p. 280; vol. III, p. 363.

[45]Smiles, *Men of Invention*, p. 128. Hence Smiles' belief that inherited experience and work-skill was worth as much as the capital accumulated by past generations, in forwarding industry.

[46]Smiles, *Lives of the Engineers*, vol. IV, p. 456. Smiles (ed.), *James Nasmyth, Engineer; An Autobiography* (Popular edition; London, 1912), p. (vi). Smiles, *Industrial Biography*, p. 209 (the context refers to the "machine breakers" of the Luddite persuasion).

[47]*Ibid*, p. 211.

[48]Smiles, *Lives of the Engineers*, vol. I, p. (xvi).

[49]*Ibid*, vol. I, pp. 348-49; vol. II, p. 271; vol. IV, p. 118. Smiles once wrote that "genius is more than intellect; it is inspired instinct," Smiles, *Life and Labour*, p. 74.

[50]Smiles, Lives of the Engineers, vol. I, p. (xxii); vol. V, p. 364; vol. I, p. 159. Smiles, Industrial Biography, p. 228.

[51]Smiles, Lives of the Engineers, vol. IV, p. 111. Smiles, Industrial Biography, pp. 251, 153. Smiles, Josiah Wedgewood, F.R.S., his Personal History (New York, 1895), p. 79. Smiles, Robert Dick, p. 252. Smiles, Thomas Edward, p. 296. Smiles, Robert Dick, p. 42.

[52]Mayhew, Benjamin Franklin, pp. 278, 279. To prove his point Mayhew uses a whole page, 279, to list the classifications of insects, birds, fish, etc.

[53]Smiles, Life and Labour, p. 7; Smiles, Lives of the Engineers, vol. III, p. 394; observation, experience and experiment related to the successful inventors' three personal requirements, disciplined by work-experience, their "mind, eyes and hands . . ." ibid, vol. IV, p. 51.

[54]Charles Kingsley. His Letters and Memories of his Life, ed. Mrs. Kingsley (2 vols.; London, 1877), vol. II, pp. 162-63.

[55]Smiles, Life and Labour, p. 6. Smiles, Self-Help, p. 27.

[56]Smiles, Lives of the Engineers, vol. IV, pp. 12-13; vol. I, pp. 306-307. Smiles, Men of Invention, pp. 354, 364. Smiles, George Moore, p. 155 (the only mention Smiles makes of this episode in his life).

[57]Smiles, Men of Invention, p. 378. Smiles, Lives of the Engineers, vol. II, p. 30.

[58]Smiles once pointed out that "civilisation . . . does not necessarily accompany the rapid increase of wealth. On the contrary, higher earnings, without improved morality, may only lead to wild waste and gross indulgence." Ibid, vol. I, p. 330.

[59]Ibid, vol. I, p. 306; vol. III, pp. 349, 250. Smiles, Men of Invention, pp. 274-75. It is also noteworthy that Smiles believed this

meritocracy was recruited almost entirely from the country and not the cities, for the country boy "has to rely upon himself" and life in the country "is full of practical teachings." *Ibid*, p. 348, and also Smiles, *George Moore*, p. 67.

[60]Smiles, *Life and Labour*, p. 40. It seems likely that Smiles thought he too belonged to the 'aristocracy' of brains and work.

## CHAPTER V

## CHALLENGE TO AN IDEAL: SOCIALISM AND THE NEW ATTITUDE TOWARD WORK

In 1875 Smiles reported the sale of 10,000 copies of _Thrift_, 3,200 copies of _Self-Help_ and 1,500 copies of _Character_, and in 1877 noted that _Self-Help_ had sold more copies that year and the previous year than in the last twelve years. But by 1896 his publishers, John Murray, told Smiles that the sales of many of his books had fallen off, and as the next two years confirmed the trend, refused to publish his sixth and last book in the self-help series, _Conduct_. Perhaps no other test could measure so objectively the decline of the ideal of self-help, or indeed the decline of the Victorian work ethic, as the falling sales of _Self-Help_.[1] There were many reasons for this decline. These included the changing technical basis of industry and its demand for a more specialised form of education than that of self-help; the growing alternatives to self-help, including the increase of social legislation and the Socialist and Trades Union movements; the rediscovery of poverty and industrial abuses; the simple failure of both political economy and the economic system itself to respond to the condition of the great mass of the people; and perhaps most important of all, a loss of faith in established principle. Beatrice Potter noticed this situation in 1886: "General principles, whether they be those of the decalogue, or the abstract thinkers on social facts, or of the political economist, are all alike for the time discredited as practical guides . . ."[2] This loss of faith seems to have been prompted partly by the economic depression of the 1880s, but also by a change of value which embraced the whole spectrum of moral and social conduct.[3] Work was just one of these values that underwent a change, and was related to other social attitudes in flux, including sex, clothes, the role of women, the family, social structure and the nature of man.[4] Smiles was well aware of this alteration of values, as were the Socialists, who took advantage of the situation to put forward new ideas on work and society - ideas that were often diametrically opposed to Smiles' position.

In 1883 Smiles acknowledged that much of the "feeling and loyalty between workmen and their employers has now expired. Men rapidly remove from place to place. Character is of little consequence. The mutual feeling of goodwill and zealous attention to work seems to have passed away." The society of fixed principles and accepted social structure seemed to be crumbling, and Smiles voiced his dismay in various ways. In 1880 he attempted to fix man's place in society once more by proclaiming that "we have it not in our choice to be rich or poor . . ." but only worthy or worthless, and wondered whether the "ever-extending tide of democracy is bearing down the best fruits of domestic discipline and moral character." Consequently Smiles warned in 1884: "Some people forget that the giver of all good gifts requires us to seek them by industry, prudence and perseverence," and returned to his simple solutions for poverty, advising the Irish for example that they could "only be levelled up by industry and intelligence."[5]

But in fact Smiles had been moving in a conservative direction from the 1860s, soon after the success of Self-Help. More accurately, the country had moved beyond the confidence and complacency of the 1850s, while Smiles had simply stood still. Gladstone's efforts at franchise reform in the 1860s annoyed him, as did John Stuart Mill's brief episode in Parliament, and so prospects for the 1868 election did not arouse his enthusiasm: "The extreme men are mostly kept out," he wrote to his son, "including Mill and his meddling . . . I suppose Gladstone will have a majority . . . but he will soon make mincemeat of his party." Smiles therefore planned "to abstain from voting . . ."[6] However, Smiles reserved his strongest censure for the Irish, probably because he had started to invest capital in his son's ropeworks in Belfast, and certainly because of his strong Protestant feeling against Catholicism.

There were only two ways to settle the Protestant-Catholic conflict in Ireland, Smiles told his son in 1872, "ropes or grape. The local magistrates are humbugs - afraid to act for fear of losing the favour of the mob . . . This comes from giving the roughs votes." Smiles had much advice for his son in Belfast over work, wages and strikes. In 1874 he wrote regarding a failed strike: "You will pay less wages now. What fools these work people are. The boot is now on the other leg." And in 1878 he remarked that "the wages of workmen will have to be lowered to the Continental Standard, and the hours of Labour will have to be lengthened, before we can compete with the foreigners . . ." Another strike at his son's plant in 1880 produced a predictable analysis: "Your poor spinners are doing what other ignorant workmen usually do. When they see a place busy, they think the proprietors are making fortunes, and then they strike." In light of these views it was not surprising that Smiles did not favour Irish Home Rule. In 1892 he wrote to his son in Belfast: "You see that the atrocious whirligig Gladstone will have a majority in the new Parliament . . . He will never get Home Rule for Ireland - never, never!" Gladstone's attempt to get Home Rule "must be the result of mania. Yet there are 'Liberal' members to cheer on the maniac. Alas! Alas! for Liberalism." However Smiles assured his son that "Rome Rule" was opposed by "the most industrious, thriving and loyal population of that country

[Ireland] . . ." In the end, it was inevitable that Smiles should desert the Liberals and support the future Conservative Prime Minister, Balfour, whose speeches in 1894 were "splendid. Balfour improves from day to day. He will be Prime Minister yet."[7]

Smiles' refusal to move beyond the principles of Self-Help, and even it appears, to back-track on the franchise question, coupled with changing attitudes toward social and moral questions in the country as a whole, meant that his position was being undermined on all sides. Thus in Duty (1880) Smiles found himself compelled to raise the basic question of authority in society, which for him rested on the two sanctions of religion and inherited principles of conduct. Hence Smiles attacked the new Art and Culture movement, believing that its adherents "sneer at the old fashioned virtues of industry and self-denial, energy and self-help." Similarly Smiles criticised the female suffrage movement, "the outcries of women who protest against their womanhood, and wildly strain to throw off their most lovable characteristics." Smiles wanted women in the Home, teaching work-discipline and authority, for the Home was "the best school of discipline . . ." Most of all Smiles worried about the loss of religion, and the sad sight of men, "and even women . . . theorising and gossiping over the great principles which their forefathers really believed . . ." This was important not only because Smiles sincerely believed in those principles, but because he considered that religion was a stabilising element in society, helping to provide sanctions for work and moral conduct, and without which "the deluge" of Revolution might come to England as it did to France in 1789.[8] For when belief in religion died out in France, the reign of materialism and atheism began, moral stability was swept away, and the Revolution ensued.[9]

By the 1880s therefore Smiles was emphasising the authoritarian side of his attitude toward man's work and place in society, although he had always conceived of work to be assigned by God as an arduous, if beneficial, part of the natural order and discipline of society. Work reminded man of his dependence upon God (who "requires" man to seek all good things by work) while idleness, by opposing this law of existence, was "a thorough demoraliser of the body, soul, and conscience. Ninetenths of the vices and miseries of the world proceed from idleness." Thus work was a moral antidote to idleness - work moralised and idleness demoralised man and his religious conscience. Indeed the activity of work itself had less value for Smiles (apart from its function of material progress) than the moral results that work produced in forming character and a disciplined society. Hence Smiles did not stress the role of work in overcoming difficulty and achieving results so much as the role of difficulty in evoking work and producing the attendant moral values. Smiles insisted that George Stephenson liked encounter with difficulty because it had made him a stronger and better character, and he "would not have the road of knowledge made too smooth and easy" for his pupils. Smiles also stated, without any evidence, that the early railway engineers would "probably have been disappointed if they [difficulties] had not presented themselves."[10]

One basic criticism of Smiles, therefore, is that because he focussed his attention on the discipline, character and nature of individual man and on the progress of the nation, rather than on what actually occurred inside the factory, he overlooked a most important point - the differences in the kind of work done in Britain, and the different conditions under which various kinds of work were carried out. That is, Smiles tended to lump all sorts of work together ("head and hand"), believing that attitude toward work was more important than the work situation itself. So he wrote to his daughter in 1885 with reference to a school prize: "I do not esteem [John's prize] the least, as it is for work. If man could only work and do his best, he will do a great deal."[11] Thus Smiles was inclined only to make the distinction between work and idleness, and not between pleasant and unpleasant work, or socially desirable and undesirable work. This was one of the many differences between Smiles' attitude toward work and that of the late Victorian Socialists, for the latter, brought up in a different tradition, were able to distinguish, as in the case of William Morris, between useful work (necessary work that produced food, clothing and shelter) and useless work (luxury articles), while again Smiles could only differentiate between productive (working) and unproductive (idle) classes. In fact, Smiles' ideal of self-help was thought to be so diametrically opposed to the Socialists' position on mutual help and State action that the editor of his Autobiography (1905) claimed the 'Gospel according to Smiles' was a familar "commonplace in the Socialists' invective against the existing order of things."[12]

Socialism was not of course a new phenomenon in Britain. Smiles had taken note of the socialism of Robert Owen in the earlier part of the 19th Century (and had even written for the Owenite journal, The Union, in 1842 and 1843), had approved of the efforts at working class cooperation in the 1840s, and had written favourably of the French socialist-anarchist Fourier, in the Leeds Times of September 17, 1842. But in Self-Help, Smiles was already complaining in typical fashion of the social reformers, obviously Owenites, "who will have us established in parallelograms, and ripened into men by abnegation of all the hopes, struggles, and difficulties, by which men are made." And by the time Smiles was writing his Autobiography (the 1880s) he voiced more clearly his two objections to Owenism, firstly its atheism, and secondly its reduction of the individual to an impotent, characterless cog in the mechanical "spinning jenny" of the Owenite universe. Smiles really objected to the way in which Socialism seemed to take away the individuality of man, and so it was inevitable that the ideal of self-help (as with the individualism of Spencer and Bradlaugh) should stand diametrically opposed, in public opinion, to Socialism. Hence, the arch opponents of Socialism, the Liberty and Property Defence League, labelled one of their pamphlets Self Help versus State Help (1883), and when Smiles' editor claimed that the message of self-help was a popular object of derision among the Socialists, he was quite correct.[13]

Perhaps this editorial claim was somewhat exaggerated in regard to the frequency of the Socialist invective against Smiles, but a sampling of Socialist literature shows that Smiles' stand on self-help was used as an antagonistic polar position. Thus in a Socialist pamphlet of 1897 the Rev. Percy Dearmer, a Christian 'Socialist', criticised the gospel according to Smiles:

> I know that money is the main cause of the awful temptations of these modern times, which have seriously made a new gospel, not of good-will towards men, but of "Self Help;" and I want not only be be freed from this temptation myself, but I want "us" to be freed from it, for I know that it is rapidly destroying all our nobility of character.

William Morris' journal, the Commonweal, also criticised the self-help ideal. Morris himself declared in 1885 that "Philanthropy has had its day, and is gone; thrift and self-help are going . . ." although another article by J.H. Smith seemed to be ambivalent, claiming that "under Socialism the motives 'to energetic self-help' would be less impaired than in existing Society . . ." Annie Besant's periodical, Our Corner, completes the sample of Socialist literature. Here too Smiles is cast as the villain. Graham Wallas saw the period after the extinction of Chartism (roughly 1851) as a difficult time for the working class, while the "middle and upper classes wallowed in the horrors of the time of crinolines, Miss Yonge, and Mr. Samuel Smiles." Bernard Shaw also ridiculed the hopes aroused by Smiles, believing that the success of an individual worker was irrelevant to the larger question of social reform:

> Here then is the opportunity of the cunning Proletarian, the hero of that modern Plutarch, Mr. Samuel Smiles. Truly, as Napoleon said, the career is open to the talented. But alas! the social question is no more a question of the fate of the talented than of the idiotic.[14]

Generally speaking then, Smiles was used by the Socialists as a convenient straw man, but their criticism, apart from Bernard Shaw's article, was usually destructive rather than comprehensive and reflective.

However, the Labour journal, The Pioneer, ran an article on Thrift in 1889, criticising Smiles in a more basic way. This was that Smiles held a double standard - one for the rich and one for the poor. Although this was not strictly true on the theoretical level, since ideally Smiles wanted all classes to work in one way or another, yet in practice it worked out as a double standard. As noted earlier, Smiles' criticism of the aristocracy did fall short of genuinely radical suggestions, and he also did make in practice a distinction between those that apparently need never work or save, and those that would always have to work and save. Thus in 1887 he wrote: "The life of man in this world is for the most part a life of work. In the case of ordinary men, work may be regarded as the normal condition . . ." The inference was that there existed others of the non-working and non-ordinary variety. The Pioneer article went on to criticise the equation of wealth and well-being in view of the equal increase of both poverty and wealth, and recommended that Smiles' Thrift be "relegated to the library shelves where lie cobwebbed books distinctly out of date."[15]

However, Socialist attitudes toward work also undercut Smiles' ideal of work and self-help in an even more fundamental way - by proposing a different concept of the nature of man, and hence of his work. For a more accurate assessment of this challenge to the ideal of self-help, it will be useful to look more closely at three Socialists, representing roughly the left, centre, and right wings of the Socialist movement, Edward Carpenter, Robert Blatchford and Sidney Webb.[16]

Edward Carpenter (1844-1929) was a Socialist who belonged both to the Fabian Society and the Socialist League. His abandonment of the religious life (he had prepared for clerical orders at Cambridge as an assistant to F.D. Maurice) together with a complete opposition to Victorian materialism, science and commerce, led him to live an individualistic life of manual labour on an isolated farm near Sheffield. His ideas were an amalgam of Christianity, Platonic and German idealism, Walt Whitman, and most important for his vision of the nature of man, Eastern religion. However an early essay, written in 1866, reveals his debt to the mid-Victorian era. Like Smiles, he could not "doubt that energy is all important; energy as opposed to luxury, as opposed to the want of healthy occupation and to the want of persevering industry" while "idleness is a continual source of sedition and a continual drag on progress." Moreover Carpenter valued man's work, as did Smiles, because "we may be sure that the effect of every historial event is not lost, but is felt everywhere, through all succeeding time." Finally, Carpenter also conceived of the possibility of a civilisation's advance and decay, and advocated a spirit of "healthy morality" among the people. Even so, Carpenter queried the value of the progress of Commerce and Railroads, Education and the Telegraph, asking "are we any the better for all this?"[17]

The emphasis in the 1866 essay had been on the innate energy of man, seeking to express itself through the powers and capacities of the individual, much in the Smiles tradition. Under the influence of Greek art, however, Carpenter came to a key point - the sensuous nature of art, he claimed, "only serves to show how difficult or impossible it is to draw any marked dividing line between our higher nature and our more animal instincts." This was a position that Smiles could never have taken, because although he did think in terms of Greek "forms," each human containing "the ideal of a perfect man, according to the type in which the Creator has fashioned him . . ." yet Smiles went on to advocate education as the development of "the germs of a man's <u>better nature</u> . . ."[18] In other words Carpenter conceived of man as a harmonious whole, while Smiles thought of man as divided into a higher and lower nature, so that while Carpenter's man could express his energy in work freely, confidently and happily, Smiles' man perforce utilised work as a necessary and severe task or difficulty to discipline his lower nature, form his character, and advance material progress, thus giving work a far more earnest purpose, and denying the possibility of work undertaken as pleasure.

Carpenter visualised work as therefore involving the whole individual: "As the blow which the skillful workman gives with his hammer sums up and transmits all the forces of his system - the energy of his aim, the poise of his legs, the intelligence of the eye, - so does the whole soul energise itself into the truthful word and . . . action." Carpenter's ideal of the harmonious individual led him to the same attitude toward work as William

Morris, namely that there could be instinctual pleasure in work, an attitude again that Smiles' divided man could not achieve. In an 1883 lecture on Cooperation, Carpenter declared:

> Every man who has done honest work knows that such work is a pleasure - one of the greatest pleasures . . . For there is no doubt now that Labour, under right conditions, is a blessing and not a curse. In fact, to use your skill and your strength in producing that which is beneficial to yourself and to others, to look back afterwards on the work of your own hands, to see that as far as may be it has been well done, that it will serve its time and the purpose for which it was intended - these things in themselves cannot but be a pleasure.

Carpenter called for cooperation, not as Smiles did (to preserve the working class from poverty), but to fulfill the inner motivations of man as a social animal, for these desires and needs, though hidden, "are . . . the agents which construct and create our social life as it is . . ."[19]

Carpenter was not fearful of the inner instincts, needs and drives of man as the Calvinist trained Smiles was. Yet both in their own way wished to elevate the dignity of labour; Smiles for an external reason, as a means of undercutting the aristocratic ideal and giving some dignity to the working classes, and Carpenter for an internal reason, to make work enjoyable, and so "above all to have done . . . with this ancient sham of fleeing from manual labour, of despising or pretending to despise it." Manual labour was important for Carpenter because the result of the work of one's hands was the true source of ownership (the labour theory of value intellectualised). In this way property ". . . is a product of my _work_. I have entered into the closest relationship to it; I have put _myself_ into it; it has become part of me - one of my properties."[20] Smiles too adhered to some kind of labour theory of value, yet because he was more interested in work as part of the natural order of the world, as a necessary link in the Divine plan, he ignored the possibility of work as freely chosen and so ignored the precise nature of the act of labour itself.

Carpenter wanted a new society which would include "the liberation of labour to dignity and self-reliance . . ." By this he meant that once the individual was freed from compulsion "a spontaneous and free production of goods wd. [sic] spring up, followed of course by a spontaneous and free exchange . . ." The present industrialisation, wage slavery and machinery represented a system whose "key note is Anxiety . . ." But if all food, clothing and housing were miraculously provided for, Carpenter postulated, in his notes for an 1890 lecture,

> I suppose 9/10ths wd. say 'Never work again.' . . . Yet you would. Give you as long as you like - a year's travel - Yet after that 9/10ths of us here wd. begin to produce. But being no compulsion, each wd. take his own line of work according to taste and skill - and mark you! quite in a difft. spirit, potatoes, tables, chairs, houses.[21]

Work would thus be done spontaneously to fulfill the real needs of internal and external man, once the material and social pressures had been removed. In comparison, Smiles did not, and could not, have trusted the nature of man as Carpenter did, for Smiles' individual required an essential training in moral discipline through the Home, School and Workshop as a counterpart to the spirit of self-help.

Carpenter's desire to liberate the internal forces of the individual for a true ideal of work through the "expression of inner meanings into outer form" was linked to another important idea - the unity of man with Nature. He wanted to see "the Greek ideal of the free and gracious life of man at one with Nature and the cosmos - remote from the current ideals of commercialism and Christianity!" But for this to be conceivable it was necessary to dispel the worship of "modern Science," because it was not possible to be one with Nature in an atomistic and mechanical world. So Carpenter attacked two of Smiles' assumptions, the value of facts, leading to the "patient and arduous observation of facts" and also "the supposed Laws of Nature . . . which were accounted immutable and ever lasting." Once Nature was freed from the compulsive laws and objective facts of Victorian science, then man could hope to overcome the alienation between himself and Nature, and the alienation within himself. In a letter to a friend in 1873, Carpenter wrote: "I fancy there is a crack all down creation . . . and that the more nearly people come to understanding creation the more do they feel this crack in themselves. Life is the bridging of this crack."[22]

Alienation was real to Carpenter and not to Smiles because Carpenter did not have the atomistic preconceptions about the sharp distinctions between man, nature, work, and society that Smiles did. Carpenter was also able to see the fall of man in terms that were extra-religious as well as religious. In 1886, Carpenter visualised the fall of man as a loss of unity with Nature, and called for man to "undo [the] wrappings and mummydom of centuries," whether they be houses, clothes, fetishes or work compulsions. By 1889 Carpenter thought of the fall of man as the onset of self-consciousness and the division of self into two, when the concepts of sin, sex and property all began. He called for man's return to the natural life, "the very wrestling with the great Mother for his food . . . to restore that relationship [with Nature] which he has so long disowned . . ." Such a life, contended Carpenter, would bring about a natural spirit of mutual help between men - to replace the individualism of the Commercial Age, and thus obviously bring an end to Smiles' ideal of self-help.[23]

Carpenter revised his theory of alienation again in 1889, and arrived at a concept of alienated production which bears remarkable similarities to Marx's theory of alienated labour, then unpublished in England. Carpenter found that

> the growth of property through the increase of man's powers of production reacts on the man in three ways; to draw him away namely, (1) from Nature, (2) from his true Self, (3) from his Fellows.

In regard to Nature, "as man's power over materials increases he creates for himself a sphere and an environment of his own . . ." By creating houses and cities and living in them, man "shuts Nature out," and by using his powers in defiance of Nature, man creates a world in which Nature has no part. Secondly, alienation from his own self occurs when the growth of property draws man from his true self by creating artificial, instead of simple, natural wants. And lastly, by creating and possessing property man comes into conflict with his fellow men, and thus abandons his "organic" relationship with the whole body of his fellows.[24]

Carpenter's effort to restore the unity of man, and hence enable man to unfold his whole nature, physical and mental, in his work, was in direct contradiction to Smiles' idea of holding back and disciplining the instincts and inner drives. That is to say, although Smiles conceived of the harmonious development of the faculties of the tripartite individual; physical, moral and intellectual; yet in practice he stressed the need for self-control over instincts of man, making the process a two-way struggle between the lower (physical) faculties and the higher (intellectual and moral) faculties: the "selfish desires have to be restrained, and the lower instincts repelled," wrote Smiles, advising self-conquest, and the Roman qualities of manliness, courage and virtue.[25] In this process Smiles' emphasis was on the calculation, holding back, and saving up of energy, sex, money, time and leisure, and on the use of work as both a barrier to the instincts (moral discipline) and a safe channel for the engagement of energy in the long-term, carefully controlled pursuit of occupation or purpose. Carpenter, on the other hand, despised the Roman virtues, and advocated the Greek ideal of expressing and liberating the instincts:

> Forms are continually being generated from feeling and desire; and, gradually acquiring . . . definition, pass outward from the subtle and invisible into the concrete and tangible. This process . . . [is] from Emotion to Thought, and from these again to Action and the External world . . . And not only the Artist and Musician, but every workman who makes things does the same.[26]

The denial of man's integrity and the pressures that produced degrading work on a massive scale elicited other responses that were similar to Carpenter's, with the same desire to reintegrate man's divided nature. These included William Morris, A Dream of John Ball, and News from Nowhere; Havelock Ellis, The New Spirit (London, 1890); Richard Jefferies, The Story of My Heart (London, 1883); and, in his own way, Robert Blatchford.

Robert Blatchford (1851-1943) was a Socialist who joined the Fabian Society, but who also preferred to take an independent line in Labour politics. This was possibly due partly to the enormous success of his small book, Merrie England (1893), which sold well over one million copies by 1904 and two million by 1910; partly to his Socialist magazine, The Clarion, which built up a strong following from 1891 on; and partly to the support which he had developed in the North of England through his brightly written 'Nunquam' column in the Manchester Sunday Chronicle, from 1887 to 1891. Blatchford's ideas owed a great deal to Carlyle, whose Heroes and Hero Worship apparently had a powerful impact on his thinking; and also to his brief spell in the British Army, which gave him the ideals of team-work and mutual respect. Lastly, Blatchford's life in Manchester while working for the Sunday Chronicle awakened him to the ugliness of industry, the drudgery of work, and the sheer lack of pleasure in the monotonous and poverty-stricken lives of the workers.[27]

Socialism, declared Blatchford, "will dignify no self-made man; will erect no statutes to Hudson, or Arkwright or Jay Gould or Masham. Will rather honour . . . the man-helper than the self-helper; will put the names of John Ruskin, Thomas Carlyle, Walt Whitman, and Erasmus Darwin above those of all the money-spinners . . ."[28] Despite his rejection of the "self-helper," Blatchford had a somewhat ambivalent attitude toward Smiles, because on the one hand he believed strongly in the value of work (as befitted an admirer of Carlyle), while on the other hand he disliked the individualism and competitive spirit inherent in what he considered to be Smiles' gospel of "getting on" and "success."

Initially in 1888 Blatchford warned "the working men that party politics were of no use to them, and that their chief hope lay in combination and self-help." But in January 1890 he disputed the ideal of self-help, valuing honour more highly, because "we worship success, we honour and extol 'self-help.' The man most admired in England is the man who fights his way to the front." And in May 1890 Blatchford attacked Smiles more specifically: "Of course you have read Smiles' 'Self-Help.' A most bewitching book." Bewitching because Smiles' idealisation of various workers and inventors had intrigued Blatchford in his youth, especially the example of Arkwright, but now Blatchford considered Arkwright to have been greedy and selfish, and not a great man:

> When I was a boy Arkwright was one of my heroes. He was a man who had 'got on,' and I had been taught to

> revere the art of getting on. He was a clever man, and I admired industry. But of late years my views have changed. I have become the prey of the philosopher. I have acquired a dreadful habit of searching for motives. I have begun to doubt whether men of Arkwright's stamp are 'great' men . . ."

Then in June 1890, on the occasion of the House of Lords' debate over sweated labour, Blatchford lumped together "fat bishops" and "wine drenched lords" with "Thrift" and "Self-Help" as particular objects of derision. And finally in 1898 Blatchford called for a higher standard of conduct in public life, complaining that too many were "extolling self-help and competition, and putting every possible premium upon the basest nature and the most selfish conduct."[29] Such was one particular Socialist's path toward the rejection of the self-help ideal.

Curiously, Blatchford evidently re-read Self-Help in the 1920s, and thought more highly of the book. Smiles' message was not selfish success, Blatchford now believed, but "to do our duty manfully, to make the best of our faculties and opportunities, and to be diligent and faithful in the doing of good deeds." Moreover, Baltchford praised Smiles' concept of work, "for work is a thing that is well worth doing . . . There is no finer food, exercise, or medicine than work - not even play." But having separated the value of work and the doing of good deeds from unworthy selfishness and success, Blatchford was still cautious: even if Self-Help was "a good book," perhaps "Smiles does attach more value to fame and promotion than some of us do . . ." And in his 1931 autobiography Blatchford is still not sure if "Smiles and other didactic teachers" were not really "success" teachers after all.[30]

However, returning to the late 1880s and 1890s, it is clear that Blatchford's approach toward, and eventual rejection of self-help, presaged a new attitude by Blatchford toward work and the nature of man. At the end of the 1880s, Blatchford still sounded very much like Smiles: "Man has two natures - the beastlike and the godlike. Let us take this for granted. Man has some qualities in common with the brutes. Such are his appetites and passions." A corresponding attitude toward work was therefore indicated and expressed: "Work itself is a fine form of moral and mental discipline and training, and contact with nature and the facts of life is, I think, more effective culture than can be got from books or lectures." Blatchford thought that "all the ills that the flesh is heir to spring from the imperfection of human nature . . ." and so man's condition could not be improved "until man's nature has slowly and painfully worked out its highest development." Meanwhile there could be "no wealth without industry, nor any prosperous state without labour."[31] Like Smiles too, Blatchford sometimes seemed more concerned with work as an antidote to idleness: "Idleness brings misery and death. Men must live by work, and what is more, they must in a great measure depend upon work, not only for sustenance, but for enjoyment." And Blatchford thought (as did the 'real' Smiles) that the important thing was not the search for fame and success, but to "us who are men, Duty and Work and Truth are good enough. Let a man do the work nearest his hand, and do it with all his heart and soul and strength."[32] In other words, a suspicious view of the lower of nature of man seemed to require a "hard line" attitude toward work as both necessary and a discipline.

Yet Blatchford differed from Smiles in dismissing the "iron law of supply and demand," and also saw that the object of life was not the patient struggle against adversity because "suffering is our enemy, happiness is our object." To this end he criticised "the political pack yelping 'Thrift, Thrift!' on the one hand, and the clerical pack growling

'Humility, obedience, and hell-fire' on the other hand," and called for "innocent pleasure" and "every natural gaiety." Blatchford was not so worried as Smiles over man's desire for pleasure:

> Would that I had the power and the eloquence to plead for rest and recreation as Carlyle pleaded for work! Such pleading is much needed. Really, folks seem to think it folly, even wickedness to enjoy themselves . . . That they live to work - instead of working to live.[33]

It is true that Smiles also asked for leisure and recreation, but he would have baulked at pleasure as an ideal of life, believing that it was "not ease, but effort, - not facility, but difficulty that makes men." But from the grime of Manchester, it was pleasure that Blatchford advised: "The people want more amusement, more change, more pleasure, more excitement. They have enough of labour and trial and care, and enough of sermons - God knows."[34]

The difference was that Smiles visualised the formation of character as the primary aim, in which the higher nature of man, aided by the environment, subdued man's lower nature, while Blatchford appeared to be moving toward a concept of the nature of man as good, and, like Carpenter, one harmonious whole. Blatchford contended that "the general tendency of men under ordinary conditions is to good . . ." and felt that the internal man did not require charcter formation since man was already and unchangeably one unit:

> The body is the soul and the soul the body. Violate one and you violate the other . . . [B]lood . . . brain . . . eye . . . - these things are the soul and the body - these things are man; these, and all the passions, all the desires, all the failings . . . You cannot botch and tinker the creature. You must take him as he is.

Consequently Blatchford was optimistic over the chances of a future Utopian society, and speculated that if people were taken from the slums and put "in a new country where they must work to live, where they can live by work, where fresh air and freedom and hope can come to them . . . in a generation you will have a prosperous and creditable country."[35]

Blatchford's Utopian speculations included the same hopes as Edward Carpenter over the potential of men's energies when released from external compulsion, and the same belief in the unity of man with Nature, while at the same time Blatchford was perhaps closer to Smiles on the need for men to be trained to work: "If all were disciplined to work, and all were granted love and leisure, what a wealth of nobleness, of strength, of beauty would be released from the chains of bondage in which they now rot and languish." It was commerce and modern civilisation that had driven a wedge between man and Nature, for when man divorces himself from Nature, Blatchford wrote, "he renounces a part of himself, and ceases to be a complete human being." For man to work well, then, he should be reunited with Nature, and reunited within himself. "He must be his _whole_ self before he can entirely make good the faculties of himself."[36] Civilisation and industrial society had therefore alienated man, and the answer was a return to Nature, pleasure, and work for all.

Like Smiles, Blatchford considered that labour was the basis of everything valuable, "everything in this earth worth having is the outcome of labour," and further, that "Labour _must_ produce good." But what was it that was likely to make all men work? Smiles' answer was conscience, duty and necessity, but Blatchford realised that there were different kinds of work, and that not all work was to be recommended, on account of its drudgery and uselessness. He therefore desired that work be made useful, honourable and respected, that it be made artistic, pleasant and elevating, and that constant change and pleasure be introduced.[37] If all this could be done, Blatchford felt that men would work, because for Blatchford, as for Morris, work was a pleasure rather than a Smilesian duty:

> By Saint Thomas of Chelsea [Carlyle], what a glorious and thrice-blessed thing is work . . . To be fit for work, to have work to do, and to do it - are not these the chiefest boons of life? To be idle by necessity or habit, to have work to do and be too lazy or feeble to do it, to be eager for work and find none to be got at, to have strength and opportunity for work, and to leave it undone - are not these among the blackest and most blasting curses? What is comparable to the delight of the strong man using his strength worthily and well! . . . Give me another draught of that strong nor'-western wind, with a sunbeam in it. There is one good thing in the world while there is work in it. There is something to live for while there is something to be done. A benizon on thee, stern Saint Thomas of Ecclefechan, apostle of labour.[39]

The romanticism of the sensuality and joy of labour could only be realised outside of the factory, and in some future Utopia, which is exactly where Blatchford placed it.

Whereas Smiles hoped that the future civilisation of Britain would operate with the tested work values of the past, Blatchford's Utopia was supposed to operate with the theoretical work values of the future. In <u>The Sorcery Shop</u> (1907) Blatchford posited two sanctions for work in his Utopia: sheer pleasure, and the influence of public opinion. A visitor transplanted into this future society was surprised to learn that

> one of their chief amusements is work.
> Work!
> Yes. For work is a pleasure when it is not imposed as a toil. Even in our England many find recreation in work . . . [I]n this country almost every man or woman works at several trades . . .

The essence of Utopian work was a spontaneous community effort:

> When a new road is to be made, or an old one mended, all the men will pour out of their workshops and houses and set about the job as if they were preparing a lawn for a garden party. They can all work, and they all like to work. To them work is sport.

This was because "they work for the general good and their own pleasure. There are no masters and no servants here." And people worked for the general good because fundamentally they desired the approval of their fellows, their incentive was the "love of approbation."[39]

Blatchford's theory of work differed from Carpenter's because although work was often (and in Utopia nearly always) pleasant, yet it was not necessarily a creative unfolding or instinctual activity as with Carpenter, but rather work became pleasant through the motives or reasons for working, and through the kind of work undertaken.[40] On the other hand, Blatchford's unified man did not have the inner tensions of Smiles' divided man, nor did he approach work in the same spirit of earnest purpose. In effect Blatchford did not quite reach Carpenter's concept of the ideal and trustworthy nature of liberated man, but he did go very much further than the ideal of self-help, because it no longer seemed that such guides to conduct were valid. "What a mad scramble life seems," wrote Blatchford in 1888. "What a mysterious and apparently objectless and unanswerable confusion prevails in the whole scheme of human nature." And to make matters worse, he found that "the printed guides . . . the religious and scientific and political charts of the way, how useless are they, seeing that the more one studies them, the less able one is to find the clue to the complex labyrinth . . .which men call 'life.'" Blatchford's answer was an effort to find the underlying simplicity and the natural dignity of human life and labour in visions of a future society - of man in harmony with Nature, released from the slavery of civilisation. For "human life is a very simple thing. It is become complicated through . . . an unnatural and unrighteous civilisation. The wants - that is, the bodily wants - of man are few, and may be easily supplied . . ."[41]

Thus Carpenter and Blatchford came to the same basic conclusions in regard to the nature of man and his work - a release from the repression of industrial civilisation coupled with the parallel release of man's unified potential for work on his own terms would enable a return to the simple life of harmony with himself and Nature. Such an ideal evidently undercut the self-help ideal, and in Blatchford's case very successfully, in terms of numbers of books and pamphlets sold, since Blatchford's highly popular Merrie England (Penny edition; 1894) appeared just at the time that Self-Help was suffering a sharp decline in sales. It was in the 1890s too that the London Fabian Society began to expand in numbers, and it was in 1892 that the first six Fabians were elected to the London County Council. Among those elected was Sidney Webb (1859-1947), recently married to Beatrice Potter, and one of the three or four leading members of the Fabian Society.[42] Sidney Webb's particular brand of functional Socialism offered a peculiar challenge to the ideal of self-help because although Webb started with many of the same values as Smiles, he was able to incorporate these values into a completely different ideal.

Sidney Webb's rejection of Smiles and the ideal of self-help was made explicit when he gave a lecture entitled "Socialism: True and False" to a Fabian Society meeting in January 1894. Liberal and Conservative capitalists, Webb declared,

> delighted in reminding the working men of all the future possibilities of self-advancement, when land should be "free," food cheap, and industrial competition unrestricted. The epics of this faith have been written by that unconscious corrupter of youth, Mr. Samuel Smiles, and are still fresh in the memories of most of us.[43]

By his use of the word "memories" Webb implied that Smiles was no longer being read, although it was only some nine years previously (1885) that

Webb himself had found "self-help" valuable, and only four years since (1890), that he had considered Smiles' edited autobiography of Nasmyth valuable for its discussion of the change from manual labour to the tending of machines.[44] In fact in the early 1880s Sidney Webb often sounded very like Smiles in his earnest strictures on work, duty and the passions of man, and, like Smiles, he found his early attitudes difficult, if not impossible, to shake off.

Sidney Webb was influenced by various traditions, including Utilitarianism; Malthusian and Ricardian political economy; the organic evolutionism of Herbert Spencer; Comtean Positivism; and not least, a strong sense of religion. He believed (in the late 1870s) that God had created the laws of Nature, which were therefore permanent, and like Smiles, conceived of a mechanical universe based on those laws, so that a man's work and activity influenced his own future life and character, that of his neighbours, the world in general, and "future humanity for ever and ever . . . [extending] in ever larger circles down the ages, inevitable and unalterable, multiplying in extent while diminishing in intensity . . . [and persisting] to eternity in some form or other."[45] Further, with Smiles, Webb thought that man's power over Nature was "the outcome of the labours of all the past ages . . ." and that because the present generation represented an investment by the past, so "they are in debt to the world to this extent; or rather that they are trustees of that skill and energy for the world."[46]

Sidney Webb also believed in the need for work, giving two basic reasons. One reason derived from early 19th Century political economy: Webb claimed that "Malthusians know that it [is] quite visionary to suppose a time when severe labour will cease to be necessary for the maintenance of the race," and in 1882 conceded the harsh reality of Nature's opposition: "Humanity finds itself under the same imperious necessity now as heretofore of satisfying the needs of organic life, and becomes merely more conscious of its subjection to the iron bonds of Nature."[47] The second reason for labour approached Smiles' position more closely, for Webb felt that man had a duty to work, to learn "the same great lesson of Work, Renunciation and Submission." There was a "universal obligation to work for the world in some way or another . . . The daily bread of the rich man is none the less the product of . . . daily toil, and unless he works in exchange he robs the toiler."[48]

As befitted a political economist of the old school, Webb believed in capital accumulation. But like Smiles he also saw added benefits in personal saving:

> Thrift, where voluntary, is thrice blessed: both the act of saving and the result of saving are fruitful in personal satisfaction, as well as social advantage, and the habit of due economy is itself so beneficial in its durable result upon personal and social character that it would be well worth acquiring even if provision for the future became unnecessary.

However, Webb's stress on capital accumulation and increased production turned out to be a reaction to one major issue - the increase of population coupled with a niggardly Nature. A buttress for this argument was the minor premise of the need to keep pace with the unlimited wants and desires of the population - a characteristically Utilitarian position, which contrasted with Carpenter and Blatchford's ideal of man's simple and few wants, and was similar to Smiles' belief in man's internal wants and desire for improvement.[49] Webb also believed in the rigid relationship of the wage fund to the numbers of the population, at least as late as 1888.

> If the iron hand of capital be uplifted ever so little, so that the market wages rise above normal,

> fewer of the families of the crowded toilers succumb to the misery of their lot; and the number of their class automatically rises, so as quickly to bring down wages again.[50]

With attitudes such as these it is not surprising that Webb counselled patience in well-doing, although contending in much the same optimistic way as Smiles that although "the main conditions of man's life are practically beyond his control, he can by patient and persistent effort, indirectly so modify the operation of these conditions, as enormously to increase his freedom."[51] But the significant difference between Smiles' ideal of work and Webb's is that while Smiles believed work produced both a moral discipline of character and an individualism of the spirit, Webb hoped that work would break down the individualism of man, and reduce him to a soldier in the cooperative army of society:

> The progress of industrialism has bound everyone of us into one great army of workers, in which each of us no longer fights for himself, but for the whole, and receives no longer what he individually produces, but a share of the whole. We fight the battle of life shoulder to shoulder, throughout the whole Universe: by this marvellous system of unconscious industrial co-operation we are all of us at each moment, in doing our own tiny work, producing a thousand different things, taking part in a thousand different productions.

Webb's faith in the industrial system of production was based therefore on the hope that the confrontation with Nature would be beneficial in eradicating individualism, and so, just as Smiles needed difficulties to help form the individual character, Webb needed the opposition of Nature to help form society:

> . . . the present struggle with nature, no longer in single units, but side by side throughout the whole world, as one industrial army gloriously fighting with and conquering the difficulties of existence on this unsatisfactory planet and triumphing each generation in a greater and greater degree by virtue of the

> constant breaking down of the remnants of isolated individualism still left among us.[52]

Webb opposed individualism partly as a result of the Socialist struggle against _laissez-faire_, but also because he saw man as divided between a higher and lower nature. Webb's motto was "Thou shalt renounce, renounce, renounce," for man's obstinate will to live an individual life was the "survival of the brute in man." Equally, strong law was necessary, since "the apes and tigers must be restrained by sanctions . . ." and those who have not yet "let the ape and tiger die" within them must perforce either accept the "rule of others or themselves rule those others." This was certainly Darwinian, and in truth Webb never felt that man could ever restrain his lower self and become a harmonious whole:

> Now if progress continues there is at any moment always a higher, and therefore also a lower nature. The lower of the future will be nobler than our present highest, but there will still be a higher. Man never _is_, but always _to be_ blest.

And hence there would always have to be law "partly to reinforce our own higher instincts against those lower ones which survive as relics of ancestry."[53] This suspicion of the nature of man, together with a Darwinian view of society as a biological entity, led Webb to a corresponding theory of work that did not free man's instincts, but like Smiles, repressed them.

Webb believed, for example, that the history of Rome was "a Sociological instance of the biologic truth that organisms of any but the smallest size must necessarily possess a well developed structure of a certain rigidity . . ." Webb accepted man's "perfect state" as one of "constant subjection," in which the role of the individual was to fill "his humble function in the great social machine . . . even if the individual be somewhat cramped . . ." Indeed the survival of the fittest meant that the individual should be prepared to work for only one reason - the survival of the society and the social good:

> Pegasus must to the plough, and, to get the ploughing well done, will perforce gradually become less and less of a Pegasus. A low development of a high type is often fitter to survive than a higher development of a low type.[54]

Whereas Smiles had advocated self-imposed moral discipline and duty to society as sanctions for work (and had used work as a means of achieving that discipline), Webb considered that the individual was required to perform his particular function in society according to the function prescribed by political economy. Hence Webb thought that social function actually preceded social structure, although he sometimes also talked as if moral duty transcended function: "Thy ability, produced by Society, is due to Society, to whom thou owest an account of the uttermost farthing paid for its use."[55]

Nevetheless, function was Webb's ideal, and he divided economic function into the traditional areas of Capitalist, Landholder and Labourer. These three groups corresponded roughly to Smiles' middle, upper and lower classes, although without Smiles' twofold division of workers and non-workers, and so, unlike Smiles, he gave the aristocracy a definite role: "Both the Middle and the Upper Classes have a definite function to perform . . ." the former as the "management of our vast industrial machine . . ." and the latter as investors of rent and capital in a socially beneficial way, "as stewards and trustees for the community." The third group, the labourers, had an obvious function, to find their "position in the great machine," and by becoming "a wheel in the great machine" of society, to work for the good of society.[56] Webb considered his own function as that of "an effective servant of the world . . ."

(indeed he was a civil servant), ready to answer the demands of the "public welfare." He professed himself prepared "to accept whatever may come to be done . . . a soldier in the great army of humanity, ready to execute whatever order comes . . . [for] we are not isolated units free to choose our work; but parts of a whole . . ."[57]

However, by 1891 Webb considered that while the work of society had to be done, at least it might be distributed better: "When we consider how the work of the world is now shared, and how it might be shared," he told Beatrice Potter, "you may be able to forgive me for some impatience when I come into contact with the idle rich . . ." For, like Smiles, and the Socialists in general, Webb wanted all in society to work, and on a personal level certainly lived up to his ideal. Whereas Smiles often remarked with a sense of guilt that he "could not be idle," it was with a definite sense of service to the social welfare that Webb restrained his personal pleasures, noting:

> I do not number my hours of work, because I do nothing else. I see no friends, save in the work. I have not read a book for months. I have not been to the theatre or concert or picture gallery in London for years. I have holidays but save for these I am at work from morning till bedtime.[58]

Perhaps the most striking aspect of Webb's letters and personal reminiscences is that he evidently did succeed in subordinating his internal desires and feelings to his work, perhaps as much because they were likely to prevent his efficient functioning as a servant to the public, as for reasons of their inherent evil. "I have very little knowledge of what has happened to me internally," he once told an interviewer. "Things impinge on me and I react to the impact . . . I can supply nothing but a series of disconnected accounts of impacts and reactions."[59]

Webb's answers to the problems of man and society were, it seems, basically Malthusian, Utilitarian, Spencerian and Positivist. He dealt in terms of the scarcity of Nature; of rationalism and calculation by the individual operating according to simple formulas of economics - an abstract man balancing pleasure and pain; and at the same time helping society to survive by fitting into the work of the social organism as efficiently as possible. Moreover Webb evidently considered that work did not have the instinctual value that it did with Carpenter; nor the pleasure and social approval that it gained with Blatchford; nor yet the quality of forming character, advancing civilisation, and existing as traditional "duty" in quite the same sense as Smiles. But there were some comparable attitudes between Blatchford and Carpenter on the one hand and Webb and Smiles on the other. Where the nature of man was seen as harmonious and unified (Carpenter and Blatchford), work was the valuable outcome of man's liberated energies and instincts, and was freely chosen by the individual according to his aptitudes. Where the nature of man was seen as divided and in conflict (Webb and Smiles), an authoritarian attitude to work developed, in which work was seen as the a priori human condition (divine retribution), and work-roles or functions were assigned to particular social classes and groups,[60] while various work sanctions were seen as supernaturally imposed - such as the scarcity of Nature, the fear of social decay and regression, the 'law' of God, and social or religious command and conscience in the shape of "Duty."[61]

However Webb went beyond Smiles on one important point. Responding partly to his vision of society as a (biological) unit, partly to the reality of industrial Britain in the 1880s and '90s, and partly to his personal experience in anaesthetising his own feelings and desires to the extent of internal blankness and numbness, Webb denied any meaning to work. "The desirability of work for its own sake," wrote Webb in 1889, "is now heard only as regards the West Indian 'Son of Ham,' or the colonial 'native.'" He concluded that "the better side of life . . . only begins at the moment when the daily bread has been ensured . . ."[62] Smiles could not have devalued work to this extent (although curiously he was not so far distant in promoting the self-culture aspect of self-help, for self-culture obviously did take place outside working hours), but in any case the corollary of Webb's position was the transfer of work from the purview of the individual to the depersonalised control of the state and Industry - a far cry from the personalised work of Self-Help. Sidney Webb's position was reinforced by Beatrice Potter, who married Webb in 1892, and who followed the same process of utilising work and the Socialist cause to repress her personal feelings and achieve internal blankness,[63] and who with Sidney Webb reached the same conclusion in regard to the subordination of work and the individual worker to the ideal of efficiency and discipline. In a book, written jointly, and published in 1897, the Webbs stated that individually chosen work was incompatible with the "economical use of steam power, the full employment of plant, or . . . specialisation . . . [through] division of labour." Work no longer belonged to the individual but to the industrial economy, for "there is no longer a choice between idiosyncrasy and uniformity. A common standard [of work], compulsory in its application, is economically inevitable."[64]

Thus the attempt by some English Socialists to find a new meaning for work went down to defeat in the 1890s, partly because of industrial needs, but also at the hands of the Fabians,[65] and it occurred at the same time as Smiles' own popularity declined. For if the ideal of self-help had been undercut by those Socialists who believed in the harmonious nature of man and his freely expressed work, equally it was undercut by those Socialists who believed that work had no meaning at all, and that the real life of the working man only began after work had stopped. This was the meaning of the agitation for the eight hour work-day that began toward the close of the 1880s. Thomas Burt, for example, a Liberal-Labour M.P., wrote in 1890 that although his own bias was "very strongly towards self-help and mutual assistance," yet the "determination of the workmen to be no longer mere tools of production . . . [led them] to demand leisure in order that they may cultivate and develop what is best in them."[66]

Of course the ideal of self-help declined not only because of the Socialist movement, but because of changing attitudes toward social values which the Socialists responded to and represented, and which they utilised to present an alternative ideal to that of self-help. As one somewhat biased commentator noted in 1895, the wage earning classes were learning that instead of improving their lot through "frugality, temperance and faithful industry" it was easier and more pleasant to use political power in transferring property to themselves. And another observer remarked in 1890 that "self-reliance seems gone, and every effort towards improvement, all initiative, are expected from Government. The Government is called upon to supply work . . ."[67] Moreover, both the radical and gradualist wings of the Socialist movement represented the new conviction in society that leisure and enjoyment were equally as important as work, and in some cases, worthy as an end in themselves. Again the late 1880s and the 1890s seem to mark the parallel decline of self-help and the wide-scale acceptance of this ideal of leisure (although with some reservations). One author accepted the concept of pleasure, but referred in 1895 to the "problem" of how to allow the working class to enjoy themselves without vulgarity. "One thing then that the Labour Movement has brought into prominence," wrote T.S. Peppin, a writer on working class clubs, "is the Leisure Problem . . ." The 'New Liberal' J.A. Hobson, complained in 1895 that work had become differentiated from enjoyment, and by 1914 could state that the

> chief justification for leisure does not consist in its contributions to the arts of industry but rather in raising the banner of revolt against the tyranny of industry over human life.

And Hobson irrevocably emphasised his distance from Smiles by proclaiming: "We should not be so terribly afraid of idleness." A final example among many is that of Sidney Webb and Harold Cox, who believed that the demand for shorter working hours was not for higher wages or health reasons, but because of "the strongly felt desire for additional opportunities for recreation and the enjoyment of life . . . in all classes the demand for leisure grows keener and keener."[68]

The decline of Smiles' ideal of self-help was due, therefore, to a number of causes. The Socialist movement, however, represented a major challenge to the ideal because it actually articulated an alternative attitude toward the morality of work and man's place in society. As with Smiles, work was given a positive value, but it was isolated and investigated as a specific problem, so that the tendency to see work in religious and moral terms was supplemented (rather than totally replaced) with the ability to view the work process objectively rather than subjectively. Thus even Sidney Webb, who came closest to Smiles' attitude to work, ended by criticising self-help and reducing work itself to an objective, depersonalised - and from the point of view of individual character and self-culture - valueless function. Other Socialists such as

Blatchford and Carpenter (and William Morris) showed that a new attitude toward the nature of man meant a new attitude toward work and man's function in society. Thus, if the nature of man was not thought to be divided, as in faculty psychology or Calvinist anthroplogy, then pleasure and enjoyment were an acceptable part of the life of every man, and work itself could be enjoyable.

So it was that the ideal of self-help had been supplemented, and to a large extent contradicted, by the concept of state help, the acceptance of leisure, the possibility of pleasurable work, and even the complete devaluation of the meaning of work. The idea of individual moral reform as advanced by Smiles and others (reform from within) had been replaced by the idea of reform from without, albeit in a somewhat impulsive and haphazard humanitarian fashion - "we are all Socialists now," said Sir William Harcourt in 1889.[69] Smiles' indirect pleas for the internal moral reform of the individual had depended on the idea that there was a moral character or standard (including a positive attitude toward work) to which the individual should conform, and on the belief that the individual would have to struggle internally to reach that standard. Such an attitude was widespread (Chapter III) and was still alive in the 1880s and beyond, as one reformer's implicit reference in 1888 to a moral standard makes clear: legislation was needed "to make the worthless classes realise that they must work, if not in freedom, then under compulsion" since the main task of working class reform was "the raising of their moral condition."[70] The difference between this desire for the moral reform of the individual from within (character formation), and social reform from without (an improved environment) devolved, it is argued, upon the question of how the nature of man was conceived.

On the one hand the proponents of the morality of work and the need for character-formation, such as Smiles and to some extent the Webbs, visualised an introspective man, struggling with the internal conflict of appetites (the brute in man) versus reason, which in turn required self-discipline and conflict with the environment (work) to achieve the required regularity of conduct and character. On the other hand the proponents of the 'new' integrated man (and the 'new' woman too), such as Carpenter and Blatchford, supported by the decline of faculty psychology and religious morality, and utilising the model of evolution, saw man as an outward looking, dynamic bundle of energies seeking to cooperate with and use a favourable environment. Oscar Wilde had a vision of such a harmoniously evolving man:

> It will be a marvellous thing - the true personality of man - when we see it. It will grow naturally and simply, flower like, or as a tree grows. It will not be at discord.[71]

Hence the emphasis came to be not on self-help and character, but on state help and the preparation of a favourable environment, for there could be no question of character formation in an integrated personality evolving naturally. Thus Blatchford wrote Carpenter: "It seems to me that our duty is to bring about the industrial change first"[72] - the other changes of work-attitudes and personality would therefore follow the creation of a suitable environment - and not, as Smiles maintained, that external change would only follow internal reform.

Chapter V - Footnotes

[1]Smiles to Jack Hartree, 6 Nov. 1875, Smiles Correspondence, SS/AI/66; Smiles to William, 24 July 1877, ibid, SS/AII/81; A.H. Murray to Smiles, 1 Sept. 1896, ibid, SS/AVII/34; J. Murray to Smiles, 9 June 1897 and 25 July 1898, ibid, SS/AVII/35 and SS/AVII/38. See Appendix F, for graph of Self-Help sales.

[2]Beatrice Potter [Webb], May 24, 1886, Diary, vol. IX, p. 30, in typescript of B. Webb, Diary (British Library of Political and Economic Science (B.L.P.E.S.), London).

[3]Some of these explanations occur in Perkin, Origins of Modern English Society, pp. 437-454; Royden Harrison, "Afterword," pp. 269-272; Samuel Hynes, The Edwardian Turn of Mind (Princeton, 1968), p. 55, on the discovery of poverty through into the Edwardian era. A.M. McBriar, Fabian Socialism and English Politics, 1884-1918 (Cambridge, 1966), p. 7. Henry Pelling, Origins of the Labour Party (2nd edition; Oxford Paperback; 1966), Chapter I.

[4]For changing moral values see P.T. Cominos, "Late Victorian Sexual Respectability and the Social System," International Review of Social History, 1963, vol. VIII. Edward Carpenter noted the many new movements of the 1880s, falling generally under the headings of Socialism, Humanitarianism, and return to Nature, E. Carpenter, My Days and Dreams (London, 1916), pp. 237-40. The truth of the statement regarding work as part of a mosaic of values is also illustrated by the youth movement of the 1960s in the United States, which besides rejecting the work and success ideal, also had new attitudes toward clothes and appearance, the family, religion, sex, social structure, etc.

[5]Smiles (ed.), Nasmyth, p. 12. Smiles, Duty, pp. 12, 14, 51. Smiles, Men of Invention, pp. 270, 263.

[6]Smiles to William, 18 Nov. 1868, Smiles Correspondence, SS/AII/19; and 20 Nov. 1868, ibid, SS/AII/20.

[7]Smiles to William, 24 Aug. 1872, ibid, SS/AII/33; and 15 July 1874, ibid, SS/AII/56; and 12 Nov. 1878, ibid, SS/AII/89; and 2 April 1880, ibid, SS/AII/101; and 16 July 1892, ibid, SS/AII/216; and 26 March 1893, ibid, SS/AII/226; and 12 March 1893, ibid, SS/AII/231; and 12 April 1894, ibid, SS/AII/273. For investment in Belfast, see Smiles to William, 16 June 1873, ibid, SS/AII/48.

[8]Smiles, Duty, pp. 47, 50, 52.

[9]Smiles, The Huguenots . . . in England and Ireland, pp. 413, 430-431. It should be added that Smiles thought the basic cause of 1789 was the corrupt priesthood of Jesuits which paved the way for Voltaire and Rousseau. The pupils of the Jesuits were the Communists of 1871 as well as the sans-culottes of 1793, Smiles, The Huguenots in France (New edition; New York, and London, 1893), p. (xii).

[10]For Smiles on God 'requiring' work see note 5 above. Smiles, Duty, p. 37. Smiles, Lives of the Engineers, vol. V, pp. 230, 312.

[11]Smiles to Janet Hartree, 8 Aug. 1885, Smiles Correspondence, SS/AI/182a. The furthest he went in appraising work conditions after the 1840s was to concede that the "lot of labour is indeed often a dull one . . ." Smiles, Industrial Biography, preface, p. (iv).

[12]Thomas Mackay, "Preface," in Smiles, Autobiography, p. (xii).

[13]Smiles, Self-Help, p. 321; Smiles, Autobiography, p. 106. Self Help versus State Help (Liberty and Property Defence League; London, 1883) (pamphlet in B.L.P.E.S.). In the same library there is an undated and

unidentified pamphlet entitled Self Help and Personal Rights, No. 2, possibly a sequel to the 1883 pamphlet.

[14] Rev. Percy Dearmer, Christian Socialism: Practical Christianity (Clarion Pamphlet No. 19; London, 1897), p. 9. William Morris, "Unattractive Labour," Commonweal (London), May 1885, vol. I, p. 38. J.H. Smith, "Prof. Sidgwick and Political Economy," ibid, Jan. 1887, vol. III, p. 12. Graham Wallas, "The Chartist Movement," Our Corner (London), Sept. 1, 1888, vol. XII, p. 140. G.B. Shaw, "The Economic Aspect of Socialism," ibid, Dec. 1, 1888, p. 356. One other article attacked self-help specifically in Our Corner, and this was E. Fairfax Byrrne, "The Bishop's Anti-Sweating Demonstration," ibid, Sept. 1, 1888, p. 161. This sample of Socialist literature was chosen to represent three wings of the Socialist movement: The Commonweal, vols. I-III, 1885-1887 (Socialist League); Clarion Pamphlets, 1-30, 1895-1899, and The Pioneer, vol. I, 1889 (Independent Labour); Fabian Tracts, 1-58, 1884-1894, and Our Corner, vols. XI-XII, 1887-1889 (Gradualists).

[15] Smiles, Life and Labour, p. 1. J.H. Clapperton, "Dr. Samuel Smiles on Thrift," The Pioneer, Jan. 1889, vol. I, pp. 1, 3, 8. See also J.B. Glasier, Working Men, Indeed! "Honest Toil" (Aberdeen, 1890), p. 10 for a similar assessment on the double standard of preaching work, and at the same time doing one' best to avoid it.

[16] See Appendix G.

[17] Edward Carpenter, On the Continuance of Modern Civilisation (1866) in Carpenter Collection (Sheffield Public Library), MS essay, pp. 24, 25, 5, 28, 3. Carpenter's intellectual debts can be found throughout his autobiography, Carpenter, My Days and Dreams, e.g. p. 143 for Oriental philosophy. Carpenter has been claimed for the Fabians (McBriar, Fabian

Socialism, p. 364), but it is not generally known that he joined the Socialist League as well, William Morris to Carpenter, Sept. 13, 1885 in Carpenter Collection (Sheffield Public Library), MS 386-21.

[18]Edward Carpenter, The Religious Influence of Art (Cambridge, 1870), p. 32. A more explicit statement occurs in 1889 - one should not "divide the virtues (so-called) from the vices (so-called) . . . but . . . see the character as a whole," Carpenter, "Defence of Criminals," To-day: the Monthly Magazine of Scientific Socialism (New Series; London), Feb. 1880, vol. XI, p. 41. Smiles, Life and Labour, p. 82 (emphasis mine).

[19]Edward Carpenter, "Truth," n.d., but early 1870s, in Carpenter Collection (Sheffield Public Library), MS essay, p. 1. Edward Carpenter, Co-operative Production (2nd edition; London, 1886), pp. 3, 11-12 (lecture first given at Hall of Science, Sheffield, 1883).

[20]Ibid, p. 15. Carpenter, "Private Property" (Lecture in London and Edinburgh, 1886) in E. Carpenter, England's Ideal (London, 1895), p. 147.

[21]Carpenter, My Days and Dreams, p. 127. E. Carpenter, Transitions to Communism (1897) in Carpenter Collection (Sheffield Public Library, MS 69; E. Carpenter, The Future Society (1890), ibid, MS 48.

[22]E. Carpenter, The Art of Creation (Hanley, 1903), p. 21. Carpenter, My Days and Dreams, pp. 67-68, 203 (Carpenter's attack on Science was first printed as Modern Science: A Criticism (Manchester, 1885)). Carpenter to C.G. Oates, April 2, 1873 in Carpenter Collection (Sheffield Public Library), MS 351-10(1).

[23]E. Carpenter, Civilisation: its Cause and Cure (1886), ibid, MS 31. Carpenter, "Civilisation: its Cause and Cure," The Pioneer, 1889, vol. I, pp. 20, 28, 31.

[24]Carpenter's rewriting of the'Civilisation' essay is in Civilisation: its Cause and Cure (1889) in Carpenter Collection (Sheffield Public Library), MS 41. The final version cited here is from Carpenter, Civilisation: its Cause and Cure (2nd edition; London, 1891), pp. 27-28. Marx's theory of alienated labour sees three main forms of alienation: (a) alienation from Nature, through production of alien objects; (b) alienation from man himself, being denied free expression in work; and (c) alienation from the "species" man and from other men, because his labour belongs to others. Carpenter had read in Marx, Engels, Lewis Morgan, Hegel, Schopenhauer, Hyndman, Carlyle, and Oriental philosophy, each of which may have contributed to his theory of alienation.

[25]Smiles, Life and Labour, p. 35.

[26]Carpenter, The Art of Creation, p. 20. The whole question of Roman "individualism" and Greek "expression" as a touchstone for 19th Century attitudes toward the nature of man is interesting; in general Socialists and Radicals idealised the Greeks, while those who favoured a divided man and the need for self-control, normally the conservative factions, cited the Romans. See section on Sidney Webb below.

[27]For information on Blatchford, see Laurence Thompson, Portrait of an Englishman: A Life of Robert Blatchford (London, 1951), pp. 98-99 for Merrie England circulation, and Robert Blatchford, My Eighty Years (London, 1931). On Carlyle, Blatchford to Alec Thompson, October 1885, in Blatchford Correspondence (Manchester Public Library), Autograph Letters, MS vol. I: "I have read Heroes and Hero Worship through about six or seven times. Slowly and carefully. I have studied Sartor Resartus and some others."

[28]Blatchford, The New Religion (Clarion Pamphlet, No. 20; London, n.d., but 1897), p. 5.

[29]Blatchford, column in the Manchester Sunday Chronicle, Nov. 11, 1888, p. 2; Jan. 12, 1890, p. 2; May 18, 1890, p. 2; June 15, 1890, p. 2. Blatchford, Altruism (Clarion Pamphlet No. 22; London, 1898), p. 13.

[30]Blatchford, "Of Samuel Smiles and Self-Help," The Clarion, July 13, 1923, p. 3, cutting in Alf Mattison Papers (Leeds Public Library), Folder 34. R. Blatchford, My Eighty Years, pp. 215-17. Asa Briggs' statement that Blatchford was one of Smiles' "unexpected admirers" should take account of Blatchford's rejection of self-help in the 1890s and his caution in the 1920s and '30s, Asa Briggs, Victorian People, pp. 137-38.

[31]Blatchford, Manchester Sunday Chronicle, Feb. 16, 1890, p. 2; Nov. 25, 1888, p. 2.

[32]Ibid, Aug. 4, 1889, p. 2; Feb. 19, 1888, p. 2.

[33]Ibid, Jan. 20, 1889, p. 2; Sept. 30, 1888, p. 2; Oct. 6, 1889, p. 2.

[34]Smiles, "What is doing for the People in Public Amusement and Recreation," People's Journal, July 4, 1846, vol. II, pp. 13-14. Smiles, Self-Help, p. 330, and for a warning against too much pleasure, p. 325. Blatchford, Manchester Sunday Chronicle, Oct. 19, 1890, p. 2.

[35]Ibid, April 28, 1889, p. 2; Oct. 27, 1889, p. 2; April 21, 1889, p. 2.

[36]Ibid, Jan. 4, 1891, p. 2; July 26, 1891, p. 2.

[37]Ibid, May 10, 1891, p. 2; Oct. 12, 1890, p. 2; Oct. 26, 1890, p. 2.

[38]Ibid, Oct. 12, 1890, p. 2.

[39]Blatchford, The Sorcery Shop: An Impossible Romance (London, 1907), pp. 99, 100, 111.

[40]Blatchford, Merrie England (New York, 1895), pp. 124-126.

[41]Blatchford, Manchester Sunday Chronicle, Oct. 14, 1888, p. 2; Aug. 31, 1890, p. 2.

[42]For details on Fabian Society numbers and Webb's election to the London County Council, see McBriar, Fabian Socialism, pp. 165-67, 198.

[43]Sidney Webb, "Socialism: True and False," lecture delivered to Fabian Society, Jan. 21, 1894, in Sidney and Beatrice Webb, Problems of Modern Industry (London, 1898), p. 257. Also Fabian Tract No. 51.

[44]Sidney Webb, "Lectures to Working Men's College," Autumn 1885 in Passfield Papers (B.L.P.E.S., London), Section VI, Item 23a, p. 25. Sidney Webb to Beatrice Potter, c. 21 Aug. 1890, ibid, Section II, Item 3(i), no. 14, f. 76.

[45]Sidney Webb, "The Existence of Evil," lecture, n.d., but probably 1878, ibid, Section VI, Item 1, p. 29; and "Heredity as a factor in Psychology and Ethics," lecture dated March 22, 1882, ibid, Item 5, p. 34.

[46]Sidney Webb, "The Factors of National Wealth," lecture, c. 1889, ibid, Item 38, p. 9; Sidney Webb, "The Ethics of Existence," lecture, c. 1880 or 1881, ibid, Item 3, p. 45.

[47]Ibid, p. 17; Sidney Webb, "Factors of National Wealth," ibid, Item 38, p. 6.

[48]Sidney Webb, "George Eliot," lecture, c. 1881, ibid, Item 6, p. 8; Sidney Webb, "The Way Out," lecture, c. 1884, ibid, Item 19, p. 52.

[49]Sidney Webb, "Factors of National Wealth," ibid, Item 38, p. 55; this same lecture also dealt with the exiled Huguenot's loss to France in terms of "the deterioration of the national character, reputation and international influence;" it seems likely that Webb had read Smiles' book on the Huguenots, ibid, p. 145. On the limitless wants of man, Sidney Webb, "The Need of Capital," lecture, c. 1886, ibid, Item 28, p. 20, and on

the limits of Nature, Sidney Webb, "What Socialism Means," lecture, 1886, ibid, Item 30, pp. 91, 93. Smiles, Thrift, p. 112 and above, Chapter II.

[50]Sidney Webb, The Rate of Interest and the Laws of Distribution (London, 1888), p. 14.

[51]Sidney Webb, "Factors of National Wealth," in Passfield Papers (B.L.P.E.S.), Section VI, Item 38, p. 8.

[52]Sidney Webb, "The Growth of Industrialism," Sunday Lecture Society, 1883 or after, ibid, Item 11, pp. 63-64, 54.

[53]Sidney Webb, "Rome: A Sermon in Sociology," lecture delivered at Hampstead as part of a course on the Development of the Social Ideal in European History, printed in Our Corner, Aug. 1, 1888, vol. XII, pp. 89, 83; Sidney Webb, "Considerations on Anarchism," lecture, c. 1884 or 1885, in Passfield Papers (B.L.P.E.S.), Section VI, Item 18, p. 8.

[54]Sidney Webb, "Rome: A Sermon in Sociology," Our Corner, Aug. 1, 1888, vol. XII, pp. 81, 89, 88.

[55]Sidney Webb, "The Economic Function of the Middle Class," lecture delivered to Argosy Society, 6 Feb. 1885 in Passfield Papers (B.L.P.E.S.), Section VI, Item 20, pp. 35, 49.

[56]Ibid, pp. 91, 12; Sidney Webb, "Lectures to Working Men's College," notes for the lectures, Autumn, 1885, ibid, Item 23a, pp. 9, 14, and for the function of Capitalist, Landholder and Labourer, p. 28.

[57]Sidney Webb to Beatrice Potter, 14 July 1890, ibid, Section II, Item 3(i), no. 8, ff. 55-56. Webb to Potter, 29 June 1890, ibid, no. 7, f. 49.

[58]Sidney Webb to Beatrice Potter, 6 April 1891, ibid, no. 9, f. 43. Webb's account of overcoming internal weakness occurs in Webb to Potter, 16 Dec. 1891, ibid, no. 100, f. 405; and Webb to Potter, 27 Dec. 1891, ibid, no. 107, f. 430. For Smiles' remark, Smiles, Autobiography, pp. 48, 347.

[59]Sidney and Beatrice Webb, "Reminiscences," St. Martins Review, October 1928, no. 452, p. 478. Sidney Webb commented on work and occupation as necessary to repress internal feelings of grief, melancholia, pessimism, and even sex, Webb, "The Ethics of Existence," 1880 or 1881 in Passfield Papers (B.L.P.E.S.), Section VI, Item 3, pp. 8-13.

[60]The description of male-female work roles is a case in point; for example Smiles did not believe in the liberated woman: "As for women taking the place of men in the work of active life," he wrote, "and becoming either sailors, soldiers, surgeons, barristers, or other occupations or professions, the thought is unworthy of serious consideration," Smiles, Life and Labour, pp. 302-303.

[61]An excellent example of sanctions is used by W.H. Mallock who contended that the majority of men must work or starve, for "Nature, not modern Capitalism is responsible for that necessity," W.H. Mallock, Labour and the Popular Welfare (London, 1893), p. 127.

[62]Sidney Webb, "The Regulation of the Hours of Labour," originally published in the Contemporary Review, Dec. 1889, in Sidney and Beatrice Webb, The Problems of Modern Industry, p. 112.

[63]Beatrice declared in 1887: "Before my work can be perfectly true, vanity and personal ambitions must die. Why need I despair of overcoming these vices . . . I must love my work and not myself . . ." Her affair with Joseph Chamberlain produced the same result: "Now to work - try to forget that which it is useless to remember, and work while the day lasts . . .", Beatrice Potter [Webb], Diary, July 2, 1886, vol. X, pp. 11-12; and June 9, 1887, vol. XI, p. 41.

[65]A.J. Penty remarked that the struggle between the two kinds of Socialism in the 1880s, William Morris' and Sidney Webb's, resulted in a

victory for Webb, A.J. Penty, Old Worlds for New (London, 1917), p. 182. The victory of gradualism can be dated quite accurately to the 1890s and particularly 1895, the date of Oscar Wilde's trial, and of a general election in which Socialist candidates ran poorly. One friend of Edward Carpenter's thought that Wilde's trial "had set the world back fifty years . . ." And another recognised the more gradual growth of Socialism in 1899, while "several years ago we all thought by this time we should be living in the ideal state of society . . .", R. Thurman to Edward Carpenter, Sept. 15, 1895 in Carpenter Collection (Sheffield Public Library), MS 386-58 and Lucy Henderson to Edward Carpenter, Aug. 22, 1899, ibid, MS 271-63.

[66]Thomas Burt, M.P., Parliament and the Regulation of the Hours of Labour (London, 1890), pp. 13, 11. Other Socialists who reached this conclusion included, of course, Sidney Webb, An Eight Hours Bill (Fabian Tract No. 9; London, 1889) (republished in 1890 and 1891 as Fabian Tracts Nos. 16 and 23); The Legal Eight Hours Question (debate between G.W. Foote and G.B. Shaw; London, 1891); and H.M. Hyndman, Mr. Gladstone and the Eight Hours Law (London, 1892). (Hyndman regarded the Eight Hours Movement as a diversion).

[67]Goldwin Smith, "The Manchester School," Contemporary Review (London), Jan.-June 1895, vol. LXVII, p. 387; "Power and Poverty," Saturday Review, Oct. 25, 1890, vol. LXX, pp. 476-477.

[68]T.S. Peppin, Club Land of the Toilers (London, 1895), p. 9; J.A. Hobson, The Evolution of Modern Capitalism (London, 1895), p. 379; and J.A. Hobson, Work and Wealth: A Human Valuation (London, 1914), pp. 241, 239; Sidney Webb and H. Cox, The Eight Hours Day (London, 1891), pp. 1-2. There is a great deal of further evidence for the decline of the work ethic, and

the rise of the leisure ideal in the late 1880s and the 1890s, for example, George Gissing, The Nether World (London, 1889); Sir Walter Besant, Autobiography (London, 1902), p. 244, and the rise of organised sport and recreation during these years. For a wide-ranging discussion on the working class need for art, leisure, education and amusement, see Transactions of the National Association for the Promotion of Social Science, Birmingham, 1884 (London, 1885), pp. 637 ff., 674 ff., 728 ff.

[69] Cited in Pelling, Origins of the Labour Party, p. 11.

[70] Francis Peek, "Workless, Thriftless, Worthless," Contemporary Review, Feb. 1888, vol. LIII, pp. 283, 284 (emphasis mine).

[71] For the decline of faculty psychology and the model of evolution in regard to creative man, Robert Thompson, The Pelican History of Psychology (Middlesex, 1968), pp. 28-30, 100. Appropriately the last major work in faculty psychology (by Alexander Bain) was written in 1859. The decline of religious morality is discussed by Alisdair MacIntyre, Secularisation and Moral Change (Oxford, 1967), pp. 58, 63. Oscar Wilde, "The Soul of Man under Socialism," (1891) in The Essays of Oscar Wilde (Bonibooks edition; 1935), p. 17.

[72] Blatchford to Carpenter, 11 Jan. 1894 in Carpenter Collection (Sheffield Public Library), MS 386-46(i). Some support for the thesis of the relationship between the nature of man and his work is found in C.B. Macpherson, "The Maximization of Democracy," in P. Laslett and W.G. Runciman (eds.), Philosophy, Politics and Society (Oxford, 1967), pp. 84-85.

## CHAPTER VI

## CONCLUSION: THE DECLINE OF SELF-HELP, AND THE PRINCIPLES OF AUTHORITY AND DEVELOPMENT

Toward the end of the century, there was another challenge to the ideal of self-help. This time it was not a confrontation, as with the Socialist view of work, nor a reversal of values, as with the acceptance of the validity of leisure, but a disguised challenge from within by the authors of books that really did advocate success - not the "best" kind of success espoused by Smiles - but straightforward advice based on an appreciation of the qualities required for advancement in a technolocigal society. The opening shot was fired by Henry Curwen in 1879, who proposed to write about his heroes without preaching or "tugging on any moral verbosities. Once moralise, and you are sure to trim your biography to suit your moral." This can be contrasted with the didactic element in Smiles' books, or with a comment by H.A. Page in 1875: "success in life depends, after all, more on moral and religious elements, which may be cultivated by all . . ."[1] Curwen's work was followed up by other books which discussed success in a frank and neutral manner, although still putting forward the qualities of industry and perseverence as the most likely avenues to financial success.[2]

On the other hand, many books with "success" titles published during the second half of the century still hesitated to offer outright and unadorned the possibilities of financial and social success. As in Smiles' books, the emphasis was on character, moral reform and the cultivation of the powers or faculties of the individual. James Hogg declared in 1859 that "success itself signifies really nothing . . .", and in 1879 the message of W.H. Davenport Adams' The Secret of Success was still much the same, not

> worldly prosperity, no extraordinary phase of fortune, but rather the acquisition of a 'sound mind in a sound body,' the complete culture of the physical, moral and intellectual faculties of the individual . . .

In 1883 Joseph Johnson could not promise success, although tedious labour might avoid failure, but with the aid of hard work he did promise one type of success to all: "culture and character. The building up of the man is a work infinitely more important than the accumulation of wealth . . ."[3] So far nothing that would have embarrassed Smiles and his ideal of self-help.

Indeed some authors found it difficult to move beyond Smiles' position and say anything new. W.H. Davenport Adams conceded that his book was similar in many respects to G.L. Craik's Pursuit of Knowledge

> and the admirable "Self-Help" by Mr. Smiles. To some extent, no doubt, it traverses the same ground. On the other hand, it devotes a considerable space to . . . the departments of "business" and "commerce" - departments which have hitherto . . . been comparatively overlooked . . .

Adams met the objection that he had only repeated the "truths which have become the commonplace of moralists and the stock-in-trade of our social teachers" by saying that such truths needed repeating, and went on to criticise G.L. Craik and Smiles for not pointing out the difference between liking a vocation and having a real talent for it, and for their glowing but false pictures of "fame and opulence." Nevertheless, Adams labelled his Chapter VIII "Self Help," and his book carried the same message - "self-help, self-elevation or self-culture - call it what you will . . ." with the "first element of self-help" being the "recognition of our duty . . ."[4]

Those authors who were prepared to move beyond Smiles' middle position between adherence to the old virtues and the possibility of self-culture and self-development, still referred frequently to his books or to the self-help idiom.[5] An anonymous work published in 1881 and entitled The Way to Fortune took a curious backhand swipe at Smiles by accusing him of not liking the medical profession, and merely using it as a pathway to authorship, but the book continued to use self-help as the basic theme: "all true workers are self-helpers and self made men. All the best men recognise what they owe as regards character . . . to self-help."[6] Nevertheless there were certain signs by the 1870s and '80s among the "self-improvement" and "success" books that the limited aims of self-help were outmoded. One book recognised that the time for individual feats and personal prowess was probably "now past," and another plainly stated its content in the title Fortunes Made in Business. But only from approximately 1890 on was there less pretense at combining success with a well-rounded character, or in seeking an acceptably slow and virtuous way of making money, instead the aim was clearly Money! Money! Money! (1890).[7]

The distance between Smiles and the 'new' self-help was underlined by the short lived appearance in 1901 of a magazine entitled Success - a Monthly Magazine of Inspiration and Self-Help, which purported to encourage social mobility, and by such new titles as How to Get Rich Quick (1907) and How to Grow Rich (1911). But perhaps the final (and unconscious) challenge to Smiles' ideal of self-help came from Ernest A. Bryant, who, some fifty years after the original, put out A New Self-Help (1908). While Bryant carefully avoided Smiles' name, he attempted to resurrect some of the original message, and his failure to do so showed only too clearly that the days of self-help belonged to the 19th and not the 20th Century. In the first place, despite disclaimers, Bryant did propose to write a genuine success book. Thus Bryant was forced to acknowledge that success was due to more than early rising and perseverence, and that new methods were called for: "The success of tomorrow lies with those who can devise new methods." He also granted that the modern lack of difficulties to overcome "might act almost as a discouragement to the aspirant of to-day were he to find that all the successes of this character belonged to the past . . ." Moreover Bryant was excited by the rise of two sets of heroes that Smiles did not concern himself with - the new Imperialists such as Rhodes, and the great American financiers, such as Carnegie and Rockefeller. Probably the greatest difference between the two Self-Helps is the admission by Bryant that examples of education obtained under difficulties were "unnecessary now, seeing that education is nominally free and compulsory . . .", and thus "every year the spread of education renders the way of nascent genius a little less difficult."[8]

The change that Bryant's book registered was reflected in the declining sales and popularity of the original Self-Help. According to Smiles' own account book, the sales of Self-Help were already deteriorating in the late 1880s, after a remarkable upsurge in the late 1870s. So, for example, while 23,049 copies of Self-Help were sold in the five year period, 1880-1884, in the next five years, 1885-1889, only 13,580 were disposed of. And in another section of his account book, Smiles noted that the annual income from the sales of all his books had dropped from £3143 in 1881 to £1009 in 1889.[9] Perhaps these figures are the most accurate indicator of both the lessened status of the ideal of self-help and the erosion of the high importance attached by Victorians to the meaning of independent, manly work.

It was not even so much that the status of work itself had declined, although this too had happened, but that the concept of the individual struggle toward independence through the time honoured path of self-denial and hard work no longer had the same social appeal or relevance in a more professional and technical world. This changed attitude was particularly visible in a book published in 1905 - one year after the death of Smiles - by H.G. Wells, then a Fabian Socialist. The book was entitled A Modern Utopia, and in it Wells proclaimed the end of labour and toil through the scientific application of machinery to the tasks of society. Wells proposed in fact the elimination of the working class, for the "whole trend of scientific mechanical civilisation is continually to replace labour by machinery . . ."[10] Ironically, it was just those inventors and builders of machines, whom Smiles had once lauded, that were seen by Wells as the advance guard of social change, putting an end for ever to that persevering and manly work which Smiles had thought to be such an essential (and indeed pre-determined) part of the human condition. Moreover, Wells' Utopia was fundamentally different from Smiles' vision of society, even when the latter projected a future civilisation, since Smiles had tried to find a meaning and value for work within a previously accepted and divinely granted framework of morality and natural order, while Wells had rejected the rule-book and had created his own framework of work values and possibilities.

In fact Smiles' ideals of work and self-help were based largely on the values of his early years, and in particular, the Calvinist Dissenting tradition of individualism, self-discipline and the formation of character. Nevertheless such a tradition fitted in well with a Utilitarian and reforming attitude toward society, including an opposition to the landed aristocracy and their control of the government. Indeed, Smiles' solution of self-help was strongly related to Utilitarian individualism and the Benthamite calculus - the "man who improves himself," wrote Smiles, "improves the world. He adds one more true man to the mass. And the mass being made up of individuals, it is clear that were each to improve himself, the result would be the improvement of the whole." But by improvement, Smiles meant moral (and also intellectual) improvement rather than the rational calculation of pain and pleasure, and so when he asked why thousands of middle class men were educated, comfortable and independent, he answered his rhetorical question in terms of moral qualities: "Why, by the practice of those very virtues . . ." namely, "industry, frugality, temperance and honesty."[11]

Smiles' attempt to instill these virtues in others was a life time effort, for he deeply felt that man's time on earth should be committed to usefulness and improvement. He summed up his own life and philosophy when he declared that "no life need be useless unless its owner chooses. We can improve and elevate ourselves, and improve and elevate others." The problem came when Smiles tried to define this elevation and improvement, for as he once said, the range of most men in life was so limited, that very few had the opportunity of being great. The vast majority had to give up ideas of success, fame or money, and stick to their honest and laborious duty.[12] For, unlike the potential of H.G. Well's machinery, Smiles was limited in what he could promise the working man by the experience of his early years. That is to say, Smiles did not believe that men (and certainly not women) should have the arrogance to rely on their own suspect "cleverness" and intelligence in changing the "rules" on which he considered the human condition to be organised. The struggle to overcome ever-present (and indeed necessary) difficulties and adversity; the formation of habits, virtues and character as part of that struggle; work and labour as the law of life and the fundamental basis of society; self-discipline and self-reliance; - these were the authoritative rules by which Smiles lived, and by which he wanted others to live. The message of Self-Help was simply that the reform of society could only be achieved if the individuals that composed society were to follow the rules and virtues exemplified in Smiles' brief biographies - in Smiles' mind there was no other way to improve the condition of society and of the working class - and the middle class had proved that it could be done.

Like Robert Owen, Smiles was sure that each individual was susceptible to rational persuasion and the force of example, and that once persuaded, the individual would change his life for the sake of himself and society. Part of the attraction of Self-Help for contemporary readers must have been its air of certainty, and just as the parallel example of the etiquette books provided a set of rules, which if followed, would enable the individual to achieve outward improvement, so too did Smiles offer an equivalent set of rules aimed at improving the lot of the individual - although he wished to emphasise internal improvement rather than external respectability. The remainder of the 'self-help' series reinforced the message - learn the predetermined order of life, and then adapt to it. Smiles' certainty about the route to improvement was reinforced by the belief that an underlying order and harmony existed in the world, as the laws of nature, economics and society seemed to prove, so that his first objective had been to discover those laws, and then to explain them to all who would listen.[13]

Like most reformers (again Robert Owen is an apt comparison) Smiles' ideal of self-help was a somewhat uneasy blend of the principles of authority and social development, of order and progress. Smiles had inherited certain Enlightenment principles - the power of reason, the potential of education inherent in Lockean psychology, the idea of progress and the perfectibility of the individual. Thus far his concepts of social development were similar to the reforming beliefs of the Utilitarians, and further coincided with the Utilitarian opposition to the aristocratic 'interest.' But the Calvinist Dissenting tradition, while comparable to the Utilitarian position in favouring the religious, economic and political freedom of the individual, also gave Smiles a somewhat severe morality. And in common with other middle class radicals of the 1840s, Smiles normally opposed government intervention, although pressing for political reform and permitting "preventive" legislation. Mankind was perfectible, but to be efficacious the perfection should germinate naturally within the individual - external legislation was an unnatural plant and hence unlikely to take hold. Moreover, the common faculty psychology of the early 19th Century and a Calvinist morality led Smiles to visualise human nature as divided and in conflict, requiring a self-imposed harmony, and hence needing the discipline of work and a continuous self-control. Such a view militated against the progress of the individual through the unrestrained drive for financial success and social mobility; while working class advance was also limited by the productive work of society, which was always present and would always require a large scale labour force.

The ideal of self-help therefore contained both authoritarian and progressive elements. Contrary to the belief that self-help was a message designed to encourage success, Smiles in fact favoured a middle way between the _status quo_ and an open society, encouraging individual self-culture and the improvement of character, rather than the pursuit of wealth and social status. In fact _Self-Help_ was aimed principally at the moral reform of society through the moral reform of the individual. Moreover the moderated _via media_ of self-help contained within it Smiles' answer to the comparable Victorian effort to find "the balance between regulation and liberty . . ."[14] Self-help implied an individualism of activity sanctioned by Adam Smith's identity of interests, but if Smiles came down strongly on the side of the freedom of the individual, he did so by imposing an internalised moral order based upon principles, character and self-discipline. As he once wrote, "Character . . . is moral order embodied in the individual."[15] Furthermore, the ideal of self-help was also related to the wider Victorian attempt - within the framework of Victorian individualism - to impose an internalised and acceptable set of values upon the largely independent working class. (As Chapter I noted this Protean attitude could also apply to the 'secular' challenge of commercialisation.) In fact Smiles may well have obtained the idea of basing external freedom upon internal discipline from R.W. Emerson, who also built his freedom of the individual upon obedience to an internalised moral and intellectual order.[16]

The ideal of self-help as an acceptable medium of regulated and moderated social change was exemplified not only by the concept of social progress through individual self-discipline and moral reform, but also by Smiles' faith in the emergence of a classless "natural aristocracy" of intelligence, hard work, moral worth and social usefulness. The idea of a "natural aristocracy" as the spearhead of social and moral change was not original to Smiles, being somewhat similar to a number of other suggestions, including Coleridge's "clerisy," Matthew Arnold's "remnant," Emerson's "class of power," and Carlyle's "Aristocracy of Talent" - to say nothing of Marx's future vanguard of the proletariat. Unlike Marx, however, Smiles and the others hoped to initiate a peaceful moral revolution, which in Smiles' case was aimed against the unnatural but lingering power of the idle aristocracy. Smiles wanted to undercut the status of the aristocracy with a new social and moral leadership based upon his meritocracy of engineers, inventors, scientists and philanthropists. As with his models in Self-Help, Smiles was confident that, once presented, the genuine worth of the meritocracy would be so obvious to rational men that social acceptance would speedily follow. However, as before, his confidence was misplaced, for the aristocracy retained their social and, in general, their economic power, while engineers remained low on the social scale.

Smiles' interest in the achievements of the "natural aristocracy" was not merely a reflection of the claims of the manufacturing middle class against the idle aristocracy, although something of this was present, for he disliked class interests and specifically included all classes among his industrial and inventive heroes. It was, in fact, part of the Victorian faith in the ability of man to achieve material progress. The 18th Century idea of a mechanical universe was still strong, and Smiles' remarks on the cumulative effects of quantified work, power and machinery, the universal operation of cause and effect; and the underlying order and harmony of nature (symbolised by the neat classification of facts by amateur geologists and naturalists) - all this provided a solid framework for material progress through the manipulation of an evidently understandable and penetrable environment. And in the process, Victorians were often compelled to give to work and machinery a Promethean and spiritualised task in order to bring such new and unnatural power within the bounds of Victorian religion and understanding.

In the last analysis, the ideal of self-help, and the concept of the "natural aristocracy" with its potential for material progress and moral leadership, were reactions to change. It was pointed out in Chapter III that Smiles' ideal of self-help was not an isolated bolt from the blue, but part of a self-help tradition, answering in a moderated way the challenge of industrialisation and the expectations of the new reading public, and suggesting that work and self-help were more valuable qualities than those displayed by the aristocracy and landed gentry. In the same way, as described in Chapter I, the Victorian work ethic was to a considerable extent a reaction to, and a compromise with, change, rather than a positive and original set of attitudes. For many reasons, some selfish, some genuine and some alarmed, Victorians were emphasising the value of work in an attempt to stabilise the social effects of industrialisation. The ideal of self-help was Smiles' post-radical answer to the same problems and hence falls within the larger pattern of the Victorian work ethic in its attempt to give a new and acceptable meaning to both the industrial worker and his often tedious work and poverty stricken life. Thus Smiles was reaching for certainty in an age of flux - offering an old and tried solution to the demands of the working class - individual moral reform and the practice of the necessary virtues. It was not his intention to promise success to the individual, but only the more realistic (and in view of his exposition of cause and effect, and his belief in the bounty of nature) more certain goals of moral, social and economic independence.

If the story of Smiles' life and its relationship to the Victorian work ethic has merit, it is as a microcosm of the formation and evolution of a generation of Victorian radicals and reformers. Born one year after John Bright (1811-1889) and eight years after Richard Cobden (1804-1865), Smiles belonged to their reforming and 'improving' generation. At the time of the Reform Act in 1832, Smiles was twenty years old, a Dissenting radical, ambitious, well-educated as a professional surgeon, and bitterly resentful of the injustices practiced by the aristocracy and their representatives in Parliament. The rest of his life is the story of how a young radical, disciplined by an early Calvinism, and inspired with the rationalism and optimism of the Enlightenment, continued to try to reform society (or rather the individuals within it) until his powers waned at the end of the century. Fired with enthusiasm for reform, Smiles' generation of radicals were both frustrated by their efforts to achieve certain reforms in the 1830s and 1840s, and mollified by the reforms they did achieve (in particular the repeal of the Corn Laws). Further placated by the economic improvement of the 1850s, the radicals outran their desire for organic change, and only dimly realised that their inherited assumptions and models of social reform had become largely irrelevant. Holding to their rationalism, and clinging to the old certainties of perfectibility and the power of education, Smiles' generation of radicals foundered among the complexities and differing circumstances of the later Victorian years. Among these radicals, many like Smiles turned to moralising. Such was the fate of William Lovett and Harriet Martineau, although one did move with the times - John Stuart Mill. But like most of the others, Smiles found his own particular rock of certainty and remained with it - the divine order and harmony of the world and the power of work and self-help.

Smiles' faith was ultimately challenged at the end of the 19th Century by those like H.G. Wells, who tried to reduce work by employing machines and not men, and by Sidney Webb, who bypassed Wells' solution because he believed machinery would enslave and degrade men "below the level of monkeys . . ." Webb's solution was simply to "limit the period of monkeydom."[17] Sidney Webb's acceptance of the devaluation of work was that of a _fait accompli_, for the problem of work in industrial society continues to plague the 20th Century. In Russia the leadership cannot raise productivity, even with common ownership and the glory of the state at stake, and many Russians despise and are "psychologically unprepared for physical labour." In America a new generation has become cynical about the opposite incentives of material and financial reward. In Britain the goal of industrial efficiency is still related insistently to the pliability of character and "human behaviour."[18] In short, industrialised nations desperately need a new attitude towards work, and thus a new attitude towards life.

For a time, in the 19th Century, Victorians tried to do what the 20th Century has by and large not attempted, namely to give a positive meaning to work and to the life of the worker. In this campaign, Smiles' _Self-Help_ arrived at a favourable juncture, and his faith in the value of work and its potential enjoyed great popularity. Before his views and the opinions expressed through the Victorian work ethic recede into the past, it would be well to consider that the question of incentives and sanctions to work does not belong only to the 19th Century,[19] and that in fact the problems discussed and solutions offered by the Victorians actually reflected a consciousness, in the first country to be industrialised, of the restructuring that industrialisation brings both to society, and to the relationship between the meaning of work and the meaning of life - a problem that the 20th Century has only too visibly inherited.[20]

## Chapter VI - Footnotes

[1]Henry Curwen, Plodding On: or, The Jog-Trot to Fame and Fortune (London, 1879), p. iv. Page, Noble Workers, p. 409.

[2]For example, The Printer (London, 1884), p. 24; and J. Hogg, Fortunate Men, How they made Money and won Renown (2nd edition; London, 1885), p. 1.

[3]James Hogg, Men who have Risen: A Book for Boys (London and Edinburgh, 1859), p. 222. Davenport Adams, Secret of Success, p. (xiii). Johnson, Self-Effort, p. 21.

[4]Davenport Adams, Secret of Success, pp. (xv), (xvi), 37, 303, 306. Smiles also found a good deal of piracy of his literature, Smiles, Autobiography, pp. 380-81.

[5]For example, Darton, Brave Boys, pp. 116, 247; A.H. Japp, Labour and Victory (London, 1881), p. 51.

[6]The Way to Fortune: A Series of Short Essays, with Illustrative Proverbs and Anecdotes from many sources (London, 1881), pp. 9, 56.

[7][James Hogg], Brave Men's Footsteps: A Book of Example and Anecdote in Practical Life for Young People (London, 1872), p. 89. Fortunes Made in Business, A Series of Original Sketches Biographical and Anecdotic from the recent history of Industry and Commerce (3 vols.; London, 1884-1887). Money! Money! Money! How to Get Money and Rise to Independence (London, 1890), pp. 6-7 for a defense of money making. The exception that makes the rule is the surprisingly early How to Get Money Quickly (London, 1866).

[8]Success - A Monthly Magazine of Inspiration and Self-Help (London), July 1901. How to Get Rich Quick (London, 1907), p. 3 (mail order advertising). How to Grow Rich (London, 1907), pp. 8 ff. (essentially to

maintain a careful gap between income and expenditure). Ernest A. Bryant, A New Self-Help (London, 1908), pp. 115, 121, 128, Chapters V, VI, and XIII, and pp. 24, 123.

[9]Account Book, Smiles Correspondence, SS/B/71, ff. 244-45, f. 328. See Appendix F, for further details on Self-Help sales.

[10]H.G. Wells, A Modern Utopia (London, 1905), pp. 102, 152. Wells did not mean that all work should be abolished, only work of a laborious kind. In 1912 he still believed in "hand operations" as "invigorating" and "attractive" to the "urban population," H.G. Wells (ed.), The Great State (London, 1912), p. 35.

[11]Smiles, Thrift, p. 34. Smiles, Self-Help, pp. 267, 266. In an 1849 article Smiles saw education as the getting together "in a common fund, as it were, the moral and intellectual possessions of a large number of persons, and opening this fund for the free use of all . . ." [Smiles], "Young Men's Mutual Improvement Societies," ECJ, May 19, 1849, vol. I, p. 34. Even education could be quantified.

[12]Smiles, Life and Labour, pp. 5-6. Smiles, Character, p. 14; Smiles also declared that life should be useful and devoted to others, but if used "for self-seeking, pleasure and aggrandisement, it will be full of toil, anxiety and disappointment," ibid, p. 372.

[13]For Robert Owen, V.A.C. Gatrell, "Introduction," in Robert Owen, A New View of Society and Report to the County of Lanark (Pelican edition; Baltimore, 1970), p. 79. for Smiles' view on law see Chapter II generally; and Smiles' lavish praise for Paley's Natural Theology (a paradigm argument for the existence of God from design) in Smiles to Billio, 23/10/1868, Smiles Correspondence, SS/AII/14. This argument is supported by the more

general discussion of order and authority in E.E. Hagen, On the Theory of Social Change (London, 1964), pp. 152, 106.

[14]Burn, Age of Equipoise, p. 132.

[15]Smiles, Self-Help, p. 376.

[16]Smiles had read Emerson in the 1840s. For Emerson, Cawelti, Apostles of the Self Made Man, pp. 87 ff. The question of liberty and order was of course a common problem in the 19th Century; apart from J.S. Mill, a striking example is Auguste Comte's dialectic of Order and Progress, in which Progress is the development of Order.

[17]Webb and Cox, Eight Hours Day, p. 243.

[18]Kyril Tidmarsh, "Russia Runs out of Labourers," London Times, Oct. 8, 1968, p. 11. Fair Deal at work, p. 10. A 1968 article notes that for the young American generation work has lost its attraction, Frank C. Porter, "G.E. Forecasts a Hippie Future for All," The Washington Post, June 10, 1968, p. A2.

[19]A latter-day exponent of the work ethic emerged in Argentina, advising the youth of that country "that the way to get ahead in the world is to be honest and hard-working." This as an antidote to economic stagnation, New York Times, Oct. 20, 1967, p. 21. Leisure and recreation are not alternatives since there is no indication that technology is substantially reducing the material need for work, while psychologically the desire for involvement, usefulness and status through meaningful work is undiminished.

[20]For a general statement on the malaise that industrialisation brings, see Harrington, The Accidental Century.

## APPENDIX A

### Work - A definition:

H. Arendt makes the distinction between Work, which endures as a witness to productivity (production of articles), and Labour, which is repetitive and is aimed only at providing subsistence (H. Arendt, The Human Condition, Chapter 1). Work has the Promethean connotation of erecting a man-made world against nature, while Labour has the meaning of endless and sometimes hopeless toil. Arendt's distinction is itself based on John Locke's discrimination between the labour of the body, and the work of the hands, so that in the 20th Century the phrase "manual labour" [of the body] comes more easily than "manual work" [of the hands]. In the 19th Century it is relevant that two contemporary encyclopedias (Encyclopedia Metropolitana (London, 1845) and Penny Cyclopedia of the Society for the Diffusion of Useful Knowledge (London, 1843) discuss Labour and not Work. However, both 'work' and 'labour' were in use, and the former was evidently thought of as less onerous that the latter, for one analysis claimed "there is small merit in doing thoroughly and well what it pleases us to do. Work done without strife, almost, indeed without labour, is but a shadow or delusion of work," ([Sir John Kaye], "Work," Cornhill Magazine, Nov. 1860, vol. II, p. 609). Nevertheless, law court decisions used both terms indiscriminately to describe all kinds of activity; for example during the case of Peate versus Dicken (1834), the occupation of the defendent is seen as "the exercise of the worldly labour, business, or work of the ordinary calling of the defendent . . ." (1, Crompton, Meeson & Roscoe, 423); and in Scarfe versus Morgan (1838) the question of value is debated:

> "If any value is communicated, it is unimportant that it was not through any immediate application of skill

> or labour to the chattel . . . for instances may be cited where a lien [legal claim] has been held to exist though no work is done upon the chattel . . ." (4, Meeson & Welsby, 277-278).

For the purposes of this thesis 'work' will be used as a generic term to cover all definitions. Work may be defined to mean activity directed toward some end, particularly in the pursuit of a trade or profession. Normally 'work' connotes that activity which is undertaken for the sake of subsistence, remuneration, reward, or honour, although it may also be undertaken for its own sake, or for the pleasure involved. The definition obviously does not include activity for the sake of relaxation or the replenishment of body and soul, in the sense of leisure activity.

# APPENDIX B

## 19th Century titles as heuristic device:

An indicator of this trend may be found in the numbers and titles of books published according to Sampson Low's Index to the British Catalogue of Books (vol. I; London, 1858) covering the years 1837-1857, Sampson Low's Index to the English Catalogue of Books (vols. II-IV; London, 1876, 1884, 1893) covering the years 1856-1889, and according to the British Museum Catalogue. There is no way of knowing how complete these lists are, nor of weighing the intent of the book by its title. But as a heuristic device the titles of the books were divided into three groups, comprising "Success" titles, "Work" titles (excluding "Working Class," but including "Working Men" titles), and a broader group including "Self-Education" and "Self-Culture" titles (but excluding "Self-Help" titles as too ambiguous). The breakdown in numbers of titles published in decades shows that from 1840-1850 Self-Culture and Self-Education predominated (7); from 1850-1860 Success achieved 8, to 14 for Work and 6 for Self-Culture; from 1860-1870 Work jumped to 22, to 6 for Self-Culture and 2 for Success; and that Work predominated from 1870-1880 (9) and 1880-1890 (17); but that the period 1890-1910 saw 10 for Work and 14 for Success. These numbers can only be approximate, and their evaluation would be another dissertation, but they can serve as a guide.

# APPENDIX C

## E.L. Bulwer, Lucretia, 1853:

Bulwer wanted to delineate a "principal vice in the hot and emulous chase for happiness or fame, fortune or knowledge, which is almost synonymous with the cant phrase of 'the March of Intellect,' in that crisis of society to which we have arrived. The vice I allude to is Impatience. That eager desire to press forward, not so much to conquer obstacles, as to elude them; that gambling with the solemn destinies of life, seeking ever to set success upon the chance of a die; that hastening from the wish conceived to the end accomplished; that thirst after quick returns to ingenuous toil, and breathless spurrings along short cuts to the goal, which we see everywhere around us, from the Mechanics' Institute to the Stock Market, - beginning in education with the primer's of infancy - deluging us with 'Philosophies for the Million,' and 'Sciences made Easy' . . . seem . . . to constitute a very diseased and very general symptom of the times. I hold that the greatest friend to man is labour; that knowledge without toil, if possible, were worthless; that toil in pursuit of knowledge is the best knowledge we can attain; that the continuous effort for fame is nobler than fame itself; that it is not wealth suddenly acquired which is deserving of homage, but the virtues which a man exercised in the slow pursuit of wealth, - the abilities so called forth, the self-denials so imposed: in a word, that Labour and Patience are the true schoolmasters on earth."

E.L. Bulwer, Lucretia; or the Children of the Night (London, 1853), pp. (vii)-(viii).

# APPENDIX D

## Attribution of articles in Eliza Cook's Journal to Smiles:

In his *Autobiography* (pp. 164-65) Smiles remarks that during the first year (1849) of *Eliza Cook's Journal* he contributed one article per week. These increased until in the fourth and fifth volumes (April-October 1851), Smiles was contributing "at least one half of the articles in each number." Smiles continued to write articles at this rate until the middle of 1854. Thus one may compute that in 1849 Smiles wrote thirty-five articles for thirty-five numbers (May-December 1849), and even discounting any increase, fifty-two articles in 1850. But by April 1851 Smiles was writing approximately three articles per week, since the usual number of articles per number was between five and seven. Thus, if twenty-five articles are allowed to Smiles from January to April 1851 (one per week), from April to December Smiles wrote approximately eighty-one (three per week). Adding 1852 (156 articles) and half of 1854 (75 articles), at which time Smiles ceased contributing, it is reasonable to estimate that Smiles wrote a grand total of some 580 articles for *Eliza Cook's Journal*. Unfortunately all this computation is necessary because Smiles did not put his name to very many of these articles, and a publishers list does not appear to exist.

Nevertheless, many of the articles can be identified through various means. Firstly, Smiles did what a number of other Victorians did who wrote articles - he republished them. But whereas most authors republished their articles in book form and largely unchanged, Smiles simply took many of his articles from *Eliza Cook's Journal* and inserted them in his 'self-help' series of books. The articles are usually reworked, but often long sections from his articles in the *Journal* appear *verbatim* and are easily recognised. This is particularly true of Thrift (1875), less so of Self-Help (1859) and Dutyr (1880), and least so of Character (1871). The first sections of Life and Labour (1887) also originated in Eliza Cook's Journal. These facts account for the sometimes puzzling prefaces by Smiles, for example, Life and Labour (p. vii): "The early chapters were written many years ago . . ." and Thrift (p. 6): "Much of this book was written, and some of it published, years ago . . ." It was partly for this reason that Smiles discontinued writing for the Quarterly Review, since "the articles [could not] be reprinted without the consent of the publisher. when I suggested the republication of my articles in the Quarterly, my proposal was declined." (Autobiography, p. 303, footnote.)

One way of identifying Smiles' articles in Eliza Cook's Journal, therefore, is to compare those that seem likely to have been written by him with his later 'self-help' books. This is simpler than it appears, for the reader who is familiar with the 'self-help' books and Smiles' own style, turn of phrase, and favourite subject matter, will readily pick out his articles from the others in Eliza Cook's Journal. Moreover, in most volumes of the Journal, Smiles wrote at least half the articles in each number, and many of the non-Smiles articles can be discounted through articles either signed or written under a pseudonym (i.e. "Silverpen" was Eliza Meteyard). Thus, all that is necessary is for the reader to be steeped in the 'self-help' books, and hence be able to recognise Smiles' Journal articles, at which point they may be compared, with the aid of indexes and tables of contents, to likely chapters in the 'self-help' books. So, for example, an article entitled "Competition" in the April 24, 1852 number of Eliza Cook's Journal may logically be referred to the most 'economic' of Smiles' books, Thrift, and a brief search through the index of that book directs attention to pp. 200-201, where a comparison soon reveals a verbatim repeat of much of the earlier article. Nevertheless, it is stressed that no articles are identified as Smiles' merely on the basis of subjective judgement and internal evidence. They had to reappear in recognisable form (meaning sections of verbatim prose) in one of the 'self-help' books, and are so attributed, with evidence, in the list below.

Secondly, Smiles did identify a number of his articles for Eliza Cook in his Autobiography, pp. 161, 164-65. Thirdly (and this applies particularly to the early numbers of Eliza Cook's Journal), Smiles actually did put his name to some of the articles that he wrote, and these are identified in footnotes as his name appears in the Journal; thus, S. Smiles, "Music in the House," ECJ, Jan. 31, 1852, vol. VI, pp. 208-11, as opposed to unsigned articles, which, if used, are all identified in the list below as Smiles' work and are reproduced in the footnotes as [Smiles], "George Stephenson," ECJ, June 2, 1849, vol. I, pp. 65-67. Fourthly, there are articles that can be identified as Smiles' work through references in other articles, through remarks in his private correspondence, and through some kinds of specific evidence; for example, his trip through Holland to gain a Leyden degree and see the country is recounted in a series of articles entitled "Dutch Pictures" with dates and places visited identical to Smiles' description in the Autobiography. Lastly, it may be mentioned that the list below does not contain all the identifiable articles (these would run to about 100), but only those cited in the text.

The following is a chronological list of unsigned articles attributed to Smiles, with evidence of authorship:

1. [Smiles], "Young Men's Mutual Improvement Societies," ECJ, May 19, 1849, vol. I, pp. 33-34.
   Evidence: Smiles, Autobiography, p. 161.

2. [Smiles], "George Stephenson," ECJ, June 2, 1849, vol. I, pp. 65-67. Evidence: Smiles, Autobiography, p. 161.

3. [Smiles], "Industrial Schools for Young Women," ECJ, June 9, 1849, vol. I, pp. 81-82. Evidence: Smiles, Autobiography, p. 161.

4. [Smiles], "Railway Travelling," ECJ, June 16, 1849, vol. I, pp. 97-99. Evidence: The author of this article stated that he also wrote the article on George Stephenson, see No. 2 above.

5. [Smiles], "Gibson and Thorburn the Artists," ECJ, Sept. 22, 1849, vol. I, pp. 333-335. Evidence: Correlation with and reproduction of Smiles, Self-Help, pp. 158-160.

6. [Smiles] "Providing Against the Evil Day," ECJ, Oct. 6, 1849, vol. I, pp. 353-355. Evidence: Smiles, Autobiography, p. 161.

7. [Smiles], "Home Power," ECJ, Dec. 29, 1849, vol. II, pp. 129-131. Evidence: Correlation with and reproduction of Smiles, Thrift, pp. 383-84, Smiles, Self-Help, p. 353.

8. [Smiles], "Nobody Did It!" ECJ, Aug. 2, 1851, vol. V, pp. 223-224. Evidence: Correlation with and reproduction of Smiles, Thrift, pp. 357-358.

9. [Smiles], "Earnest Purpose," ECJ, Aug. 30, 1851, vol. V, pp. 285-86. Evidence: Correlation with and reproduction of Smiles, Self-Help, pp. 189, 193-94, 317.

10. [Smiles], "Helps to Self-Culture," ECJ, Oct. 4, 1851, vol. V, pp. 365-67. Evidence: Correlation with and reproduction of Smiles, Self-Help, pp. 95, 101.

11. [Smiles], "Drill!" ECJ, Nov. 8, 1851, vol. VI, pp. 17-19. Evidence: Correlation with and reproduction of Smiles, Thrift, pp. 148 ff.

12. [Smiles], "Don't Care!" ECJ, Dec. 20, 1851, vol. VI, pp. 127-28. Evidence: Correlation with and reproduction of Smiles, Duty, pp. 262-63.

13. [Smiles], "Competition," ECJ, April 24, 1852, vol. VI, pp. 407-408. Evidence: Correlation with and reproduction of Smiles, Thrift, pp. 201-202.

14. [Smiles], "Quite the Gentleman!" ECJ, May 22, 1852, vol. VII, pp. 62-63. Evidence: Correlation with and reproduction of Smiles, Self-Help, pp. 381, 390-92, Smiles, Life and Labour, pp. 26, 32, 35.

15. [Smiles], "Dutch Pictures," ECJ, Sept. 25, 1852, vol. VII, pp. 343-345.
Evidence: Smiles' trip to Holland in 1838, Smiles, Autobiography, pp. 66 ff.

16. [Smiles], "Ignorance is Power," ECJ, Nov. 6, 1852, vol. VIII, pp. 30-31.
Evidence: Correlation with and reproduction of Smiles, Thrift, pp. 72 ff.

17. [Smiles], "The Lot of Labour," ECJ, Nov. 13, 1852, vol. VIII, pp. 46-47.
Evidence: Correlation with and reproduction of Smiles, Thrift, pp. 16-17.

18. [Smiles], "Heads!" ECJ, Dec. 4, 1852, vol. VIII, pp. 89-92.
Evidence: Internal evidence, discussion of phrenology; citation from Dr. Fletcher, Smiles' teacher at Edinburgh; citation from Paley on human organisation that corresponds to Smiles' questions in an early letter (Samuel Brown to Smiles, SS?AIX/30a-c, n.d., Smiles Correspondence); discussion of development of human brain and mental faculties that paraphrases Smiles, Physical Education, pp. 12, 23; knowledge of Blumenbach in Smiles, Life and Labour, p. 119; circumstantial evidence includes the title, "Heads!", the pithy style of which is typical of many of Smiles' titles: for example, nos. 11, 12, 20, 21; and the interest that Smiles always took in racial theories, e.g. Smiles, Autobiography, pp. 320 ff.

19. [Smiles], "Gifts of Memory," ECJ, Dec. 4, 1852, vol. VIII, pp. 94-95.
Evidence: Smiles rewrote this article for an American magazine, Dr. Smiles, "The Gift of Memory," Youth's Companion (Boston) March 20, 1884, vol. V, pp. 113-14. This is noted in a letter from Smiles to Janet Hartree, Feb. 14, 1883, Smiles Correspondence, SS/AI/154.

20. [Smiles], "It's All the Same!" ECJ, March 12, 1853, vol. VIII, pp. 313-14.
Evidence: Correlation with and reproduction of Smiles, Duty, pp. 394 ff.

21. [Smiles], "Patience is Genius!" ECJ, March 26, 1853, vol. VIII, pp. 350-52.
Evidence: Correlation with and reproduction of Smiles, Self-Help, pp. 304-305.

22. [Smiles], "Success in Life," ECJ, May 7, 1853, vol. IX, pp. 30-31.
Evidence: Correlation with and reproduction of Smiles, Self-Help, p. 289.

23. [Smiles], "Attend to Little Things," ECJ, Sept. 24, 1853, vol. IX, pp. 344-45.
Evidence: Correlation with and reproduction of Smiles, Thrift, pp. 177-181.

24. [Smiles], "Parvenus," ECJ, Feb. 11, 1854, vol. X, pp. 254-55.

Evidence: Correlation with and reproduction of Smiles, Life and Labour, pp. 236-39.

25. [Smiles], "The Scottish Borders," ECJ, March 6, 1854, vol. X, pp. 293-95.
Evidence: George Reid, the artist and friend of Smiles', wanted to illustrate for publication a series of six "Scottish Borders" articles which Smiles had written for Eliza Cook's Journal, George Reid to Smiles, Sept. 13, 1878, Smiles Correspondence, SS/AV/83.

# APPENDIX E

G.L. Craik, _Passages of a Working Life_, 1864;
and G.L. Craik, _The Pursuit of Knowledge under Difficulties_, 1830-1831:

I. "Our concern . . . is neither with individuals who have _in any way_ been exalted from one region of society to another, nor even with such as have been chiefly the authors of their own exaltation, - for the fact of their exaltation is not at all the one upon which we wish to fix attention, even although we should make it out to have been in every case the consequence of their abilities and attainments. What then is our subject? Not the _triumphs_ of genius, nor of perseverence, nor even of perseverence in the pursuit of knowledge, because it is not the _success_ of the effort, at least in a gross and worldly sense, we would point attention to: nor is it by any means what is called _genius_ to which we are exclusively to confine ourselves, while we still less mean to include every _species_ of perseverence. But we want a category which shall embrace . . . all . . . who, whether in humble or in high life, have pursued knowledge with ardour, and distinctly evidenced, by the seductions they resisted or the difficulties they encountered and overcame for her sake; that she was the first object of their affections; and that the pursuit of her, even without any reference to either the wealth, the power, or the distinction, which she might bring them, was . . . its own sufficient reward . . . [O]ur title must be, not Anecdotes of Self-Taught genius at all, for that is greatly too limited, but _Anecdotes of the Love of Knowledge_ . . ."

G.L. Craik to Charles Knight, Autumn 1929, cited in _Passages of a Working Life_ (3 vols.; London, 1864-65), vol. II, 1864, pp. 133-134.

II. "His (Mr. Craik's) idea of the line to be drawn as to self-educated men in modern times, is also quite correct; but we must, nevertheless, confine the examples to cases which are quite plainly those of men who have greatly altered their situation by force of merit. As Watt, Arkwright, Franklin, . . . making the ground of division or classification <u>self-exaltation</u> rather than self-education, though they often will coincide . . . The work might be followed by another . . . including all self-taught Genius in the larger sense. To give an example - I should certainly exclude Newton . . . also Granville Sharpe, though he raised himself by his merit to great fame; but he was grandson of the Archbishop of York, and could not be said to alter his station in life."

Lord Brougham to Charles Knight, September 1838, <u>ibid</u>, p. 134.

III. "If some of the individuals we have mentioned have risen to great wealth or high civil dignities, it is not for this that we have mentioned them. We bring them forward to shew that neither knowledge, nor any of the advantages which . . . flow from it, are the exclusive inheritance of those who have been enabled to devote themselves entirely to its acquisition from their youth upwards."

"Their example also shews that many of these impediments, which, in ordinary cases, altogether prevent the pursuit of knowledge, are impediments only to the indolent or uninspiring, who make in truth, their poverty or their low station bear the blame which ought properly to be laid upon their own irresolution or indifference. It was not wealth or ease which these noble enthusiasts sought; it was [emancipation from] the bondage and degradation of ignorance . . ."

"With regard to the great mass of the population, any counsel or exhortation which would attempt to raise them above the rank in which they have been born and reared, must, from the nature of things, be totally inoperative."

G.L. Craik, The Pursuit of Knowledge under Difficulties (S.D.U.K.; 2 vols.; London, 1830-31), vol. I, pp. 53, 55.

# APPENDIX F

## Sales and Printing of SELF-HELP, 1859-1894:

| Years | No. Printed | | No. Sold | |
|---|---|---|---|---|
| 1859 | 6,000 | 6,000 | 1,921 | 1,921 |
| 1860 | 14,000<br>15,000 | | 15,057<br>16,344 | |
| 1861 | 10,000 | | 7,317 | |
| 1862 | 5,000 | | 7,914 | |
| 1863 | 5,000 | | 5,661 | |
| 1864 | 5,000 | 54,000 | 3,867 | 56,160 |
| 1865 | - | | - | |
| 1866 | 5,000 | | 5,555 | |
| 1867 | 5,000 | | - | |
| 1868 | 2,500<br>2,500 | | 3,721<br>3,857 | |
| 1869 | 3,500 | 18,500 | 3,499 | 20,037 |
| 1870 | 3,500 | | 2,683 | |
| 1871 | - | | - | |
| 1872 | 4,000<br>4,500 | | 3,701 | |
| 1873 | 4,000 | 20,000 | 4,132<br>4,567 | 19,980 |
| | | 98,500 C/F | | 98,098 C/F |

| Years | No. Printed | | No. Sold | |
|---|---|---|---|---|
| | | 98,500 B/F | | 98,098 B/F |
| 1875 | 7,000 | | 6,083 | |
| 1876 | 10,000 | | 6,238 | |
| 1877 | - | | 5,698 | |
| 1878 | 5,000 | | 6,083 | |
| 1879 | 3,000<br>6,000 | 31,000 | 5,331 | 29,833 |
| 1880 | 5,000 | | 5,141 | |
| 1881 | 4,000 | | 5,205 | |
| 1882 | 5,000 | | 4,720 | |
| 1883 | 5,000 | | 4,320 | |
| 1884 | 5,000 | 24,000 | 3,663 | 23,049 |
| 1885 | 5,000 | | 3,790 | |
| 1886 | - | | 3,280 | |
| 1887 | 5,000 | | 3,342 | |
| 1888 | - | | - | |
| 1889 | 4,000 | 14,000 | 3,168 | 13,580 |
| 1890 | 5,000 | | | |
| 1891 | 2,000 | | | 164,560 |
| 1892 | 5,000 | | | |
| 1893 | 1,000 | | not available | |
| 1894 | 2,500 | 15,500 | for 1890-1894 | |
| | | 183,000 | | |

Account Book, Smiles Correspondence, SS/B/71: 1859-1880, ff. 25-50; 1881-1889, ff. 244-249. Ibid, SS/B/100 (1890-1894).

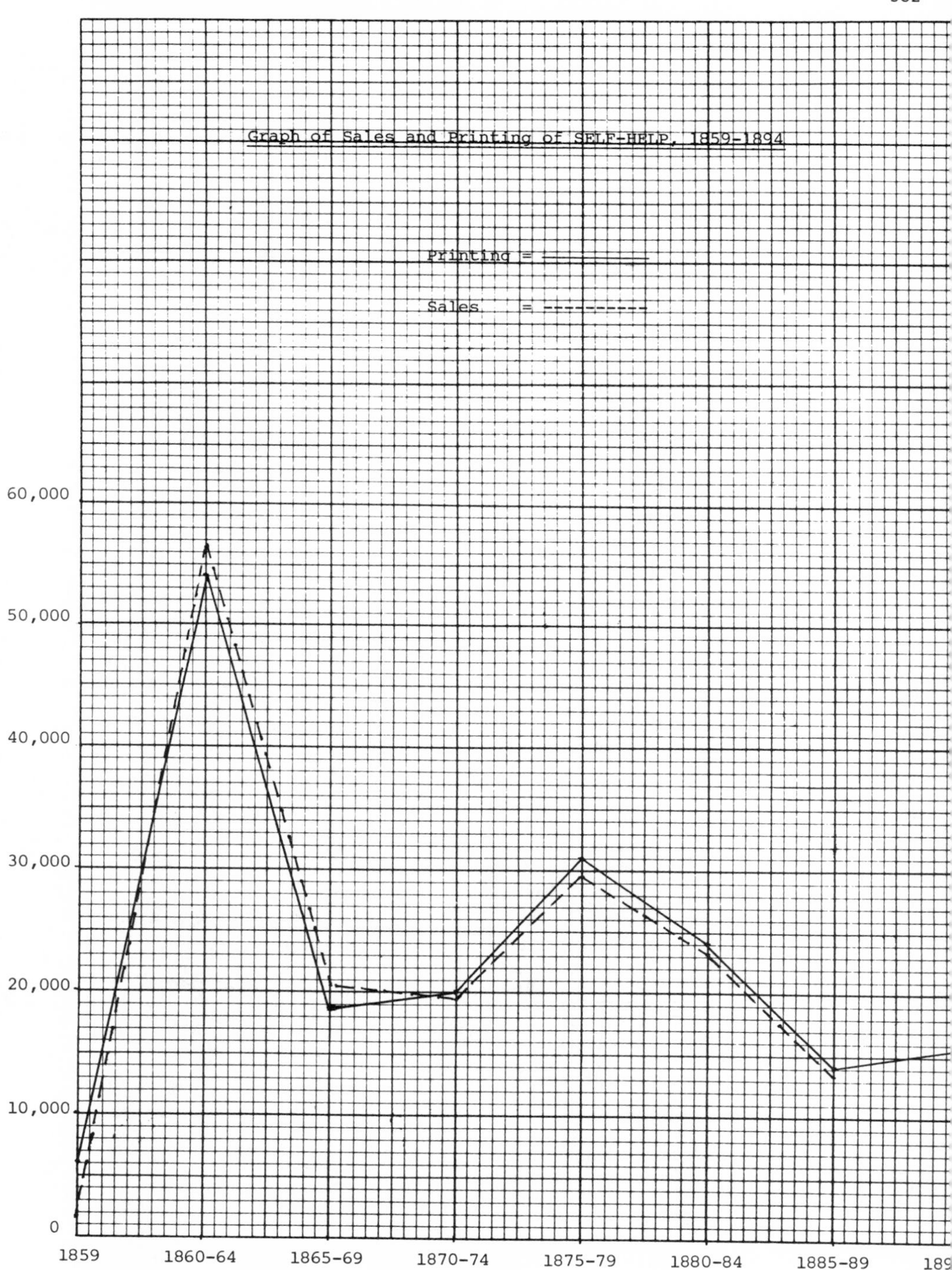
Graph of Sales and Printing of SELF-HELP, 1859-1894
Printing = ———————
Sales = -----------
60,000
50,000
40,000
30,000
20,000
10,000
0
1859
1860-64
1865-69
1870-74
1875-79
1880-84
1885-89

Smiles' records of Self-Help sales and printings cease by 1895. However, further research kindly undertaken by Lt. Col. T.H. Travers in the files of Smiles' publisher, John Murray Ltd., London, reveal that the sales of Self-Help achieved a remarkable renaissance in the late 1890s. For example, Self-Help sold 13,304 copies in 1896 and 16,310 in 1897, compared with 2,083 in 1895 and around 3,000 per annum in the late 1880s. Very possibly this renaissance is connected with the reaction against radicalism and Socialism that occurred in 1895 and the following years (see footnote 65, Chapter V). Had this story continued beyond 1890, the final decline of Self-Help would have been postulated from 1900 and following years, when again the sales fell back to the 2,000 mark per annum. The figures from the files of John Murray Ltd. (who were good enough to let the research take place) are as follows:

| Years | No. Printed | No. Sold |
|---|---|---|
| 1895 | 2,500 | 2,083 |
| 1896 | 13,000 | 13,304 |
| 1897 | 16,000 | 16,310 |
| 1898 | - | - |
| 1899 | 10,000 | 9,232 |
| 1900 | - | 2,809 |
| 1901 | 5,060 | 2,747 |
| 1902 | 5,000 | 2,757 |
| 1903 | 5,060 | - |
| 1904 | 5,000 | 2,380 |
| 1905 | 10,481 | 10,109 |

# APPENDIX G

## Edward Carpenter, Robert Blatchford, Sidney Webb:

Carpenter, Blatchford and Webb have been chosen because they did represent three Socialist positions. Edward Carpenter was from the 1880s on a champion of that blend of individualism and Socialism that always threatened to turn to Anarchism. Closest in thought to William Morris and the Socialist League in the ideal of work as pleasure, Carpenter ranged fearlessly through the ranks of Fabians, Marxists and Trades Unionists, defending his intellectualised left wing Individualist-Socialist position. Never a violent revolutionary, Carpenter did advocate a radical change, and his books, songs and lectures made him a well known figure in Socialist circles. He corresponded with leading Socialists and intellectuals, and on his 70th birthday (1914) received an address signed by Galsworthy, Havelock Ellis, G.B. Shaw, H.G. Wells, Sidney Webb and many others. His largely forgotten popularity is also recalled through the number of books written about him in the early years of the 20th Century - Tom Swan, _Edward Carpenter: The Man and his Message_ (Manchester, 1902); Edward Lewis, _Edward Carpenter_ (London, 1915); A.H. Moncur Sime, _Edward Carpenter: His Ideas and Ideals_ (London, 1916); and G. Beith (ed.), _Edward Carpenter_ (London, 1931).

Robert Blatchford's contemporary popularity, rather than any lasting intellectual originality, has made him into another somewhat neglected figure. Influenced by Carlyle, and determined to improve the quality of life for the working classes, Blatchford fought for half a century to introduce a deeply-felt, but occasionally 'Tory' Socialism, rather in the style of H.M. Hyndman. Blatchford wanted to produce Socialists, to convert men and women (successfully in the case of the Countess of Warwick) to Socialism. Hence his bent of mind was practical, rather than intellectual, and he came to support an independent Labour movement - once running as a candidate himself. Thus Blatchford represented the centre of the Socialist movement - to elect Labour candidates and introduce Socialism through writing and organisation.

Sidney Webb hardly needs introduction, but his position in the Socialist movement puts him to the right of Blatchford, for while the Fabians also relied on electioneering and influence, Webb's training as a political economist and his intellectual background generally (as Chapter V shows) gave him a most detached and almost dehumanised attitude to the individual - with overtones of _1984_. Webb was really interested in results, and although he was committed to evolutionary Socialism and the improvement of the _material_ conditions of life, he disregarded the pleasures of the spirit and nature that Blatchford was so aware of. Perhaps the greatest difference between Webb and Blatchford was Webb's tendency to an elitist and functional Socialism, to which Blatchford (for all his reading of Carlyle) was immune.

# A CRITICAL BIBLIOGRAPHY

Three basic areas of material were used to research this study. These were: the Smiles material (MS and secondary), Victorian work ethic literature (mainly secondary), and Socialist material (largely MS, but also secondary).

Since this study was written, a certain amount of new material has appeared. The new material relates mostly to recent articles concerning Samuel Smiles, and to further studies of the Socialist movement. A number of Victorian working class autobiographies have also been published, together with oral history interviews. All of this recent material is reviewed in a new introduction, pp. xiii ff., which therefore supplements the following Critical bibliography, itself written in 1969-1970.

## (a) Samuel Smiles

The major source of MSS material for Samuel Smiles is Smiles' private correspondence (approximately 1,000 letters) deposited in the Leeds Public Library. These are mostly post 1860, and are invaluable for Smiles' political opinions, and for an assessment of the earnest meaning and purpose he gave to life. Probably the most significant letters are the few early examples, including the long letter from Samuel Brown, reflecting Smiles' religious doubt and 'materialist' questions in about 1834. This collection is accompanied by MSS relating to the sales of Smiles' books and various details of finance. Three other collections of MSS are useful: the Eva Hartree collection in the Fitzwilliam Museaum, Cambridge; 20 or 30 scattered letters in the National Library of Scotland at Edinburgh; and a brief but politically revealing series of letters from Smiles to Cobden in the Cobden Papers, West Sussex Record Office. The Hartree Collection (Mrs. Hartree's husband was the son of Smiles' daughter Janet) contained some further Cobden-Smiles correspondence, useful for Smiles' politics, and the Ruskin letter, while the National Library of Scotland contained the surprising Smiles-George Combe letters, and others of less value, including Smiles' correspondence with Jane Welsh Carlyle. Further Smiles MSS were scattered around, particularly in the Place Collection, British Museum, where Smiles' commitment to radicalism in the 1840s is confirmed, and in the British Transport Historical Records, in which Smiles has an interesting letter on the subject of character. The author also holds a collection of Smiles letters, dating from 1880-1904.

Of Smiles' printed material, the most important were the six hundred odd editorials he wrote for the _Leeds Times_ (1839-1842), particularly in regard to his early radical stance (1839-1840) which had discernibly shifted by 1842. In general these editorials concentrated on the Corn Laws, the suffrage, and reforms of various kinds. Smiles' articles for _Eliza Cook's Journal_ (1849-1854) filled in a hitherto blank period in his life, and were of most use in marking his 'retreat' from radicalism to self-help. The _People's Journal_ (1845-1847) and _Howitts' Journal_ (1847-1848) contained some useful articles on the question of Short Time and political reform. A journal which contained some new and interesting 'sensationalist' psychology articles by Smiles was _The Union_ (1842-1843). Of Smiles' twenty-seven odd published books, the most intriguing was the earliest, _Physical Education_ (1838), which again revealed a strong _tabula rasa_ psychology, and also some insights on Smiles' view of the physiology of man. The _Lives of the Engineers_ (1861-1862) showed unusual ideas on history, technology and the means of invention, while his two books on the

Huguenots confirmed Smiles' strong anti-Catholic bias. Finally the Autobiography (1905) was useful for Smiles' childhood, schooling and later resentment at the lack of British acceptance of his books and reputation. It should, however, be used with caution, for it was written with the prejudices of his old age.

There has been one monograph on Smiles, written by his granddaughter, Aileen Smiles, Samuel Smiles and his Surroundings (London, 1956). Aileen Smiles is concerned to rescue her grandfather from the charge of advocating a selfish pursuit of individual interest. She does this competently enough, and is able to use some of the family correspondence. However, she does not attempt to use all the correspondence, nor the other collections of Smiles material. Furthermore her account may be criticised on three points. Firstly, she pays little attention to the early formative years of Smiles, particularly his education, and his first book, Physical Education. Secondly, her evident admiration for her grandfather, and her professed intention of setting the record straight, does not lend itself to objectivity. This is the more evident because she appears to share many of Smiles' own feelings in favour of individualism. And thirdly, her explanation of the ideal of self-help as one of self-education, while partially true, by no means registers Smiles' attitudes toward the aristocracy, the government, economics, psychology, the Utilitarian-Unitarian axis, social structure, and the moral reform of the individual and society, to say nothing of the question of work and character, and the other aspects of the post-1859 books on engineers and various individuals. In short, Aileen Smiles' monograph, while entertainingly written, is superficial, uncritical and thus unreliable.

Asa Briggs has devoted a chapter to Smiles in his Victorian People: A Reassessment of Persons and Themes 1851-1867, first published by the University of Chicago in 1955. Briggs also provided an introduction to the centenary edition of Self-Help (London, 1958). Asa Briggs' statements on Smiles have the same sense of multitudinousness that radiate from the 'self-help' series of books - Smiles' inclusion of hundreds of brief biographies do have a way of mixing up the message. Consequently Briggs is not sure what Smiles really was trying to say, although among his suggestions are: success, the self-made man, individualism based on character, thrift, and socially desired economic behaviour. This variety is understandable in view of the fact that Briggs had not consulted the Leeds Times, the Smiles MSS material, or even Smiles' books apart from the 'self-help' series and the Autobiography (and even here Briggs does not include Life and Labour in the 'self-help' series to which it belongs). Asa Briggs' essay is an introduction to the study of Smiles rather than an analysis.

Among other historians who have considered Smiles, are J.F.C. Harrison, "The Victorian Gospel of Success," Victorian Studies, December 1957, vol. I (repeated in his book, Learning and Living 1790-1960 (London, 1961), pp. 203-211); and K. Fielden, "Samuel Smiles and Self-Help," Victorian Studies, December 1968, vol. XII. Harrison places Smiles among the proponents of success, and so misinterprets the message of self-help. Fielden, on the other hand, is a great deal more cautious in regarding Self-Help as success literature, stating correctly that duty, character and knowledge were also important. Fielden also makes one or two interesting points, claiming, for example, that Smiles remained throughout his life a country man, disliking crowds, cities and 'mobs.' However, Fielden is mistaken in his analysis when he remarks that Smiles was Janus faced (requiring character, duty, and knowledge to supplement business success) for as this study points out, Smiles was not interested in success at all, but in the moral reform of character and the achievement of 'independence.' Fielden's difficulty seems to arise from his belief that Smiles changed from addressing literate workers in the 1840s to addressing culture-lacking middle class achievers. This theory is difficult to accept because Character, Thrift, and Duty (and to a lesser extent Life and Labour) were only too obviously aimed at the working classes - the middle classes were part of Smiles' solution, not part of the problem.

As in the case of Asa Briggs, J.F.C. Harrison and K. Fielden were unable to do justice to Smiles and his message because their articles were necessarily limited in scope, and they were familiar with only a small fraction of Smiles' written work, to say nothing of his private correspondence. In particular, the Leeds Times, Eliza Cook's Journal, and Smiles' books outside of the 'self-help' series were not consulted. Royden Harrison's brief "Afterword" to the 1968 Sphere Books edition of Self-Help should also be mentioned. These last limitations necessarily apply to Royden Harrison also, although his essay places Smiles nicely within the Victorian context. Royden Harrison can be criticised for various slips - that Self-Help was largely concerned with industrial biography, that women played little or no role in Smiles' thought (whereas he considered mothers as vitally important educators), and that Smiles wanted to encourage individual social mobility and success.

Indeed the erroneous idea that Smiles was principally an author of success literature seems to have gained widespread, if not total acceptance, and become enshrined as a myth. Two examples have already been given at the start of Chapter II, J.F.C. Harrison's Learning and Living, pp. 204-205, and Harold Perkin's The Origins of Modern English Society, p. 225. Similar statements can befound in Robin Winks' edited Age of Imperialism (Englewood Cliffs, N.J., 1969), p. 72, where Smiles is regarded as the "British Horatio Alger;" T.K. Derry and T.L. Jarman, The Making of Modern Britain, Life and Work from George III to Elizabeth II (Collier Books edition; New York, 1962), p. 171, where Smiles "used the careers of the earlier industrial pioneers to point an attractive road to fortune . . ." Raymond Chapman, The Victorian Debate: English Literature and Society, 1832-1901 (London, 1968), pp. 41 and 231, in which Smiles stands for "personal [financial] betterment," and an "optimistic assertion that all was well" (the latter a particularly erroneous notion); Walter E. Houghton, The Victorian Frame of Mind, 1830-1870 (New Haven and London, 1957), p. 191, who sees Self-Help as "Samuel Smiles' handbook to success . . ." David Riesman, The Lonely Crowd (Yale Paperbound edition; New Haven, 1961), pp. 92, 149, considers Smiles' output as "success biographies;" and R.D. Altick, Lives and Letters, A History of Literary Biography in England and America (New York, 1969), p. 88, which considers Smiles as the "great master" of the Victorian "literature of success." The list could be extended, but the point is made, and if myths can be destroyed, perhaps this study may go some way towards destroying the myth of Smiles as a paradigm British 19th Century "gospel of success" author. (Part of the problem may be that the 20th Century, which equates work incentives with promises of reward, financial and otherwise, has read this equation back into 19th Century England, a century which was remarkably reluctant to concede 'success' as a result of work.)

Finally, a series of more recent books and articles are considered in the Introduction. These reflect a more sympathetic and well researched view of Smiles.

(b) Victorian work ethic

The second basic area of research was Victorian work ethic literature. This was investigated in the British Museum and approached through the subject listings of 'Work,' 'Success,' 'Labour,' 'Self-Help,' 'Self-Effort,' etc., in Sampson Low, *Index to the British Catalogue of Books* (vol. I; London, 1858) covering the years 1837-1857, and Sampson Low, *Index to the English Catalogue of Books* (vols. II-IV; London, 1867, 1884, 1893) covering the years 1856-1889. The result was a wide survey of what may be termed Victorian 'sub-literature,' perhaps not always of enduring value to English literature, but certainly evocative and representative of what a wide variety of Victorians were thinking and writing about in relation to the subject of work. This approach seemed to be the more useful because the best known description of Victorian attitudes toward work, in Walter Houghton's excellent book on Victorian thought, concentrates largely on Carlyle, and one or two other major figures; certainly a legitimate approach, but necessarily limited. Thus, while investigating Carlyle and other well known figures, this study also used a large number of often unknown authors, who frequently turned out to be Dissenting clergy of various persuasions, or writers for religious groups such as the Religious Tract Society and the Young Men's Christian Association. Moreover, considerable numbers of journals and periodicals were consulted, some previously unused, for example, *The Journal of Health* (1851-1867). Of especial interest were those authors such as E.P. Hood, who anticipated Smiles' ideal of self-help, and who showed that Smiles and

Self-Help were part of a tradition rather than something unique. At the same time a large number of Victorians were emphasising the value of work for their own reasons, independent of the impact of Carlyle, who is usually taken as a paradigm of Victorian attitudes to work.

Literature on the Victorian work ethic is exceedingly scanty, and as noted, one useful source exists, Walter Houghton's The Victorian Frame of Mind, 1830-1870 (1957). This book is an admirable investigation of mid-Victorian thought, and contains a concise twenty page analysis of the work ethic. Houghton believes that "Puritanism, business and doubt met together to write the gospel of work," and substantiates his claim largely with reference to Carlyle. There were business needs, and the revival of the economic virtues (rather than Houghton's continuum of "Puritanism" or "Puritan tradition") can be argued, but it often seemed that those who advocated work as a solution to doubt either had ulterior aims (conversion to religion) or were those with their own special problems and time on their hands to consider them (i.e. the sexual problems of Carlyle and Charles Kingsley). It is highly unlikely that the already hard-working middle and working classes could find the time and energy to contemplate doubt and dispel it with yet more work. Nevertheless, Walter Houghton's Victorian Frame of Mind is an excellent background to the study of any Victorian intellectual topic, and his twenty pages on 'work' are a useful introduction to the problem of the work ethic.

One other work should be mentioned, T.D. Diehl, "The Gospel of Work and Four Victorian Poets" (unpublished Ph.D. thesis; Columbia University, 1966). Diehl studies in an exhaustive and interesting way the attitudes of four poets, Browning as the arch-individualist, Tennyson and the will to work, A.H. Clough's "service" and humble toil, and Matthew Arnold's desire for "true work;" but has difficulty with the 'gospel of work,' which he sees as a middle class substitute for religion. Again this seems to stem from the top-heavy influence of a few literary figures such as Carlyle, for in the first place the middle class, by and large, kept their faith during the 19th Century, as opposed to the working classes, half of whom had lost theirs by mid-century, K.S. Inglis, Churches and the Working Classes in Victorian England (London and Toronto, 1963). In the second place, if most of the 'gospel of work' was written by the upper and middle classes it was aimed not at themselves, but at the lower classes. Again, the Introduction provides an up-to-date evaluation of the literature on 'work.'

(c) Late Victorian Socialism

The third area of material used was concerned with the late Victorian Socialists. Three Socialists were chosen as representative (see Appendix G), Edward Carpenter, Robert Blatchford and Sidney Webb, and a number of other Socialists were investigated, including G.B. Shaw, William Morris, and H.G. Wells. The extensive Carpenter collection in the Sheffield Public Library provided the majority of material for Edward Carpenter, including lectures, sermons, note books, notes for lectures, and a wide correspondence. There was also a smaller collection of Carpenter correspondence in the Brotherton Library of the University of Leeds (noteworthy for Carpenter's correspondence with the British anarchist movement). Until the 1970s, there were no modern studies of Carpenter, except for a brief mention in Samuel Hynes, The Edwardian Turn of Mind (Princeton, 1968). Robert Blatchford's MSS material in the Manchester Public Library proved a little disappointing, apart from one or two letters to Carpenter, but Blatchford's 'Nunquam' articles for the Manchester Sunday Chronicle (1887-1891) were an excellent source. Blatchford's unusual, but forgotten Utopian novel, The Sorcery Shop (London, 1907) elaborated what he had said in the Sunday Chronicle. There is one secondary work on Blatchford, written by the son of his old friend Alec Thompson, and this is a biography by Laurence Thompson, Robert Blatchford (London, 1951). It is brightly written and sound on the main outlines, if a little preoccupied with personal and anecdotal details.

A study of Sidney Webb must rely on the large and fascinating quantity of MSS correspondence, lectures and notes for lectures in the Passfield Papers of the British Library of Political and Economic Science (London School of Economics). A useful series of articles by Sidney and Beatrice Webb are in their Industrial Democracy (2 vols., London, 1897). Curiously enough there is no single biography of Sidney Webb, one of the originators of modern British Socialism, apart from joint studies of the Webbs such as Mary Hamilton, Sidney and Beatrice Webb (London, 1934), and Margaret Cole (ed.), The Webbs and their Work (London, 1949). Hamilton's account is only adequate, but recently Kitty Muggeridge and Ruth Adam have produced a sensible and partially psychoanalytic biography of Beatrice Webb involving, of course, Sidney Webb. A more general background to the Fabians, minimising their role, is achieved by A.M. McBriar, Fabian Socialism and English Politics, 1884-1918 (Cambridge, 1962). For the Socialist movement as a whole, one of the best introductions is still Henry Pelling, The Origins of the Labour Party 1880-1900 (2nd edition; Oxford, 1965). Once more, the Introduction evaluates recent studies of the three socialists.

(d) Victorian Britain - general

Lastly, a number of books were found to be particularly useful as introductions to the study of Victorian Britain. Raymond Williams' Culture and Society 1780-1950 (New York and London, 1958) helped to point the way toward an understanding of the relationship between culture and education. Asa Briggs' The Age of Improvement, 1783-1867 (London, 1959) provided a solid but not always inspiring framework for the study of institutional, economic and social change. Walter Houghton's Victorian Frame of Mind was especially valuable in accounting for concepts such as "The Worship of Force" and "Hero Worship." In The age of Equipoise, A Study of the Mid-Victorian Generation (London, 1964), W.L. Burn neatly sorted out the arguments over laissez-faire; and a series of articles in Ideas and Beliefs of the Victorians (New York, 1966) concerning science, man and nature, illuminated Victorian ideas on quantification and scientific laws. Harold Perkin has produced a synthesis of politics, class, economics and social thought in The Origins of Modern English Society, 1780-1880 (London and Toronto, 1969); and while the book is somewhat burdened with a heavy structure that relates class ideals to class roles, Perkin has evolved an integrated account of Victorian society, grounded solidly in economic and political needs and realities. And a book by Herbert Sussman, Victorians and the Machine, The Literary Response to Technology (Cambridge, Mass., 1968) showed that Samuel Smiles was not the only Victorian fascinated by the power of machinery. Finally, the Introduction relates Smiles more firmly to mid-Victorian trends, and to recent literature concerning this area.

INDEX

THE LIBRARY
ST. MARY'S COLLEGE OF MARYLAND
ST. MARY'S CITY, MARYLAND 20686